RARY

MW01028397

Praise for *The Achievement of Wendell Berry: The Hard History of Love*

"Wendell Berry's life and works are a sustaining oasis amid the turmoil and alienation that mar the moral landscape of our time. Fritz Oehlschlaeger has provided a brilliant guide to Berry's fiction, nonfiction, and poetry, tracing the consistent themes of good work, faith, patriotism, agrarian values, and love of the land and its people that flow through Berry's writings. To read this book is to fully understand why Wendell Berry is the conscience of modern America."
—David Ehrenfeld, author of *Becoming Good Ancestors: How We Balance Nature, Community, and Technology*

"A nearly comprehensive engagement with the work of Wendell Berry, who is without question one of America's most important contemporary writers. This book will remain a significant contribution to scholarship on Berry for some time to come."
—Joel James Shuman, coeditor of *Wendell Berry and Religion: Heaven's Earthly Life*

"If you want to learn from Wendell Berry, you must read him. After that, Fritz Oehlschlaeger's remarkable book on Berry's work is the next best thing. This is because he writes not to characterize or peg Berry as a writer, but because he has learned from him and come to share deeply in his loves. Oehlschlaeger's thematic ordering of Berry's extraordinarily imaginative and extensive corpus not only preserves the force of Berry's blazing insights but enhances them, providing connection and context. Berry's many gifts to our time, gifts that awaken and alarm, are here unwrapped with the deepest fidelity and love. Read Berry, then read Oehlschlaeger, and you will know why you must read Berry again, equipped with the understanding that what you are doing is a revolutionary act."
—Charles R. Pinches, author of *A Gathering of Memories: Family, Nation, and Church in a Forgetful World*

"Oehlschlaeger's careful and respectful reading of Wendell Berry is a boon to anyone who values clear thinking, clear writing, and the empathic imagination. If reading Berry helps us see ourselves and our web of interactions with sobering clarity, reading Oehlschlaeger redoubles our appreciation of the mastery of Berry's expansive art and redemptive vision. Read both with pencil in hand."
—Morris A. Grubbs, editor of *Conversations with Wendell Berry*

THE ACHIEVEMENT OF WENDELL BERRY

Culture of the Land: A Series in the New Agrarianism

This series is devoted to the exploration and articulation of a new agrarianism that considers the health of habitats and human communities together. It demonstrates how agrarian insights and responsibilities can be worked out in diverse fields of learning and living: history, science, art, politics, economics, literature, philosophy, religion, urban planning, education, and public policy. Agrarianism is a comprehensive worldview that appreciates the intimate and practical connections that exist between humans and the earth. It stands as our most promising alternative to the unsustainable and destructive ways of current global, industrial, and consumer culture.

Series Editor
Norman Wirzba, Duke University, North Carolina

Advisory Board
Wendell Berry, Port Royal, Kentucky
Ellen Davis, Duke University, North Carolina
Patrick Holden, Soil Association, United Kingdom
Wes Jackson, Land Institute, Kansas
Gene Logsdon, Upper Sandusky, Ohio
Bill McKibben, Middlebury College, Vermont
David Orr, Oberlin College, Ohio
Michael Pollan, University of California at Berkeley, California
Jennifer Sahn, *Orion* Magazine, Massachusetts
Vandana Shiva, Research Foundation for Science, Technology, and Ecology, India
Bill Vitek, Clarkson University, New York

THE ACHIEVEMENT OF
WENDELL BERRY

The Hard History of Love

Fritz Oehlschlaeger

THE UNIVERSITY PRESS OF KENTUCKY

HOCUTT-ELLINGTON MEMORIAL LIBRARY
CLAYTON, NC 27520

Copyright © 2011 by The University Press of Kentucky

Scholarly publisher for the Commonwealth,
serving Bellarmine University, Berea College, Centre
College of Kentucky, Eastern Kentucky University,
The Filson Historical Society, Georgetown College,
Kentucky Historical Society, Kentucky State University,
Morehead State University, Murray State University,
Northern Kentucky University, Transylvania University,
University of Kentucky, University of Louisville,
and Western Kentucky University.
All rights reserved.

Editorial and Sales Offices: The University Press of Kentucky
663 South Limestone Street, Lexington, Kentucky 40508-4008
www.kentuckypress.com

15 14 13 12 11   5 4 3 2 1

Library of Congress Cataloging-in-Publication Data

Oehlschlaeger, Fritz.
  The achievement of Wendell Berry : the hard history of love / Fritz
Oehlschlaeger.
      p.   cm. — (Culture of the land)
  Includes bibliographical references and index.
  ISBN 978-0-8131-3007-1 (hardcover : acid-free paper) — ISBN
978-0-8131-3009-5 (ebook)
  1. Berry, Wendell, 1934– —Criticism and interpretation. I. Title.
  PS3552.E75Z79 2011
  818'.5409—dc22

                    2010053736

This book is printed on acid-free paper meeting
the requirements of the American National Standard
for Permanence in Paper for Printed Library Materials.

Manufactured in the United States of America.

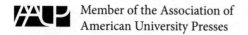 Member of the Association of
American University Presses

MOUNT OLIVE COLLEGE MOYE LIBRARY
OLAY TON, NC 27520

Contents

Acknowledgments

I wish to begin by thanking Wendell Berry for the rich and honest work he has given, and continues to give, to his readers. I thank him, too, for his permission to quote more fully from the poems "Dante" and "Sabbath VII, 2008" than fair scholarly use customarily allows. I am also grateful to my editors at the University Press of Kentucky, Laura Sutton, Ann Malcolm, and Ila McEntire, and to the press director, Stephen Wrinn, for their wonderful encouragement and kind suggestions about the book. The readers of the manuscript offered careful criticism that has helped me to make this a better book than it would have been otherwise, and for this I thank them.

Stanley Hauerwas and Norman Wirzba of Duke Divinity School read the manuscript and gave me important suggestions. My colleagues at Virginia Tech, Tom Gardner and Peter Graham, have been wonderful conversation partners over the years on all literary matters. I have learned a great deal from three groups of graduate students who have taken seminars with me devoted, in part, to Berry's work. In particular, I wish to thank Sarah Parker-Clever, from whom I learned much about *Remembering* as she did her master's capstone essay on that novel. I also want to thank Linda Patino and Jared Gibbs for their fine work as research assistants at different stages of the project.

The English Department and College of Liberal Arts and Human Sciences at Virginia Tech provided me with research assistance and a sabbatical leave that enabled me to finish the work. I especially thank my chairperson, Carolyn Rude, for her support. The staff of the Interlibrary

Loan Department of the Virginia Tech Library helped me to find materials I needed, just as they have done so competently and cheerfully for the past thirty years. Finally, I wish to thank my wife, Deb, for her unfailing encouragement and kindness in all things.

Abbreviations

ECCA "The Ecological Crisis as a Crisis of Agriculture," in Wendell
      Berry, *The Unsettling of America*
EP   "Economy and Pleasure," in Wendell Berry, *What Are People For?*
FBM   "Feminism, the Body, and the Machine," in Wendell Berry, *What
      Are People For?*
FW   "The Failure of War," in Wendell Berry, *Citizenship Paperes*
GGL   "The Gift of Good Land," in Wendell Berry, *The Gift of Good Land*
HW Wendell Berry, *The Hidden Wound*
ILE   "The Idea of a Local Economy," in Wendell Berry, *The Art of the
      Commonplace*
KJV   The Bible, King James Version
LF   "The Loss of the Future," in Wendell Berry, *The Long-Legged House*
LH   "The Landscaping of Hell: Strip-Mine Morality in East Kentucky,"
      in Wendell Berry, *The Long-Legged House*
LM Wendell Berry, *Life Is a Miracle*
LU   "The Loss of the University," in Wendell Berry, *Home Economics*
LWJ   "Letter to Wes Jackson," in Wendell Berry, *Home Economics*
NAR   "Notes from an Absence and a Return," in Wendell Berry, *A
      Continuous Harmony*
NH   "A Native Hill," in Wendell Berry, *The Long-Legged House*
NR   "A Nation Rich in Natural Resources," in Wendell Berry, *Home
      Economics*
NRSV The Bible, New Revised Standard Version
OYC   "Out of Your Car, Off Your Horse," in Wendell Berry, *Sex,
      Economy, Freedom, and Community*
PLC   "People, Land, and Community," in Wendell Berry, *Standing by
      Words*
PM   "Poetry and Marriage: The Use of Old Forms," in Wendell Berry,
      Standing by Words
PPND "Property, Patriotism, and National Defense," in Wendell Berry,
      Home Economics
RH   "Renewing Husbandry," in Wendell Berry, *The Way of Ignorance
      and Other Essays*
SBW   "Standing by Words," in Wendell Berry, *Standing by Words*
SE   "Sex, Economy, Freedom, and Community," in Wendell Berry,
      Sex, Economy, Freedom, and Community

SFP	"Solving for Pattern," in Wendell Berry, *The Gift of Good Land*
SOP	"The Specialization of Poetry," in Wendell Berry, *Standing by Words*
SP	"A Secular Pilgrimage," in Wendell Berry, *A Continuous Harmony*
TC	Wendell Berry, *A Timbered Choir*
TE	"Two Economies," in Wendell Berry, *Home Economics*
THC	"Toward a Healthy Community: An Interview with Wendell Berry," in Morris Allen Grubbs, ed., *Conversations with Wendell Berry*
TL	"Think Little," in Wendell Berry, *A Continuous Harmony*
TPF	"Thoughts in the Presence of Fear," in Wendell Berry, *Citizenship Papers*
UA	"The Unsettling of America," in Wendell Berry, *The Unsettling of America*
WBC	Anne Husted Burleigh, "Wendell Berry's Community," in Morris Allen Grubbs, ed., *Conversations with Wendell Berry*

Introduction

To attempt a work of literary criticism devoted to the writings of Wendell Berry might seem foolhardy. After all, Jayber Crow has warned critics off in no uncertain terms in the "Notice" posted "BY ORDER OF THE AUTHOR" at the beginning of the novel bearing his name: "Persons attempting to find a 'text' in this book will be prosecuted; persons attempting to find a 'subtext' in it will be banished; persons attempting to explain, interpret, explicate, analyze, deconstruct, or otherwise 'understand' it will be exiled to a desert island in the company only of other explainers."[1] At least the critic is not to "be shot," as he no doubt deserves and as Mark Twain threatens at the outset of *Huckleberry Finn*.[2] In self-defense, I can think of only two things to say. One, regarding exile, is to remind Berry of his own poem "Dante," from *Given*: "If you imagine / others are there / you are there yourself."[3] The other is to say that while this is a work primarily of literary criticism, it is also one of affection that seeks to be faithful to what Berry has himself said the work of criticism should be.

Berry concludes his 2004 essay "Imagination in Place" with a brief paragraph that richly suggests his moral commitments as a writer and human being and offers a standard by which to judge his work: "I have tried (clumsily, I see) to define the places, real and imagined, where I have taken my stand and done my work." He speaks of making "the imagined place of Port William" in an "attempt to honor the actual place" where he has lived and then, "by means of the imagined place," learning "to see [his] native landscape and neighborhood as a place unique in the world, a work of God, possessed of an inherent sanctity that mocks any human valuation that can be put upon it." "If anything I have written," he concludes, "can be taken to countenance the misuse" of the place, "or to excuse anybody for rating the land as 'capital' or its human members as 'labor,' my writing would have been better unwritten. And then to hell with any value anybody may find in it 'as literature.'"[4]

This last comment suggests a dilemma felt keenly by many writers. The writer will make use, necessarily, of people and places. In this, he or she is not much different from the rest of us. We all "get our living," as Thoreau put it, from people and places.[5] Nevertheless, there is great intuitive force to our sense that people, and perhaps also places, deserve to be regarded as ends in their own right and not merely as means.[6] If writers are sometimes particularly sensitive to this requirement, it is because they are aware of the degree to which their work does depend on making use of its subjects. Berry's insistence is that there is no independent aesthetic judgment of value by which he would have his writings justified if they were to violate these moral requirements.

As the writer must use, the question he faces becomes how to "use kindly." Berry uses the word "honor" to describe how he has regarded his actual place, and he frequently makes use of the word "love" as well, as when he remarks in the preface to *The Way of Ignorance* that the work he "feel[s] best about" has been done "as an amateur: for love."[7] To love and honor a place is to be married to it, which is to recognize that one's life is bound up with it, for better or worse, as Berry did when he returned to Kentucky to live in 1964. But what does it mean to say that a writer loves and honors the people and places he imagines? To answer that is difficult, perhaps finally impossible, but I do think we can make a start. It means first that he will not oversimplify, that he will approach his work knowing that there is always more to know. He will recognize himself to be a perennial amateur of sorts, as we are in marriage, that analogous discipline that we enter into necessarily in ignorance. Knowing the need to avoid reduction and excessive abstraction, the writer will seek to "complexify" his work, much as the good farmer learns to allow the infinite particularities of his farm to guide what he does. To treat his people lovingly involves continually extending the contexts in which their actions are to be understood— much as Berry recommends that both scientist and humanist must learn to extend the contexts of their work if they are to learn to talk to each other.

To be continually aware of his own ignorance will require certain virtues of the writer, perhaps especially humility and patience, the willingness to allow time to reveal what can only be understood in time. In the meantime, the writer who honors his place and people will be compelled to defend them against the clear threats to their integrity and existence. Berry has been doing this, particularly, but not exclusively, in his nonfiction writing now for roughly forty years (taking the publication of *The Long-Legged House* in 1969 as a marker). In defending his people against stereotyping and their home places against the industrial agriculture that has damaged rural life in America and everywhere, Berry has become a major voice in the argument for a new agrarianism. I would argue he passes the moral test he sets for himself: nothing that he has written "countenances" the misuse, the reduction to mere means, of the people or places he treats. We must remain in ignorance ourselves as to whether the value of Berry's work will, in future, be found in it "as literature." Berry has himself pointed out the absurdity of reading and teaching the Bible "as literature," and the kind of argument he makes applies to his own work as well. The biblical writers did not think of themselves as writing "literature." They were trying to write the truth, and so is Berry. That we teach any text merely "as literature" is a function of the overspecialization of our disciplines, particularly in the universities, and a way of insulating ourselves from the hard questions these texts pose.[8] Having lived more of my life "in school" than Berry, I see no way we can give coherence to our learning and teaching without a broad disciplinary category like "literature," but I think we must correct for what he fears by insisting—as he suggests—that we study a writer's work with an eye toward learning from it, not simply about it. I hope it will be evident in this book how much I have learned from Berry's work.

One reason we might want to adopt Berry's standard of "kindly use" in our relations to people and places rather than one framed in terms of ends and means is that "kindly use" specifically resists a too sharp separation of these terms, something whose dangers Berry has warned about. In "Discipline and Hope," for example, Berry argues that we have "come to attribute to ends a moral importance that far outweighs that which we attribute to means." As a result, we lose discipline and hope, for "the discipline of ends is no discipline at all," and "hope lives in the means, not the end." "The end is preserved in the means," and a good or "desirable end may perish forever in the wrong means."⁹ To preserve a good end, we must seek endlessly to purify our disciplines, knowing our hope lies in them.

If the end is to be preserved in our discipline, then it must somehow be there before us as well, for a discipline is a teaching and must be learned, at least at first, from others. The end for Berry, as he's described it in "Imagination in Place," is what we might call the development of a comprehensive charity, the virtue that sees and acts from an ever-deepening regard for the unique particularity of every created thing. There is nothing soft about this quality, which is eminently practical. Working through the virtue of prudence, "real charity calls for the study of agriculture, soil husbandry, engineering, architecture, mining, manufacturing, transportation, the making of monuments and pictures, songs and stories."¹⁰ But it will not study any of these things in complete abstraction from the whole, for "by its nature," charity "cannot be selective." Everywhere discovering the bonds that exist among creatures, charity cannot stop short of the Kingdom of God, that term Berry invokes to describe the widest economy, the most inclusive order. Charity will discover, or perhaps comes fully into being *as* it discovers, that it only makes sense "to love all Creation" as a "response to the Creator's love for it."¹¹ Charity will understand itself as moved by, and participating in, the love of God, there at the beginning, along the way, and at the end. That love is the end that informs the discipline and must be preserved in the means.

But how does the writer, as Berry claims, come to see his actual place more accurately through the imagined place? As significant charity in the disciplines mentioned above requires a "constant criticism" of skills, so, too, the writer engages to tell and retell the history of his people and their place, considering it from a variety of viewpoints and pondering how actions and motives resonate over time. In this, his work resembles that of Andy Catlett as he tries to understand the murder of his uncle Andrew in *A World Lost* by sifting through the accounts that have come to him and reconstructing a narrative. The love in a place has a history, a good bit of it "hard," as the young Mat Feltner begins to sense in "The Hurt Man (1888)"¹² The writer's task is to tell that history as lovingly as possible, in the process discovering depths in it that only the patient work of imagination, assisted by time, can reveal. The writer reminds us that all history is a *"history of souls,"* as Andy says in *Remembering,* and souls—whether fictional or real—can only be understood through imagination.[13] To understand "what is going on," then, in any actual place, there is no substitute for imagination guided by love.

We can see, then, why Berry is so rightly wary of attempts to "explain" works of literature. To do so is uncharitable and potentially tyrannical, for it is to substitute abstractions for life itself, or at least for what Henry James called that "illusion of life" created by the best works of imaginative literature.[14] Berry rejects unequivocally the idea put forth by E. O. Wilson in *Consilience*—that works of criticism can somehow substitute for, or replace, the "works of art" they seek to understand. He does acknowledge, however, a more modest, "useful" role for criticism of a kind we once knew as "practical": "I don't mean at all to say that criticism is impossible, or that it cannot be useful. Obviously, we need to talk about works of art. We must test our ways of knowing about them. We must learn them and teach them and describe them and study the ways they are made. We must compare them with one another, and evaluate them by whatever standards we can make applicable."[15] I take this as a description of the kind of criticism I have tried to practice in this book. To it I would add two further precepts, themselves derived from Berry. Part of the critic's charitable practice is to enlarge the contexts in which a writer's work can be considered and also to demonstrate how one can learn from it, to point out directions for its further use.

It's perhaps best to start out with a word about audience. I suspect Berry's work has several, partially overlapping audiences, and part of my purpose here is to help members of each of those audiences to see Berry's work as the integrated whole I believe it to be. I hope those who are familiar primarily with his agrarian essays will find helpful insights here in my discussions of the fiction and poetry and that those who have come to him primarily through the "literary" side will be attracted to the agrarian and political vision. The book's organization is by genre and topic. The first three chapters focus primarily on Berry's nonfiction. Conceived as an introduction into Berry's world, chapter 1 suggests how the roots of his ideas may lie in his learning the discipline of the teamster. It stresses the centrality of practices, particulars, and virtues to Berry's thinking, connecting these terms to a host of matters in the essays. Chapter 2 addresses Berry's political and economic thought, broadly construed. Berry has been particularly perceptive, I believe, in analyzing the ways our increasingly "total economy" undermines community life, the private-public distinction, and the institution of marriage. To counter this detrimental influence, he reasserts the importance of household and local economies. Since September 11, 2001, he has written more explicitly as a citizen and patriot, but it is my contention that these roles, and their accompanying obligations, have always been important to him—although he gives to them particular meanings that are at odds with what they too often seem to mean. Chapter 3 takes as its starting point a question once posed to me by a student: is Berry's work dependent on Christianity? Without attempting to answer that question definitively, I use it as a frame, suggesting at least a half-dozen Christian emphases in Berry's work.

In treating Berry's agrarianism, I have decided not to give it a chapter of its own but to allow it to be the implicit—and often completely explicit—context and condition for everything I am doing. This decision derives, in part, from my sense that Berry's agrarianism is the one feature of his work that has been most fully addressed by previous scholars and critics. I have tried throughout to make use, in fact, of the excellent work on Berry and agrarianism by Kimberly K. Smith, Norman Wirzba, Allan C. Carlson, Eric T. Freyfogle, and many others.[16] Berry's agrarianism is "new" in the sense articulated by Wirzba when he says that agrarianism must be understood as a "compelling and coherent alternative to the modern industrial/technological/economic paradigm" and not as "a throwback to a never-realized pastoral arcadia."[17] On the other hand, there is much that is "old" about agrarianism in that it draws upon sources of wisdom rooted in the oldest of human practices and on natural ones much older. Agrarianism, then, is a work of retrieval and rediscovery as we aspire toward something new that also acknowledges the perennial force of the best of the old. To achieve an "authentic agrarianism"—something Wirzba defines as "the sustained attempt to live faithfully and responsibly in a world of limits and possibilities"—would be to become "authentically settled" in America at last, something Berry believes we have yet to accomplish.[18]

Chapters 4 through 6 consider Berry's fiction, each focusing on an individual genre. The subject of chapter 4 is Port William's "hard history of love" as it is told in the short stories collected in *That Distant Land*. That story is complex, and, as with most things, all the interest lies in the details. But perhaps the overall arc of the story can be described as one from hurt to charity—from the hurt young Mat Feltner sees in the face of the man his mother assists in the opening story to the charity of sight and knowledge evident in Wheeler Catlett and Danny Branch in the last story, "The Inheritors (1986)." The volume's stories work together to suggest how a good community prevents hurt from compounding endlessly as pain and anger, how it provides a place and context for the development of charity. Obviously crucial to this process is memory, which provides the organizing idea for a discussion of Berry's five short novels in chapter 5. The chapter is framed by Andy Catlett's recognition—in Berry's most recent novel, *Andy Catlett: Early Travels*—that telling the stories of his grandparents is part of the necessary enactment of the gratitude by which he lives. The way the loss that necessitates gratitude comes into the world is part of Berry's subject in his first novel, *Nathan Coulter. A World Lost* suggests the way a child responds to the death of a beloved other through narration, the concerted attempt to re-create the wholeness of what is truly "a world" lost. *Remembering* traces the way the mature Andy becomes utterly lost to himself and then found again through a process of return that involves the mysterious presence of the other, the beauty of the world, and the deep recognition that what lies before him is worthy to be lived because of the way it has been lived already by his ancestors. Devoted to a life that has become almost entirely memory, *The Memory of Old Jack* depicts one who comes to the end of his life, sees what is worthy, and recognizes it to be enough. Jack Beechum's life may seem a failure in some ways, but I think it actually suggests how trivial terms like failure and success are when applied to a life like his—a life given passionately and thus, in some sense, never lost, to himself or to those who come to love him.

Chapter 6 is devoted to Berry's three longest novels, *A Place on Earth, Hannah Coulter,* and *The Life Story of Jayber Crow, Barber, of the Port William Membership, as Written by Himself.* Again the richness of these novels lies in their details, but I suggest that they can be helpfully read together as novels of love set in time of war. Each contributes to our understanding of the practical kind of peaceableness that may yet enable us to imagine alternatives to war. My final chapter offers a consideration of Berry's work as a poet, a task he has understood, in traditional terms, to be one of renewing the language. The chapter examines Berry's thoughts on the unspecializing of poetry; distinguishes his work from the so-called language poetry; draws out the rich analogies he traces between poetry, on the one hand, and other disciplines of the real like marriage and farming; and concludes with a look at the Sabbath poems in his two most recent volumes. Above all, poetry is, for Berry, the art of the particular and thus the art through which we learn the goodness and grace of being here.

What Berry says of his friend the painter Harlan Hubbard in "Sabbath XV, 2005" might well be said of Berry himself. In painting places that he knew along the Ohio River, Hubbard thought of himself as "painting Heaven," for the particulars of those places were such that he could "never" see "them clear enough / to satisfy his love, his need / to see them all again, again."[19] Berry has worked from a similar love now in all the genres for fifty years, in the process helping his readers to come to know their own places on earth more truly by showing them what it means to imagine "in place." In doing so, he has contributed immensely to that "great general work of criticism to which we all are called," as he has put it in "The Loss of the University."[20] At the risk of sounding as old-fashioned as Berry himself when he talks about virtues like "thrift" or "patience," I will say that he has given us what we rightly expect from a writer of his stature: a serious moral vision of life rooted in care, affection, and honesty. The critic's task is not so much to "explain" that vision—certainly not in any reductive way—but to point out ways in which it might be used kindly. I hope to have done a little bit toward that here.

Chapter 1

Practices, Particulars, and Virtues
What Mules Taught Wendell Berry

Wendell Berry remarks in "A Native Hill" that he was born in "the nick of time." If he had been born only five years later, he "would have begun in a different world, and would no doubt have become a different man." Born in 1934 in Kentucky, where the Depression and later World War II "delayed the mechanization" process, Berry became "less a child of [his] time" than his contemporaries born in cities or in areas of the country where machine farming was closer to being the norm. He received the paradoxical grace of anachronism, grounded in memory of earlier and alternative ways of living. His "acceptance of twentieth- [and now twenty-first-] century realities"—when he does accept them—has thus had about it "a certain deliberateness."[1] Here Berry's language recalls Thoreau, who "went to the woods" because he "wished to live deliberately," to ask quite consciously what he needed for life and what he was better off without—irrespective of what his contemporaries assumed.[2] Berry has brought similar deliberateness to his examination of contemporary American life, a deliberateness grounded in his sense that things have been, and can always be, different. His greatest similarity to Thoreau, with whom he is often compared, lies precisely in the radical quality of his questions and his hope. He is not one of the thousands who hack at the branches of evil, but one who tries always to go to the roots.

"One of the first disciplines imposed on me was that of a teamster" (NH, 171), Berry writes, and I believe thinking about this discipline offers us a particularly illuminating entry into Berry's world. His learning as a boy to work teams of animals has much to do with a whole host of matters:

his way of thinking about the integrity of farming, his love of the essay as a literary form, his emphasis on the virtues, his disdain for the word "environment," his way of placing himself in relation to other American writers, perhaps even his being a Christian. The chapter takes up each of these matters in turn, showing the connections among them and their connections to Berry's learning to work with mules. I do not mean to suggest that Berry consciously reflected on his history as a teamster when he decided to write essays or even that he "decided" to write essays. It would be more accurate to say that these are analogous practices or disciplines. Gravitating toward the essay as a form reflects a way of thinking about how and what we know that is grounded in practices like those of the teamster. To think about what it would mean for farming to regain its integrity depends first on our understanding it as a set of practices now subject to external forces inherently alien to its disciplines. Skill at a practice requires the ability to differentiate among particulars, a quality dependent on the cultivation of virtues like humility and patience. What the first part of the chapter explores, then, is a way of entering Berry's world through a language of practices, particulars, and virtues. I use Alasdair MacIntyre's analysis of practices as a way to clarify the concept and focus particularly on Berry's understanding of farming as a practice.

The chapter's second part explores the virtues Berry espouses in both his nonfiction and his fiction. My list, which is certainly not exhaustive, includes prudence, courage, justice, equity, friendship, and the three theological virtues of faith, hope, and love or charity, along with the humility and patience mentioned above. The latter part of the chapter extends this introduction to Berry's world by looking at three additional matters related to his decisions to return to Kentucky from New York in 1964 and to use draft animals—horses, not mules—in the early 1970s. These decisions represent the "free acceptance of proper limits" that Patrick J. Deneen has said lies at the heart of Berry's conception of liberty.[3] I consider first his resistance to using the popular term "environment" and why this has important implications for our thinking about our places on earth. One can see why the term would seem so inadequate to one who thinks of his own farm not just as something surrounding him, but as the source of his own life. Next I look at the way Berry tells the story, in "A Native Hill," of his decision to leave New York, using that piece as a way to explore his relationship to other American writers who have decided either for or against deep connection to their native places. The final part of the chapter develops the idea that even Berry's religious understanding may have its roots in his earliest experiences with Grandfather Berry's mules.

We begin our entry into Berry's world with his full description of the way he began to acquire the skills of the teamster:

> One of the first disciplines imposed on me was that of a teamster. Perhaps I first stood in the role of student before my father's father, who, halting a team in front of me, would demand to know which mule had the best head, which the best shoulder or rump, which was the lead mule, were they hitched right. And there came a time when I knew, and took a considerable pride in knowing. Having a boy's usual desire to play at what he sees men working at, I learned to harness and hitch and work a team. I felt distinguished by that, and took the same pride in it that other boys my age took in their knowledge of automobiles. (NH, 171–72)

First it bears emphasizing that learning to work a team is a "discipline," the acquisition of a teaching, and one that inherently involves learning and accommodating limits. Mules have ways of letting people know what the limits are. People working them will likely become not-so-naive realists, philosophically speaking. People thinking they are working their ideas of mules have probably gone into other trades by now.

The second thing to notice is that the discipline was "imposed on" Berry by his elders, who had had it, no doubt, imposed on them in turn. Ultimately it was imposed on all of them by mule nature and by the demands of making a living on relatively small, often hilly farms. There was nothing unfeeling about such imposition. It would have been irresponsible, even unloving, not to have imposed this discipline on Berry rigorously. Bringing a child up without the skills needed for life in a difficult world is irresponsible, and, as there are inherent dangers in working with mules, the loving thing to do is to make sure that a boy knows how to do so as safely as possible. Probably Berry felt at times that such discipline was punishment, but he could always see that there was nothing arbitrary about it. He could see that what the men insisted he learn was part of what they did every day. They were right before him all the time doing what they were teaching him to do. They seemed also to enjoy it, to do their work as part of a life they considered worth living and passing on, and so, in time, the

≂ HOCUTT-ELLINGTON MEMORIAL LIBRARY
CLAYTON, NC 27520

child could be pleased and proud to have acquired the disciplines that made their life possible.

The third thing to notice is that no mule is like any other mule. Having different qualities, strengths, and temperaments, they must be known as particulars. One must learn what and how much each can do and how to match them properly. Learning what's necessary will involve, especially at the beginning, direction by one who has had a long history of working with mules—a master—for only through such history does one learn what to look for in a mule, to know what makes a "good one." As one works more and more with the animals, the good learner—the one who learns to pay the right sort of attention—will become an increasingly skilled teamster. But he or she will know, too, that there is always more to learn about managing teams and caring for the animals and that even the best knowledge of this kind is largely proximate. It cannot be known with the degree of certainty that one can achieve in other kinds of pursuits. The best standard for being a good teamster will always be those acknowledged to be the most skilled in the work.

What Berry was learning was a "practice," in the sense defined by Alasdair MacIntyre. In *After Virtue*, MacIntyre defines a practice as "any coherent and complex form of socially established cooperative human activity through which goods internal to that form of activity are realized in the course of trying to achieve those standards of excellence which are appropriate to, and partially definitive of, that form of activity." One result of such activity is that "human powers to achieve excellence, and human conceptions of the ends and goods involved, are systematically extended." Thus, tic-tac-toe and "throwing a football with skill" are not practices—because there can be no "systematic extension" of excellence in these—but the games of football and chess are. Or, to take an agricultural example, "Planting turnips is not a practice; farming is."[4]

Several qualities of MacIntyrean practices are helpful in thinking about Berry's work. First, as we have seen in regard to Berry's learning the teamster's art, the acquisition of a practice requires an authoritative teacher—the skilled practitioner—and a certain amount of prereflective training. Some things have simply to be learned first before they can be thought about. Second, practices involve external and internal goods. We might, to use one of MacIntyre's examples, teach a child to play chess by rewarding her good performance with candy, but we hope that eventually "the

ROCKHURST UNIVERSITY MEMORIAL LIBRARY
CLAYTON, MO 87200

achievement of a certain highly particular kind of analytical skill, strategic imagination and competitive intensity" will become reasons for the child to do her best at the game. Her happiness will thus lie in a certain kind of excellence "internal" to the practice itself (*AV,* 188). Or, as Berry puts it, "there came a time when I knew, and took a considerable pride in knowing" how "to harness and hitch and work a team" (NH, 171–72). Third, practices involve "standards of excellence and obedience to rules as well as the achievement of goods." The standards need not be fixed and unchanging. Practices have histories; standards are "not themselves immune from criticism." But "to enter into a practice is to accept the authority" of the "best standards" current; to be willing "to subject" one's "own attitudes, choices, preferences and tastes" to those standards; and to judge one's own performance "inadequate" when it fails to meet the standards (*AV,* 190). When practitioners are no longer willing to be judged by the standards, a practice risks losing authority over itself. This may happen because the lure of external goods is greater than fidelity to a practice's internal goods, as it has been, for instance, for steroid-using baseball players.

This example specifically illuminates Berry's discussions of what has happened to farming under the model of industrialized agriculture. Berry clearly understands farming as a practice, a discipline with its own evolved standards of good and bad work. "All good human work remembers its history," he says in "Feminism, the Body, and the Machine," and yet much of modern farming has sought to make its history irrelevant.[5] Farming, like baseball, has been unable to prevent external goods from destroying its very status as a practice with an integrity of its own. This destruction of farming's integrity is what Berry objected to as early as *The Unsettling of America* in response to then-secretary of agriculture Earl Butz's proclaiming food "a weapon." "Food is *not* a weapon," Berry insists. Moreover, "to foster a mentality willing to use it as such" is to "prepare, in the human character and community, the destruction of the sources of food." This conclusion may seem counterintuitive; after all, using food as a weapon depends upon either producing it or being capable of doing so. But for Berry the conclusion follows because the character of farmers and the health of farms are matters that cannot be left out of account. To begin thinking of food as a weapon, Berry suggests, is evidence that already the "fundamental integrities" of the practice of farming have been "devalued and broken."[6] It is not an overstatement, I believe, to suggest that the most important thrust of all of Berry's work has been to help farming reacquire linguistic authority over itself, to give it again a way of understanding itself that will enable it to reestablish its integrity as a practice.

A good place to look for further understanding of how farming's "fundamental integrities" came to be broken is Berry's recent essay "Renewing Husbandry," which focuses on another "landmark" moment in his past involving mules.[7] The moment is in summer, 1950, and he is mowing a field with a "nearly new Farmall," when his father sends a hired man with a "mowing machine and a team of mules to the field" where Berry is working. Berry notes again that he "had been born" into "the way of farming represented by the mule team" and "loved it," and he knew, too, "irresistibly," that these "mules were good ones" as they stepped "along beautifully at a rate of speed" only slightly slower than his own. Nevertheless he remembers how, "from the vantage point of the tractor," he now "resented their slowness," seeing them primarily as "in my way" (91). It has taken Berry a "long time" to learn how to read this incident, largely because the fifty-four years between its happening and his writing about it "have widened the context of the scene as circles widen on water around a thrown stone." He now understands that the "team belonged to the farm," to a kind of farming that had its own integrity because it could be sustained from its own resources, from "free solar energy." The tractor, on the other hand, "belonged to" an "alien" economy dependent on "distant supplies," "long supply lines," and petroleum. The life made possible by the team, the life of Berry's mule-working grandfather, was one "of limits, both suffered and strictly observed, in a world of limits." With the tractor, and the apparent promise of "limitless cheap fossil fuel," we "had entered an era of limitlessness," or, at least, "the illusion thereof" (RH, 94–95).[8]

Berry's point is not that all farming be done again with mules or horses, although these do have a place in today's farming, and their role is likely to increase as we come to the unavoidable conclusion that we must depend less on fossil fuels and more on free solar energy. Berry does some of his own farming with horses, having made the decision to do so in the early 1970s, a decision he describes in *The Gift of Good Land* almost as a kind of *metanoia:* "Now I was turning around, as if in the middle of my own history, and taking up the old way again."[9] This language suggests Berry's description in "A Native Hill" of another turn in the middle of his history, one we'll look at in a moment, the decision to return to Kentucky from the cosmopolitan center of New York. Both decisions represent the free consent to limits, perhaps deriving from the intuition that freedom involves for any of us the trustful and ever-deeper exploration of the history and places that have made us who we are. We might think of the decision to farm with horses as Berry's way of going deeper into the logic of his earlier decision, deeper into the fund of trust he had opened in his ancestors' way of life.

To use terms Berry has adopted from Wallace Stegner, we might say he had decided to be a "sticker" rather than the literary equivalent of the American "boomer."[10] Or to use analogous terms, he decided for "nurture" rather than "exploitation," concepts Berry has used to explore fundamental tensions in our attitudes toward the land. The exploiter asks of a "piece of land only how much and how quickly it can be made to produce," whereas the "nurturer asks a question that is much more complex and difficult: What is its carrying capacity?" (UA, 7). To think of food as a weapon, as Secretary Butz proposed, is to go wholly over to exploitation in the treatment of land: to consider the farm as merely one variable in a vast quantitative and calculative effort of output whose goal is national empowerment. To do so is to introduce so many alien valuations into farming that it inevitably destroys the integrity of farming as a practice and the health of farms along with it. If farming has one advantage over other practices—baseball, for example—in its attempt to reclaim its integrity it is that the ultimate authority in farming is not human beings, but the land itself. For fifty years we have treated the land otherwise, but ultimately we must learn to bring our actions into harmony with the "disciplines imposed" upon us by nature. We must learn again to live within limits, a fact whose growing acceptance no doubt contributes to the growing audience for Berry's work. If we are to read Berry not as an elegist, but rather as a "futurist," as David W. Orr suggests, we can do so by attending to how that work offers an extended exploration, an opening up, of the practices, particulars, and virtues of a way of life that understands itself to be limited.[11] Berry's work offers opportunities, on all sorts of levels, for the kind of creative retrieval that is at the heart of the new agrarianism, one based on finding analogous ways to use the best practices of the past to create a sustainable future.

Learning to manage and care for teams of mules taught Berry an Aristotelian lesson: that pursuits of different kinds of knowledge carry with them different degrees of certainty. "It is a mark of the trained mind never to expect more precision in the treatment of any subject than the nature of the subject permits," Aristotle writes in Book 1 of the *Nicomachean Ethics*. We cannot reasonably demand "logical demonstrations" from a teacher of rhetoric any more than we would accept "mere plausibility from a mathematician."[12] We might argue, in fact, that failure to understand such elementary matters has led to the crisis in farming, at least as Berry depicts it: experts trained in the scientific farming of the agricultural colleges have sought degrees of certainty in the management of farming practices that are inherently inconsistent with the "nature of the subject." Fortunately, mules taught Berry early on that managing animals is an inherently uncertain practice, knowledge he has carried over not only to his farming but to his writing.

In the "Preface" to *Home Economics,* Berry explains his fondness for the essay in terms that perhaps suggest his memory of mules: "I have thought, sometimes, of my essays as trials, not because I think they render verdicts, but because they make attempts, trying out both their subjects and my understanding. Often, too, they try my patience." Each trial is but a piece of a larger argument whose subject is "the fact, and ultimately the faith, that things connect—that we are wholly dependent on a pattern, an all-inclusive form, that we partly understand." Each piece is an "effort to describe responsibility," and thus it is "necessarily an *essay*—a trial or an attempt," risking error always and committing it often. "The idea that it could produce a verdict is absurd, as is the possibility that it could be concluded," for this would be to expect of the inquiry a certainty inconsistent with the subject.[13] One essays again and again, hoping each time to learn a little more while knowing, too, that what one learns often leaves the subject even more mysterious, the inquiry more uncertain.

Living within limits in a world of uncertainties requires discipline. It implies a turning for wisdom to local and traditional sources too often dismissed by formal education. As Berry hears from the experienced horse farmer Nick Coleman when he asks for advice about using horses, "Find somebody who knows how. . . . You can't learn it by yourself, and you can't read it out of a book. A book is all right, but you need to know something before you start reading."[14] Some things can only be learned from those "who know how," from those who have become experienced and proficient in practices. Reading can lead to reflection on those practices, and perhaps some modification of them, but only if one first has a grounding in the practices themselves. Skillful practitioners must be able to differentiate among particulars, and this requires the cultivation of virtues like patience and humility. Living within limits requires other virtues as well, and these, too, must be learned, as Aristotle made clear, from those who know how to do the right thing at the right time and in the right way and for the right reason. In addition to humility and patience, a brief list of the virtues about which Berry has written would include prudence, courage, justice, equity, friendship, and the three theological ones, faith, hope, and love or charity. It is to these I turn now.

Consideration of the virtues in Berry's work appropriately begins with humility, the willingness to acknowledge the limits of what we can know. The practice of humility involves learning "to co-operate" in the world's "processes, and to yield to its limits." Even more crucially, it involves learn-ing to "acknowledge that the creation is full of mystery," that "we will never entirely understand it" (NH, 196). Its antithesis is the intellectual or "aca-demic hubris" represented by doctrinaire materialists like Edward O. Wilson who elevate scientism to religious status and argue that everything can be explained—and will be, in Wilson's view, when the scientific disci-plines can be unified in the process he calls "consilience." One disturbing implication of Wilson's thinking is that it seems inherently totalitarian, as Berry argues in *Life Is a Miracle,* for if "any social theory" were to be, for instance, "general, consilient, and predictive," what possible reason could there be not to put it into force? "If you know with certainty what is true," Berry asks, "should you not *enforce* the truth?"[15]

Humility requires patience as an accompanying virtue, for if we are to pursue what Berry has recently called "The Way of Ignorance," we will need to learn what Berry says he learned from the African American man who taught him to hunt squirrels: "to look and to listen and to be quiet" (NH, 197). Berry has borrowed the phrase "The Way of Ignorance" from T. S. Eliot, believing it to be not only "the way that is appropriate for the igno-rant" but also what Eliot understood to be the way "recommended by all the great teachers."[16] Part of this "way" is to remember how our knowledge may itself distort our ways of perceiving experience. Thus, we must develop an almost infinite patience toward reality as we seek its patterns while knowing that our discernment is likely to be, in some sense, false and dis-torting. As Berry points out, Americans have never been very patient as a people. The myth of the frontier has been one way of talking about our impatience. The "unsettling of America" is a perpetual tendency, our habit of being constantly on the road to somewhere else. Even reaching the end of the geographical frontier brought no end to this process, only its displacement into an economic life premised on constant growth.

Humility and patience support each other, and both are closely related to prudence. The rehabilitation of the virtue of prudence seems a consequence of much of Berry's writing. Prudence, for us, often means a quality of self-interested, self-protecting calculation. The Prudential is an insurance company: prudence is that quality that enables us to manage risk. The prudent person knows how to maximize effort, to distribute time wisely, to position herself not only to be productive but to seem so.[17] But prudence once meant something quite different, as for Thomas Aquinas, who considered it, in Josef Pieper's words, "nothing less than the directing cognition of reality."[18] Prudence was the practical wisdom by which one knew, as Pieper put it in *The Four Cardinal Virtues,* "both the universal principles of reason and the singulars with which ethical action is concerned" (9). Rather than being narrowly self-regarding or defensive, prudence, in this sense, depends on the silencing of "egocentric interests" in order that one "may perceive the truth of real things, and so that reality itself may guide [one] to the proper means for realizing [a] goal" (20). The structure of prudence as Aquinas outlines it is something Berry comes back to again and again. We live in a world of "singulars," unique events, and in such a world we need to be guided in action by practical wisdom that allows reality itself to show us how to reach our goals. That is a virtual definition of good farming as Wendell Berry sees it. Of course we can generalize, abstract, draw up rules and laws, express certain kinds of truths in mathematical equations. But when we attempt to apply our abstractions without a proper willingness to understand that reality is always a matter, too, of unique singularities, then we get distortion and sometimes disaster—as Berry insists we have by applying excessively abstract models of industrialized farming to the unique particularities of individual farms.

Berry's "People, Land, and Community," from *Standing by Words,* can be read as a primer in the virtue of prudence in the older sense. Berry begins by declaring his intention to speak "precisely" of the "connections that join people, land, and community," things often separated and oversimplified in the separation. He will do this by focusing on a complex example:

how to make "the best human use of a problematical hillside farm." But he will do this as well by suggesting an analogy between marriage and farming, two practices with enough overlap that we can see something about how to act in each by looking at them together. Before beginning the inquiry, we must first get over some of our prior assumptions: one, "that knowledge (information) can be 'sufficient,'" and two, "that time and work are short."[19] Both of these are assumptions of the oversimplifying, industrialized approach to problem-solving, one that would treat people, land, community, and marriage as separable problems for analysis and action. What we will find in the course of the inquiry—or better yet, assume as matters of prudence, humility, and patience—is that knowledge can never be sufficient and had better thus be applied cautiously and that time and work are short only in relation to our own egocentrism. If we think of ourselves as living in God's time, not our own, or if our goal is to act only in ways that do not diminish the earth's capacities to sustain itself, then we are likely to see that work and time are long indeed.

Berry's exploration of the analogy between marriage and farming begins with a subtle point about knowledge in marriage. "As a condition" marriage "reveals the insufficiency of knowledge, and as an institution it suggests the possibility that decisions can be informed in another way that *is* sufficient, or approximately so." What this means is that no one can "know enough to get married"—something Berry considers axiomatic—because no one knows what is involved until one gets married. In marriage one enters into a practice or discipline marked by commitments, vows, and promises that are unlike those one enters into anywhere else—and does so in relation to a unique other who is simultaneously doing the same. Where else does one come together with another to make "one flesh"? How can one who has always been his or her own flesh even begin to know what that will mean? The institution can provide guidance, rooted in a history of practice, as a couple lives the unique process of their marriage. Such guidance and discipline may prove to be sufficient, or at least "approximately so," practically wise enough, that is, to help the couple sustain their life together until they discover that marriage, "or something like it, is the only possible answer" to the "inescapable condition of loneliness and ignorance" in which it was made (PLC, 66).

In a passage meant perhaps to distinguish himself from Thoreau, who went round and round the farm but did not buy (saying finally that he had his seeds still ready),[20] Berry suggests that one's connection "to a newly bought farm" almost always begins in love, and in a love that is, as in marriage, "more or less ignorant." "Something different" happens "when one buys the farm," and "thoughts begin to be translated into acts." One's "first vision" of the place "invariably turns out" to have been "to some extent an imposition on it." But what can happen, then, is the development of something more wonderful, the beginning of a kind of practical wisdom, of prudence in the older sense:

> If one's sight is clear and if one stays on and works well, one's love gradually responds to the place as it really is, and one's visions gradually image possibilities that are really in it. Vision, possibility, work, and life—*all* have changed by mutual correction. Correct discipline, given enough time, gradually removes one's self from one's line of sight. One works to better purpose then and makes fewer mistakes, because at last one sees where one is. Two human possibilities of the highest order thus come within reach: what one wants can become the same as what one has, and one's knowledge can cause respect for what one knows. (PLC, 69–70)

One can see here how prudence—the practical wisdom that enables sound proximate judgment in a world of unique yet complexly related singularities—depends upon patience and humility (as well as something like constancy or fidelity). "Correct discipline" and "enough time" are, for Berry, "inseparable notions." Good work is premised upon patience; it cannot be made "answerable to haste, urgency, or even emergency." Because distraction is also "inimical to correct discipline," the farmer must consider questions of scale, and questions of "propriety of scale" are "invariably associated with propriety of another kind: an understanding and acceptance of the human place in the order of Creation—a proper humility" (PLC, 70–71).

At the time of his writing "People, Land, and Community," Berry had worked seventeen years at restoring a "once exhausted hillside."[21] He came to know that "*good* work" on the hillside required both "*good* intention and *good* (that is, correct) information." But he came to know, too, that fully restoring the hillside would require work beyond his lifetime and that the restoration could be destroyed at any time by someone's shoddy or hasty work. In short, good work requires community, which itself must embody "*character*: the sort of knowledge that might properly be called familiarity, and the affections, habits, values and virtues (conscious and unconscious) that would preserve good care and good work through hard times" (PLC 72). We see here how additional virtues come into play in the maintenance of good community. Courage is certainly vital to the preservation of good care through times of hardship. It's courage, together with faith, that keeps Marce and Dora Catlett working their farm even when their whole year's revenue from tobacco fails to pay the commission on its own sale—as we learn from Andy Catlett in *Remembering*. Moreover, a deep courage may be continually required of the farmer who must learn to act against his own most immediate interest in the service of the longer-term health of farms and communities. The farmer who acts in that way illustrates the connections among the virtues in a particularly striking fashion, for while his action displays courage, his courage is itself rooted in justice, in what he owes others and the land itself, both immediately and in the long term.

Justice must operate throughout a good community as people consider what is due to each in his or her turn. Otherwise resentment is likely to tear the community apart. A sense of equity must also be present somewhere if the right stewards—those capable of good care—are to come into possession of the land. Supplementing the law with equity in regard to the passing of land is the role of Wheeler Catlett in "It Wasn't Me (1953)" and "The Wild Birds (1967)"—though, in the latter story, Wheeler himself learns that equity must sometimes be overridden by generosity and fidelity in the life of a "membership." We have for too long "voted for information as a safe substitute for virtue," Berry argues, "but this ignores—among much else—the need to prepare humans to live short lives in the face of long work and long time" (PLC, 76). The "futility of a dependence on information" lies ultimately in the fact that "we cannot contain what contains us or comprehend what comprehends us" (PLC, 74). Living sustainably in a nature that contains and comprehends us—rather than the other way around—will depend on the virtues, those habits of character that make good human life possible in the face of uncertainty.

Berry has written less about friendship in his essays than about other virtues, but his fiction throughout offers extended treatment of the subject. Perhaps this reflects a sense that friendship requires narrative display, but I suspect something more basic is going on: that Berry does not think of himself as writing *about* friendship at all. Friendship is simply such an obvious feature of any life worth living that Berry cannot help but write about it. There is little doubt he would subscribe to Aristotle's first remark about friendship in Book 8 of the *Nicomachean Ethics*: "It is a kind of virtue, or implies virtue, and it is also most necessary for living. Nobody would choose to live without friends even if he had all the other good things."[22] I suspect that most postmodern autonomous consumers would accept this latter claim: that no one would choose to be friendless. Their participation in digital "communities" suggests at least the desire for friendship. But what I suspect they are largely without is awareness of the contexts in which friendship weighs in the balance as something that makes life worth living. Berry's depiction of Port William is an extended display of such a world: one where friendship is not just a pleasurable activity or choice among others, but necessary sustenance. We discover happiness in being good friends because friendship—like marriage, which includes but transcends it—enables us to escape the loneliness and fear that are the real marks of our condition. We find comfort, even joy, in friendship without lying or needing to lie about what I suspect we mostly lie about: our deaths.

Berry's many scenes of communal work offer a place to begin thinking about friendship in his fiction. Port William's men routinely gather at planting or harvest to assist one another in work requiring communal effort. Such times are ones of camaraderie marked by banter, joking, storytelling, and mythmaking designed to ease the hardness of the work. There is no shirking, unless by someone like Mat Feltner's hired hand Lightning, whose relationship to others is a matter of contract rather than friendship.[23] The banter often focuses on the men's different capacities for the work—their relative speeds in getting down the tobacco row at cutting time, for instance. Yet there is no grumbling or resentment that some end up doing more of the task than others. What is expected is simply that each man do what he can. As the aged Jarrat Coulter says of his diminished abilities, "I'm old and wore out and not worth a damn. But every row I cut is a cut row."[24] Every man's effort contributes to relief from a necessity that the ritual transforms into common wealth—a wealth not measurable in dollars, as these will go, individually, to each owner in relation to his holdings. The common wealth is a more complex achievement by which the affliction of labor is transformed through mutual care, affection, respect, and humor into a kind of joy, the deep happiness that comes from knowing one has done one's part in the world to assist others to bear their burdens and to live. There is no question of justice among them. They illustrate exactly what Aristotle observes when—in showing how friendship "seems to be the bond that holds communities together"—he remarks that "between friends there is no need for justice."[25] It would be unthinkable for Elton Penn to calculate exactly what he owed the Rowanberrys for work they did to assist him. One who would raise the question in terms of the quid pro quo of contractualism would prove himself thereby incapable of the friendship that sustains the community and provides friends a reason for living.

Friendship in the common task is the subject of Berry's story "A Friend of Mine (1967)." Forty-seven years old, three weeks into tobacco-cutting time, Elton Penn is beginning to understand what older men have meant when they've said they are tired. He is happy to have some brief errands to do one Saturday morning before going to work at the Rowanberrys. When he arrives there, Mart asks him to begin cutting a piece apart from where the others are at work, warning him comically not to eat any of the "dead ripe" watermelons he'll find in a patch at the far end of the tobacco rows. The work is a "dread": Elton is tired, and it is hot, difficult effort. But there is nothing to do except to pitch in, finding as he goes a "moment by moment" satisfaction. Of course, he eats the watermelons, discovering again, as he does so, a "gift" in himself "for such moments," the ability "to have a good time."[26] The watermelons are neither an incentive nor a payment from the Rowanberrys, but a gift, one they know their friend loves, one that may make this day of work memorable. As Elton continues, he finds increasingly the satisfaction of work accomplished. "Leaving a harvested patch," he thinks, "is like leaving a house where you have lived. For you *have* lived there, and suffered and rejoiced, and looking back, you see that it was after all a good time, and you like to remember it" (329). He can look on his work and repeat the original affirmation of Genesis 1: it was good. In part, he is able to do this because it is work accomplished in suffering, together with others and in a way that is not for pay. If he were paid, he might very well look back on it and say, "Well, it wasn't very good, but at least I got paid for it." Perhaps because he was not to be paid for it, he had to find it good and therefore did. He has the satisfaction to be derived from taking on himself his share of the general human burden and proving himself equal to it, at least for this day. It is, for Elton and the Rowanberrys, a memorable day. At its finish, Elton comes walking toward the barn where the other men are, "eating one melon and carrying two," grinning in feeling again his competence before the task: "Boys," he said, "all I want is a good day and a long row" (335). Seven years from that day Elton would be dead, but those left would remember him, "along with the others who were gone," during their pauses in the new year's work. Mart especially remembers Elton standing "with them in the barn door in the long shadow, sweaty and soiled, exultant and graceful, eating that sugary little melon." "He was a friend of mine," Mart would say, "accenting lightly the final word, 'A friend of mine'" (335–36).

Many characters in Port William act from an affirmation like Mart's about Elton. In *Jayber Crow,* Burley Coulter joins Jayber in filling the grave of Mat Feltner, silently honoring his longtime friend. In "Watch with Me (1916)," Sam Hanks, Braymer Hardy, Tom Hardy, Walter Cotman, and Burley Coulter all join Tol Proudfoot as he follows Nightlife Hample in an effort to prevent Nightlife's suicide. Each of those men takes on a risk to his life out of a necessity that arises only from friendship for Tol and Nightlife. In "Pray Without Ceasing (1912)," Jack Beechum acts instinctively from love for Mat Feltner—thereby committing himself to the younger man for life—when he holds Mat back from vengeance after his father's murder. In "A Jonquil for Mary Penn (1940)," the group of neighbors surrounding Mary support one another through hard poverty, providing her with practical help and affection she cannot do without, especially after her rejection by parents who have expected her to make a better marriage. In *A Place on Earth,* Mat Feltner and Jasper Lathrop find that the friendship they had prior to World War II becomes a necessity for them both after their sons are called into service. Joined by Jack Beechum, Burley Coulter, and Jayber Crow, they meet every afternoon to sustain one another through an endless gin rummy game in which nobody keeps score. What is at stake cannot be reckoned. Finally, in "The Wild Birds (1967)," Burley insists to Wheeler Catlett that real friendship turns on a depth of connection as close as brotherhood. As Burley becomes seventy and wants to bring all his doings into the open, he insists that Wheeler forgive and accept him as a brother and not just tolerate him as he has as a friend. They have been friends of a sort, but full truth to each other requires they become brothers.

Burley Coulter may seem an odd figure to place at the center of a consideration of the three theological virtues, but that's just where he belongs.

His pressing Wheeler to acknowledge him is an act of love, as is his coming to Wheeler, in the first place, to make formal recognition, long past due, of his love for Kate Helen Branch and his paternity of Danny. But it is also an act of hope and faith. As he approaches his allotted three score and ten years, Burley must "turn it loose," and he knows Wheeler needs some turning loose as well.[27] Wheeler is committed to the best of human arrangements, the law, and his concern is that Burley's land go to both the rightful and the most able steward—in his judgment, Nathan Coulter. But Burley knows both that Danny is the rightful heir and that Wheeler is a little too afraid of the "wayward" in human experience. Burley knows what must be done—what fidelity to the past, at last, demands—and he is willing, in hope and faith, to let the future take care of itself. Danny's own fidelity to his father is at the heart of the story "Fidelity (1977)," in which he rescues Burley from an anonymous death amid the death-delaying technology of the modern hospital. Danny's fidelity allows Burley a death that is faithful to his life, and the membership of Port William—which Burley had always waywardly preached—answers with faithful witness to both the goodness of Burley's life and the fidelity of his son. Wheeler himself concludes the eulogy for Burley, pronouncing him a "faithful man." This does not mean he was utterly consistent, as if he knew the truth with certainty and acted from it always. It means something much more wonderful, something that made Burley, in Wheeler's words, "exceptional." Burley was able to do what we all find difficult, to change, to "become a different man from the one he started out to be." Wheeler is not sure when this change began in Burley, but he thinks it probably started "when Nathan and Tom started following him around when they were little boys, after their mother died." Caring for them, he took on a good part of their rearing, then cared for his mother when his own father died and did "his proper part in raising" Danny. Burley often said he had never intended to stay in Port William, but as the years went by, he found himself liking to stay. As Burley responded to what he saw of need, he found himself loving and being loved, and thus eventually he recognized that faithfulness to what he needed to be required him to change. Love moved a kind of fidelity in Burley and overcame in hope the inertia that weighs so heavily against change. Burley was no paper saint. He "never gave up his love of roaming about." He was more like the prodigal found by love and wise, or maybe just puzzled, enough to know that he was found. He preaches the widest extension of the "membership" in Berry's work, and that is no doubt because he knows that only the widest membership could possibly include him.[28]

Berry's fondness for the concept of "membership" can help us to understand his perhaps surprising wariness of the word "environment." Often Berry uses "membership" to refer to the human community, as in the membership of Port William, and surely the word's resonance derives from its echoing St. Paul's assertion that "we, being many, are one body in Christ, and every one members one of another."[29] But Berry thinks, too, of membership as involving not only humans but all of creation, as Edwin Muir put it in lines Berry likes to cite: "Men are made of what is made, / The meat, the drink, the life, the corn, / Laid up by them, in them reborn."[30] "Environment," on the other hand, simplifies more complex concepts like "country, homeland, dwelling place," or membership, reducing them to "what surrounds us." But this divides us from the world, and we begin to lose the capacity to think of ourselves and our country as creating one another, as being so thoroughly part of one another that it is impossible for any single part "to flourish alone."[31] What concerns Berry is how we will respond to the "ecological crisis" if we see it as a problem of "the environment." The ecological crisis is a crisis of "character," one that involves us— our indiscipline, our inflated consumerist expectations, our seemingly inexhaustible appetite for cheap energy. Changing our character must be a part of the way we address the ecological crisis. If we think of the problem as one involving primarily "the environment," we will be likely to turn over its solution to specialists, possessors of the right expertise and information. Such approaches are unlikely to produce much in the way of lasting results, primarily because they rest on false analysis. The crisis is not in "the environment," understood as that which surrounds us, but rather in the whole membership of things, including—ineluctably—us.

Berry's sense that the membership includes all the living may have its roots in his early experiences with mules. As he reflects on his work with draft animals in "Renewing Husbandry," he notes that one of the things lost in the transition from team to tractor is the practical ground of sympathy in the farmer for other creatures. Going over the ground behind a team is to see "the farm in a different way" than one does from the tractor; it is to understand the "cost" of working the farm differently. As the tractor never tires, the farmer comes to see the ground as something "to be got over as fast as possible." A team, however, "grow[s] weary," just like the boy working them, a weariness that serves as a "living connection that enforce[s] sympathy as a practical good" (RH, 95). The boy working the team is never able to forget his own embodiment in the way possible for one on the tractor—an embodiment he shares with his animals. Dependence on machines encourages an understanding of the world as a machine; working with creatures makes it more likely that we will see the world "as a living creature." That creaturely understanding is essential to good "husbandry," a word that names a "connection," the acceptance of "bondage to the household" (RH, 95–96).

It is the sense of connection to a place and its particularities that is lost in what Berry calls "that idiotic term 'the environment.'"[32] None of us lives in "the environment"; we live in and from particular places, which we treat either well or badly according to the degree to which we care for them precisely as particulars. This involves coming to know their possibilities, limits, and requirements in an intimate way. If one were to mediate between Berry and defenders of the term "the environment," I think one could usefully say that he has insisted on pressing further some of the original intention of popularizers of the term. Surely defenders of "the environment" have wanted us to understand that the web of life sustaining us is much more complex and delicate than it appears ordinarily to the Western urban or suburban consumer. What Berry wants to insist on is that our analysis and cultural habits must take into account an even greater degree of complexity. He proposes the concept of "kindly use" as one "that can dissolve the boundaries that divide people from the land" and encourage a necessary broadening in our approaches to its care. The land itself requires this broadening, for it is simply "too various" in its characteristics "to prosper under generalized treatment." The use of land "cannot be general and kindly."[33] Conservers or defenders of "the environment" might hear Berry simply asking them to take the next step: to learn to care for all the particulars of specific places in ways that will allow for them to be healthy indefinitely.

A shift from focusing on "the environment" to the health and kindly use of particular places would imply a whole set of revaluations. Local knowledge and local culture would take on renewed importance, for these carry "the knowledge of how [a] place may be lived in and used." A revival may occur in local control of education as it becomes clear that healthy localities are necessary for the nation's health. Berry rejects what he characterizes as "the prevailing assumption" that "if the nation is all right, then all the localities will be all right also," suggesting further that the nation's current ill health is related to its inattention to—if not destruction of—the health of its localities.[34] Change might occur, too, in our ways of understanding knowledge itself. Particular country understood and cared for as one's sustaining context will come to be beloved country, and thus any knowing about it will have to be wedded to sympathy and affection. No longer will it be possible to discount a family's love for its farm, for it will become obvious that discounting people's affection for the land leads to practices that are ultimately destructive. As "minutely particular love" of places comes to be prevalent—comes to be understood, indeed, as part of knowledge itself—the sciences and humanities will "have to come together again in the presence of the practical problems of individual places, and of local knowledge and local love in individual people."[35]

More insistence on particularity of knowledge will necessitate a "greater range of species and varieties of plants and animals, of human skills and methods, so that the use may be fitted ever more sensitively and elegantly to the place" (AD, 114). A model of this kind of elegant ecological appropriateness is the Andean farming around Huancayo, Peru, that Berry observes in the opening essay of *The Gift of Good Land.* There very intense farming takes place in tiny fields on steep hillsides whose soil seems generally "well conserved."[36] Fields distinguished by individual names are planted, tilled, and cultivated according to patterns discerned and established over centuries. Fallowing, polyculture, and planting in the sod to avoid erosion are crucial to maintaining the health of these places. The Andean farmers have learned to listen to the questions being posed them by their places; that their answers work is because they are developed in the presence of the land and by those on the land. Thus, a focus on "kindly use" of land implies a politics. A society concerned to see its land used in kindly fashion will endeavor to see it in the hands of those who will regard it with the right sort of stewardship. This means making sure that households can stay on the land and that farmers can earn a living from farms small enough to be recipients of affection and particularized care.

We begin to see how much is at stake in Berry's seemingly prickly rejection of the term "the environment." He takes the position he does because he sees connections among all those spheres of our lives that we are tempted to separate (if only, sometimes, for the sake of thinking clearly about one problem at a time). In this he is like nobody so much as Thoreau with his sometimes maddening awareness of how everything is connected to everything else. He refuses, we might say, to be alienated from, or within, himself. He wants, as the title of one essay puts it, "The Whole Horse."[37] This is why he has aligned himself primarily with "kindly use" in the conversation about environmental matters rather than with the preservation of wilderness. I do not want to be misunderstood here. Berry has been unequivocal in saying that "the concern for wilderness must stand at the apex of the conservation effort" and "probably" at "the apex of consciousness in any decent culture" (ECCA, 29). But he also believes "we cannot hope" to "preserve more than a small portion of the land in wilderness." "Most of it we will have to use," and therefore we will have to think about, develop, and work toward "kindly use" (ECCA, 29–30). Only by doing so can we hope to put people back into touch with the resources on which they depend and begin to move them toward policies of sustainability.[38]

Berry may fear that an environmentalism focused primarily on wilderness preservation will not change our politics to the degree he believes it needs changing. The goal is not only to allow urban consumers to know that somewhere wilderness still exists. It is to bring an end to American empire and restore the republic, a change dependent on large numbers of people coming to understand themselves as something other than consumers with unlimited license to deplete what sustains them—or as beneficiaries of technology that enables infinite production of what we need. If we are to have widespread change toward sustainability, it will have to come from our thinking about the processes on which we all depend most directly and obviously—and these are agricultural.

Questions of agriculture are inevitably questions of scale. Perhaps one of the things the land can teach us, in fact, is that all questions are questions of scale. A human being can only know and do so much. We often presume to know more than we can, generally through excessive abstraction, leaving out too much detail.[39] Often damage done by ill-informed policy can be hidden, particularly by those positioned to control information. Damage to the land is harder to conceal. Bad agricultural and ecological practices force themselves on our awareness. Perhaps carrying the corrective to our hubris is what both agriculture and wilderness can contribute to our politics. The land and wilderness are the best sources of resistance to our nearly incurable self-deceptions. What they can teach is that knowledge tempered by proper humility must learn to leave out as little as possible. We cannot avoid abstraction, but keeping our abstractions responsible requires fidelity to the particulars. Honest writing requires fidelity, and that requires a choice about scale. The writer will have to ask himself: To what can I be faithful? What can I write about with integrity and without the danger of self-deception? He will also have to ask to whom he is writing. This is not just a question about who will be interested in his work, but one about who knows enough to keep him faithful. For Berry, of course, at a crucial point in his career, these questions of scale meant leaving the cosmopolitan center in New York for a return to Kentucky. He was seeking a place where his writing could be—and be held—responsible. Or, if you prefer, where it could be—and be kept—faithful.

When Berry tells the story, in "A Native Hill," of his leaving New York University (NYU) for Kentucky, he does so in a way that places his decision in a history of such choices by American writers. Writing of the way in which his "own life is inseparable from the history and the place" of his birth and rearing, Port Royal, he recalls Henry James, who famously remarked, "It's a complex fate, being an American."[40] "It is a complex inheritance," Berry writes of being a Kentuckian, "and I have been both enriched and bewildered by it" (NH, 171). It seems likely Berry is thinking of James, who was born, we should remember, in the very Washington Square where NYU is located.[41] James made the choice to leave America to spend most of his adult life in Europe, doing so in order to find the "texture" necessary for his fiction. Yet the cosmopolitan James remained always deeply American, always himself "enriched and bewildered" by America, to adapt Berry's remarkably appropriate phrase. In writing about Hawthorne, James argued that the older writer's strength lay precisely in his own deep commitment to his native, ancestral materials. James made one choice, leaving then-provincial America for cosmopolitan Europe; Hawthorne had made the other, remaining, for the most part, in his native place—one so lacking in significant surface that he was driven deeply into his history and psyche.[42]

While in New York, Berry was discovering what Henry James's career bears out: that he could not escape his fate. Berry had reached "the greatest city in the nation," had a good job and reason to hope that he might have a significant part "in the literary life of that place." Yet, as he explains,

> I knew I had not escaped Kentucky, and had never really wanted to. I
> was still writing about it, and had recognized that I would probably

need to write about it for the rest of my life. Kentucky was my fate—
not an altogether pleasant fate, though it had much that was pleasing
in it, but one that I could not leave behind simply by going to another
place, and that I therefore felt more and more obligated to meet directly and to understand. (NH, 174)

We might think of Berry as making a choice quite unlike James's, but for
Jamesian reasons: turning away from the cosmopolitan center in order to
find the place, and also the scale, in which he could hope to come as close
as possible to living out the terms James established for the young writer:
"To be one of the people on whom nothing is lost!"[43] What one particularly does not want to lose is one's fate, for if one is ever to write anything
sufficiently deep to be satisfying, it will be by confronting, not avoiding, it.

The faculty elder who urges Berry not to leave New York alludes "to
Thomas Wolfe, who once taught at the same institution. 'Young man' he
said, 'don't you know you can't go home again?'" Berry grants that he knew,
like Wolfe, "that there is a certain *metaphorical* sense in which you can't go
home again," but that the phrase also carries a "self-dramatizing sentimentality that was absurd" (NH, 174). His home, place, and countryside were
still there, and there was no reason he could not go back. Doing so was not
a kind of "intellectual death," as is often assumed by urban cosmopolites
who regard "the life of the metropolis" to be "*the* experience, the *modern*
experience." Other writers had made choices similar to Berry's: "If there was
Wolfe, there was also Faulkner; if there was James, there was also Thoreau."
It seemed "false and destructive and silly," Berry recalls, to consider everything apart from the urban centers irrelevant and archaic (NH, 175–76).

In addition to those Berry mentions specifically, other American writers seem also strongly present just under the surface of "A Native Hill."
Berry's discussion of his own fortunately anachronistic upbringing suggests that of Sherwood Anderson, whose father was a harness maker who
lost his business in Clyde, Ohio, during the 1880s, when farmers lost their
taste for his "individually crafted harnesses" and began to buy "products
turned out by factories specializing in agricultural implements."[44] Anderson
struggled throughout his career with the tension between commerce and
the city, on one hand, and the deep background of his writing in small
Ohio towns. Berry's decision between New York and Kentucky reminds
one also of the career of Willa Cather, who made "her way by stages" from
the Nebraska "Divide, to Red Cloud, to Lincoln, to Pittsburgh, and finally

to New York," where she resided for the last forty-one years of her life—part of that time at Washington Square.[45] But Cather made frequent trips to the West, particularly to Red Cloud, and in her fiction she followed the advice to write about her own country, the Nebraska of her youth, given her in 1908 by Sarah Orne Jewett. Jewett, who of course wrote from her own country, the Maine of pointed firs, advised Cather to depend less on James, to avoid the exhaustion and distraction of her own "good job" working for S. S. McClure, and to find her own "quiet centre and write from that to the world." Unless Cather did so, she would be able to "write about life, but never write life itself." "To write and work on this level," Jewett said, "we must live on it."[46] Jewett's advice to Cather seems nearly the reverse of that Berry received from his well-meaning colleague at New York University. Berry has himself attested to Jewett's attraction for him, calling *The Country of the Pointed Firs* "the one American book I know that is about a beloved community—a settled, established white American community with a sustaining common culture, and mostly beneficent toward both its members and its place."[47]

Cather and Berry arrived at different resolutions of the conflict between their grounding in the life of specific places and the attractions of the literary center. Their work, though, evinces some suggestive comparisons. Cather would surely have subscribed to Berry's sense that he could never escape his own place; that it was his "fate"; and that, moreover, one had finally to speak about one's attraction to it as a kind of love. "Deep love for the place I had been born in," Berry explains in "A Native Hill," was "perhaps even more important" in his decision to return to Kentucky than his felt sense of obligation and the need to understand the place's life (174). Jim Burden articulates a similarly deep sense of fate and love of country at the end of Cather's elegant *My Antonia* as he remembers Antonia and his coming to the Nebraska prairie when they were children: "For Antonia and for me, this had been the road of Destiny; had taken us to those early accidents of fortune which predetermined for us all that we can ever be." Jim has "the sense of coming home" to himself, "having found out what a little circle man's experience is," and yet he will, as Cather did so many times, return to his home in New York.[48]

Cather's sense of the determining quality of very early experience is undoubtedly even more powerful than Berry's, which is perhaps why she needed to remain at a greater distance from it—geographically and aesthetically—in order to write about it. Where she and Berry are very close, however, is in their sense of "country." When Jim in *My Antonia* studies Latin at the University of Nebraska, he is drawn to the *Georgics* of Virgil, whose third book he contemplates one night: "'*Primus ego in patriam mecum . . . deducam Musas*'; 'for I shall be the first, if I live, to bring the Muse into my country.'" From his teacher, Gaston Cleric, Jim has learned

> that "patria" here meant, not a nation or even a province, but the little rural neighborhood on the Mincio where the poet was born. This was not a boast, but a hope, at once bold and devoutly humble, that he might bring the Muse (but lately come to Italy from her cloudy Grecian mountains), not to the capital, the *Palatia Romana,* but to his own little "country"; to his father's fields, "sloping down to the river and to the old beech trees with broken tops." (169–70)

In similar fashion, Berry's *patria* is the rural neighborhood and landscape around Port Royal, Kentucky, small enough to be known intimately and loved. The source and end of Port Royal's life is the river, not the capital in Frankfort or the Palatia Americana in Washington. Berry wants to be a citizen of the republic, but the place of his affection will always be his own local world, broadened enough perhaps to take in Kentucky. Once again this is a matter of scale. One can only give a truly loving attention to so much. Cather speaks of Jim's way of remembering the land in terms that suggest beautifully what Berry is calling for in commending an intimate knowledge of the particulars of a place. Watching what once seemed very barren land become fruitful, Jim says, "I found that I remembered the conformation of the land as one remembers the modelling of human faces" (197).

One writer forever connected to a particular place deserves extended attention for his role as a conversation partner of Berry's, and that, of course, is Thoreau.[49] Writing about Edward Abbey, Berry has joked that "every writer who has been as far out of the house as the mailbox" has been compared to Thoreau. In Berry's case, however, the comparison is no empty conventional gesture. In the same piece on Abbey, Berry begins his "defense" by linking Abbey and Thoreau as writers he "*want[s]* to argue with."[50] These are writers fiercely enough committed to their integrity as to be unavoidable. They are writers one can learn from, not just learn about, as in literary classrooms. Berry has learned so much from Thoreau that I cannot do much more here than just sketch out a few themes of their conversation, but I hope these will be suggestive.

Nothing connects Berry to Thoreau more closely than the unwilling-ness to settle for conventional ways of framing issues, irrespective of ideo-logical stripe. What Berry calls "a broader deeper criticism" is always possible, usually "necessary," as when he calls for such in regard to conven-tional feminism in "Feminism, the Body, and the Machine."[51] Such willing-ness to examine everything derives from what Berry and Thoreau call faith, the "faith," as Berry says in the preface to *Home Economics,* that "things connect—that we are wholly dependent on a pattern, an all-inclusive form, that we partly understand." Believing this, Berry conceives the essay as an attempt to "describe responsibility" (ix), to understand and hold ourselves accountable for what we are doing within our part of the pattern as we try to discern more of the whole. Thoreau invokes faith in this sense in his answer to those who ask him whether he can subsist only on vegetable food: "There is a certain class of unbelievers who sometimes ask me such questions as, if I think that I can live on vegetable food alone; and to strike at the root of the matter at once,—for the root is faith,—I am accustomed to answer such, that I can live on board nails" (*Walden,* 108). Thoreau's response seems at first a little odd, for it's not immediately obvious that this is a question of faith rather than one of diet, or physiology, or comfort and convenience. But for Thoreau it is one of faith because it involves his will-ingness and ability to be responsible, to do, within his part of the pattern, what is right and necessary for the health of the whole.

"If a man has faith," Thoreau adds later in "Economy," "he will cooper-ate with equal faith every where; if he has not faith, he will continue to live like the rest of the world, whatever company he is joined to. To cooperate, in the highest as well as the lowest sense, means *to get our living together*" (*Walden,* 115). Thoreau, like Berry after him, gives an extensive meaning to economy; indeed, he would surely object to our talk today of "the econo-my," as if it were some separate, isolable realm of existence. We are always involved in getting our livings together, and thus, if we are people of faith, we must be continually thinking about what that means for our local part of the pattern and how that relates to the whole. Asking those questions requires faith, for we may find that our actions need radical modification: responsibility to our part of the pattern may require us to live on board nails. Thus, we can see how faith is closely related to hope, both for Thoreau and Berry, and how both are related to discipline.

Thoreau tells a story in the "Visitors" chapter of *Walden* that pertains to the connection between hope and discipline. The story draws on the New England history of Edward Winslow, later governor of Plymouth, and concerns a visit of his and a companion to Massasoit when the latter's people had no food. On the day of their arrival, "nothing was said about eating." On the next day, Massasoit, in Winslow's words, "brought two fishes that he had shot," and "these being boiled, there were at least forty looked for a share in them. The most ate of them. This meal only we had in two nights and a day; and had not one of us bought a partridge, we had taken our journey fasting." One detects a hint of resentment in Winslow, but Thoreau admires the way Massasoit and his people maintained their discipline: "As far as eating was concerned, I do not see how the Indians could have done better. They had nothing to eat themselves, and they were wiser than to think that apologies could supply the place of food to their guests; so they drew their belts tighter and said nothing about it" (188–89). They shared what they had and offered no lies to falsely mitigate the hardness of the times. Thoreau's is a story of loaves and fishes with a difference: here there is no miraculous multiplication, but there is faith moving Massasoit's people to get their livings together with others as well as possible. Faith, discipline, and hope go together, as they do, too, for Berry in his fullest treatment of these matters, "Discipline and Hope," in *A Continuous Harmony*.

"Hope lives in the means, not the end," Berry writes; indeed, one of the dangers of too much consequentialist thinking is that it destroys hope. "We expect ends not only to justify means, but to rectify them"—that is, once we have achieved a "desired end," the means will come to seem justifiable. This "vicious illusion" masks the fact that "the discipline of ends is no discipline at all." Rather, the end must be "preserved in the means; a desirable end may perish forever in the wrong means." Or, to put this otherwise, we can lose everything that is good about an end by allowing wrong means to transform us in their image. If this is a thought difficult for postmoderns to conceive, that is simply an indication of our nearly complete hopelessness. Hope resides in our disciplines, in our purification of means, in faith that enables persistence in the disciplines that define us. That "good ends are destroyed by bad means" is a theme of such sources of wisdom as the *I Ching*, Confucius, and the Sermon on the Mount. As the *I Ching* puts it, we must even be on guard not to "combat our own faults directly," for "as long as we wrestle with them, they continue victorious." The discipline must be instead to make "energetic progress in the good."[52] Or, to give a further example, Berry cites the experience of a sheep-breeding friend who is told "he could 'make money' by marketing some inferior lambs." The man refused, "saying that his purpose was the production of *good* lambs, and he would sell no other kind." What Berry's friend meant was "that his disciplines had to be those of a farmer, and that he would be diminished as a farmer by adopting the disciplines of a money-changer" (DH, 126).

The sheepman also gives witness to faith, the "ultimate discipline," which includes, at the very least, faith "in the propriety of one's disciplines." The test of such faith is "consistency," not the "fanatic consistency" that repudiates knowledge, but "rather a consistency between principle and behavior" (DH, 150). These comments recall Thoreau's pervasive language of principle, as in "Civil Disobedience": "Action from principle, the perception and the performance of right, changes things and relations; it is essentially revolutionary, and does not consist wholly with anything which was. It not only divides states and churches, it divides families; ay, it divides the *individual*, separating the diabolical in him from the divine."[53] This passage suggests why it is difficult to place Thoreau or Berry on the political spectrum. Action from principle is revolutionary, but primarily because it resists the pressure of expediency, which can be exerted either in favor of the status quo or against it. The really revolutionary quality of principled action—whether it be that of Thoreau's civil resistor or Berry's sheep breeder—lies in its insisting that right action must be independent of immediate circumstances and consequentialist calculation.

Berry's comments on principle also suggest Thoreau's essay "Life Without Principle," one frequently quoted by Berry. That essay reads almost like an anticipation of what Berry has worked at not only in his essays but also in his fiction and poetry. Thoreau opens the piece by noting how often others want only his "shell" and not his "meat," how "a man once came a considerable distance to ask [him] to lecture on Slavery," but that as they conversed, Thoreau discovered that "he and his clique expected seven-eighths of the lecture to be theirs, and only one-eighth" his. "I declined," Thoreau remarks, adding that he was committed forthwith to giving his audiences a "strong dose of myself"—and not just what they already thought or wanted to hear.[54] Here is the heart of Berry's insistence that he is not a spokesman for "environmentalism" or any other "ism." Part of this insistence, for Berry, lies in the desire to give as honest an account of his own experience as he can. But part of it also lies in his conviction that movements like that for the environment stand no chance of succeeding unless they involve the deep private commitments of people. As Thoreau continues in "Life Without Principle," he notes the constant busyness of Americans, so engaged in "infinite bustle" that "there is no sabbath." And he notes later that "there is nothing, not even crime, more opposed to poetry, to philosophy, ay, to life itself, than this incessant business"(198). The logic is clear: destruction of the Sabbath is contrary to "life itself." That, I suggest, is the context in which we should read the Sabbath poems that Berry has been writing for nearly the last thirty years. Finally, Thoreau notes, too, that "it is remarkable that there is little or nothing to be remembered written on the subject of getting a living: how to make getting a living not merely honest and honorable, but altogether inviting and glorious; for if *getting* a living is not so, then living is not" (201). One might say that hardly any writer (besides Thoreau himself) has devoted so much good work to the subject of getting a living as Wendell Berry. And his conclusions—while much more detailed—may not be too far removed from the spirit of Thoreau's remark that "you must get your living by loving"(201).

How we get our living together—economy—has been a central concern of both Thoreau and Berry. *Walden* begins with "Economy," derived from *oikos nomos,* the rule or management of the household, and that chapter—as well as all of Thoreau's book—ponders the requirements of a healthy household. Thoreau fears the incursion of an increasingly industrial economy on the household economies of his neighbors. What he sees developing in the 1840s in New England is an economy based on an increasingly specialized division of labor, the stratification of classes, the multiplication of luxuries, and onerous personal and familial debt. Berry has similarly placed the household at the center of his economic thinking, arguing that a healthy and sustainable economy requires healthy households. His assessment of the destruction of the household economy essentially confirms Thoreau's sense of what was already beginning to happen in his own time. "I do not believe that there is anything better to do than to make one's marriage and household, whether one is a man or a woman,"

Berry argues, in "Feminism, the Body, and the Machine" (182). He indicts American men in a jeremiad worthy of Thoreau himself for "submit[ting] to the destruction of the household economy" and thus rendering themselves "helpless to do anything for themselves or anyone else without money"—a fact that leads, in turn, to their doing "for money" whatever "they are told" (184–85). Here Berry comes close to Thoreau's most searching criticism of money: that, as he puts it, it "comes between a man and his objects," eroding one's character, removing the need to stake oneself on what one believes.[55] The substance of Thoreau's whole notorious attack on philanthropy and charity, as these had come to be understood by the mid–nineteenth century, is that they, too often, involve so little of one. The charity Thoreau endorses, that which "hides a multitude of sins," derives from the whole person, from a goodness that is not a "partial and transitory act, but a constant superfluity, which costs him nothing and of which he is unconscious" (*Walden,* 120).

Thoreau wants, like Berry, the "whole horse." His concern about labor under the industrialized system is that it is increasingly meaningless in human or personal terms—the familiar problem of "alienation." He is particularly close to Berry in his sense that what we give up as we enter into ever more specialized roles is pleasure—the pleasure to be found, for example, in such seemingly natural work as building one's house. "Shall we forever resign the pleasure of construction to the carpenter?" Thoreau asks (*Walden,* 89). Berry similarly insists that economy must be addressed from the "standpoint of affection" or "pleasure," that is, "affection in action."[56] He argues that our "great variety of pleasure industries" indicates that our economy is actually "divorced from pleasure and that pleasure is gone from our workplaces and dwelling places"—given over increasingly to production and consumption respectively (EP, 139). Too much of our addiction to the pleasures of consumption comes at the expense of the future, while we do too little to enjoy the "pleasures that are free or without a permanent cost"—such pleasures as those "we take in our own lives, our own wakefulness in this world, and in the company of other people and other creatures—pleasures innate in the Creation and in our own good work" (EP, 138).

It may be a startling idea in this age of utilitarian seriousness "that God created all things for His pleasure" and that he meant for us to enjoy them. As he develops this point, Berry quotes Thoreau's graduating speech to his class at Harvard in 1837: "This curious world we inhabit is more wonderful than convenient; more beautiful than it is useful; it is more to be admired and enjoyed than used."[57] Berry shares Thoreau's liberating sense that we are not primarily required to devote ourselves to making the world better, however bad we might find it. "I came into this world, not chiefly to make this a good place to live in, but to live in it, be it good or bad," Thoreau remarks in "Civil Disobedience" (396). We hear the same accent in Berry's elegantly simple comment, "My wish simply is to live my life as fully as I can. In both our work and our leisure, I think, we should be so employed" (FBM, 190).

It remains to suggest what learning to team animals has to do with Berry's being a Christian. A way to begin is by recalling that living "sympathy" between the animals and the teamster whose loss Berry charges up to the tractor in "Renewing Husbandry." That living connection is essential to "husbandry," which is, in Berry's definition, the "art of keeping tied all the strands in the living network that sustains us" (RH, 97). The renewal of husbandry depends upon the extension of sympathy. Appropriate care for creation presses one to an ever-enlarging sympathy for all that is, for every creature in the Kingdom of God, which signifies for Berry the all-inclusive order. When joined to the word "animal," husbandry means good care both for our fellow creatures and for what sustains them. "Animal science," with its denial of the "sanctity of animals," has led us to the "animal factory," whereas "animal husbandry . . . comes from and again leads to the psalmist's vision of good grass, good water, and the husbandry of God" (RH, 99). To understand God in this way is to understand "analogically," as Berry has characterized his own way of seeing how "the things of time relate to the things of eternity." "My approach to religion has pretty much been from the bottom up," Berry has said. "I never was very good at the top-down version." Surely one source of that "revelation from below" was the sympathy the boy acquired in going over the ground with animals whose possibilities and limits he had to respect, whose work made possible his family's life, and whose bodies tired just like his own.[58]

We should remember Berry's sense that the discipline of the teamster was anachronistic. He was born in the nick of time, but not in the same nick as his contemporaries. Perhaps by its very anachronism, the discipline involved in farming with animals made possible for Berry some contact with the perennial world and thus with the concerns of a *philosophia peren-*

nis. No isolation can be more complete than that in our own moment in time. We might see it as an extraordinary gift of those mules to have saved Berry from the current technological obsession with what we are doing right now to invent our moment and the future. Living with and in dependence on other animals seems, too, an essential part of coming to understand what it means to be a creature. Animals resist us; they have their own purposes. In fact, living with other animals may be our first introduction into the fact that the world abounds with mysterious purposes not our own. We need the other animals; we depend on them. They can become something like our friends, but only through our disciplining them and through a remarkable gift of their own, one we cannot repay. This is to say that learning to team mules or horses at an early age is to be initiated into a world whose terms are flesh and will and mutual dependence, energy, generosity, gift, and gratitude. Those are surely the background terms for coming to understand oneself—along with the other animals—as creatures of a God who has looked on this world and called it good.

To learn the practice of the teamster is to learn that one has not invented the terms of one's existence. One must discover what works within a practice that one depends upon but whose possibilities and limits one did not create. To learn a practice in this way is to find oneself in the midst of an ongoing history. The practice must be learned from others; what one learns, in fact, is the history of others' experiments in the practice. One comes, in short, to think of learning as a matter of discovering what is appropriate or fitting within the limits inherent in the practice. As one can also see that this practice is vital to the lives of those for whom one cares, one comes to care about the practice or discipline. Learning it becomes an act of love, a way of giving allegiance to those who have come before one and found it good. One can see that those who are concerned to transmit the practice do so not because they want to bind or enslave the future to the past but because they care about passing on a way of life they have found to be good. Education becomes inseparable from love. When this process takes place within the context of rural or agricultural life, it is inevitably fleshly, embodied, particular. Mules differ; pieces of land differ; hillsides differ; bottomlands differ. These are things good farmers know. These are things that people who want to continue to live in the good land *must* know.

In "A Praise," a short poem from *Farming: A Handbook,* Berry gives homage to one, now dead, by acknowledging how "certain wise movements of his hands, / the turns of his speech / keep with me. His hope of peace / keeps with me in harsh days."[59] The man remains present with Berry, his hope a part of him, his wisdom carried in his movements. What one learns from such a man or woman is embodied knowledge, inseparable from the one who bears it. Moreover, to recognize that what one knows has been forever shaped by the memory of "certain wise movements" of another's hands is to know that one resides ultimately in mystery. For one can never know, nor be able to explain, what lay behind those movements. A distinction between mystery and problem is important to Berry, as in *Life Is a Miracle,* where he finds that the "most unscientific and disturbing thing" about Edward O. Wilson's theory of "consilience" is the way it destroys this distinction by the simple device of "not yet." This device accomplishes a "tyrannic" reduction by redescribing all mysteries as problems "not yet" understood, but scheduled for solution when the principles and methods of science become sufficiently sophisticated (36). To resist such reduction is at the heart of Berry's intellectual, political, and religious commitment. His way of doing so is to ceaselessly remind us of what is left out by the abstractions of our specialized knowledges, not because he fears those knowledges—though there is reason to fear some of what they have produced—but because he believes, much like Thoreau, that freedom for both scientists and artists lies in continually enlarging the contexts of their work.

A real, nonreductive enlarging of the contexts of artistic or scientific work must depend, however, on a knowledge of particulars. That knowledge requires the virtues, especially patience, humility, the courage to begin a practice like marriage that one cannot understand prior to its practice, hope, faith, the willingness to rest in ignorance. Knowledge of particulars requires love, perhaps especially in our time when the horizon of technology enframes everything as so much "standing reserve" to be converted into something else.[60] To be continually enlarging the context of one's work, then, without diminishing the weight of particulars, requires the continual extension of one's love. To think of love in this way is to understand it as a history—sometimes, perhaps even often, hard. Surely it is something one did not invent, if for no other reason than that one is so inadequate to it. As Hannah Coulter puts it, love does not "come out of thin air. It is not something thought up. Like ourselves, it grows out of the ground. It has a body and a place."[61] We find ourselves in the midst of it; we know it as it is conveyed to us by those particular people and animals with whom we share a place; we come to think of ourselves as unique singularities as we come to know we are loved and somehow able to love in turn. Berry has said that he takes "literally the statement in the Gospel of John that God loves the world," meaning by that, among other things, that love is "the opening of a mystery in which our lives are deeply, dangerously, and inescapably involved."[62] When that mystery begins to open for each of us is a part of our singular stories. Perhaps, for Berry, as I have tried to suggest, it began to open when he learned from those who loved him how to care for and manage those half-ton concentrations of energy as eternal delight, those refractory, real-making creatures Adam named mules.

Chapter 2

Toward a Peaceable Economy for a Beloved Country

Berry as Agrarian, Citizen, and Patriot

I want to begin this chapter with the improbable proposition that the Mad Farmer of Wendell Berry's poetry and his character Burley Coulter have something to contribute to the salvation of political life in America. In "Manifesto: The Mad Farmer Liberation Front," Berry's Mad Farmer urges us to "every day / do something that won't compute":

> Love the Lord.
> Love the world. Work for nothing.
> Take all that you have and be poor.
> Love someone who does not deserve it.
> Denounce the government and embrace
> the flag. Hope to live in that free
> republic for which it stands.[1]

The alternative seems to be continuing the lives so many of us have been encouraged to live, those of unrestrained, largely debt-financed consumption in the search for private satisfactions. The opening of the "Manifesto" should resonate particularly with the baby boom generation, described so aptly by Christopher Lasch as settling down after the political forays of the 1960s to go about the serious business of claiming their class privileges.[2] Paraphrasing the voice of the culture and economy, Berry's Mad Farmer begins:

> Love the quick profit, the annual raise,
> vacation with pay. Want more
> of everything ready-made. Be afraid

to know your neighbors and to die.
And you will have a window in your head.
Not even your future will be a mystery
any more. Your mind will be punched in a card
and shut away in a little drawer.
When they want you to buy something
they will call you. (*CP,* 151)

Reading this, one is reminded of George W. Bush's imploring Americans to go out and shop after 9/11 in order to show the world that our national life was going on unimpaired. Or perhaps one is reminded of network pundits projecting the behavior of the red and blue states on election nights. Doing so is simply a matter of knowing how many people from which microareas have gone to the polls, there to express the preferences punched on their cards, preferences largely created for them by government, media, and corporations. One thing is certain. However people in the red and blue states are behaving, they are behaving, not acting, if by acting we mean something more inaugural, unpredictable—something on which one's character, not simply one's preferences, is staked. That we each have windows in our heads suggests our transparency, our openness to analysis and manipulation by today's "reality instructors."[3] Berry has argued that we have nearly destroyed private life in this country, a claim with which I largely agree. Perhaps if we are to think of restoring it, we should each resolve to be more opaque, to give our own turn to the Mad Farmer's concluding advice: "Be like the fox / who makes more tracks than necessary, / some in the wrong direction. / Practice resurrection" (*CP,* 152).

What we can learn about political renewal from Burley Coulter might be seen by looking at his role in "The Wild Birds (1967)." When Burley reaches his appointed three score and ten years, he comes to Wheeler Catlett to make changes in his will, to ensure that Danny Branch will inherit from him what would otherwise go to Nathan Coulter. Burley is, in effect, acknowledging Danny as his son and Kate Helen Branch as his wife—while also insisting that Wheeler forgive and accept him as a brother rather than merely tolerating him, with some bemusement, as a friend. "When you have rambled out of sight," Burley says, "you have got to come back into the clear and show yourself."[4] He has been a man of the woods, of the darkness, one who has not always behaved in either sense of the word. He has also been a placed man, one who characteristically insists he is never lost in the woods. Whenever a companion, sensing they may be lost, asks Burley where they are, Burley answers simply with the words of biblical faith, "Right here" (347). He is where he is, present to the moment and the place.

Burley's decision to "come back into the clear and show" himself is suggestive for our political thinking. He will, and must, come into the open, to be accountable for his life before others, to be known as he is and has been. He is greatly blessed to have Hannah and Nathan, who accompany him to Wheeler's office, as witnesses to his action. He is also blessed to have a respectful antagonist in Wheeler, one whose commitments are sufficiently different from Burley's as to have caused him to wrestle with his own doings and find a way to explain them to one he loves. Burley can also come into the open because he comes from a place that is not already transparent. It makes no sense to speak of an "open," a clearing, unless there is a place that is closed, opaque, dark. Another way to put this would be to say that a viable public space depends upon private space.

Berry has emphasized the problems with both private and public spaces in contemporary American life. If we have largely destroyed private life, part of that destruction has been accomplished in the name of the "public," a word Berry wrestles with, finding its definition difficult. Berry does define a legitimate and limited sphere he designates public, but he also suggests a more negative and destructive sense of the concept. "Public" can, for instance, mean "simply all the people, apart from any personal responsibility or belonging," he comments in "Sex, Economy, Freedom, and Community."[5] Thus, "public" seems the most abstract of terms, for there is no one in particular whom one could point to as the "public." As Berry says elsewhere that "abstraction is the enemy *wherever* it is found," it follows that the concept "public" might also be suspect.[6] Often, Berry suggests, "public" serves as the leading-edge abstraction of forces whose goal is to uproot people from every particular identity—seemingly in the name of emancipation, but actually only so they can be remobilized as workers, consumers, and taxpayers in our increasingly "total economy." Thus, for Berry, the term we must insist on in order to protect the private and properly limit the public is "community." This is more, however, than a matter of terms. It is rather a matter involving every feature of our lives, beginning perhaps with "economy," understood in the classic sense as the ordering of the household. When Burley brings his doings into the open, it is perhaps more accurate to say that he moves into the communal rather than the public space. And he is truly blessed to have what so few of us any longer have: a community in which to act in the presence of others and whose expectations make it possible for him to give an account of his doings.

Exploring the relationship of the private, communal, and public spheres offers a way to begin a consideration of Berry's political thinking, broadly construed. I have divided that consideration here into three parts, hoping that readers will understand that too clean a separation of ideas is difficult when treating as holistic a writer as Berry. The first part focuses on Berry's case for community as the indispensable source of virtues necessary to keep the private and public spheres in proper relationship. Part of the discussion focuses on Berry's analysis of the forces that undermine community life in America: our addiction to debt, private and public; our tendency to identify freedom always as escape from restraint; our education system, including the universities; our public media culture, particularly in its pimping for an increasingly devalued sexuality; and a general failure of what I will call loving or sympathetic imagination.

The second section turns to Berry's constructive account of an alternative to the "total economy" in which we increasingly find ourselves. Here my focus is on his advocacy of household economy, his rich treatment of marriage as a condition of mutual helpfulness, and his proposals for the redevelopment of local economies. This part of the chapter closes with a discussion of Berry's insistence that the question of the family farm is critical not only to our agriculture but also to our politics. In her study of Berry's relationship to agrarianism, Kimberly K. Smith divides his political from his ecological thinking, arguing that the small farmer is less the repository of essential republican virtues than the carrier of environmental values critical to the country's ecological health.[7] This is, in my view, to divide what is indivisible. Ecological and political values are interconnected for Berry, and both are tied also to religious convictions—as my next chapter explores. For Berry, as for other new agrarians, agrarianism represents an order toward which to aspire: one concrete, particular, communal, balanced in private and public commitments, richly spiritual yet not at the expense of the bodily, always gratefully aware of the sources of its life. Like Allen Tate, Berry has always wanted "The Whole Horse," and he's always regarded it as holy.[8] What he seeks is a peaceable economy for a "beloved country," one appropriate to people who have come to be "authentically settled" at last in their own places.

The final part of the chapter focuses largely on Berry's writing as a citizen and patriot since September 11, 2001. Berry has sharply criticized American policy since 9/11, arguing especially that the provisions for preemptive strikes contained in the National Security Strategy are inconsistent with democracy. He is aware that some argue we have entered an unprecedented period in which the threat of terrorism requires us to give up "some measure of freedom in return for some increase of security."[9] But he is unwilling to grant this claim, at least not without serious inquiry into what "real security," "true patriotism," and freedom "require of us" (CR, 3). Here, as elsewhere, Berry asks us to enlarge the contexts in which we consider these matters. He argues for the practical pursuit of peaceableness, whose beginning must depend upon the creation of a healthy, sustainable, and self-sufficient polity and economy at home. One thing I hope will emerge from this discussion is that Berry has been writing as a citizen and patriot all along, not just since 9/11. He has exercised the "eternal vigilance" required to defend liberty, and he has done so, in part, because of his attachment to the *patria,* not the nation, but his own beloved local country. In answer to the title question of an essay by Alasdair MacIntyre—"Is Patriotism a Virtue?"—I suggest that patriotism is, for Berry, indeed a virtue, but not one to be equated with the kind of idolatrous identification with the nation that often goes by that name today.[10]

One of Berry's fullest treatments of the relationships among the private, public, and communal is the title essay of *Sex, Economy, Freedom, and Community.* Here Berry defines a clear role for the public sphere, granting what seems unexceptionable, namely that "a public government," founded "on democratic suffrage, is in principle a good thing." Its specific function is justice: to adjudicate disputes among communities and allow individuals a place for appeal outside their own communities when they feel they have been wronged. Such justice will have mostly to do with individuals, whereas living and healthy communities will have the family and household as their central terms. The relationship between the two spheres, public and communal, is a delicate one. Potentially "compatible," they are, "in the present economic and technological monoculture," often "at odds." Both community and public "are founded on respect—the one on respect for the family, the other on respect for the individual." Both these "forms of respect are deeply traditional," and, while "not fundamentally incompatible," they are "different," in ways that "can be the source of much damage" (SE, 148–49).

These are important propositions to consider not only for understanding Berry's thinking but also for estimating the circumstances behind it and its possible applications to current political and economic life. In his comments on the centrality of family, Berry sounds like a cultural conservative, and of course, in one sense he is a conservative, for he knows that our life is dependent on a whole set of givens—from topsoil to marriage—that we must actively cultivate and preserve or put ourselves in peril. But Berry has argued that "the conventional public opposition of 'liberal' and 'conservative'" is "perfectly useless."[11] What Berry criticizes particularly in the so-called conservative defense of the family is its inadequate critique of our economic life and its effects on the family. He wants to revive the economic importance of the family—and its related term, the household—in order to change our politics and economics. This is a far larger goal than that of conservative defenders of the family who seem to see it as a refuge of something called "values" in the middle of an otherwise amoral world. Berry might feel sympathy for such a defense, just as he sometimes speaks sympathetically of fundamentalism, understood as part of a local or regional culture's attempt to defend itself against intrusion and colonization from outside.[12] Berry believes, however, that the family must not be allowed to become simply a "haven in a heartless world," as Christopher Lasch called it.[13] Family and household are vital moral and economic institutions, essential for the maintenance of healthy communities and the places to which they are necessarily attached. They are also vital to the formation of the moral habits required by good communities and by a healthy, appropriately limited public sphere.[14]

Unfortunately, much that justifies itself under the name "public" can be destructive of communities:

> When a public government becomes identified with a public economy, a public culture, and public fashions of thought, it can become the tool of a public process of nationalism or "globalization" that is oblivious of local differences and therefore destructive of communities. (SE, 148)

Public economy, culture, and thought are almost contradictions in terms, for the word "public" means to Berry that which attaches to nobody in particular—and the thought or culture of nobody in particular seems unlikely to be thought or culture at all. Exalted notions of national community are simply nonsense, for a nation is much too large and abstract to elicit the feelings of belonging that are vital to community identification. It may require a village to rear a child, but if a nation attempts to rear one, it will produce nothing but an economic subject. That one hears frequent talk of national community means only that we are well along in the process of uprooting so well described seventy years ago by Simone Weil in regard to her beloved France: "The State is a cold concern which cannot inspire love, but itself kills, suppresses everything that might be loved; so one is forced to love it, because there is nothing else."[15] Public government, thought, culture, and education have too often simply served the industrial and now postindustrial economy as it has uprooted people from every particular attachment and identification.[16] The goal has been "economic and technological monoculture" (SE, 148), the nation analogous to a vast flat Midwestern cornfield, with no house or trees in sight, only miles and miles of nearly uniform units of corn. Change might begin with an alternative act of agricultural and political imagination: perhaps the nation as a Kentucky hillside farm, infinitely diverse in particular localities, each with its own shapely, beautiful life—some under cultivation, some as pasturage, some timbered, some left simply growing wild.

The difficulties involved in maintaining the appropriate balance of community and public can be illustrated by considering Berry's statement that both depend upon respect—in the case of community, respect for the family, in that of the public, respect for the individual. Worth considering is whether community and public are equally capable of forming the respect they require or whether one is parasitic off the other. Surely family and community provide the basic contexts in which we learn respect, understood here, for purposes of definition, in the Kantian sense as "the *maxim* of limiting our self-esteem by the dignity of humanity in another person."[17] This definition seems problematic today when there is so much concern about ensuring the self-esteem of children—presumed, apparently, to be without adequate self-esteem. Kant argues it is a matter of virtue to learn to will the limitation of our self-esteem before the dignity of the other. But how can we do that without losing our self-esteem? What is required is a context in which we are so thoroughly loved, so thoroughly esteemed, that we can learn to limit our self-esteem appropriately because we know that it is not fully at risk. I can limit my self-esteem when I know that I cannot lose it. Thus, the family or relatively small community where such bonds of love are possible provides the necessary context for the development of respect. If we ask, too, what kinds of situations are likely to impress on one the need to limit self-esteem, we again think of the family. We see the need to limit self-esteem when its exercise or expansion hurts or wounds another whom we ourselves esteem. If I hurt a sibling, I may see that it would be better for me to limit my self-esteem than to give pain to one I love. If my sibling continues to love me and our parents to love us both, I see further that I can limit my self-esteem without losing it: I am still esteemed. Moreover, I will have begun the process, so crucial to respect, of holding myself to an impersonal standard, for I will have seen that it is better for me to limit my self-esteem than to simply give it free reign if that means wounding the self-esteem of those with whom I wish to live peaceably. To cite Simone Weil again, I will have begun to learn how to love, if "belief in the existence of other human beings as such is *love*."[18] I will begin to regard myself, too, as a "human being as such"—as another—both respectful and worthy of respect, accountable always for treating others and myself in ways consistent with the dignity of human beings (as such).

I have opened up this matter of respect to show how the family and small face-to-face community can contribute to the formation of virtues needed by both the community and the public sphere. Surely the public sphere, at its best, can uphold and reinforce standards of respect. But if it becomes too closely allied to economic life, then the public undermines the very sources of respect required for its proper functioning. Berry thinks that we are already far along in using up the "moral capital built up by centuries of community life" (SE, 143) in the same way that we have used up the topsoil and our other natural gifts. In populist fashion, he regards the destruction of local communities to be part of the larger colonization project managed by government and corporations, whose alliance becomes more visible every day. Government's extension of massive debt ought to be seen, I believe, as the surest sign that the oligarchy has no understanding of, or interest in, real sustainability—at the heart of an understanding of sustainability is the awareness that nothing comes without using up something else. When we understand this fact, we become careful to conserve and restore those sources on which we depend. If there's any place Berry sounds exceedingly old-fashioned—and yet now of course perennially relevant—it's when he speaks, as he has often, of the virtue of "thrift." Thrift is the commitment to conserving both what one has earned and the sources on which one has depended to earn it—and recognizing that freedom lies in doing so. Berry says that "thrift" is a "better word than productivity" because "it implies a fuller accounting."[19] Debt, on the other hand, produces a prison of illusion, resentment, and necessity: illusion that something can be had without something else being used up, resentment of the justifiable claims of others to be paid, and the necessity of endless growth and ever-increasing efficiency—unless the necessity of servicing the debt can be relieved by extending even more debt, itself justified by the promise of an even brighter future for those to whom we will leave our debts.

Our addiction to debt has produced what Berry calls, in "The Idea of a Local Economy," "an era of sentimental economics and, consequently, of sentimental politics." In both its communist and capitalist forms, sentimentalism requires the sacrifice of whatever is good in the present for some "unprecedented security and happiness" in the future.[20] The "trick" is to "define the end vaguely," make it sound grandiose enough, and keep it sufficiently "at a distance." To believe these things, I would argue, has become a kind of necessity for us, a form—false, of course—of generational accounting and accountability. The load of debt we leave for our children to pay will be more than compensated by their greater, more abundant future—or so the official mythology goes. As Berry points out, the implicit devaluing of the present—the only real moment in which people can be happy—"contradicts the principle" common "to all the religious traditions—that if ever we are going to do good to one another, then the time to do it is now; we are to receive no reward for promising to do it in the future" (ILE, 251–52). One hears behind this remark, to cite just one tradition, the well-known line of Rabbi Hillel: "If I am not for myself who is for me? and when I am for myself what am I? and if not now, when?"[21]

The modern idea of freedom has been too exclusively, however, one of my being only "for myself." Berry traces the idea to the Romantics, identifies it as the goal of "contemporary liberation movements," and points out how freedom as escape from constraint is now demanded by "almost everybody" (SE, 150).[22] Freedom is understood as the relentless search for the elusive goal of self-fulfillment. Berry tends, I believe, to undervalue the importance of negative liberty, but what seems unexceptionable is that thinking of freedom so exclusively as escape from restraint cannot help but undermine the constraints required by community life. Paradoxically, Berry maintains, the increased "emphasis on individual liberty" has been accompanied by a decline in the power of most individuals to make significant life choices. "Ordinary people" find it "steadily harder," for example, to "choose a kind of work for which they have a preference, a talent, or a vocation, to choose where they will live, to choose to work (or to live) at home, or even to choose to raise their own children" (SE, 151). The point about vocation is a key one, as "justice and vocation" are "inseparable." The "principle and practice of vocation" is the way that "sanctity and reverence enter into the human economy" (ILE, 258). We might measure the health of a culture by the degree to which people are able to work at something to which they feel called; to abandon that idea altogether, as we seem increasingly to do, is to abandon people to the sheerest kind of economic determinism.

Education and the media also bear responsibility for the destruction of community life in America. Too much of public education is devoted to unfitting children for community life. With regard to rural life, this has been accomplished by disseminating the message that physical labor is demeaning and that rural people are largely unworthy of respect. Berry is fond of pointing out how many professors in the agriculture departments of land-grant universities identify themselves as "old farm boys," escapees from the places they presume to redesign and improve in the name of efficiency, too often understood along industrial models. Or, with even greater edge, he notes how it has remained acceptable to use "'redneck' and 'hillbilly' and 'hick'" long after similarly demeaning terms for other groups have ceased to have any place in public discourse.[23] Particularly destructive to small-town life is school consolidation, which Berry treats along with busing in the "Afterword" to *The Hidden Wound*. However much Berry supported the racial integration supposedly served by busing, he came to believe, largely based on his own children's experience, that it primarily served the larger process of social disintegration that was the real effect, perhaps the aim, of school consolidation. Busing the children put them "under school discipline" an additional two hours a day, reducing by that amount their "home discipline" and their time for work or play at home. They were being taught primarily how to behave according to the school authorities. Berry points out, too, that the distances to the consolidated schools were "well beyond the range of close or easy parental involvement" (*HW,* 133–34). Thus, one thing busing and consolidation served was the separation of the school world from that of home and community.

Berry's complaint is that the school exists now "in reference only to itself and to a theoretical 'tomorrow's world.'" "Neither teachers nor students feel themselves answerable to the community" (*HW,* 134), for the school exists to assist students to leave their communities for a place in the larger world, which too often means simply someplace in the government-corporate complex. Berry might well say of the public schools what his friend Wes Jackson has said of the university: that there is only one remaining major, "upward mobility."[24] Such exclusive focus on individual development—perhaps most benignly called "empowerment"—cannot help but be destructive of community, which depends upon young people's coming to understand their lives "in terms of membership and service" (SE, 149). Thus, Berry suggests the possibility that "the future of community life" may "depend on private schools and home schooling" (SE, 157), for perhaps only these can transmit the virtues and the locally particularized knowledge required to sustain community.

Berry has been even more critical of the university than of the public schools. Two features of his critique are particularly salient here: the first involving his specific analysis of the effects of reigning assumptions in the agriculture schools, the second his more general concern with the excessive specialization of the disciplines and the commoditizing of university education.[25] First, in both his essays and his fiction, particularly *Remembering,* he has charged the agricultural departments of the land-grant universities with contributing to the destruction of rural life. They have consistently assumed, Berry argues, that the success of American agriculture can be demonstrated by the productivity of the individual "farmer" measured by the number of people he or she can feed. Thus, the most successful agriculture is marked by having the fewest possible farmers feed the greatest number of consumers. The underlying assumption of this assessment must be that the life of the farmer is undesirable. Among the consequences, predictably, of the approaches to productivity developed by the schools has been the radical reduction of the number of farmers, the virtual disappearance of the family farm, and the destruction of rural communities. These consequences have been accompanied by ecological degradation, itself largely the product of practices urged by the agribusiness complex and their allies in university departments. Why these consequences have come about is complex, but Berry understands them largely as matters of scale. There is no doubt that in industrial enterprises certain kinds of economies can be achieved by increasing scale, particularly if one can externalize many of the costs. But the application of this industrial model to agriculture leads to ecological and communal disaster. Rectifying things must begin with a better accounting of what we have simply been treating as externalized costs: coming to understand, in short, just what we have done to land and people in the process of making American agriculture a model for the world (measured by the fact that hardly anybody is needed to do it!).

Here, as elsewhere in his analysis of the university, Berry sees the problem as grounded in the excessive specialization of the disciplines.[26] Agriculture has been treated as if it were simply a specialized science, rather than the fundamental way human beings support themselves on the earth. What must happen is for that specialized science to become more widely cognizant of agriculture's connections to everything in life and more responsive to a wider group of stakeholders. It seems, to me, that this is what Berry's writings have sought to do, and done so well, from *The Unsettling of America* onward.

"It is a mistake," however, as Stanley Hauerwas has said, to accuse Berry of "being anti-technological or against all forms of specialization"—or of being antiscience.[27] It might be said of him that he wants to apply very rigorously Thoreau's standard of accounting, articulated in *Walden* as he ponders the difference between the Native American's way of providing his shelter and that of so-called civilized man: "If it is asserted that civilization is a real advance in the condition of man,—and I think that it is, though only the wise improve their advantages,—it must be shown that it has produced better dwellings without making them more costly; and the cost of a thing is the amount of what I will call life which is required to be exchanged for it, immediately or in the long run."[28] Admirable here are Thoreau's insistence that we must regard costs as both immediate and long-term matters—which, for the relentlessly eschatological Thoreau, means even to the last day—and his keeping the measure of cost, "what I will call life," very loose, thus open to a great deal of imaginative construal. Perhaps the kind of accountability suggested here could be a gathering notion for a revived university, one in which the now extraordinarily specialized disciplines would have to at least imagine what it would mean to be accountable to one another.[29] Practitioners of the disciplines would need, at the very least, to become more imaginative about the consequences of their work, particularly the longer-term ones, and to develop ways of explaining that work to practitioners of other disciplines, especially those furthest removed methodologically. They would also need to learn to listen, to learn as much as possible of the language of a quite different discipline in order to see where there might be not only shared areas of concern but also imaginatively different ways of counting costs.[30]

What seems apparent to Berry is that currently there is no such notion of accountability in the university. Nor is there likely to be any time soon. I think he would assent to the proposition that American universities lack the resources—personal and intellectual, not financial—to change along lines that he thinks desirable. Pressured by various clienteles, universities will continue to develop in accord with the consumerist model: offering upward mobility to careerists who see themselves in increasingly individualized ways while providing space to faculty engaged in research deemed worthy by the willingness of external grantors to fund it. As public universities move increasingly toward "career preparation," they will continue to suffer from decreased public financing, for such preparation "is an improper use of public money," since it "serves merely private ends."[31] The work that should really "unify a university" is "that of deciding what a student should be required to learn," but this question is eclipsed by the emphasis on specialization and career preparation (LU, 83). Or, to put this another way, there simply is no authority resident anywhere in the university to answer the question meaningfully, as anyone who has ever sat on a core curriculum committee knows. "Underlying the idea of a university," Berry claims, must be "the idea that good work and good citizenship are the inevitable by-products of the making of a good—that is, a fully developed—human being" (LU, 77). This humanistic ideal means that students in all fields should graduate with a capacity for broadly informed and responsible judgment; an imagination sufficiently varied and developed to allow "for the great general work of criticism"—of all kinds—"to which we all are called" (LU, 96); and the "indispensable interest in the question of the truth of what is taught and learned, as well as the equally indispensable interest in the fate and the use of knowledge in the world" (LU, 90).[32]

Increasingly given over to the business model, the university plays its role in promoting competitive private ambition and self-realization at the expense of the virtues and attachments required by community life. Deprived of its "communal supports," public life "becomes simply the arena of unrestrained private ambition and greed"—a development we have come to understand all too well (SE, 121). What Berry discerns is a process by which individuals are simultaneously "atomized" and then "congealed into one public"—a process accelerated greatly by the "electronic media," whose particular role is to "blur and finally destroy all distinctions between public and community" (SE, 123–24). Here one hears a Tocquevillean quality in Berry's critique of our national life. His concern for the health of subsidiary institutions—marriage, family, community, church—reflects his judgment that we are being simultaneously alienated from one another—atomized—and then congealed into that "innumerable crowd of like and equal men" imagined by Tocqueville as he pondered how democracy might evolve into despotism. "Revolv[ing] on themselves without repose," "stranger[s] to the destiny of all" except their "children" and most "particular friends," the members of the crowd will be all too willing, Tocqueville feared, to be governed by "an immense tutelary power," which "takes charge of assuring their enjoyments and watching over their fate." "Absolute, detailed, regular, far-seeing, and mild," this benign power "provides for their security, foresees and secures their needs, facilitates their pleasures, conducts their principal affairs, directs their industry, regulates their estates, divides their inheritances." Can it not also, Tocqueville asks, "take away from them entirely the trouble of thinking and the pain of living?"[33]

Berry comes close to the heart of Tocqueville's analysis when he insists that a people cannot remain free when they have become almost completely unable to do anything for themselves. Berry also confirms a Tocquevillean insight when he points to our growing condition of "total economy." Tocqueville argued that most of the passions of people who "live in democratic times" will "end in love of wealth, or issue from it." This is not because "their souls are smaller," however, but because they recognize "that the importance of money really is greater then." For "when fellow citizens are all independent and indifferent, it is only by paying them that one can obtain the cooperation of each; this infinitely multiplies the use of wealth and increases the value of it" (587). A condition of "total economy," then, might be the logical outcome of a liberal social order, where each is understood to pursue his or her own self-interest in "indifference" to others. Politics under such an arrangement will come increasingly to resemble our own, not so much simply futile, but empty, on the domestic side, as being about little more than how either to grow the pool of available money or move it from one group to another. If we accept something like this line of analysis, we can see the potential for a revitalization of our politics in the emphases of Berry's work and that of other agrarians. We can diminish the importance of money in our lives by being simultaneously more independent—thereby less dependent on the "tutelary power" of state and corporation—and less indifferent to one another, that is, more committed to real community solidarity and its basis in local life. If we can diminish the importance of money in our lives, then perhaps it can become less important in our politics, and we can begin to talk about other kinds of questions.

Tocqueville thought that disciplinary power would operate largely through negation, blocking "the most original minds and the most vigorous souls," by establishing a "network of small, complicated, painstaking, uniform rules" (663). These become seemingly necessary, as Berry points out, when implicit communal understandings can no longer be counted upon to produce restraint. "Losing kindness," Berry quotes from Lao Tzu, "they turn to justness" (SE, 139). Disciplinary power "does not destroy, it prevents things from being born; it does not tyrannize, it hinders, compromises, enervates, extinguishes, dazes," reducing "each nation" to a "herd of timid and industrious animals of which the government is the shepherd" (663).[34] I think we should consider whether, in our own time, the primary instrument by which the nation exercises this power is the debt. For it is the debt, after all, that necessitates our industriousness, our need to regard ourselves as so much output requiring maximized efficiency, our compulsory participation in networks that increase this efficiency at the expense of any sort of individualized deviation (creativity), our faith in competition as the promoter of efficiency and thus abundance, our increasing intolerance of natural limitation understood only as condemning one to being a low-quality functioner, our muted criticism of the projection of American military power when it is understood as guaranteeing the stability required for global economic growth.

Debt "prevents things from being born." The question that should be raised about it is not how much the nation can bear—the exclusive focus of our policy makers—but what it prevents, what it makes inconceivable. Is there any doubt, we might ask in Berry's idiom, that the worship of growth, efficiency, and mobility so devastating to rural life derives from the necessity we have laid upon ourselves in the form of our national and personal debts? Or that the tutelary power has gained the degree of control it exercises over us because we assent to the rationalization of effort required apparently to service our debts?[35] The debt guarantees that we will be, first and foremost, subjects of a money economy whose increasingly global scale makes possible the multiplication of wealth—or at least of the leverage that can, for a time, be made to pass for it. The long-standing wisdom of the agrarian tradition, being discovered again by new agrarians, is that land is the one source of value that enables some independence from a money economy and the disciplinary power that necessarily accompanies it.

One of Berry's specific criticisms of the electronic media focuses on television's exploitation of sexuality. No matter what network executives decide about promoting "safe sex" or the "use of condoms"—or how sanctimoniously news anchors denounce the indiscretions of politicians—the networks continually "pimp for the exceedingly profitable 'sexual revolution'" (SE, 124). Berry's treatment of the way sexual liberation contributes to community disintegration must likely seem offensive, or even repressive, to some feminist readers and will probably be nearly incomprehensible to today's young people (judging from my college students). Berry's argument may look to the feminist reader suspiciously like an ill-disguised worry about a liberated female sexuality. The critic will suggest that Berry's seeming idealization of the kind of community that existed before "sexual liberation" may, unwittingly, simply reinforce the older double standard prevalent in such communities. Ordering sexuality toward reproduction as thoroughly as Berry does may always run the risk of subordinating women. Perhaps, indeed, the triumph of industrial—and now information—economies has been a necessary development in the liberation of women from their often repressive placing in the kinds of communities Berry might seem to defend.

It is certainly not Berry's intention to argue for institutional arrangements or understandings that oppress or repress anyone. Nevertheless, his
desire to defend and reinvigorate community life may sometimes cause
him to neglect the way that life did entail restricted horizons for whole
classes of people, minorities as well as women. One question I think Berry
needs to address more directly concerns the internal weaknesses of community life in America. His basic argument has been to suggest that community life was all destroyed from outside by forces collectively describable
as the "industrial economy." But surely there must have been something
defective in American communities, something limiting in rural life, that
caused at least some Americans to opt for alternative ways of living.[36] Or,
to put this more constructively, what do we need to know about the way
communities were in order to rebuild and reinvigorate them without the
weaknesses that made them so susceptible to emigration and colonization?

To see how we would put Berry's analysis of sexuality to constructive
use, let me begin by amplifying something I said above about my students.
I do think my largely suburban, affluent, electronically networked students
would find Berry's account of sexuality incomprehensible. For them sexuality is a source of pleasure and, probably, distraction, a technique to get
something they want, another thing to be thought about in means-end fashion. It is wholly disconnected from its natural function. It may seem extreme to think so, but I doubt there is even any significant memory that sex
is naturally ordered to reproduction. Of course they know that, but as living
knowledge, it is meaningless. Another way of putting this might be to say
that sex is thought about entirely from within the horizon of technique.

Berry presents sexuality as a gift, a trust, and a source of responsibility—all of these grounded in the natural reality toward which it is ordered.
We might say he wants to put the risk back into sexuality for a society that
has tried to make it safe, primarily by bringing it within the horizons of
exchange of the total economy. For Berry "there is nothing 'safe'" about
sexuality or about its proper context, marriage. These are at the center of an
alternative human economy, one based on gifts, rather than on profitable
exchanges. Giving the self in marriage involves "an unconditional giving,"
a commitment to finding one's "life by losing it." Such giving is a joyful and
fearful thing, for it carries with it the knowledge that "time and mortality
will impose their inescapable conditions" (SE, 136). Those who give them-

selves unconditionally affirm something like Dante's pledge in *La Vita Nuova*, "Of a surety I have now set my feet on that point of life, beyond the which he must not pass who would return" (SE, 137).[37] Or, to adapt the language of the young Mat Feltner in "The Hurt Man (1888)," lovers giving themselves unconditionally begin to understand that all this is "real."[38] The community must be able to celebrate and protect "this giving," Berry maintains; otherwise it "can protect nothing" (SE, 138). If we increasingly exist in a condition of "total" economy, it is because the public economy has nearly destroyed the economy of gift on which community depends—which is to say also, of course, that marriage is in a bad way.

The unconditional self-giving of marriage places it in a sphere of relations that cannot be made subject strictly to justice or the adjudication of rights and claims. "Marriage, family life, friendship, neighborhood, and other personal connections" must "try" for justice, but they "do not depend" on it. These connections depend rather on virtues Berry gathers together as the "*practice* of love": trust, patience, respect, mutual help, forgiveness (SE, 139). Schooling in these will come, for most of us, from marriage and the care of children. Part of that schooling involves the practice of imagination, that breaking out of the "solitary self" that enables us to "cross over the differences between ourselves and other beings." "In sex, as in other things," however, we "have liberated fantasy but killed imagination, and so have sealed ourselves in selfishness and loneliness." As a result, we have "arrived at" a "sexual brutality" analogous to our "economic brutality." Sex can never be made safe, because it involves a self-giving "that if not honored and reciprocated, inevitably reduces dignity and self-respect" (SE, 143). My only qualification to this would be to say that the proponents, purveyors, and pimps of a commoditized sexuality have succeeded in making it partially safe precisely by diminishing its stakes—that is, by undermining the ideas of dignity and self-respect themselves, making them dependent on little more than competitive measures like economic status. If the self is little more than a locus of desires created by the various shaping fantasies of postmodern life, then there is not much to be gained or lost in sexual encounters. Reclaiming the rich idea of marriage espoused by Berry will involve reclaiming also a sense of self capable of being given. And we must not underestimate the difficulty of this task, for the difference between the self capable of radical self-giving and the consumerist self is great, perhaps irreconcilably so. The self that gives itself entirely finds all it needs, and a self that has found all it needs is not the one required by an economy fueled by ever-increasing consumption.

We can now see why Berry has emphasized the household as the center of a revitalized agrarian economy. One of Berry's strongest defenses of the household is "Feminism, the Body, and the Machine," which begins with a recounting of the negative responses he received after republishing an earlier essay in *Harper's*. In that piece, "Why I Am Not Going to Buy a Computer," Berry gave his reasons for refusing to buy a computer and mentioned that his wife types his manuscripts and gives him advice about them. These statements elicited a number of critical letters, condemning Berry either for being a Luddite or for exploiting his wife. Berry's response is to make a strong statement for "marriage as a state of mutual help, and the household as an economy."[39] Berry is well aware that the word "economy" itself refers to the ordering (*nomos*) of the household (*oikos*), a term contrasted in political thinking since the Greeks with the *polis*. Michael Ignatieff has said that it is characteristic of the "Western political imagination" to be "haunted" by these classical conceptions of citizenship, and Berry is perhaps no exception.[40] He has, after all, written both *Home Economics* and *Citizenship Papers*. But Berry's way of correlating the household and the realm of the citizen shares little with Greek political thinking. In fact, it is articulated by way of distinction from that thinking.

For the Greeks, the *oikos* was an inferior realm, the material infrastructure in which women managed the slaves, whereas the *polis* was, as J. G. A. Pocock has said, "the ideal superstructure in which one took actions which were not means to ends but ends in themselves." What we are haunted by specifically, according to Ignatieff, is the Aristotelian notion that human beings become what they most truly are—political animals—through participation as citizens in a public realm. For Aristotle the movement into the *polis* meant specifically leaving behind the *oikos*, the inferior realm of the household, the place for matters of *oeconomia*, but not for the free exercise of judgment that defined one as a citizen and fully rational nature. Feminist anger at Berry's comments regarding his wife's typing his manuscripts, then, may have less to do with the Berrys' specific division of labor than it does with his general defense of the household—a term haunted with reminders of patriarchal arrangements in which women did the managing while men participated in the rational life of the *polis*.

Today, however, when one escapes from the *oikos,* one does not escape into a realm in which one practices the art of politics as the good in itself. Rather, one enters the modern economy, generally designated "industrial" by Berry, but now perhaps more accurately labeled postindustrial or information based. Here there is nothing like the free exercise of judgment to which the Greeks aspired, but rather only a more complex and abstract realm of instrumentality—in which everyone is subject to becoming the instrument of economic purposes exercised by people far away and only vaguely comprehensible by those affected. Some of Berry's most stringent criticisms of our economic life are made by way of asking what women have gained by entering the industrial or symbolic economy in mass numbers. "What are we to say," Berry asks, "of the diversely skilled country housewife who now bores the same six holes day after day on an assembly line? What higher form of womanhood or humanity is she evolving toward?" Or how, he asks, "can women improve themselves by submitting to the same specialization, degradation, trivialization, and tyrannization of work that men have submitted to?" (FBM, 184).

In part, then, Berry's defense of the household is intended to redraw the distinction between *oikos* and our political-economic life. His assumption is that the relationship between these realms is radically out of balance and that marriage is made to bear extraordinary pressures as a result. No longer understood as an economy, a condition of mutual help in response to necessity, marriage becomes a place for private emotional fulfillment, a matter of "relationships" involving "(ideally) two successful careerists in the same bed" (FBM, 180). Berry's analysis has many affinities to the story of the modern family's decline told by Christopher Lasch, who argued that the family has been under siege for over a century as part of the process of socializing reproduction. The "deterioration of domestic life," Lasch maintained, can be attributed in part to "public policy, sometimes conceived quite deliberately not as a defense of the family at all but as an invasion of it." The family has not simply evolved into its current condition; it has been "deliberately transformed by the intervention of planners and policymakers," including educators, reformers, ministers, and other members of the helping professions.[41]

Lasch develops a complex analysis of the way sociological theory in the twentieth century either failed to understand or exacerbated the problems of the family. Two points of that analysis are particularly salient to Berry's argument for household economy. First, as sociology developed a theory of the family's "function," within a larger understanding of the differentiated functions of modern, largely urban society, it tended to defend the family for "the indispensability of the emotional services it performed" (37). Defending it in those terms, however, "simultaneously justified the transfer of its other functions to other agencies" (37). Second, the very differentiation of functions within the family cannot help but weaken it, for "the family form[s] an integrated system." The "only function of the family that matters is socialization; and when protection, work, and instruction in work have all been removed from the home, the child no longer identifies with his parents or internalizes their authority in the same way as before, if indeed he internalizes their authority at all" (130). The family comes to rest "on the parents' services to the child," but this is a "shaky footing" since families can no longer "provide even the basic necessities" without state assistance or shelter the child from "the encroachments of the outside world" (131). Following this line of analysis, one is irresistibly led to the kind of conclusion Berry presents: that the recovery of the health of the family depends on its ability to reintegrate its so-called functions and reclaim its role in the socialization of the child—all of which depend upon its achieving some measure of economic security as a household in its own right.

Marriage and the household are crucial to learning to "think little," which we must do if we are to "rebuild the substance and the integrity of private life."[42] Berry is unequivocal in his conviction that there is nothing better one can do "than to make one's marriage and household, whether one is a man or a woman" (FBM, 182). No employment is more "valuable" than "employment at home, for either men or women." Children need the daily care of both parents, they need to see their parents work and to learn "to work with their parents," and they need to understand that the work done has "the dignity of economic value" (FBM, 182). Whereas we have been largely persuaded by the powers—governmental, corporate, educational—that all meaningful political action involves Thinking Big, Berry insists that the kinds of change necessary to preserve the world require habits of mind and heart that can only be learned through the discipline of Thinking Little:

> A man who is trying to live as a neighbor to his neighbors will have a lively and practical understanding of the work of peace and brotherhood, and let there be no mistake about it—he is *doing* that work. A

couple who make a good marriage, and raise healthy, morally competent children, are serving the world's future more directly and surely
than any political leader, though they never utter a public word. A
good farmer who is dealing with the problem of soil erosion on an
acre of ground has a sounder grasp of that problem and *cares* more
about it and is probably doing more to solve it than any bureaucrat
who is talking about it in general. (TL, 77–78)

No doubt these assertions are difficult to believe, for the large institutions
that dominate our lives would have us believe otherwise. I doubt many of
the young people I teach would agree with Berry, perhaps because they
have rarely had any experience of being able to make a discernible change
in anything. Perhaps the most important change to be promoted, then, by
the reclamation of marriage and household—and of the placed intelligence
that would come with them—is the ability to believe again in the large
resonance of the little things that most of us spend our lives doing.

    Marriage and household are matters treated throughout Berry's work
and with far too many implications to draw out fully here. Nevertheless,
several of these deserve additional comment. First, these matters are related to Berry's concern for the meaningfulness of work. In his early "Notes
from an Absence and a Return," written in 1968, Berry remarks on a change
in his thinking regarding meaning. Whereas he had thought of it "as something that one had recourse to—a touchstone or a base," it now seems to
him "that unless an act or an occupation is suffused with meaning, constantly and indivisibly meaningful, it is meaningless." One cannot "work at
meaningless work" and then "go home or to church or to a museum and
experience meaning, as one would recharge a battery."[43] A couple making
their marriage, rearing children, and building up a supportive household
engage in acts capable of being suffused throughout with meaning. (This is
not, of course, to suggest that these are exclusively the ways toward meaningful work.) Already in this early piece Berry presses the political ramifications of building family and household, quoting from Ezra Pound's
Confucian translations: "One humane family can humanize a whole state;
one courteous family can lift a whole state into courtesy; one grasping and
perverse man can drive a nation to chaos" (NAR, 39).[44] We are no doubt
less likely to assent to the positive propositions here than we are to recognize the validity of the warning, situated as we are this side of the adminis-
trations of one grasping and perverse man after another. The key to

understanding the Confucian affirmation is to recognize the way it insists we cannot dodge self-discipline. To quote Pound's translation further, "Thinking of this self-discipline [one] cannot fail in good acts toward his relatives; thinking of being good to his blood relatives he cannot skimp his understanding of nature and of mankind; wanting to know mankind he must perforce observe the order of nature and of the heavens" (NAR, 40).[45] The thinking of "professional reformers and revolutionaries," on the other hand, tends toward the machine analogy symptomatic of "military and other coercive thinking." Reflecting on the popular 1960s slogan "Power to the People," Berry hears "Power to *me*," the one man who has determined himself to be "their benevolent servant-to-be, who knows so well what is good for them." The slogan is a sample of the "diseased speech" that always threatens politics and whose only cure is firm commitment to the discipline of details, discipline the Confucian mind accepts (NAR, 40).

An economy of the household depends upon acceptance of this discipline of details and is thus likely to conserve local intelligence of the kind so apparent to Berry during his journey to Ireland in 1982. Ownership of property by alien landlords, corporations, or banks tends to invite neglect and abuse and "unavoidably degrades the managerial abilities and virtues in the local people."[46] Widespread distribution of ownership will not, in itself, guarantee "good care" of property, but "there is no hope of it" otherwise.[47] Committed to a place and embedded in a local economy, the agrarian household remains the best possible locus for our learning the habits and requirements of good care for the land that sustains us. As a way of promoting respect for the necessary sources of our life, Berry urges us to understand "our ubiquitous word, *resource*," according to its "Latin root, *resurgere*, to rise again," rather than as "means that can be used to advantage." This latter definition treats a resource as "something that has no value until it has been made into something else."[48] The right kind of economy, however, will learn to treat the resource as something that can always be replenished—that can resurge—if it is not asked to do too much. Understanding resources in this way implies small-scale, household management; intimate knowledge of possibilities and costs; and long-term horizons. Moving toward sustainability will involve a basic change in our understanding of value and time from that implicit in the industrialized concept of the "resource," which, by valuing things only according "to their future usefulness," effectively empties "the living present" of value (NR,

136). What results is a practical nihilism: the assumption that everything and everybody is at least "theoretically replaceable by something (or somebody) more valuable." The country we "had thought to make our home" becomes "instead 'a nation rich in natural resources'" (NR, 136). Berry has suggested that the "rapidly deepening" division in our country is "between people who are trying to defend the health, the integrity, even the existence of places whose values they sum in the words 'home' and 'community,' and people for whom those words signify no value at all."[49] Thinking about our division in this way might well lead to a richer sense of what is going on than the blue state–red state paradigm so fondly insisted upon by our current elite class, left and right.

The goal of Berry's politics, we might say, is that our country—not the nation or the flag—again become beloved. Only when we learn to speak of "a beloved country"—that is, of "a particular country, particularly loved"—will we start to raise the question about how it is to be used. The question about "ways of use will arise" because, "loving our country, we see where we are, and we see that present ways of use are not adequate," in great measure because they have destroyed the local cultures and economies on which proper stewardship of the land depends.[50] Berry has been an advocate of local food economies, pointing with hope to the "growing concern among urban consumers about the quality and the purity of food."[51] There is clearly a "politics of food," and it "involves our freedom." While "we still (sometimes) remember that we cannot be free if our minds and voices are controlled by someone else," we have "neglected to understand that we cannot be free if our food and its sources are controlled by someone else."[52] As a means of urging people to participate in local food economies, Berry has encouraged consumers to rediscover the "pleasures of eating," the superior taste and appearance of fresh foods locally grown. Perhaps eating with delight should be understood as the culminating phase of a "loving economy," one that remembers and honors the source throughout the process of good use so that the source is never simply used up in transformation into something else.[53]

The question of the family farm, then, is not only agricultural but also "political and cultural."[54] Our relationship to the land is "ruled by a number of terms and limits" that are "set not by anyone's preference but by nature and by human nature"—and that Berry sets down as seven precepts in "Conservation and Local Economy." Those precepts insist that proper care for land can only be accomplished by those with a "direct, dependable, and permanent" interest in it. The motivation for proper care is greatly strengthened by "mutuality of belonging" between people and land, itself encouraged by nothing so much as the expectation that not only one's own generation but also one's children and grandchildren will live on the land. Ownership is "an incentive to care," but the scale of ownership must be small enough that the "*quality* of attention" required by good care can be maintained. Finally, "a nation will destroy its land and therefore itself if it does not foster" the "sort of thrifty, prosperous, permanent rural households and communities that have the desire, the skills, and the means to care properly for the land they are using" (CLE, 3–4). The conservation of sustainable sources of food depends upon our recognizing the "preeminent and irrevocable value" of "*familiarity, the family life that alone can properly connect a people to a land*" (DFF, 164). Without family farms and dependable local sources, Americans become increasingly "dependent on money" and on that "total economy" that is hardly an economy at all, but rather a bloated, overextended financial system. Both the future of democracy and the kind of people we will be are at stake in the question of the family farm. If the many own no "usable property," they will have to "submit to the few who do own it," and they will neither "eat" nor "be sheltered or clothed except in submission" (DFF, 165). It goes without saying that the prospects for a republic of the self-ruled are small when people must submit in order to procure even the most basic necessities.

Berry began enlarging the contexts for our discussion of national defense as early as 1984 in "Property, Patriotism, and National Defense," arguing, as he has more recently in *Citizenship Papers,* that "sound policy" must begin with "thriving local communities" capable of living "indefinitely" from "local sources," even in the direst "adversity" (109). Such communities are not only the "prerequisites" of sound national defense; they "*are* a sound national defense," for they "defend the country daily" by "giving it the health and the satisfactions that make it worth defending, and by teaching these things to the young." If military defense of the country were to be needed, it would spring from these sources "as if by nature," as "our Revolution suggests" (PPND, 109).

To lose the ability to supply ourselves necessities is to become vulnerable in at least three ways. First, in a passage eerily suggestive of our current, post-9/11 awareness, Berry pointed out, in 1984, how "our national livelihood is everywhere pinched into wires, pipelines, and roads," all that we now call infrastructure. As a result, a few "well-placed sticks of dynamite" have the potential to hurl us into "darkness, confusion, and hunger." This fragility in turn leads to an "obsession with megatonnage," or, if that sounds dated, with the godlike capacity to inflict "shock and awe." Moreover, the awareness of national vulnerability encourages a debased version of patriotism rooted in fear and easily aroused by "a leader sufficiently gifted in the manipulation of crowds" (PPND, 108). A people thoroughly dependent on the globalized economy is likely to react with terror to any perceived or possible disruption of its sources of support. Thus, the too great interdependence of the globalized economy may produce an inflexibility or exaggeration in our responses to conditions or players seeming to threaten it.

Berry argued further in "Property, Patriotism, and National Defense" that a degree of fatal abstraction had entered our politics through our dependence on nuclear weapons. Focused on Cold War realities, this part of Berry's essay may seem somewhat dated. Yet I would suggest that it is not, for we are still dependent on nuclear weapons, even if the possibility of global nuclear conflict seems more remote than it once did. Moreover, what Berry says about the attitudes that must be fostered in us in order for us to contemplate using nuclear weapons seems now at least partially applicable to the so-called War on Terror. His claim is that government's asking citizens to commit themselves to a strategy of nuclear defense—with the concomitant assumption of nuclear attack—is inherently "ruinous of the political health" of the nation. We were being asked in 1984 "to accept and condone the deaths of virtually the whole population of our country, of our political and religious principles, and of our land itself, as a reasonable cost of national defense" (PPND, 98). "Good citizenship," in such circumstances, absurdly becomes the acceptance of policies whose results are too brutal and devastating even to contemplate. One political result is the driving of "wedges of disbelief and dislike" between "citizens and their government"—as well as between different groups of citizens (PPND, 98). Those citizens who properly give a high value to loyalty must seem utterly irrational to those who find the nuclear strategy absurd. Those who find the strategy indefensible must seem cowardly to those willing, at least in imagination, to make the sacrifices required by what seems, to them, the only realistic defense alternative. It is difficult to see how either side could profitably engage the other—a situation perfectly suited to the loss of democratic control over military policy and its seizure by ideologically driven power elites.

In taking up nuclear weapons, we become "tools of [our] tools," to cite a danger Thoreau warned about regarding technology in *Walden*. Once we choose to rely on nuclear weapons, Berry argues, there is no choice left but "*not* to rely on them": we have ceded other choices. As they "articulate a perfect hatred" of our enemies, that hatred becomes a necessity for us. Yet the hatred required by nuclear weapons is "such as none of us has ever felt, or can feel, or can imagine feeling." No one of us—as an individual—could ever intend the destruction produced by nuclear exchange. Thus, we can only be brought to "belief in the propriety" of the use of such weapons by "personal abandonment to a public passion not validated by personal experience" (PPND, 99–100). Government policy must necessarily devote attention to manufacturing the passions required to sustain the perceived propriety of the means of defense it has adopted. Thus, our tools have shaped the discourse so thoroughly that it requires a different kind of intelligence altogether to raise questions about defense strategy. That kind of dissent requires a "particularizing intelligence," one that begins by asking "first what kind of country is defensible"—and then assuming that appropriate defense will arise when and if we have that kind of country (PPND, 100, 103). Only by developing that kind of intelligence, and with it moral imagination, will we be able to raise questions about the "determinative" power our weapons hold over us.

In the opening chapter of *Citizenship Papers,* published in 2003, Berry notes that Thomas Jefferson "justified general education by the obligation of citizens to be critical of their government: 'for nothing can keep it right but their own vigilant *and distrustful* [Berry's emphasis] superintendence.' " "An inescapable requirement of true patriotism, love for one's land," is, it follows, "a vigilant distrust of any determinative power, elected or unelected, that may preside over it" (CR, 5). The first task of the patriot, then, is to identify what determinative powers preside over our country, to ask whether this need be the case, and to probe the consequences of that determination. I hope it is clear from this chapter that Berry has been working at this patriotic task throughout the whole of his career. What he has done in his writing since 9/11 is to give a more explicitly political focus—in the ordinary sense of the term—to his vigilant identification of the powers that determine us, self-created as well as external. His argument that sound defense policy begins with healthy, self-sustaining local communities is designed precisely to insist that the way to freedom from determinative powers is to remain as capable of self-determinism as possible. There is perhaps some danger in my putting things this way, as self-determinism means to some the ability to project American power anywhere in the globe at any time. Obviously, for Berry self-determinism has less to do with the ability to project power than it does with being free of the need to do so—and aware of how possession of such power exercises its effects on us and our politics.

The title of *Citizenship Papers* is a claim of standing, an insistence on the dignity one possesses and exercises in a free republic where one rules and is ruled in turn. The first essay of that volume takes vigorous exception to provisions of the "National Security Strategy" issued by the White House in September 2002. Berry focuses on what he deems the "central" statement of the document, the announcement that "we will not hesitate to act alone, if necessary, to exercise our right of self-defense by acting preemptively" against terrorists. What is at stake here is nothing less than our democracy. Commenting on the "we" that here announces its right to act, Berry suggests that this "we" can be neither that referred to in the Declaration of Independence nor that evoked in the Constitution since there is nowhere any appeal to the "consent of the governed." Rather, this new "we" can only be a "royal" one, declaring its intention to act in a way that cannot, by definition, be open, public, or extensively discussed (CR, 1–2). Any preemptive action discussed beforehand would obviously risk being preempted in turn by acts of those against whom it is planned.

What we are being prepared for is "acceptance of war as a permanent condition" (CR, 7) of our national life. This is implicit in our declaration of the right and intention to act alone in preemptive ways that cannot, in principle, be subject to discussion. Such a policy would seem to require "the acquiescence of a public kept fearful and ignorant," likely through "manipulation by the executive power" and the "compliance of an intimidated and office-dependent legislature" (CR, 2), for which Berry shows appropriate republican scorn. Sounding much like Thoreau, who said of himself that he "was not born to be forced," Berry calls for a kind of civil disobedience: a conscious, active, and immediate withdrawal from the "we" of the "National Security Strategy," with the intention of promoting a higher, truly legitimate civility and insisting that the "consent" of democratic citizens cannot be "coerced or taken for granted" (CR, 2).[55]

Berry does not deny the threat of terrorism nor diminish the importance of security. His criticism of the "National Security Strategy" insists that it will make us less democratic without making us any more secure. Here, as everywhere in his thinking, he offers a wider, deeper criticism based on enlarging the contexts of the work. The starting point is to insist on the "contradiction between national security and the present global economy" (CR, 11). It is axiomatic that a nation's independence can "be maintained only by the most practical economic self-reliance" (CR, 10). At a minimum, this means the nation "should be able sustainably to feed, clothe, and shelter its citizens, using its own sources and by its own work." This will require citizens who are "patriotic" in "the truest sense": those who will "love their land with a knowing, intelligent, sustaining, and protective love" (CR, 10). Thus, a true policy of national security might begin with "practical measures" of conservation and thrift, the goal being to reduce "the nation's dependence on imports" and the "competition between nations for necessary goods." Security—and freedom, in this view— depends upon the widespread cultivation of the virtues required to build a sustainable domestic economy. There must be "due concern" for the long-term health of everything on which we depend: soils, forests, watersheds, the whole gamut of natural systems.[56] Commitment to this truer, harder version of national security depends, first, on unmasking the assumption that the unlimited expansion of global capitalism makes conservation of all kinds unnecessary. While our national security is certainly connected to global economic conditions, it is naive to assume, as the authors of the "National Security Strategy" do, that the world's "economic wrongs can be righted merely by 'economic development' and the 'free market'" (CR, 11). It is wrong to believe that these offer an automatic cure for poverty, and it is doubly wrong not to recognize that economic development will be greatly impeded by the very policies the "National Security Strategy" espouses: those of "a war against terrorism or a preemptive war for the security of one nation" (CR, 11).

"Thoughts in the Presence of Fear" continues Berry's argument that national security depends upon the creation of a healthy, sustainable polity and economy at home—themselves dependent upon healthy local communities and environments. Among the unpleasant realities brought home to us by 9/11 was one regarding innovation. Prior to that day, reigning doctrine had been that endless growth could be fueled by continual "innovation." What we had not foreseen is that all our innovations "might be at once overridden by a greater one: the invention of a new kind of war." We now find ourselves "trapped in the webwork of communication and transport that was supposed to make us free."[57] We discovered specifically that a globalized economy also means a globalized arms trade and that it is impossible to keep the "weaponry and the war science that we have marketed and taught to the world" out of the hands of those who would use them against us (TPF, 18). Indeed, we need to question the legitimations of violence by those states engaged in what we call "war" rather than "terrorism"—not in order to blame states for the murderous actions of terrorists, but rather to begin to bring the process of legitimation under the most intense scrutiny. We need to ask how national governments "so uncannily" legitimate "large-scale violence" in the globalized world order: is it by inventing systems of national security and international exchange so vast and dominating that they come to seem indispensable? Have we become so imprisoned in the networks of a globalized economy that we have created for ourselves a fate that cannot be turned aside, the necessity to engage in war to protect sources of supply and to keep open the markets required for constant growth?[58]

Berry argues that we now face a clear choice. One alternative is to "continue to promote a global economic system of unlimited 'free trade' among corporations, held together by long and highly vulnerable lines of communication and supply." On this side of 9/11, it should be clear that "such a system" will require protection by "a hugely expensive police force that will be worldwide," whether maintained solely by the United States or jointly with other nations, and that the efficacy of this force will depend necessarily on its "oversway[ing] the freedom and privacy of the citizens of every nation." Berry's preferred course would be to "promote a decentralized world economy that would have the aim of assuring every nation and region a *local* self-sufficiency in life-supporting goods." International trade would continue, but it "would tend toward a trade in surpluses after local needs have been met" (TPF, 18–19). This second alternative is much more conducive, in Berry's view, to the preservation and health of the natural environments and local cultures on which a sustainable future depends.

Today's vigilant defender of liberty will ask three things of our officials. One, that rhetoric not be substituted for thought, as it was often in the days immediately following 9/11 and frequently continues to be when the subject is response to terrorism. Perhaps "serious and difficult thought" on these matters is taking place in Washington, but too often the complex problems facing us have been reduced "to issues of unity, security, normality, and retaliation" (TPF, 19). Second, we must avoid "national self-righteousness," particularly of the kind expressed by ex-President Bush at the National Cathedral on September 14, 2001, when he proclaimed our "responsibility" to "answer" the "attacks and rid the world of evil." That "anything so multiple and large as a nation" can be so unambiguously good as to take upon itself the task of ridding the world of evil is "an insult to common sense." But, more important, it is "dangerous," because it "precludes any attempt at self-criticism or self-correction." The Jeffersonian dissenter must insist "it is a sign of weakness," not of strength, for a nation to do anything to reduce the ongoing work of criticizing its assumptions, policies, and practices—criticism dependent, incidentally, on the availability of alternative self-understandings and sources of support (CR, 5). Finally, and here Berry is most specifically Christian, we must challenge the assumption that we will make war in order to bring about peace. Victory, not peace, is the "aim and result of war," and "any victory won by violence necessarily justifies the violence that won it and leads to further violence" (TPF, 19–20). Berry fears we are on the brink of a period of perpetual war necessitated by the logic of continual global economic growth. He proposes instead the practice of peaceableness: an economy founded on thrift and care, refusal to caricature our enemies, and promotion at home and abroad of "the ideal of local self-sufficiency" (TPF, 21). To make a beginning, we need to enlarge the contexts in which we see the work of conserving freedom and providing security.

In one of the best studies of Berry's politics, Kimberly K. Smith describes him as an advocate for a "*cooperative* internationalism," one in which the United States would act as a "good citizen of the global community," displaying the virtues expected of citizens themselves: "rationality, moderation, prudence, and constructive engagement." For the nation to play that kind of role, citizens must "involve themselves, deeply and critically, in public debates over foreign policy." Smith is less convinced, however, by Berry's arguments for "local self-sufficiency" and "food security," suggesting that he has been "somewhat opportunistic" in emphasizing these on the heels of 9/11. "Even more problematic," in her view, is the apparent disjunction between Berry's "argument for self-sufficiency" and the pervasive emphasis of his "philosophic framework" on "'the whole network of interdependence and obligation' in which human lives necessarily unfold." Why, Smith asks, "should we try to escape the interdependencies and vulnerabilities of the global economic system? Isn't local self-sufficiency just another misguided bid for an illusory sense of security?" Her own answer to this last question stresses the way working toward local self-sufficiency "requires *more* from us—more conscious effort, more awareness of our duties toward one another, and more active involvement in the life of the community." It makes us, in short, "better citizens, local *and* global," for "seeking local self-sufficiency is after all nothing more than preserving the community's productive capacities—which is for Berry the very definition of patriotism."[59]

Several of these carefully considered points deserve comment. First, it is no doubt true that a reinvention of local self-sufficiency will require more effort from us, making us better citizens of both our own places and the globe. But it is important to specify some of the ways in which this will happen and to recognize that these will make us global citizens of a somewhat different kind than those envisioned by most who argue for the necessary interdependence of the "global economic system." Part of Berry's argument for local self-sufficiency involves, as we have seen, our regaining control over the language of politics, our reclaiming it from that fatal abstraction into which it fell as our national policies—particularly but not exclusively regarding defense—became such that no ordinary citizen could imagine or assess them according to anything in his or her own experience. Local self-sufficiency also means resistance to the elevation of money to a position of supreme importance, one it increasingly assumes as those brought into so-called interdependence share no more than mutual economic advantage. The sources of our ecological and moral imagination are also inevitably local. It's when we are rooted enough in particular places to see the damage we do that we come to understand the damage others are capable of in their places. It seems to me highly improbable that we are, as Smith contends, "as likely to suffer abuses and injustices at the hands of our neighbors as at the hands of international terrorists or corporations" (57). Even if this were the case, there would be political hope in the knowledge that one can enter into substantive conversation with neighbors in a way impossible to do with the institutions responsible for the massive oil contamination of the Gulf of Mexico or the recent series of economic bubbles.

Perhaps most important of all, a local frame of reference is critical to our maintaining the imagination required to see the damage we have done to our country. All of us are "implicated" in a "destructive, predatory, and wasteful economy," Berry contends, a fact he attributes to a "failure of imagination" on our part.[60] "We are destroying" our country "*because* of our failure to imagine it," Berry writes in "American Imagination and the Civil War." If this seems a large claim for the imagination, it may be because that term has lost some of its force in our generally devalued speech. "By 'imagination,'" Berry writes, "I do not mean the ability to make things up or to make a realistic copy. I mean the ability to make real to oneself the life of one's place or the life of one's enemy—and therein, I believe, is implied imagination in the highest sense."[61] What we are in danger of losing in talk about globalization is precisely this ability to make the lives of people and places real to us. If we insist, in fact, that "interdependence" not become a mere abstraction, we will see that there is no necessary contradiction between local self-sufficiency and interdependence. Berry's claim is that local self-sufficiency is critical to a properly human kind of interdependence: one in which people meet one another—within or across national boundaries—as rough equals or neighbors. Having imagined that possibility, let us, to paraphrase Thoreau, set about laying the foundations needed to make it a reality.[62]

Patriotism, as Alasdair MacIntyre has pointed out, often comes under fire from liberal cosmopolitans precisely because its particularist commitments seem at odds with the impersonal stance insisted on by post-Enlightenment ethics. According to such views—not shared by MacIntyre—patriotism cannot be a virtue because it represents a kind of partiality inconsistent with morality.[63] In response to this claim, Berry might argue that patriotism—at least of the sort he advocates—is essential to moral action as a source of the ability to make the lives of others real to us. Berry's patriotism identifies the *patria* with his own fields, small enough to know with the intimacy of love. It begins with the love of family and household, extends to his neighbors, his local community, and the common wealth from which they draw support. It may take in an entity as large as the Commonwealth of Kentucky, and Berry has shown patriotic devotion to the nation through his loving criticism of American policies over the years—and most especially since 9/11. What Berry's patriotism most emphatically is not is what MacIntyre has called that "simulacrum" (225) of patriotism left to the clients of bureaucratic states for whom no particular place evokes enduring love. We might think of Berry as advocating a local patriotism for the sake of a more critical national patriotism, except that love for local beloved country is not adopted "for the sake of" anything. It rather springs from one's grateful recognition of how much one's life depends on what one has been given. Nevertheless, we see in Berry's work the way a rooted love for one's own place and community provides sources for constructive criticism of the nation.

To predict that agrarianism might revitalize our country's politics is perhaps too bold, but I think we can see how agrarians like Berry carry kinds of knowledge that lead to a shifting of the discussion—as has already occurred on countless local and national issues, particularly regarding the environment. Those rooted in their own beloved country will understand themselves as something other than the workers, consumers, and taxpayers required by today's "total economy." Knowing some things cannot be sold no matter whose interests may be satisfied, they will resist the devolution of politics into the endless invention of schemes to satisfy reciprocal self interest. Moreover, agrarians are likely to be too humble to believe themselves capable of estimating the interests of contemporary people as if these are separable from the health of the whole natural household and the good of succeeding generations. They will thus insist on traditional sources of wisdom not often reckoned in the calculations of bureaucrats and insist that good policies must always take into account the widest range of stakeholders. Because they know themselves to live in and from beloved country, the means to defense will be there if ever required, and yet because they love their country, they will not want to see it destroyed and thus will practice the everyday defense of peaceableness.

Chapter 3

Against the Church,
For the Church
Berry and Christianity

Some years ago a student of mine asked in a seminar on Wendell Berry whether Berry's ideas depended on Christianity or at least on a religious view of the world. I remember answering with considerable equivocation, first because I wanted to avoid saying anything that would encourage my non-Christian students to write off Berry's ideas, but also because I was myself uncertain. I remember saying I saw no reason why one might not reach, from a purely secular point of view, the same kinds of conclusions as Berry about a whole variety of matters: the need to conserve topsoil, the inapplicability to agriculture of industrial modes of thinking, the absurdity of our regarding food as a weapon, the inevitability of destruction to particular environments (pace Berry) in an increasingly global economy, and so forth.[1] This seemed to me an unsatisfactory answer to the student—and it still does—because there is throughout Berry's work a deep sense of our dependence as creatures on a world only rightly understood as sheer loving gift. Berry has spoken of himself, in "The Burden of the Gospels," as "first of all a literalist," as he thinks "every reader should be," meaning by this simply that he "expect[s] any writing to make literal sense before making sense of any other kind."[2] Following him in this, I want to make literal sense of his statement that he takes the Gospel of John literally, or, as he puts it in "Sabbath IX, 1999," "The Incarnate Word is with us, / is still speaking, is present / always, yet leaves no sign / but everything that is."[3] If Christianity involves not simply our assenting to a number of doctrinal positions or declaring a cultural identity, but rather our coming to understand ourselves as being drawn up into the life of God, then it is difficult to see how any question could stand completely outside of Christian reflection. I believe that Berry does understand himself in this way, and so, with that in mind, I would have to answer my student that Berry's ideas are those of one who believes, as he puts it, "that not just humans but *all* creatures live by participating in the life of God, by partaking of His spirit and breathing His breath" (BG, 66). Perhaps this means that Berry's thinking depends upon Christianity; perhaps it means that non-Christians who arrive at something like the same conclusions as Berry are acting from something like what Christianity means when it talks about our participating in the very life of God.

If I were trying to answer my student's question from Berry's own most direct comments about Christianity, I might be inclined to come to something like Huck Finn's conclusion after he'd been reading "considerable" in *The Pilgrim's Progress*: "the statements was interesting, but tough."[4] In response to a question about his "religious background," Berry has said that he "was raised as a Southern Baptist," but he's "always felt" himself "an outsider to the sects and denominations."[5] He deplores the process of exclusion by which religious groups "come into being and cohere," adding, "We know what a bloody business this is" (THC, 118). He criticizes Christianity for its lack of interest in nature, "the body's life and all that it depends on," which is "to say," as he puts it, that Christianity "has not been interested enough in our economic life," that it "has been too easy to be 'a good Christian' while destroying the world that (we are told) God loves." Moreover, modern churches "have entirely lost their artistic tradition," too often gather in buildings that are either "brutally ugly or rather tackily pretentious," and have generally sat by and "even approve[d] while our society hurries brainlessly on with the industrialization of child-raising, education, medicine, all the pleasures and all the practical arts." If "Christians quit worrying about being 'Christians' or church members" and did what Jesus "told them to do," the "church" might "sooner or later dissolve into something much better" (THC, 119). Berry confesses to being "sometimes" a "rather bewildered reader of the Bible"; argues that the "human mind too readily imposes on God," becoming "owlishly knowledgeable about his mysteries, when it needs to be humorous and forgiving"; and seeks, at times, to distance himself as far as possible from theology (THC, 119).[6] "Having written some pages in favor of Jesus," Berry writes in a Sabbath poem from his most recent volume, *Leavings,* "I receive a solemn communication crediting me / with the possession of a 'theology' by which / I acquire the strange dignity of being wrong / forever or forever right." In response to the question he's asked in the letter—"Have I gauged exactly / enough the weights of sins?"—Berry asks only for forgiveness:

> O Lord, please forgive
> any smidgen of such distinctions I may
> have still in my mind. I meant to leave them
> all behind a long time ago. If I'm a theologian
> I am one to the extent I have learned to duck
> when the small, haughty doctrines fly overhead.[7]

On the other hand, Berry responds to one interviewer's question about environmental "stewardship" by saying that the most "comprehensive understanding of the world is that it's God's property" and that if we want to insist that "human interest" cannot be "definitive," we're on less risky ground using theological language than we are otherwise.[8] When asked if he thinks "a community can exist without religious belief," Berry remarks that he has "great admiration for reason" but thinks that "ultimately, you have to have religious faith for community life to work."[9] Berry uses scripture—particularly the affirmation that "God loved the world, that the Incarnation *happened* because God loved the world"—to defend his sense that Christianity has erred when it has been too dualistic, when it has too sharply opposed heaven and earth. That dualism "always leads you to condemn the earth as something evil, as something to be suffered through in order to get to heaven." It omits not only the great pleasure made available to us through the gifts of creation but also what Berry calls the "interpenetration" of heaven and earth:

> It seems to me that there is an interpenetration, a major communication, and that to know this world at its best is to know something heavenly. And the other way around, too. To know it at its worst is to know something hellish. That's how we know what to work for and what to hope for in this world. This seems to me to be sanctioned by Scripture. (WBC, 140)

That it is "wrong to condemn the world and wrong to refuse its decent pleasures" seems to Berry, too, simply an obvious implication of God's "Sabbath rest at the very beginning" in "appreciation and approval of what he had done" (WBC, 140).

I want to use my student's excellent question, then, as a frame for this chapter, but I want to continue to leave its answer somewhat equivocal. No doubt the most reasonable thing to say is that Berry has been a voice against the church, for the church, one who has tried to call Christians to be more faithful to the affirmations of scripture and more imaginative in regard to the tradition's implications—particularly, but not exclusively, regarding the care of the earth.[10] He is part of an honorable tradition of nonchurchly American writers who have often told Christians more forthrightly what they needed to hear than voices within the church were willing or able to do—a tradition including Thoreau, Melville, Dickinson, Whitman, and Mark Twain. What I will do explicitly here is to draw out the Christian dimension of Berry's thinking in six areas of emphasis. This mapping of the territory certainly has about it a dimension of the arbitrary. The areas overlap; my focus on six is not meant to be exhaustive or exclusive; what I'm offering is only the most beginning approach to the Christian aspects of Berry's work. The focus here will be mostly, though not exclusively, on Berry's nonfiction. Later chapters will touch on similar matters, among others, in Berry's fiction and poetry.

The chapter's first section focuses on Berry's consistent criticism of forms of Christianity he regards to be life-denying; far too devoted to the language of individual salvation; and too easily co-opted by the projects of nation, economy, and technology. His criticism here bears significant resemblance to that of Harold Bloom, who defines a particular kind of Gnosticism as the reigning American religion.[11] While Christianity was busy lending itself to supporting these large cultural projects, poets, according to Berry, were often more faithful in maintaining a sense of the sacred, a feeling for the mystery of love in which we come to live and move and have our being. My second emphasis, then, is on the way some of Berry's work, especially in his earliest volumes, stresses the fidelity of poets over against Christianity, understood—at least in its cultural manifestations—as a system of belief that undermines the sanctity or holiness of the natural world and everyday life. During the course of his career, Berry seems to have become more comfortable using Christian language for his reflection, perhaps because he has come to understand the doctrine of creation differently, and in a more classically orthodox fashion, than he does, for example, in the pieces collected in 1972 in *A Continuous Harmony*.[12]

What complicates our understanding of this point is that those early pieces do, I believe, reflect a view of creation that has been held by many, possibly most, Christians—despite its not being what orthodox Christianity has meant in talk about creation. Obviously a central area of concern is our relationship to the natural world, the environment, for want of a better generalizing word. Some of Berry's early work seems similar in its assumptions to those of historian Lynn White Jr., whose essay "The Historical Roots of Our Ecologic Crisis" has exercised so much influence over our understanding of the relationship between Christianity and the environment.[13] Grounding his argument particularly in a reading of the first chapter of Genesis, White argued that the extraordinarily anthropomorphic quality of Christianity was at the root of our ecological crisis, that it provided the primary authorization for human exploitation of the environment without regard to the health of nature itself.[14] Already in 1982, however, in the title essay of *The Gift of Good Land*, Berry responded to White specifically, arguing that the biblical and Christian traditions about the "proper use" of the natural world were much more complex than White had suggested.[15] The third emphasis of the chapter, then, explores Berry's counterargument to White and his claims that the Bible and Christian tradition point toward the need for loving and sustainable use of the land.

The fourth and fifth parts of my discussion concentrate, respectively, on the importance to Berry's Christianity of two closely related terms, "body" and "mystery." Berry insists strongly on the incarnational quality of Christianity and on embodiment as our way of being in the world and with others. The body is not, for Berry, a kind of container for the soul, but rather the medium for our openness, availability, and communication with others. He works out, at times, something like a theology of the body that is reminiscent of John Paul II. "Mystery," for Berry, means something like what it does for Herbert McCabe, who speaks of mystery as referring to a "depth of meaning," to "what shows itself but does not show itself easily." Using the example of *Macbeth*, McCabe argues that great works of art draw us ever deeper into mystery, "enlarg[ing] our capacity for understanding" as we go. What mystery reveals to us finally is that we will never come, at least in this life, to an end of knowing. When McCabe writes of the "Mystery of Unity" that is Holy Thursday, he says, for example, that we "can see humankind itself as one only in mystery, in the gesture towards the reality that is to come. We can only see God in mystery, as the reality that is to come. We cannot see love except in hints and guesses of what is to come."[16] If we, on the other hand, see mystery only as a kind of intolerable limit to our certainties, to our mastery of the world, then we will never be led into the slow revealing of what is to come, now and beyond. The foreclosure of mystery in favor of materialist certainty—particularly as evidenced by E. O. Wilson in *Consilience*—is what Berry takes aim at in *Life Is a Miracle*. "Body" and "mystery" are terms for Berry, then, that point to a way of being on the earth—a way of being, I am tempted to say, by faith, one willing to rest in uncertainty, confident that more of what we glimpse now will be revealed in time and seeking to live in a way marked by "a continuous harmony" with the larger creation that supports us—what William Carlos Williams called "the body of the Lord."[17]

Such harmony is something that moderns or postmoderns will mostly experience as absent or disrupted, as increasingly almost inconceivable. Our condition is largely defined by rootlessness and exile, utter placelessness. These are central concerns throughout Berry's work, of course, and they are important biblical themes. As Walter Brueggemann has pointed out, "the Bible itself is primarily concerned with the issue of being displaced and yearning for a place."[18] The "sense of place," Brueggemann argues, "is a primary category of faith," adding that our current crisis is not so much one of meaninglessness as it is one of rootlessness, for "there are no meanings apart from roots" (4). Place is to be contrasted with space, which "may be imaged as weekend, holiday, avocation, and is characterized by a kind of neutrality or emptiness waiting to be filled by our choosing." Place, on the other hand, represents "a protest against the unpromising pursuit of space"; place is "space that has historical meanings, where some things have happened that are now remembered and that provide continuity and identity across generations" (4). These terms would serve us well in defining the intent behind all of Berry's work: to reinvent, reimagine, or reestablish a usable place for a people in exile, a people in need, first, perhaps, of being persuaded that what they have come to call freedom and progress are actually exile.

What I want to suggest, then, as my sixth focus is that Berry's understanding of the land throughout has a biblical dimension. The point is not only that the Bible can be read to prescribe and uphold practices of good stewardship of the land—as I have suggested above—but also that Berry's own imagination is sufficiently steeped in the biblical tradition that it affects the way he sees phenomena like the demise of the family farm or the loss of topsoil. To put the household at the center of one's economic thinking is not just a way of suggesting alternatives to industrialism: it is a way of insisting on the possibility of rootedness and the meaningful life that comes with it. To point to the degradation of the topsoil is not just to suggest we'll need to find other ways to feed ourselves, but rather to care about the possibility of a placed existence where love can have a history.

Harold Bloom has argued that the dominant form of religion in America is actually a post-Christian Gnosticism that "masks itself as Protestant Christianity yet has ceased to be Christian."[19] Bloom's work of "religious criticism" is maddeningly overgeneralized in its treatment of American religious life and belief, but his analysis of the experiential dynamics of what he calls the "American Religion" is highly suggestive. "Salvation" within the "American Religion" is intensely individualistic; it "cannot come through the community or the congregation," but rather involves an experience of "total inward solitude" (32) in which God reveals himself either to or in the self. The individual comes to know herself as a "spark or spirit" that is "free both of other selves and of the created world." What is "around" the isolated spirit "has been created by God," but the spirit knows itself to be "no part" of this creation and thus must be "as old as God is." Creation comes to be understood as a falling away from spirit; salvation involves a kind of reuniting of spirit with what it "already is," God or Jesus, who will come to "find the spirit," but "only in [its] total isolation" (32) from others and from the creation. What marks this as Gnostic is that salvation is identified with the "solitary act of knowledge" of a spirit escaping from creation, a spirit, uncreated in itself, that "find[s] its way back to the uncreated, unfallen world" (27). Such a scheme has two obvious consequences: it tends to devalue creation, making its manipulation or abuse more likely, and it tends to mark off spiritual elites—those who possess saving knowledge—from the rest of us.

Wendell Berry's treatment of American Christianity bears considerable resemblance to Bloom's analysis, though Berry is much too restrained to indulge in sweeping generalizations of Bloom's sort about people's faith convictions. Where Berry is not restrained is in his criticism of American Christianity's dualism, individualism, and abandonment of creation. The "most dangerous" dualism that afflicts us is "the dualism of body and soul," Berry writes in "Christianity and the Survival of Creation."[20] There he demonstrates how the creation of Adam in Genesis 2:7 points specifically to the human being as a "single mystery," not as a "creature of two discrete parts temporarily glued together." God does "not make a body and put a soul into it, like a letter into an envelope." He forms "man of dust," breathes "His breath into it," and makes "the dust live." The dust does "not *embody* a soul," it "*bec[o]mes*" one, "soul" here referring "to the whole creature" (CSC, 106). The "dominant religious view," however, has too often treated the human being not as a whole unified mystery, but rather as a two–tiered structure or a pair of competing corporations—with, in either model, the soul elevated, the body devalued (CSC, 107).

The modern church, then, becomes a specialized institution whose particular function is the saving of individual souls. We go to the dentist for our teeth, the plumber for drains, the church for our souls. The church reckons its successes according to the "industrial shibboleths of 'growth,'" counting its numbers while engaging in the "very strange enterprise of 'saving' the individual, isolated, and disembodied soul," itself regarded as a kind of "eternal piece of private property" (CSC, 114). As the unity within ourselves is broken, we find ourselves at odds with the whole surrounding household or membership of creation that sustains us. The soul is left utterly alone, as Berry comments in a passage from "The Body and the Earth" that sounds much like Bloom:

> The soul, in its loneliness, hopes only for "salvation." And yet what is the burden of the Bible if not a sense of the mutuality of influence, rising out of an essential unity, among soul and body and community and world? These are all the works of God, and it is therefore the work of virtue to make or restore harmony among them. . . . The Bible's aim, as I read it, is not the freeing of the spirit from the world. It is the handbook of their interaction.[21]

We work now by analogy, one might say, seeking to restore harmony as we know it will one day be restored in "the resurrection of the body," Christian language that points not toward the escape of soul from fallen creation, but rather to an ultimate reconciliation as God becomes all in all.

Part of Berry's effort to restore harmony by opening up the truth, however painful, is evident in *The Hidden Wound,* where he suggests that the often dualistic emphasis of his own Southern Protestantism is, to some extent, a legacy of slavery. Berry asks us to consider, for instance, the "moral predicament" of the slaveholder "who sat in church with his slaves, thus attesting his belief in the immortality of the souls of people whose bodies he owned and used." The contradiction between his profession and his practice would have proved intolerable if it had been allowed to come fully to consciousness. In order to suppress this contradiction, the master "had to perfect an empty space in his mind, a silence, between heavenly concerns and earthly concerns, between body and spirit." Preachers dependent on the white half of their congregations for livelihood would "have to honor" this "division in the minds of the congregation between earth and heaven, body and soul." Questions of "moral obligation," of "how best to live on the earth, among one's fellow creatures," were separated off from a religion focused on "the question of salvation."[22] When Berry says that there is something "personal" for him in making the case for a more earthly Christianity, as he does in *The Gift of Good Land,* he is working from the desire to heal that "historical wound" left within him by racism in America—that wound he describes so well as one "prepared centuries ago to come alive in me at my birth like a hereditary disease, and to be augmented and deepened by my life" (*HW,* 3).[23] He wants to "know," as "fully and exactly" as possible, "what the wound is," how much he suffers from it, and how "to be cured" (*HW,* 4)—and part of that cure is to recover a Christianity that refuses to compromise with unjustifiable earthly practices.

Berry's insistence on a Christianity that honors the whole human being within a whole creation is, then, part of the legacy left to him by Nick Watkins and Aunt Georgie Ashby, the African Americans whom he remembers in *The Hidden Wound.* Berry writes "about them in order to reexamine and to clarify what" he knows "to be a moral resource, part of the vital and formative legacy of [his] childhood" (*HW,* 61)—a childhood marked by experiences of kindness and affection among Nick, Aunt Georgie, and himself, and thus at odds with the lies about race he has had to learn as an adult. "Sympathy" was "involved" and "essential" to his childhood experiences with Nick and Aunt Georgie, but it was not the "great benefit" of that friendship. That benefit came instead from the "prolonged intense contact with lives and minds radically unlike my own, and radically unlike any other that I might have known as a white child among white adults" (*HW,* 63–64). Telling the stories of Nick and Aunt Georgie, then, as if he could understand or explain them would be an act of intellectual hubris of the worst sort: he can only attempt to imagine their lives in a way that honors them. The search for a membership that would include Nick, Aunt Georgie, and himself perhaps received its first impulse from Berry's childhood memories of their love. That membership would obviously have to be a great deal more capacious than that preached from many American pulpits, and it would have to be grounded in a theology capable of reconciling body and soul, those realities whose division lay at the heart of American racism. Obviously, seeking a cure for the wound of racism was primarily of importance to Berry as a person, but it was also critical for his art. For, as he puts it in *The Hidden Wound,* "the art of a man divided within himself and against his neighbors, no matter how sophisticated its techniques or how beautiful its forms and textures, will never have the communal *power* of the simplest tribal song" (49).

The church has not, however, rejected its comfortable compromise with the destructive economy that supports it, as Berry argues in "God and Country." The emphasis on individual salvation and spirituality does little to challenge economic arrangements or press us to think about ecological practices. "The ecological teaching of the Bible is simply inescapable," and thus it is a failure of Christian and scriptural practice when "church leaders" can be "born again in Christ" without being "discomfort[ed]" in their "faith in the industrial economy's bill of goods."[24] On ecological as well as other matters, Christians too often avoid the "burden" of their allegiance to the Bible or to Christ. Instead of endeavoring to read and keep Jesus's commandments, it has become "fashionable" for people to "declare themselves to be followers of Christ" and then to "assume that whatever they say or do merits the adjective 'Christian.'" Berry wants nothing to do with this kind of cultural Christianity. He compares it to that "accommodation" between Christianity and worldly power that has too often resulted in a "monstrous history":

> War after war has been prosecuted by bloodthirsty Christians, and to
> the profit of greedy Christians, as if Christ had never been born and
> the Gospels never written. I may have missed something, but I know
> of no Christian nation and no Christian leader from whose conduct
> the teachings of Christ could be inferred.[25]

Obviously, Berry offers no comfort to any who would identify America as a Christian nation or seek to ally Christianity with the purposes of American nationalism. It seems almost preposterous to need to say such things, but in today's cultural context—where there is so much ignorance of Christianity on the part of both so-called conservatives and liberals—perhaps it is best to do so. Berry does clearly object to an administration like that of President George W. Bush's "adopt[ing] a sort of official Christianity" and wishing "to be regarded as Christian."[26] But this represents no simplistic America bashing on his part. It reflects instead his conviction that the Christian Gospel must always remain independent of every worldly power in order to serve to bring those powers under judgment. In this sense it assists that "vigilant distrust of any determinative power" that is the requirement of our patriotism (CR, 5).

I confess myself somewhat wary of Berry's title "The Burden of the Gospels," believing, as I do, that human beings are burdened enough without being additionally so by the *evangelion,* the good news. But one must respect Berry's insistence that grace not become cheap. He begins by noting the abundance today of "confident" Christians, ones who claim a full understanding of the Gospels, "appear to know precisely the purposes of God," and assume that their actions are fully in accord with his will. Such Christians are confident even "that God hates people whose faith differs from their own, and they are happy to concur in that hatred" (BG, 49). It's in contrast with this kind of "confidence" that Berry's sense of the Gospels' "burden" must be read. Some of Jesus's teaching is burdensome because it is "so demanding," so contrary to our ordinary way of understanding. One such instruction is "the proposition that love, forgiveness, and peaceableness are the only neighborly relationships that are acceptable to God." This is "difficult for us weak and violent humans" to accept. Equally strange must be the "requirement that we must be perfect, like God," which Berry suggests is perhaps as "outrageous" as the "Buddhist vow to 'save all sentient beings,' and perhaps is meant to measure and instruct us in the same way" (BG, 56). Sometimes a saying seems so hard that we are tempted to say Jesus could not have meant it—like that in Luke 14:26 concerning the need for the disciple to "hate" all those to whom he or she is closest. Dismissing such a teaching is mistaken, Berry believes, suggesting that precisely here we need to "accept our failure to understand" and to recognize "a question to live with and a burden to be borne" (BG, 57).

Berry's taking seriously the "burden" of Christ's teachings has meant an increasing pacifist emphasis in his writings, especially since 9/11. "Christian" war is, for him, an oxymoron, despite his granting that Christianity has, of course, been a "warlike religion" (CR, 16). He categorically rejects any attempt to identify or reconcile policies of "national or imperial militarism" with "anything Christ said or did." The Gospel is "a summons to peace," and it "would require a most agile interpreter to justify hatred and war" in the name of its call to us "to love our enemies, bless those who curse us, do good to those who hate us, and pray for those who despise and persecute us" (CR, 14). This does overlook somewhat the just war tradition, with its roots in Augustine's interpretation of the demands of the love commandment—a tradition that would not, however, justify hatred even in legitimate war. Moreover, some passages of Berry's could be construed to be consistent with a justification of defensive war: those we looked at, for instance, in the last chapter regarding the spontaneous defense that would emerge from true patriots in a time of dire need.[27] Berry recognizes that he is "one of many who have benefited from painful sacrifices made by other people," and he "would not like to be ungrateful." Surely Berry is not ungrateful, and he declares that as "a patriot myself . . . I know that the time may come for any of us when we must make extreme sacrifices for the sake of liberty."[28] Here Berry confronts perhaps the most difficult, nearly impossible, problem for the one who takes Christian teaching seriously: how to accept gratefully the sacrifice that has been made for us, while yet retaining freedom from the compelling demand that it makes on us. Perhaps we need Christ most of all to prevent past sacrifice from compelling us to make similar sacrifice in order that we might not be judged unworthy.[29]

Berry grapples with this problem as honorably as it is possible to do, and in what I see as four distinct ways. First, he insists on the irreconcilability of national purposes and Christian teachings. The monopoly of violence that is a nation cannot be baptized with the word "Christian." Second, he argues that we must begin to think of peace as the norm. The teachings about peace in Christianity and other religious traditions must be placed at the center of our reflection and practice instead of being marginalized "in deference to the great norm of violence and conflict" (CR, 15). We must break from the belief, in short, that power and violence determine every-thing in that world we pride ourselves on calling "real." If the recipients of Christ's teachings are not willing to lead in this, then where shall we turn for hope? Third, we must recognize—as people have, "by fits and starts," since the end of World War II—that peace is now no longer simply a "desir-able condition" but also a "practical necessity" (CR, 15). Given the capacity for destruction of today's weapons, the interconnection of the global econ-omy, the internationalization of the arms trade, it is impossible to speak meaningfully of victory in military conflict. Modern war has brought about a terrifying new reciprocity, making it not only impossible to distinguish "combatants" from "noncombatants" but "impossible to damage your en-emy without damaging yourself" (FW, 23). As Berry puts it in "The Failure of War," "You cannot kill your enemy's women and children without offer-ing your own women and children to the selfsame possibility. We (and, inevitably, others) have prepared ourselves to destroy our enemy by de-stroying the entire world—including, of course, ourselves" (23). In order to sustain such preparations, we must be taught a kind of perfect hatred of the enemy or have formed in us an almost complete denial of what we are about. Thus, a fourth emphasis of Berry's is on the way Christ's teachings might break through this denial, pressing us to recognize that "the only sufficient answer is to give up the animosity and try forgiveness, to try to love our enemies and to talk to them and (if we pray) to pray for them" (CR, 16). If we cannot do any of those things, then we "must begin again by trying to imagine our enemies' children, who, like *our* children, are in mor-tal danger because of enmity that they did not cause" (CR, 16). All of this seems almost impossibly hard, impossibly unrealistic. That it does so is, in part, a measure of Christian failure and a reason why Christianity must not be allowed to remain what it has too often been for Americans: a technique for individual salvation whose language is also available, when needed, for pious consecration of national purposes.

If the official Christianity of the churches has too often focused on Gnostic escape from a devalued world, poets like Blake, Thoreau, Frost, and Yeats have carried the tradition's feeling for the holiness of all created things. "Blake," Berry writes in "Christianity and the Survival of Creation," was "biblically correct" when "he said that 'everything that lives is holy'" (98). Yeats, too, is cited repeatedly by Berry for his insisting that "body" must not be "bruised to pleasure soul."[30] Frost's accent can be heard clearly in Berry's comment on how "truth begins to intrude with its matter-of-fact" when one buys a farm and begins to translate thoughts into acts. Fact is the "sweetest dream that labor knows" for Berry as for Frost—a fact that itself can only be known through bodily labor.[31] We hear Frost again, and Thoreau behind him, in Berry's saying that an authentically local culture "would begin in work and love," an insight he presses in what can only be called a religious direction: "People at work in communities three generations old would know that their bodies renewed, time and again, the movements of other bodies, living and dead, known and loved, remembered and loved, in the same shops, houses, and fields." This "community dance" offers "perhaps the best way we have to describe harmony" (PLC, 79).

Delight in creation is an important way in to the Christian story, though it has been too often obscured by an overemphasis on duty.[32] Something Berry shares deeply with Thoreau is the sense of a free, abounding, and nonhuman joy in creation. After citing Thoreau's comment, made in his Harvard graduating speech, that this "curious world" is more "beautiful than it is useful," Berry speculates that Thoreau "may very well" have "been remembering Revelation 4:11: 'Thou art worthy, O Lord, to receive glory and honour and power: for thou hast created all things, and for thy pleasure they are and were created.'"[33] That the world was created for God's pleasure, not our use, "is formidable doctrine indeed," Berry asserts (EP, 138). At the very least, it would mean that our uses should always take into account his pleasure. That there is truth in the doctrine is something we likely know but of which we need to be reminded, as Berry does by asking, "Where is our comfort but in the free, uninvolved, finally mysterious beauty and grace of this world that we did not make, that has no price? Where is our sanity but there? Where is our pleasure but in working and resting kindly in the presence of this world?" (EP, 140). The sense of beauty for Berry here, as for Thoreau, presses in the direction of an insight of Simone Weil, who said, "The beautiful in nature is a union of the sensible impression and of the sense of necessity. Things must be like that (in the first place), and precisely, they are like that."[34] Wonder is the appropriate response to this union of things as they are and as they must be, a wonder felt and expressed most fully in silence. To "encounter the silence and the darkness of his own absence" is one of the reasons, for Berry, to "leave the regions of our conquest" and "re-enter the woods."[35] This is part of the work of becoming an "apprentice of creation," whose "privilege" is "to come with his imagination into the unimaginable, and with his speech into the unspeakable" (NH, 202). Berry does not refer explicitly to *A Week on the Concord and Merrimack Rivers*, but there is remarkable consonance between his feeling for silence and Thoreau's tribute to "her" at the end of that work: "She is when we hear inwardly, sound when we hear outwardly. Creation has not displaced her, but is her visible framework and foil."[36]

In "A Secular Pilgrimage," the opening piece of the 1972 volume *A Continuous Harmony*, Berry emphasizes the religious—or, as he proposes, "worshipful"—quality of the nature poetry of three of his contemporaries—Denise Levertov, A. R. Ammons, and Gary Snyder.[37] He suggests that the "peculiar aspiration" of much contemporary nature poetry be characterized "by calling it a secular pilgrimage." It is "secular" in that it takes place without any reference to "the institutions of religion" and is "in search of the world." But it is simultaneously a "pilgrimage" because "it is a religious quest." What it seeks is not a "world of inert materiality," but "the created world in which the Creator, the formative and quickening spirit, is still immanent and at work" (SP, 3–4). Perhaps more than any other, this piece of Berry's comes closest to reflecting something like the conclusions about Christianity and ecology often drawn from White's famous essay. Berry argues, for instance, "that perhaps the great disaster of human history is one that happened to or within religion: that is, the conceptual division between the holy and the world, the excerpting of the Creator from the creation" (SP, 4). Berry goes on immediately following to indicate his agreement with a contrast drawn by John Stewart Collis between polytheism's "intimate connection with" and "veneration" for the earth and monotheism's "extracting" of deity "from the earth." According to Collis, monotheism has meant that God goes "completely out of sight," and it becomes "possible to fear God without fearing Nature—nay, to love God (whatever was meant) and to hate his creations" (SP, 4).[38] Berry glosses this by saying, "If God was not in the world, then obviously the world was a thing of inferior importance, or of no importance at all" (SP, 4).

There are certainly ways of responding, from within the Judaic and Christian traditions, to the problems set out here by Collis and Berry. In both traditions, for example, the Creator is, of course, different from the creation, but not "excerpted from" it, as it is precisely God's creating that makes it creation. One could say that creation is our way of naming God's relationship to all that is. Moreover, the Trinitarian God of Christianity certainly does not go "out of sight": he is most decisively visible in the Cross. Nor is it possible for either Jews or Christians to love God and hate his creations. Love of God and love of neighbor are held together throughout those traditions, and it is impossible to love one's neighbor without caring for the creation that is given as the context of our lives together. In one sense, Berry is right that of course the Abrahamic traditions understand the world to be of "inferior importance" to God, but it can never be of "no importance" precisely because it is God's creation.

The point here is not to engage in a theological critique of Berry's thinking, but rather to develop the changes in his understanding of the crucial matter of creation. Berry is no doubt right, as White was, that the Judaic and Christian understanding of the Creator has been a crucial underpinning of the Western objectification of the world in the project of technology. Many of us would say, indeed, thank God that this has been so, although it is long past time we started reckoning the consequences. If White was mistaken, it was in his reading out too much from the opening chapters of Genesis. In short, he placed too much emphasis on the tradition's supposed anthropomorphism without acknowledging its affirmation that "the earth is the Lord's and all that is in it."[39] What White and Berry rightly criticize is not so much Christian orthodoxy, but rather what Charles Taylor has called "providential Deism," an "intermediate stage" in the story Taylor tells us of the rise of an "exclusive humanism" characteristic of modern secularity.[40] Taylor's claim is that the way God's design of the world is understood goes through "a striking anthropocentric shift" around the "turn of the seventeenth/eighteenth centuries" (222). This has been prepared, in part, by the development of a modern notion of moral order, rooted in the natural-law understandings of Grotius and Locke. Organized society comes to be understood as an arrangement for the mutual benefit of its constituent members. Security and prosperity are its "principal goals," much of its life is devoted to economic exchange, and the "ideal social order is one in which our purposes mesh, and each in furthering himself helps the others" (166). The understanding of Providence itself then changes to an "economistic" view in which God's "goals for us shrink to the single end of our encompassing this order of mutual benefit he has designed for us" (221). Whereas previously God had been understood to have "inscrutable" purposes for his creation, but that surely "included our love and worship of him," now his purposes can be discovered. They involve primarily human flourishing, and what we owe him is "essentially the achievement of our own good" (221–22). The sense of grace and mystery fades, and eclipsed, too, is the idea that God seeks a profound transformation in us, taking us beyond human flourishing to a participation in his very life— that "*theiosis*," or "becoming divine," spoken of by the Greek fathers and understood to be "part of human destiny" (224).

I have stayed with this section of Taylor's work a bit for two reasons: first because it explicates so well how Christianity gave rise to a Providential deism and thus to the notions of creation implicit in Berry's critique of monotheism in "A Secular Pilgrimage." But second, it seems worth pointing out how Taylor's and Berry's assessments of our disenchanted condition dovetail in many ways. Taylor provides helpful context, for instance, for Berry's claim that we are now in a condition of "total economy." It becomes possible to see that what Berry senses is not only that we have reduced everything to dollars and cents—though certainly that's important —but that we have become so committed to ordering our lives according to principles of mutually productive exchange that we risk losing a great deal: joy, grace, the free gift of being, the possibility of the sheerly gratuitous, love that knows no calculation. We have set about most efficiently to create a rationalized order for ourselves that closes us off from what we really need. Taylor wants to claim a place for mystery in our secular age, as does Berry, particularly in *Life Is a Miracle*. Berry, too, has moved over time specifically toward language that is suggestive of that concept of *theosis* whose loss Taylor points out in the analysis treated above. In "Christianity and the Survival of Creation," published in 1992, Berry quotes Greek Orthodox theologian Philip Sherrard to the effect that "creation is nothing less than the manifestation of God's hidden Being."[41] For Berry, "this means that we and all other creatures live by a sanctity that is inexpressibly intimate, for to every creature, the gift of life is a portion of the breath and spirit of God" (CSC, 98). Our life is participation in the life of God, whose desire is to draw us as deeply into that life as he can. Similarly, in "The Burden of the Gospels," Berry comments on the Good Samaritan by saying that he breaks "all the customary boundaries, because he has clearly seen in his enemy not only a neighbor, not only a fellow human or a fellow creature, but a fellow sharer in the life of God" (66). Here is a richness of theological affirmation about God's relationship to his creatures and his desire for them that is very different from Berry's earlier treatment of creation in "A Secular Pilgrimage." Perhaps paradoxically, it is the very condition of postmodern secularity so well depicted by Taylor that enables Berry and others to speak with such theological richness. No longer responsible for providing the intellectual and moral background for the order of mutual benefit, the Christian thinker is free to give maximal expression to the tradition's boldest claims.

Berry responds specifically to White's thesis in the 1979 piece "The Gift of Good Land." He begins by declaring two purposes: first, "to attempt a Biblical argument for ecological and agricultural responsibility," and second, "to deal directly at last with [his] own long held belief that Christianity, as usually presented by its organizations, is not *earthly* enough—that a valid spiritual life, in this world, must have a practice and a practicality" (267). He engages White, then, on the much-vexed matter of God's instructing human beings to "subdue" the earth and on the sense of "dominance" involved in Adam's naming of the animals. Berry contends first that "dominance" ought not to be equated with tyranny, that it ought to be understood rather in relation to the charge given Adam and Eve "to dress" and "to keep" the Garden. Nor is there any warrant for reading "subdue" as license to destroy.[42] In any case, "these early verses of Genesis can give us only limited help" since they refer to our prelapsarian condition (GGL, 268). A "more serviceable" story for a fallen people is "the giving of the Promised Land," which provides "the beginning—and, by implication, the end—of the definition of an ecological discipline."[43] Berry does not ignore the fact that Israel's coming into the land involved taking it "by force." The conquest was, like that of the American frontier, a "dark story of human rapaciousness," but there was also something else working in it, "a vein of light" originating "in the idea of the land as a gift—not a free or a deserved gift, but a gift given upon certain rigorous conditions" (GGL, 269–70).

Those "conditions" form the heart of an ecological discipline.[44] Implicit in the idea of gift is a "warning against *hubris*," the "great ecological sin." Deuteronomy 8:17 warns specifically against the folly of saying, "My power and the might of mine hand hath gotten me this wealth." The gift of the land is not permanent; it is not a transfer of possession, but rather more like the offer of "tenancy," a "right of habitation and use" granted to those who are "strangers and sojourners with me" (Lev. 25:23). Berry points out how the required "sabbath for the land" and the "sabbath of sabbaths every fiftieth year," the "year of jubilee," are ways of ritualizing the observance of "limits" on "human control" (GGL, 270–71). These are perpetual ordinances designed to remind Israel that the earth is God's and that their tenancy is a matter of gift. Israel has not merited this gift in advance, but it must "prove worthy of it afterwards" by using the land well. Responsible use involves being "faithful, grateful, and humble." It involves being "neighborly," a responsibility that is to be understood in terms not only of space but also of time. As the land is received in "inheritance" from those who come before, it is to be passed as a living inheritance to those who will come. Thus, "good husbandry" is of paramount importance, and "the inflexible rule is that the source must be preserved" (GGL, 272–73).[45] Implicit, for Berry, particularly in Deuteronomy, is something made "explicit in the New Testament": "an elaborate understanding of charity." This theological virtue is not to be limited to our sense of it as benevolent philanthropic giving. Rather, it represents our whole complex response to the givenness of creation and particularly to the "bond" among all creatures that creation establishes. Berry says of charity that "by its nature," it "cannot be selective," because it everywhere discovers the bond between creatures who exist by virtue of creation. Thus, it "cannot stop until it includes all Creation, for all creatures are parts of a whole upon which each is dependent, and it is a contradiction to love your neighbor and despise the great inheritance on which his life depends" (GGL, 273). Berry contrasts this understanding of charity specifically with White's claim that the Bible opens the world to exploitation for human purposes. Charity cannot—"any more than the Creation itself"—be "answerable to 'man's purposes'" precisely because it only makes sense as the "effort to love all Creation in response to the Creator's love for it" (GGL, 273). That effort must be practical; it requires action, knowledge, skills. "Real charity," Berry insists, "calls for the study of agriculture, soil husbandry, engineering, architecture, mining, manufacturing, transportation, the making of monuments and pictures, songs and stories." The world will "be used either charitably or uncharitably," and, as our biblical task is to use it charitably, we must know what we are doing, a knowledge requiring both skill and the constant "criticism of skills" (GGL, 274).

Berry returns to the biblical case for ecological responsibility in "Christianity and the Survival of Creation." Reading the Bible carefully, Berry notes, is apt to bring home to us several truths generally ignored by the churches. First, that "humans do not own the world or any part of it," for it is "the Lord's"; second, that "God made not only the parts of Creation that we humans understand and approve but all of it"; third, that "God found the world, as He made it, to be good, that He made it for His pleasure, and that He continues to love it"; and fourth, that "the Creation is not in any sense independent of the Creator, the result of a primal creative act long over and done with, but is the continuous, constant participation in the being of God" (CSC, 96–97). It's worth noting how much Berry continues to assume something like the rightness of White's thesis, at least as a description of the practices that have too often resulted from Christian misunderstanding of the scriptures. The burden of the argument is to point Christians and others to a fuller understanding of the biblical tradition, one that would cause them to withdraw unthinking support of the industrial economy and start to raise again real economic questions. If the biblical teaching is that all life is holy, then "the most urgent question" faced by "people who would adhere to the Bible is this: 'What sort of economy would be responsible to the holiness of life?'" (CSC, 99–100).

Berry's essay—as well as much of his work—might be seen as an effort to do what Norman Wirzba has said we are in great need of doing: recovering "the art of being creatures." Critical to this effort is understanding, as Wirzba puts it, that the biblical teaching on creation is not simply an account of "how the world began" but also a "characterization of human identity and vocation within the world." "Creation is not a once-and-for-all completed event," but an ordering of the world by God, who continues to sustain and to care for his creation. In the scriptural tradition, the "whole of creation belongs to God," but God invites us to "participate in the work of creation" in accord with his "life-giving, creating, redeeming intent."[46] Our radical dependence, together with that of all other creatures, is evident for Berry in Elihu's warning to Job that "all flesh shall perish together" if God "gather unto himself his spirit and his breath" (CSC, 97). We are at all times under a kind of biblical accounting, and wanton destruction of nature is not simply "stupid economics" but "the most horrid blasphemy," "flinging God's gifts into His face" (CSC, 98). Part of learning to live as creatures involves having the widest possible sense of economy, which is why Berry has found "The Kingdom of God" "indispensable" in thinking about it.[47] "The Kingdom of God" is our most comprehensive economic

term, for it "does not leave anything out." It points to three related and crucial principles: that we are part of the kingdom whether we know ourselves
to be or "wish to be"; that the kingdom is orderly, all things in it being
joined to everything else; and that we as humans "do not and can never
know either all the creatures that the Kingdom of God contains or the
whole pattern or order by which it contains them" (TE, 55). We are dependent on an order and on sources that will always elude our full comprehension. If we wish to avoid biblical language in speaking of this comprehensive
economy, Berry proposes the term "Great Economy," suggesting, too, that
readers steeped in Asian traditions might think of it in terms of the Tao
(TE, 56). But in Christian terms, he is laying out what it means to live
within a creaturely economy, one in which we understand ourselves as "living souls, God's dust and God's breath, acting our parts among other creatures all made of the same dust and breath as ourselves" (CSC, 110).
Understanding economy in this richly biblical sense will surely lead to different practices than those White attributed to a destructive anthropocen-
trism, whose roots lay in the limited and inadequate—though popular—deist
understanding of creation as a one–time event.

A place to begin discussing the centrality of the body in Berry's theology is
with two contrasting images of the body in motion. The first involves a
picture alluded to by Berry in "Sex, Economy, Freedom, and Community"
and remembered vividly by many of us of a certain age: "a photograph of a
naked small child running terrified down a dirt road in Vietnam, showing
the body's absolute exposure to the indifference of air war, the appropriate
technology of mechanical politics."[48] The picture was, and is, hard to take,
especially for its revelation of one consequence of what we have wrought.
Here is the utterly particular innocent and suffering body of a child exposed to overpowering force conceived by and put to the service of abstractions. A contrasting image is that of what I will call Berry's agrarian
pilgrim, for whom every bodily movement is a kind of resistance to abstraction, an experience of particularity. In "Out of Your Car, Off Your
Horse," Berry comments on the shallow reductiveness of global thinking,
telling his readers that "if you want to *see* where you are, you will have to
get out of your spaceship, out of your car, off your horse, and walk over the
ground. On foot you will find that the earth is still satisfyingly large and full

of beguiling nooks and crannies."[49] To know the earth intimately requires walking over the ground, again and again. Only in this way can one begin to acquire the sympathetic "feeling" for a farm that Berry suggests is essential to "Renewing Husbandry," the title of a piece from *The Way of Ignorance*. Berry remarks there on how "the form of the farm must answer to the farmer's feeling for the place, its creatures, and its work. It is a never-ending effort of fitting together many diverse things."[50] As the farmer comes to sense that he is arriving at a satisfyingly comprehensive fit of the farm's elements, he begins to feel the goodness of his work. Terry Cummins has expressed this feeling nicely in a passage from his *Feed My Sheep*, quoted by Berry:

> Nobody else knows or cares too much about what you do, but if you get a good feeling inside about what you do, then it doesn't matter if nobody else knows. I do think about myself a lot when I'm alone way back on the place bringing in the cows or sitting on a mowing machine all day. But when I start thinking about how our animals and crops and fields and woods and gardens sort of all fit together, then I get that good feeling inside and don't worry much about what will happen to me.[51]

Cummins's comments bear on several theological matters. First, as Berry has said elsewhere, the important work on the farm is mostly done in secret, as Jesus said that prayer and good works should be (Matt. 6:1–18). If there is a liberating dimension to Christian faith, surely it lies, at least in part, in freedom from what Kierkegaard called the ceaseless process of worldly comparison and distinction.[52] Such freedom involves arriving at a stage where one works at something that is between God and oneself, and it really doesn't matter if anybody else knows. One becomes free from envy, from the fear and suspicion that someone else has or is something that one lacks, fear and suspicion too often promoted today as the very drivers of our economic life. There is about Cummins's last remark, too, that particular kind of "unconsciousness" that Berry identifies with health. Health involves "membership," right relatedness to other human beings and to the whole household of what sustains us. Its opposite is dis-ease, a contrary state in which we are "conscious not only of the state of our health but of the division of our bodies and our world into parts."[53] What the good "husband" manages to do is to put his body back into the world, making it again part of a pattern that fits together pleasingly and well. As Berry puts it in "Solving for Pattern," the "good farmer's mind and his body—his management and his labor—work together as intimately as his heart and his lungs." "Farmer and farm are one thing," a "single organism" whose endurance is dependent on "the sufficiency and integrity of a pattern."[54] That pattern is everywhere a matter of the relatedness of embodied beings: soil, plants and animals, farmer, farm family, farm community. Arriving at "proper solutions" to the whole "complex of problems" posed by these realities constitutes "*health*" (SFP, 137).

Berry's theological model for the good husband is the Good Shepherd, who, in Matthew's and Luke's parables, leaves the ninety-nine sheep to go in search of the one who is lost. Berry uses this story in "Two Minds" to contrast the Rational and the Sympathetic Mind. The rationalist would certainly not go in search of the one who is lost, for this inevitably exposes the remaining ninety-nine to danger. He would more likely deem this an acceptable loss, a "trade-off" to be weighed against the safety of others. But the shepherd of the parable is a Sympathetic Mind who "goes without hesitating to hunt for the lost sheep because he has committed himself to the care of the whole hundred, because he understands his work as the fulfillment of his whole trust, because he loves the sheep, and because he knows or imagines what it is to be lost." "To the Rational Mind, all sheep are the same"; each is a unit of production, just like every other. But to the Sympathetic Mind of the shepherd, "each one is different from every other. Each one is an individual whose value is never entirely reducible to market value."[55] We can say that the shepherd's is a relentlessly particularizing intelligence, one that will challenge every abstraction or ideology by asking how it will affect every particular being. Elsewhere Berry has compared the story of Jesus's going in search of the lost sheep to the Buddhist commitment to saving all sentient life. Both affirm the sacred integrity of every particular being in its own right; none is to be treated as a trade-off to be discounted against some other good. It is that kind of particularizing intelligence that stands the best chance of standing against the abstractions that lead to the naked Vietnamese child's running from being napalmed by those who claim to be saving her country.

Adopting the language of Pope John Paul II, Berry asks in *The Way of Ignorance* whether we will have a "culture of life, or a culture of death."[56]

The immediate context of his question seems rather different from those in which John Paul typically used these phrases—or from those in which the American bishops spoke of a consistent ethic of life. Berry is describing the questions posed by the scientists of the Land Institute as they seek ways for Americans to farm not by going to war against nature, but by modeling their work on the patterns inherent in nature. For Wes Jackson and the Land Institute, this means especially finding and developing perennial grains that can be raised in a diverse bioculture analogous to that of the native prairie grasses.[57] Such farming is obviously in stark contrast to the government-subsidized monoculture of annuals, with its disastrous consequences for the health of soil, rural communities, and consumer bodies. It seems entirely appropriate to describe Berry as seeking here, as elsewhere, a consistent ethic of life: he wants us to see how to conceive farming as peace rather than war, harmony rather than conflict, cultivation of diversity rather than imposition of abstract models. As the scientists of the Land Institute know, the questions they pose "will reveal not only the state of the health of the landscape, but also the state of the culture of the people who inhabit and use the landscape." "Is it," Berry asks, "a culture of respect, thrift, and seemly skills, or a culture of indifference and mechanical force?" (AR, 109). The health of the landscape and of the cultures it supports most directly will also inevitably be indicative of the nation's health. We now have an "insupportable health care industry" required, in part, because we insist on treating our bodies with indifference until they become so diseased that they must be addressed through mechanical force (AR, 109). Part of any solution to the "health care" crisis will require a renewed sense of the holiness of the body, understood not as a machine subject to the mind's projects—whether of exploitation and neglect or of obsessive perfection—but rather as the lived and living context for all of our engagements with others and the world. The body is a holy member of the living household of life, one that must, like all other features of that household, be treated with "respect, thrift, and seemly skills."[58]

That skills might be "seemly" suggests an idea of "propriety," a concept Berry finds our "scientific, artistic, and religious disciplines" increasingly unable to address or even to conceive. Inherent to propriety is the idea that "we are being measured" by a "standard that we did not make and cannot destroy."[59] Propriety assumes that the world is not simply ours to design or invent as we choose. Rather, experience has about it a kind of shape or structure that dictates what is appropriate and into which we must learn to fit our conduct. Clearly, Berry is working toward something like an idea of natural law to hold up as a restraint on the totalizing pretensions of technology. The body plays a crucial role in this supplying of a standard; it is a kind of measure or limit, the most basic of the "givens" of our life. The body is a witness to our particularity and the various forms of our dependence. In it we see, in the most basic way, "that we are *not* the authors of ourselves," a perception that is at once religious, biological, and social. "There is no escape," Berry argues, from the conclusion that "the human race is a great coauthorship in which we are collaborating with God and nature in the making of ourselves and one another."[60] The body places us: that we are here and not there is largely a matter of our body. Berry's refusal to write on a computer reflects his unwillingness to divide his thinking from the life of the body in the way technology invites. The writer who works on a computer "flirt[s] with a radical separation of mind and body, the elimination of the work of the body from the work of the mind." He works in a ghostly realm that is nowhere in particular, his ideas lacking the traces and "marks of skill, care and love" that persist through the "hesitations, flaws, and mistakes" of writing that is "of the body."[61]

As the body places and particularizes us, so too it provides an important measure of the appropriate scale of our enterprises. "Scale" is notoriously difficult to define with precision. Perhaps the concept is of greatest value, in fact, when invoked, as Berry often does, to characterize an overreaching or violation: when, for example, an enterprise has gone so far beyond human scale as to seem "gigantic" or "monstrous." While themselves imprecise, these words usefully remind us of the all-too-human ability to construct systems of such size and complexity that we can no longer manage them. We are perfectly capable of building our own nightmares and prisons. Fortunately, the agrarian serves as a permanent check on our Promethean tendencies, for his is the continual experience of limit and appropriate human scale, whose ultimate term is the body. Berry develops this point in "The Agrarian Standard" by way of explaining why Jefferson thought the widespread ownership of land to be so critical to the preservation of democratic liberties.

> Everything that happens on an agrarian farm is determined or conditioned by the understanding that there is only so much land, so much water in the cistern, so much hay in the barn, so much corn in the

crib, so much firewood in the shed, so much feed in the cellar or freezer, so much strength in the back and arms—and no more.[62]

From "this understanding" come "thrift, family coherence, neighborliness, local economies," and a "sense of abundance" based on the "experienced possibility" of "renewal within limits." This is "exactly opposite" to the reigning "industrial idea" of abundance based on extracting all the "good possibilities" from a place, a people, an energy source, even a technology— and then waiting and hoping for the next one to be discovered and depleted in turn (AS, 149).

"There is an uncanny *resemblance,*" Berry asserts in "The Body and the Earth," between "our behavior toward each other and our behavior toward the earth" (124). This insight can help us to understand one feature of Berry's theology of the body that puts him at odds with at least some of his readers: his criticism of abortion. Berry has allowed that abortion "might be defensible as a tragic choice acceptable in the most straitened circumstances," but he is otherwise opposed to the practice.[63] He opposes abortion, as he says in "The Failure of War," for very plain reasons. Abortion kills a form of human life. The distinction between the supposedly autonomous baby and the dependent prebirth fetus makes little sense, as "no living creature is 'viable' independently of an enveloping life-support system." "It is wrong" to treat an innocent "living human being" as an "enemy." Considering abortion within a consistent ethic of life, Berry suggests the analogy between it and war: "If we are worried about the effects of treating fellow humans as enemies or enemies of society eligible to be killed, how do we justify treating an innocent fellow human as an enemy-in-the-womb?" None of this means that Berry opposes the right "to control one's own body," only that the right does not carry with it the freedom to dispose of other bodies as one wishes (FW, 30). That we can so easily regard the fetus as a disposable product suggests the way sexuality has become an isolated feature of our lives, one in which we no longer feel called to exercise responsibility. No longer regarded as integral to the whole person, sexuality becomes simply another industrialized activity, subject to the same measures of evaluation: quantity, efficiency, maximization of result, consumer satisfaction. To the degree that the body is understood as a machine, the goal becomes to get as much out of it as possible before it breaks down. The biological consequences of sex are to be brought under technological control as fully as possible. When those techniques fail, the consequences are eliminated.

In "The Body and the Earth," Berry declares himself "fully aware of the problem of overpopulation" and supportive of the need for contraception, but he also insists "that any means of birth control is a serious matter, both culturally and biologically" (134). "Subject[ing] fertility to moral will" has been "one of the fundamental interests of human culture," but with the advent of artificial contraception, human fertility becomes subject "to a new kind of will: the technological will, which may not *necessarily* oppose the moral will, but which has not only tended to do so, but has tended to replace it" (BE, 135). Technology has come to substitute for responsibility, eliminating the need for responsibility in one whole area of life. Here Berry closely approaches the concerns about artificial contraception that lie at the heart of the papal encyclical *Humanae Vitae,* at least as John Paul II interpreted it. As Martin Rhonheimer has argued, John Paul's insistence that every marital act remain open to conception derives not from a simplistic biologism, but from a concern to maintain marital responsibility.[64] This is why John Paul insists on such a strong distinction between natural methods of controlling fertility and artificial contraception. The first does not break the connection between the "unitive" and the "procreative" meanings of sexuality. Sexuality remains a matter to be subjected to moral will, responsibility, and the virtues. Artificial contraception, on the other hand, eliminates the need for responsibility and the virtues, substituting technological control, breaking apart "unitive" and "procreative" meanings, and encouraging the falsely subjectivist and Gnostic understandings of personhood that John Paul fears. What is at stake is obviously of the greatest importance to John Paul, for he understands marital love as a dynamic process that can lead people into a "manifold service of life."[65] Establishing sexuality's "autonomy," as Berry puts it, is likely only to lead to its becoming "frivolous" or "destructive, even of itself"—a subject for popular romance or capitalist exploitation, rather than the means to lead people out of isolation (BE, 117).[66] Clearly, Berry and the pope's positions are not the same, for they differ on the matter of artificial contraception. They are very close, however, in their sense of the body as our basic givenness to and in the world and in their conclusions about the consequences of our regarding the body as a technological project. For both, alienation from the body is profoundly implicated in our alienation from one another and from the household of life that sustains us.

A term closely connected to "body" for Berry is "mystery," a connection perhaps best approached by looking at the concluding pages of *Life Is a Miracle*. After "speaking of the reductionism of modern science," as he has throughout that book, Berry reminds us "that the primary reductionism" lies in the false "assumption that human experience or human meaning can be adequately represented" in language" (*LM*, 151). The example he gives "to show" what he means is of his four-year-old grandson "following his father" and grandfather "over some of the same countryside" that Berry had followed his "father and grandfather over." In this "familiar spectacle," Berry remarks, we see "part of a long procession, five generations of which I have seen, issuing out of generations lost to memory." The "meaning" of this "sort of family procession across a landscape" can be "known but not told," for it is "too specific to a particular small place and its history." Nor will any one person ever "know" it, for what each knows is specific to his or her place in the procession. Berry knows what he does in relation to those uniquely embodied particular persons who were his grandfather and father and are his children and grandchildren. Berry recognizes that, at present, he is perhaps the one best positioned to know the meaning and "cultural significance" of his family's procession because he is "in the middle now" between his grandfather and father. But he also knows that he "cannot tell it to anyone living," because no one else is in his place in the procession (and can never be, precisely because it is *his* place and not some other's). If, in another thirty years, his son "has the good pleasure of seeing his own child and grandchild in that procession, then he will know something like what" Berry knows now. That knowledge, however, will be personal to his son; it will resemble what his father knows now, but it will not be the same. "This living procession through time in a place *is*," Berry concludes, "the record by which such knowledge survives and is conveyed" (*LM*, 151–53).

Berry's conclusion has several important implications. First, it points to another aspect of the tragedy of "modern displacement." Uprooting causes the loss of personal knowledge that can only be gained through our understanding ourselves within a place in the procession and in relation to a specific place. Second, it suggests a powerful motive for narration, one akin perhaps to that which moved the biblical writers. If there is a kind of knowledge conveyed only by the "living procession through time in a place" (*LM*, 153), then it becomes important to narrate that procession. The narration will carry with it a kind of specific knowledge not obtainable otherwise. Our access as readers to that knowledge will never be perfect, for the narration will remind us always that what the characters know—and what we know—is relative to their and our places in the procession. Our reading will be at once a continual experience of difference together with the continual search for a way of mediating between us and the characters, a search that can lead to the enlargement of charity on our parts. Part of the purpose of narration will also be genealogy: the remembering of the names. The names are crucial because they point to particular persons, their particular places in the procession, their relations to particular places—and thus to the kinds of knowledge that may have been personal to them and thus are only remotely available, at best, to us, and then only if we approach with fear, trembling, and loving humility. Our interpretations of narratives are, we will recognize, much-belated reflections on experiences told and understood from personal horizons incommensurable with our own. This is why Berry objects strenuously in *Life Is a Miracle* to Edward O. Wilson's conflation of works of art with their critical interpretations. In his search for a "common groundwork of explanation," rooted in science and capable of unifying all the academic disciplines, Wilson tends to diminish the distinction between the work of art and critical interpretations, ones that can then "be aligned with the laws of biology and ultimately with the laws of physics" (*LM*, 112). On this view, to understand *King Lear* would be to give materialist analyses—in presumably as quantitative language as possible—of all the factors or causes that went into its production. For Berry, on the other hand, no number of explanations can ever explain *King Lear*. Only explanations are explainable, not *King Lear*, which, with the "individuating power" of great art, resists all reductions (*LM*, 113). This is not to say that criticism is impossible or useless. It is to insist that "a work of criticism is not equivalent to a work of art and cannot replace it" (*LM*, 118). The title of Berry's work derives from a line of Edgar's to his father Gloucester: "Thy life's a miracle. Speak yet again."[67] The line applies equally well to the play itself, which speaks again and again in ever fresh ways from that ultimately unfathomable depth we call mystery.

"We are up against mystery," Berry writes in "Letter to Wes Jackson," as he ponders whether "randomness," as used by scientists, points to a "verifiable condition or a limit of perception."[68] Berry suggests it should be understood as a limit, remembering that Jackson has said to him in conversation that "what is perceived as random within a given limit may be seen as part of a pattern within a wider limit" (LWJ, 4). We find ourselves within patterns that we can discern and yet also within patterns that remain mysterious to us. Thus, "mystery" is both a practical and a necessary term, one that keeps us humble and respectful of patterns that we do not understand and may disrupt. To declare what is beyond our ken "random" is, on the other hand, a way "to plant the flag by which to colonize and exploit the known." Calling a phenomenon "random" is, in a sense, to say that we need not concern ourselves with it. If we know ourselves to be "up against mystery," we "dare act only on the most modest assumptions" and thus avoid the "evil or hubris" about which both Greek and Hebrew traditions warn (LWJ, 4–5).

"An exercise in a sort of academic hubris" is what Berry calls Wilson's *Consilience,* treated at length in *Life Is a Miracle* (27).[69] By "consilience" Wilson means the process of unifying the academic disciplines by finding empirical, materialist explanations for all phenomena. Advocating an extreme version of the Enlightenment project—one with its own religious overtones—Wilson confidently looks forward to the day when science will be able to supply the answers to all questions. Mystery is for him, then, "attributable entirely to human ignorance": the unknown is simply the "to-be-known" (*LM,* 27). This strategy "appropriates mystery as future knowledge," scheduling it for solution even if the precise timing of explanation is left unclear. The mystery scheduled for solution ceases to be mystery, becoming merely a "problem," and a "tyrannic" reduction has been achieved—without, one might observe, the scientist having to produce anything more than the most abstract of theories, confidently asserted. For Berry, this extreme confidence in materialist explanation represents a "sort of moral blindness" rooted ultimately in the will (*LM,* 36). He points out repeated expressions of Wilson's that indicate a "fiercely proprietary mind" (*LM,* 31). The progress of empirical science is presented, for example, not only as the means toward our achieving some understanding and control over physical processes but as a Promethean liberation of human beings from the gods: "We can be proud as a species because, having discovered that we are alone, we owe the gods very little." Similarly, Wilson speaks of science's "proprietary sense of the future" and likens its grantors to "royal geographic commissions of past centuries," aware "that history can be made by a single sighting of coastland, where inland lies virgin land and the future lineaments of empire."[70] As noted earlier, Berry finds this language and the implicit logic of Wilson's position "almost inescapably totalitarian," for if, he asks, one were in possession of a "social theory" that was "general, consilient, and predictive" (*LM*, 31), would not one be obliged to impose it, by force if necessary? Moreover, is not the supposition itself—that there is a total, unifying knowledge waiting to be achieved—equally as dangerous as the "consilient" knowledge would be (were it possible)?

One clear danger of the supposition lies in its inconsistency with the humility required of us as we engage in enterprises that affect the natural world. Berry notes that Wilson shares his concern for conservation, but he does so with puzzlement, precisely because he considers Wilson's excessive confidence in human knowledge to be among the most dangerous threats to our natural households. A second danger lies in the way a confident scientific materialism will simply drive out every kind of question it cannot answer. Berry parodies Wilson's approach by asking, "*Why do the innocent suffer?*" and proposing a Wilsonian answer: "*We don't know yet*" (*LM*, 37). But I suspect that the real import of the search for consilience is to make the question irrelevant, even unthinkable, perhaps by so transforming the world through scientific management that neither innocence nor suffering registers any longer in the minds of the properly educated. (If something like the conditions we once designated "innocence" or "suffering" remains still observable, it can perhaps be considered "random" noise.) Surely, no one educated in the consilient university will ask the "How come?" question to the radical degree Herbert McCabe speaks of as lying at the basis of our engaging in that particular form of "research" devoted to proving the "existence of God."[71] McCabe thinks it quite legitimate to ask the "deepest question" about any particular thing, the one that is simultaneously a "question about everything" (3). Thus, if we ask about our dog, "How come Fido?," we will find that this can be asked at a series of levels, the ultimate one being, "How come Fido exists *instead of nothing*[?]" (5). McCabe considers it "a part of human flourishing" (3) to be open to this question, which is posed to us by existence.

McCabe fears, as I believe Berry does, a kind of society that we can "quite easily" imagine: a hard or soft totalitarian one "extremely keen on improving [its] technology and answering detailed questions within the

accepted framework of science, but extremely hostile" to radical question-
ing about "what everybody has come to take for granted" (2). Such a society
might paradoxically be no more open to "fundamental thinking in science"
(3) than it would be to theological research, for these, in McCabe's view, are
analogous in their asking radical questions. What is more likely, after all, to
direct inquiry only into well-established institutional ways of thinking—
and away from anything eccentric—than the assumption that we are inexo-
rably on the way to the consilience of all knowledge? "The asking of radical
questions is discouraged," McCabe points out—acknowledging the rele-
vance of his observation to the church's confrontation with Galileo—"by
any society that believes in itself, believes it has found the answers, believes
that only its authorised questions are legitimate" (3). "Mystery" may yet
prove "necessary," as Berry puts it, to save science as well as other kinds of
knowledge from the drive for consilience (LWJ, 5).

What remains is to consider the biblical quality of Berry's thinking—that
is, how the Bible provides him the language to see and describe what is
going on. His critique of Wilson offers as good a place to begin as any, particularly if we consider Berry's claim that possession of a "general, consilient, and predictive" knowledge would inevitably have totalitarian
implications (*LM,* 31). I suspect this will not seem obvious to all readers,
many of whom probably hope for disciplinary knowledges that could be
described in such terms. But it is true for Berry because he sees in the aspiration something like the drive to exclude God, to fashion a human reality
that would be completely manageable, predictable, and secure. The aspiration to total knowledge is akin to that which moves the making of images,
forbidden by the Torah, particularly if we understand images to be, in
Brueggemann's words, "controllable representations of our best loyalties
and visions."[72] Today we are told both that "image is everything" and that
"history is dead," perhaps not surprisingly if we understand the fascination
with images to be a way of "removing our land from history," of "leveling
memories and hopes into the deception that it is all present and given now"
(58). A world made timeless through the image hides a secret despair, for
it is one into which "no newness can come" (59), and something like despair may, in Berry's view, be what underlies the drive for a consilient
knowledge. Berry's critique of Wilson is only one of many places where he

resists totalizing forms of power. He warns we have entered a condition of "total economy," fears the dependence of our helpless "total consumerism," and laments that we seem to know no remedy for social disintegration except "the forcible integration of centralization—economic, political, military, and educational" (*HW*, 131). "Our aim, it would appear," he writes in *The Hidden Wound*, "is to 'integrate' ourselves into a limitless military-industrial city in which we all will be lost, and so may do as we please in the freedom either to run wild until we are caught or killed, or to do 'all the things that other people do'" (131). Here Berry very specifically reads events in our day in terms of Samuel's prophetic warning to Israel against centralization of power in the monarchy, one overridden of course by the people's "determ[ination] to have a king over us, so that we also may be like other nations, and that our king may govern us and go out before us and fight our battles."[73]

A biblical reading of our times is evident, too, in Berry's powerful early piece "The Loss of the Future" from *The Long-Legged House*. "We are a remnant people in a remnant country," Berry begins this version of the American jeremiad, one that has "used up the possibilities inherent in the youth of our nation"; carried out its destructions "on the assumption that the earth is inexhaustible, and that we, the predestined children of abundance, are infallible"; presumed itself unfallen though living in a fallen world. "Only a nation that is conscious of its own guilt can change and renew itself," Berry charges, proceeding then in a particularly biblical way to argue that our confusion lies in our own strength, our substitution of power for vision.[74] "It is deeply disturbing, and yet I think it is true, that as a nation we no longer have a future that we can imagine and desire" (LF, 46), Berry says, counting on the well-known language of Proverbs 29:18 to fill out his warning, "Where there is no vision, the people perish" (KJV). His description of what this means for our politics seems even more appropriate today than it did in the 1960s:

> We have lost the hopeful and disciplining sense that we are preparing
> a place to live in, and for our children to live in. Instead of an articu-
> late vision of a decent world, we have the bureaucracy and the rheto-
> ric of the Great Society, an attempt through organization and wealth
> to delay or avoid the obligation of new insight, a change of ways, a
> change of heart. (LF, 46)

Paradoxically, in Berry's analysis, what has caused us to lose vision is an increase in power. The danger of power lies in its compelling fascination, its ability to drive out every alternative way of approaching the problems we face, its shaping the way we see everything—so that it determines even what becomes a problem for our vaunted pragmatism to address. "Power has darkened us," Berry remarks, referring specifically, though not exclusively, to the war in Vietnam, where our presence can perhaps best be accounted for by the simple fact "that we are strong enough to be there." For some, this fact is not simply explanation but "justification." Empire, like other powers, must be exercised, according to the "rule" that "if we have great power we must use it" (LF, 47).

Berry's seeing the great danger in our accumulation of power derives, in part, from his being an exile. In "Does Community Have a Value?" Berry suggests that "the people of rural America" have been struggling now for many years "with the realization that we are living in a colony."[75] Domestic colonialism has systematically transferred wealth from those in rural America who have produced it to those in other places who have owned either the land or the right to profit from it. He has witnessed the loss of family farms for decades, understanding that loss not only as an agricultural or economic matter but as a "political and cultural" one as well. The question of who owns the usable property, the real wealth, of a country is a "version of the question of who will own the country," and with it, the people.[76] The "enlargement of industrial technology" has required "the movement of knowledge and responsibility away from home," causing the "disintegration of homes" and the "subjugation of homelands."[77] Instead of cooperating locally to "fulfill local needs from local sources," the displaced are increasingly drawn up into larger and larger economic structures in which they "deal with each other" competitively and "across the rift that divides producer and consumer" (SBW, 58). These developments have only been exacerbated by the increasingly globalized quality of the information economy. The elites best positioned to profit from such an economy envision completely linked networks of exchange in which nobody will be able to produce what he or she needs. What is lost in this process of uprooting is not only the "nature" and "character" of the places people leave or the "landmarks by which they might return." Culture also becomes increasingly difficult to preserve, for detached from place, it "is driven into the mind," where it is "hard to keep" and "harder to hand down." What "survives is attenuated" because it no longer has any practical reason to be. "That is why the Jews, in Babylon"—after their deportation into exile— "wept when they remembered Zion." "How shall we sing the Lord's song in a strange land?" Berry quotes from Psalm 137, suggesting that the psalmist's question reflects the knowledge that a culture cannot be long remembered or preserved apart from place (SBW, 58).

We can read these passages as offering insight into Berry's whole task as a writer, which has been to create the memory of a culture, of a people really, in the mind—perhaps particularly in the fiction but also in the other genres. It is the memory of a people now largely in exile, one whose exile resembles Israel's in its including a promise of land both as memory and as future possibility. Berry knows that a remnant must be stirred in order that the promise not be lost. The task is not simply elegy or nostalgia; an image in the mind will not long preserve a people. The task is to make another order of possibilities visible again and to move people to believe and take up the promise. The stakes are large and, to a great extent, known through what has been lost.

One of Berry's most gripping depictions of lost possibilities is "The Landscaping of Hell: Strip-Mine Morality in East Kentucky," from *The Long-Legged House*. The most graphic loss he treats is, of course, to the land itself, destroyed forever, beyond the "possibility of recovery," by a "few men in a short time."[78] But the destruction by the mining companies— made possible by the "broad form" deed and abetted by government greed, stupidity, and indifference—represents not only a "violence to the earth" but also a "violence to justice" (LH, 21). The rights to destroy property asserted by the companies left those on the land completely without that most fundamental right to security in their homes. "When this right is no longer defended by any power greater than himself," Berry asserts, a person's "days begin to come to him by accident, in default of whatever caprice of power may next require his life" (LH, 21). Here we can see the heart of Berry's resistance to our current condition of "total economy," in which the capricious movements of global capitalism leave us all increasingly subject to uprooting and aware that whatever days come to us are merely accidents of fortune. Berry's agrarianism is, in short, an insistence that economic life must serve the realization of authentic personal existence. Ownership of land makes possible an extended self-giving by the farmer through which he realizes possibilities in himself and in that place that can never come to be otherwise. Berry puts this matter beautifully as he describes a mountain house and garden in back of a coal camp in Hardburly, Kentucky:

> One can see, even from the height of the mine bench, that a man has taken a proud stand there, has put into the place the long and dear investment of his attention and love and work and hope; that because of the expenditure of himself there he has come to be in that place what he would not have come to be in any other place on earth. (LH, 16)

To treat land merely as a commodity is to discount the irreducibly particular way in which this man's life can come to its fullness in this place on earth. We can console ourselves perhaps with an account of the "creative destruction" of economic life—by which the farmer is supposedly liberated by his displacement into other possibilities he would not have known. But we should ask, in all cases, whether those possibilities allow for "attention and love and work and hope" in the ways those are possible for the agrarian. It seems apparent that a great deal of what we call "our work" today allows for little, if any, really "dear" self-giving.

D. N. Premnath has pointed out the way commoditization of the land was viewed by the eighth-century prophets in Israel as a violation of the Torah.[79] A key text is Isaiah 5:8–10: "Ah, you who join house to house, who add field to field, until there is room for no one but you, and you are left to live alone in the midst of the land! / The Lord of hosts has sworn in my hearing: / Surely many houses shall be desolate, large and beautiful houses, without inhabitant. / For ten acres of vineyard shall yield but one bath, and a homer of seed shall yield a mere ephah" (NRSV). Berry has given us his version of the landowner to whom Isaiah refers in the progressive farmer Meikelberger whom Andy visits in *Remembering*. A man of "exceptional intelligence, energy, and courage," Meikelberger is "the fulfillment of the dreams of his more progressive professors." He farms two thousand acres of "rich, broad land south of Columbus," Ohio, which he has "acquired by patiently buying out his neighbors." The farm is a complete monoculture in corn, worked "by a herd of machines" and managed from an office "like a bank president's" at the back of Meikelberger's "expensively and tastefully furnished" but "deserted" house.[80] Even Meikelberger's body seems to rebel against his joining of field to field, for he has an ulcer. His wife works in town, they are busy incessantly, they eat out mostly in restaurants, they will never escape debt. They are desolate, but without knowing it. As Isaiah sees, they live the result of their own desires, now alone because they have sought to eliminate neighbors. No doubt their acres in corn are productive, but this, too, is a kind of illusion, for it is based on a borrowing from the future—on the debt they will never pay off and the fertility of the land they use up without replenishing for those to come.

Berry's agrarianism turns on a perception like that Brueggemann sees at the heart of Israel's tradition: that its "involvement" is "always *with land* and *with Yahweh*." Neither Torah nor land is to be minimized or neglected; holding them together is "the central problem for Israel."[81] Moreover, since every relationship to the land is also one to God, it is simultaneously one to the neighbor. That fact provides the energizing dialectic of Berry's work, which devotes itself relentlessly to thinking out the connections between our environmental practices and our social, economic, and political ones. In his search for an alternative to many current arrangements, two biblical themes have served him extremely well: the idea of the land as gift and the practice of the Sabbath. As we have seen, land as gift offers protection against the "great ecological sin" of hubris (GGL, 270). It means we must give the greatest care to sustainable use and develop more honest means of generational accounting, for as gift the land is not meant for one generation alone but for all who follow. Land as gift suggests the absurdity of anything like a policy in which food could be seen as a weapon to be used by one people against another. Understanding the land as a gift might lead to our becoming "authentically settled" in America in a way never yet achieved, for our deeply "unsettled" condition springs from the "boomer" mentality that sees every place only as a resource to be exploited on the way to somewhere else.[82] If land is gift, it is so as a gift of love from the Creator and thus calls for loving response, that charity that Berry calls both a "theological" and a "practical" virtue. To accept and love the land as a gift to be treasured, nurtured, and passed on undiminished would be a way into the "loving economy" for which Berry has called (DC, 189). Foregrounding the idea of land as gift is a way to resist the pressure of the "total economy," to insist that economy cannot be allowed to become a purely autonomous dimension of life. Land as gift refuses the separation of economy from love; it puts love at the beginning and economy within love. Decisions about economy must be answerable ultimately to love. This means the test of economies must always lie in the way they promote the authentic development of the human person, which is not to be equated simply with the accumulation of the goods provided by technology. To regard the human person as an economic subject alone is to engage in a form of coercion, one contrary not only to land as gift but also to the keeping of Sabbath.

One could argue that Sabbath-keeping is the most fundamental of the practices required by a "loving economy," for it involves the systematic, disciplined reminder that we are to "honor" and keep holy the sources of our life. "Looking at their fallowed fields," Berry says of ancient Israel, "the people are to be reminded that the land is theirs only by gift; it exists in its own right, and does not begin or end with any human purpose" (GGL, 271). Perhaps the simple fact that something "exists in its own right," independent of human purpose, is what we most need to be reminded of in the age of near total technology. We are "accustomed to managing things," as Brueggemann says in relation to the provisions for remission of debt in Deuteronomy 15:1–11, and "as we manage things we would manage people." "We manage them by taxation and interest rates, by debts and mortgages" until finally "every one is either owner of others or part of the owned." Moreover, because we are so devoted to forgetting our history, "we think that is the way it has always been and is supposed to be." Sabbath in Israel, however, affirms "that people, like land, cannot be finally owned or managed," for they are encircled by "lines of dignity and respect and freedom" that "must be honored" by a people "who will have the land as a covenanted place."[83] Sabbath-keeping protects us from our own frantic attempts to manage every feature of our lives, to secure ourselves against every eventuality, to persuade ourselves that if we only work hard enough, we will never die. The sanity of Sabbath-keeping lies in its forcing us to acknowledge, by rule, what will take place, by rule, despite our best attempts to prevent it: change we do not desire. Thinking of the deaths of friends in a costly year, 1998, Berry begins "Sabbath VI":

> By expenditure of hope,
> Intelligence, and work,
> You think you have it fixed.
> It is unfixed by rule.
> Within the darkness, all
> Is being changed, and you
> Also will be changed.[84]

By rule of rest and sanity, we practice every seventh day the unfixing of what we try so hard to fix; we anticipate the change we know will come to all we hope to ensure against change. Sabbath-keeping disciplines us to the hard knowledge that we are creatures and not the creators of our world. It is thus a vital part of that "hard history" by which we learn that being changed by love is somehow greater than anything we could aspire to be or do on our own.

At this point I want to return to that good question of my student's that frames this chapter: how much is Berry's work dependent on Christianity? The question is so good because it suggests the student's feeling for the way Christianity's own relationship to postmodern culture is both changing and being perceived differently. In short, I offer no definite answer, only a little more complex story. We have seen clearly what Berry wants to distance himself from in various versions of what now is called Christianity. He wants no part of an official Christianity used to underwrite the purposes of American, or any other, nationalism; he criticizes heavily the tendency of some Christians to declare whatever they believe "Christian" simply because they believe it; and he insists that Christianity is not a special knowledge or technique designed primarily for the saving of individual souls. These understandings not only distort Christianity but too radically limit its claims. On Berry's reading, the Bible claims that all of creation is holy precisely *as* the creation of God. A number of conclusions flow inescapably from this: that the creation is not simply to be exploited for human purposes; that making food an element of foreign policy coercion is not only absurd but blasphemous; that the claims of neighbors, in both space and time, must always be foremost in economic decision making; that a foreign policy worthy of support by Christians must take into account the complex demands of charity. What's wrong specifically with the focus on individual salvation is that it is too narrow and that it encourages a picture of the human being as a two-tiered hierarchy of body and soul. What God intends for human beings is nothing less than to draw them up into the Trinitarian love, a love that moves and sustains all of creation and will redeem it at last.

That Berry feels free to use this maximal Christian language is perhaps one of the salutary effects of the cultural dispossession of Christianity. As Christian thinkers find themselves no longer responsible for upholding the current social order, they become free to articulate the tradition's boldest claims. Cultural dispossession may underlie, too, the increasing Christian willingness to insist on ecological discipline. Perhaps this is one way to read the growing turn of American evangelicals toward a greener politics. Renewed emphasis on the earth as God's good gift offers a way to resist the ever more totalizing claims of technology, economy, and government. What's most deeply at stake, perhaps, is maintaining a sense of the "given," both as that word points toward life's being a gift—and we gifts to one another—and as it suggests there is a structure in experience to be discovered and not simply made. Whether any sense of the "given" can endure apart from a religious tradition is something we are now in the process of discerning in this "secular age." I suspect that it cannot.

Berry makes rich use of the language of gift, in part because he writes for a people in exile—former and current rural Americans. No one is so aware of promise given as those in danger of coming to believe the promise lost. If Berry writes as an exile, however, he writes also as an inheritor, as one who believes the promise of good land will be made good at last. Coming into that promise is a "long job," one "too late to quit," to paraphrase a title of one of Berry's essays.[85] Keeping at it requires constantly looking to the "given" for reasons to go on trusting in the promise that moves one in the first place. The alternative, for Berry, is "death," that "illusion" of ours deriving from "our wish to belong only / to ourselves," which is also "our freedom / to kill one another."[86] For Berry, our most important freedom lies not in what we do or make, but in what we are given, for what we most need to be free of is ourselves. Learning this is the lifelong work of love, the everyday practice of resurrection in making the self a gift. Whether self-overcoming in self-giving is a peculiarly Christian practice is something I do not know. I prefer to say that wherever such self-overcoming is practiced, there something very like Christianity is being practiced.

Chapter 4

Port William's "Hard History of Love"

The Short Stories

In the closing story of *That Distant Land*, Wendell Berry's collected short fiction, fifty-four-year-old Danny Branch accompanies eighty-six-year-old Wheeler Catlett on a day trip to Louisville, where Wheeler is selling some of his calves. As Danny listens to the always voluble Wheeler, who seems to be "swaying on the edge of the world as if he might at any moment disappear," he sees the older man "not just with his own eyes but with the eyes of several of his elders to whom Wheeler had been a friend." "There could be nothing single-sighted in Danny's regard for Wheeler," Berry remarks, for "he felt for him an affection made manifold by its passage through the company of the dead."[1] The story is called "The Inheritors (1986)," and part of what Danny and Wheeler inherit is each other. But what they also inherit is this blend of knowledge and affection—something closely akin to charity, in its deepest sense—that can be achieved only through life in a membership that knows its history. Or perhaps it is more accurate to say that it can be achieved only by the membership itself living in time and then inherited by those fortunate enough to do so. Probably the most accurate thing to say is that anyone even approaching the virtue of charity will understand it always as primarily an inheritance and not an achievement.

What Danny and Wheeler inherit is the achievement of the Port William membership as it lives "the town's hard history of love."[2] The chronological delimitation of that history, as Berry relates it in the short fiction, is from 1888 through 1986, but the history has roots in even earlier time and also points beyond its own ending. Port William responds, of course, to the great national and worldwide events and developments of that period: two world wars, the Depression, the rise of technology and concomitant centralization of economies, the demise of the family farm. But much of Port William's history—particularly as Berry tells it in the short stories—has less to do with those developments than it does with the personal and moral histories of the membership. Those histories involve the struggles of mortal human beings learning to live as creatures in the mystery of time—time that comes to them as gift and to which they have no claim. It is the history of creatures who can be badly hurt, not least in their ability to believe that what they are meant for is the good. Sometimes, as in "Pray Without Ceasing (1912)," the response to that hurt—perhaps to the weight of time itself—is anger, even murderous anger, the ultimate oversimplifier that offers a kind of pure elated escape from the uncertainties of timeful existence. Sometimes, on the other hand, the response is a wonderful "consent" to being, as in the stories of Tol Proudfoot and Miss Minnie Quinch, who becomes his wife. Always a community needs those like Wheeler Catlett, who devotes himself, primarily through the law, to ensuring the order and continuity of the good, abundant life he sees possible for people and animals in Port William and its farms. Law is critical to the life of a people, but it is not enough. It must be supplemented by a sense of equity, by friendship, by a fidelity of members one to another, by love. A community lives by its members keeping faith with one another, and that keeping faith requires a complex responsiveness to what is going on in one's own and others' histories. The only way to know those histories is by remembering them and telling them, as Mat Feltner does first and then passes the task to his grandson Andy Catlett. Andy's father, Wheeler, is described as a "keeper of the names," and Andy, too, is one.[3] The particular form of his fidelity to Port William involves remembering and narrating the stories that have come to him, told and retold as they have made their passage through the living and the dead. Those stories carry the history of the membership's love and its gift to the future of a complex, only partially achieved charity, our best hope for deliverance from time within time itself.

   Port William's history, as told in *That Distant Land*, begins when five-year-old Mat Feltner—still wearing dresses and thus too young even to know whether he's a boy or a girl—sees a wounded man break from a crowd in the street and run toward the porch where he and his mother are sitting. As a group of booted men pursue the "hurt man" toward the house, Nancy Feltner pushes Mat inside, holds the door while the stranger also enters, and then stands outside to confront the crowd. She is dressed as Mat has always known her, in the mourning she wears for his brother and two sisters. "Surprised" that his mother has not come in with him, Mat begins to understand her separateness from him.[4] He senses she has a history of her own that requires her to shelter the "hurt man" even if it means not doing what Mat has expected of her. To understand her separateness is to begin to fathom his own. "Loss came into his mind," and he began to know "what he was years away from telling": "that his mother's grief was real; that her children in their graves once had been alive, that everybody lying under the grass up in the graveyard once had been alive and had walked in daylight in Port William" (10). Mat has passed from eternity into time, from a child's obliviousness to time to a beginning awareness that all things are in continual passage from beginning to end. With this knowledge comes the beginning of his devotion to collecting the stories of Port William—later passed to his grandson Andy—so that these might be remembered and narrated. For remembering and narrating are part of the town's "deliverance" (10), the only kind possible—a deliverance through love that does not deny loss but instead wrings from it courage, competence, and hope.

Mat observes these qualities in his mother as she tends the hurt man. The friendly crowd, now inside, defers unhesitatingly to her authority. She cleans his many wounds, reassuring him repeatedly that he's "going to be all right" (9). Simone Weil once said that each of us contains within "something that goes on indomitably expecting," even "in the teeth of all experience," that "good and not evil will be done" to us. This "profound and childlike and unchanging expectation of good in the heart" is what is sacred about us; it is what cries out from the depth of the heart in a way that even "Christ himself could not restrain, 'Why am I being hurt?'"[5] Mat sees something like the sacredness of this inextinguishable expectation of good in the face of the "hurt man," who "had shed the look of a man and assumed somehow the look of all things badly hurt" (9). He sees something from his mother that is both pity and something more than pity: a "hurt love that seemed to include entirely the hurt man." As Nancy washes, stanches, and bandages the man's wounds, her touch seemed to have about it "the promise of healing, some profound encouragement." It is "the knowledge of that encouragement," curiously, that finally overwhelms Mat, for he begins to sense "what it had cost her," or what "it would cost her and

would cost him." "He fled away and wept" (10), a little mysteriously, perhaps like Jesus at the tomb of Lazarus, moved by an awareness of just how
badly "hurt" human beings can be.[6] He learned that day that "the losses
would come"—to him and to all whom he loved. Yet he came into the possession also of a knowledge "unsurprised and at last comforted" that was
enough to sustain him, "whatever happened," until "he was gone" (11). The
closing allusion is to Rachel, "weeping" in Ramah, and refusing "to be
comforted," because the children "were not."[7] Nancy Feltner's children,
apart from Mat, are gone, but unlike Rachel's, they continue to be, active in
and through the comfort she is able to give the hurt man. They and she
participate in that love that she is able to direct to him so completely as to
include him entirely, a love capable of making credible her assurance that
he's "going to be all right." "There are few words for it, perhaps none" (10),
Mat says of what he learned from his mother that day, but I think we can
come close to it through the insights of Simone Weil quoted above. The
comfort Nancy can give, and that Mat comes to trust, derives from that
indomitable expectation that causes us to cry out in pain when we are hurt:
the expectation that, as Weil puts it, "good and not evil will be done" to us,
or, as Berry might say, that what "we are for" is ultimately the good.[8]

Nancy Feltner lives from the incarnational, non-Gnostic Christian
faith Berry commends in his essays. It is difficult to imagine how such faith
could be better exemplified than by one wounded person's competent and
hope-giving care for another's bodily and psychic hurt. Care-less unfaith
and an idolatry that refuses to acknowledge our dependence on creation
are evident, however, in the story that follows "The Hurt Man (1888)" in
That Distant Land, "Don't Send a Boy to Do a Man's Work (1891)." The
story explores the coming-of-age of Athey Keith, "who didn't intend ever
to be separated from his father," Carter, a successful farmer who also makes
"a sideline of trading in livestock, tobacco, corn, hay and other things" produced by his neighbors.[9] This business requires Carter to go to Louisville at
the same time that he has arranged for his neighbors to come to the Keith
place for a hog-killing. They are to kill two dozen hogs, sold to them in
advance, the men doing the slaughtering while Carter provides "scalding
box, gam'ling pole, firewood, and other necessities at a small surcharge per
head" (14). Athey is left by his father to preside over the slaughtering.

The story reveals the inadequacy of Athey's self-confident assumption
that he will be man enough to do this man's job. A first indication that he

overestimates himself occurs when he speaks peremptorily to Aunt Molly Mulwain, the black woman who has reared him after the death of the mother whom he never knew. "Give me my breakfast!" Athey orders her, only to be reduced in size by her sarcasm: "Now . . . ain't you something, Mister Man. You take off that cap, and square yourself to that table, and act a nickel's worth civilized" (15). What undoes Mister Man is a series of "complications" that also provide him, finally, with an opportunity for real heroism and growth. The complications involve two men uninvited to the hog-killing, Put Woolfork and Jim Pete Markman, and a keg of Jim Pete's "prime" whiskey. Athey tells this story retrospectively, from the standpoint of maturity, which enables him to see that Put "had it planned out" all along, for he was "a man who believed in thinking if it would get him something for nothing." Put planned to appear at the killing, figuring that if he "worked or appeared to work" somebody would give him something from the hogs or, at the very least, a "tub or two of guts to throw out for his chickens and dogs" (15). Now Put not only believes work and the appearance of work to be about equally good, but he also loves "the taste of somebody else's whiskey." He stops at Jim Pete's store, tells him of the slaughtering, and, at Markman's suggestion, takes a keg of whiskey while offering a promise he has no right—by either possession or labor—to make. When Jim Pete offers to supply the whiskey if they'll kill a hog for him, Put answers, "Why, sure. That'll be just fine" (16).

Carter Keith parts from Athey with an injunction and a reassurance: "See that they have what they need. They'll know what they're doing" (14). This confidence in the men is misplaced, for they do not know what they are doing. They know the business of hog-killing well enough, but they do not know themselves or their limits any better than Athey knows his. When Put arrives, "a rich man with his offering," he puts that keg on a big chopping block where it can be seen by all. It sits "in the midst of the people, like the golden calf" (16). The men do have a leader, Dewey Fields, but he is either not strong enough to resist them all or not committed enough because these have not been his hogs—entrusted to him and raised by his sweat. Moreover, it is not his place that stands to be defiled. He "eye[s]" the keg as if the golden calf is "exactly what it was," warning the men, "We ain't having none of that here" (16). But he does not destroy the idol made of human hands, the self-created image of our desire to believe that we are the creators and controllers of all that sustains us. As he tells the story, Athey admits that this is the moment "when I ought to have picked up the axe that was leaning right there and split that keg wide open." But he did not, and "after that," as he recognizes with proper humility, "I stayed a boy more or less to the end of it" (16).

By the middle of the afternoon, the men have killed, gutted, and hanged twenty-five hogs and managed to keep at least eight feet, at all times, from the keg, "as if from suspicion or respect" (17). But with the butchering still to do, the possibility of a "little warming" becomes too strong to resist, and they draw the bung of the keg. "Good-good-good-good-good" (17), it says. Now Berry is no teetotaler. There are wonderful drinking scenes throughout his fiction, mostly involving homemade Kentucky whiskey that announces its "goodness" as it's drunk from the jug or drawn from the keg. But five "goods" is at least two too many at any time. Drinking that much represents an overestimation of human ability and maybe even a failing of creaturely appreciation of the real good that is Kentucky whiskey—when drunk for enjoyment and not to induce a forgetting of one's fidelities. As the men become drunk, they become increasingly careless in their handling of the meat. The nature of good work is forgotten. Obligations to one another go by the board. Put Woolfork drops a ham "meat-side-down onto the ground," announcing that he'll eat it, "if nobody else will." Little Joe Ellis cuts a "middling with a hole in it that you could look through like a window." Big Joe Ellis "mistakenly or accidentally" cuts a "gobbet of fat" from a middling and drops it on the ground, saying, "in excellent good humor, 'Now, that there piece now, would you call that there piece sausage or skin fat? Well, God bless it, I'm a-calling it sausage. The dirt on it looks just like pepper.'" When one of the men points out to Dewey Fields that his overshoes have caught fire, he responds, "These ain't my overshoes, honey. I borrowed these overshoes offen Isham Quail" (18). What's forgotten is the cost, in sweat and life, of what sustains us. Things just come to be what we call them: fat dropped in dirt can be sausage. The work Isham Quail did to get his shoes can cease to matter. Meat from the animals we kill to sustain us can be wasted, lost through carelessness, allowed to touch the ground. This is the men's most serious failing: they fail to honor the animals on which they depend. They reject, or try to forget, their own kinship to the hogs as creatures dependent on the lives of other creatures.

The third and last "complication" of Athey's day comes "in the several persons of the Regulators," a kind of "imitation Ku Klux Klan" who take it upon themselves to prevent "sins against domestic tranquility" by regulating the drinking, sale, and making of "demon rum." Predictably, the Regulators consist of "every maker and seller of whiskey within a radius of several miles," and the group becomes a professional organization whose real function is to ruin "new or outside competitors" (19). Where the Regulators most resemble the Klan is in their self-proclaimed role of protecting "peace and the public good" against a demonized enemy. As "old man Thobe" chirps through his hood to the drunken hog slaughterers, "I reckon you all know, now, that we can't let this sort of doings go on unmolested. No woman nor child would be safe" (20). Unlike the Klan, they do not even believe their own language, unless they are so fully self-deceived as not even to realize the hypocrisy of their protecting the women and children by feasting on free pork and the remainder of Jim Pete's whiskey—after they have successfully driven all the pig killers except Athey "into the stripping room" and secured the door. The incident has a certain comic quality, but our seeing it through Athey's eyes leaves us, like him, with a "shiver" (20). The identities of the Regulators are no secret; "every boy above the age of five" (19) would recognize the horses and mules they ride. They are neighbors, known as neighbors, coming—armed—to steal from those with whom they live. What is particularly troubling about them is their speaking under the hoods "in their own voices," but not "for themselves" (20). Any justification, no matter how empty, seems able to cause men to do things collectively that they would never do alone.

Resistance to such insanity depends upon individual and communal discipline, upon law, for a people is no people at all without law. The law must be made for them in order for them to recognize the gift of law. Law that is obviously devised only for the advantage of some against others, like the "law" of the Regulators (or of Jim Crow), undermines all law. But to recognize good law as gift is also to recognize one's need for law. That is perhaps one way of thinking about why the First Commandment is "I *am* the Lord thy God. . . .Thou shalt have no other gods."[10] The commandment stresses not only that God is God, but also that human beings are not. To recognize that status is to live as a creature among other creatures, giving every thing the respect and care appropriate to it. The men's failure to respect the life they take reveals a potential lawlessness made manifest in the Regulators. To worship what is of human devising—golden calf or bourbon whiskey—is to be a rabble where no one can trust another, not a people with a life worth living. Fortunately, in Berry's story, one figure does resist the keg, Athey, who acts very well once he loses the misconception that he will be adequate for anything. When the Regulators have gone to sleep, he disarms them, burying their guns in the granary. Then later he drives off their horses and mules and releases the somewhat sobered hog killers. A fight follows, with the pig slaughterers winning an unimpressive victory, a sign of the thinness of their moral edge. Carter Keith arrives, drives the Regulators from the field, and orders coffee from Aunt Molly for those neighbors of his who have presided over a "damned nasty hog-killing" (24). The story ends, though, not with condemnation but with charity. As Athey watches the defeated Regulators, he sees them "now wholly apart from power, seniority, even meanness. They were only men." As the lame Peg Shifter hops "along like a one-legged crow," it occurs to Athey "that it might be possible to feel sorry for Peg Shifter, and, in later years he did" (24).

To accept one's creaturely status involves "consent," what Jonathan Edwards called "the consent" to "Being," the source, for him, of "true virtue."[11] One who embodies such virtue—with its original suggestion of strength or manliness—is the slightly unlikely hero Ptolemy Proudfoot. "Overabundant in both size and strength," Tol is "nothing if not a farmer"—a "good and a gifted one," not ambitious, committed to husbanding and improving "all his life" a place of ninety-eight acres without ever desiring even the additional two to make a hundred.[12] He has "consented" to participate—both by discovering and creating—the particular and inexhaustible good of a particular place. No wonder, then, that he is introduced in "A Consent (1908)," which relates a story that "is one of the dear possessions of the history of Port William" (28). The consent, however, to which the title most obviously refers is the "first consent" of Miss Minnie Quinch to Tol, "the beginning of their story together" (28). As "small and quick" as Tol is "big and lumbering" (26), Miss Minnie teaches the first eight grades at Goforth School. Loving children and books, she offers the best kind of literary education by simply "introducing the one to the other" (27). Though no one would expect tenderness of the powerful Tol, he does embody "very powerful tender feelings" (26), mostly devoted to years of admiring Miss Minnie.

Miss Minnie also admires Tol, though she tries to keep her feelings to "concern" about his being unmarried at thirty-six, for "she was conscious of being a small person unable even to hope to arrest the gaze of so splendid a man" (27). Indeed, both Minnie and Tol carefully avoid meeting one another's gaze, perhaps as much from fear that they will be seen inadequate as from the desire to keep their admiration private. One morning, however, Tol comes out of a Port William store just as Miss Minnie is entering, and she, "before she could think," says, "Well, good morning, Mr. Proudfoot!" (27). Tol gets his mouth open on this encounter but manages no sound. He does slightly better on their next meeting, which occurs one fall afternoon as he is driving his team by the schoolhouse, where Miss Minnie is outside "standing by the pump." After she smiles and greets him, Tol looks "intently into the sky ahead of him" and says, "quickly as if he had received a threat, 'Why, howdy!'" Though a "poor thing," as Tol recognizes, the conversation has begun (28).

The consent of both Miss Minnie and Tol to the love that is trying to be in them occurs at the school's annual Harvest Festival, which features recitations and readings by Miss Minnie's scholars. Tol has never gone to the festival, despite always "long[ing] to go" (28). Obviously fearful of being found inadequate in "Miss Minnie's world," he has stayed home unhappy. Even on this occasion, after he has resolved to go, he must several times consent to the feeling for Miss Minnie that is pressing him to risk her judgment. As he nears the schoolhouse, Tol stops his horse and sits in the road, his heart "quak[ing]" as he thinks about whether "to go on by, pretending to have an errand elsewhere" (29–30). When he arrives at the schoolhouse—clothes wrinkled, shirttail out, "horse manure on one of his shoes"—only women and girls are present. Tol is "embarrassed," thinking he has made "a serious mistake." Fortunately, Miss Minnie sees his dilemma and rings the schoolhouse bell, bringing in the men who have been outside and letting Tol feel somewhat "inconspicuous" (31). The program for the evening follows, the scholars reciting psalms, poems like "Thanatopsis" and "Concord Hymn," or pieces of patriotic oratory. After Burley Coulter has massacred "When the Frost Is on the Punkin'" by James Whitcomb Riley, and Kate Helen Branch has sung "In the Gloaming" in a voice "clear and true" (35), the last event of the night begins, the one that makes Tol's feelings very conspicuous indeed.

The event is an auction, for the good of the school, of pies and cakes made by the ladies, including Miss Minnie, who has contributed an angel food cake "with an icing as white and light and swirly as a summer cloud." "White as a bride," it "fairly" took Tol's breath away when he first came into the schoolroom (32). Gilead Hopple, local magistrate, opens at one dollar, expecting to be the only bidder. "Astonished to hear himself," Tol bids two dollars in a "voice far too loud" (36). The bidding goes back and forth as a "revelation" comes to Miss Minnie: "It seemed to her beyond a doubt that Tol Proudfoot, that large, strong man whom she had thought ought to be some woman's knight and protector, was bidding to be *her* knight and protector. It made her dizzy" (37). When Hopple bids, "Five and a quarter," Tol shouts out, "*Ten!*"—prompting Hopple's wife to say, "Good *lord*, Gil! I'll *make* you a cake!" Tol wins the cake but stands terribly exposed, his affection for Miss Minnie now fully public. She comes "through the crowd, looking straight at him, and smiling," signifying her acceptance of the feeling for her he has shown. As the story ends, Tol asks if he might see her home, and Miss Minnie gives her consent: "Certainly you may" (37).[13]

Miss Minnie's is the first explicit "consent" in their relationship, which leads to a marriage of many years. But as we have seen, the story suggests a series of consents by both people, the most basic of which involves both their consenting to the improbable possibility that one so seemingly different could find the other not only acceptable but lovable precisely as the particular person he or she is. They must consent to the way love seeks through them to create a new and unforeseeable possibility. Each says, in effect, "let it be."

The continuing conversation that is Miss Minnie and Tol's marriage provides the material for several fine comic tales. In one of these, "A Half-Pint of Old Darling (1920)," Miss Minnie, a Temperance supporter, gets a little too much Kentucky whiskey as she and Tol return from Hargrave one day in November 1920, twelve years after their consent. Tol's ewes are nearly ready to birth, and he has bought the "medicinal" to use as a little encourager to the weak lambs. He places the half pint under the buggy seat, only to have a horrified Miss Minnie discover it and begin a course of sacrificial sipping intended to save Tol from his own weakness. Tol is unaware of what she is doing until she begins to call out to buggies they meet on behalf of a candidate in the upcoming election. Discovered, Miss Minnie tries to retain the moral advantage by calling Tol a "drunkard" and refusing to believe his story about the lambs.[14] When they arrive home, Tol must carry Miss Minnie to the sofa, help her to remove her coat and hat, and cover her. When she awakes, she asks him again whether the half pint was just for the lambs, and when Tol responds that it was, her crying jag begins.

She mourns for her suspicion of Tol and for "the public display" she has "made of herself." "I surely am the degradedest woman who ever lived," she declares. "I have shamed myself, and most of all you." Tol merely sits quietly, patting her and saying, "Naw, now. Naw, now. You didn't do no such of a thing" (136).

The story ends with a framing comment in which the narrator, presumably Andy Catlett, tells us that Miss Minnie liked to call this, later, "a lovely time." "Oddly," she enjoys telling the tale, savoring particularly the line about her degradation. Of her husband, Miss Minnie says, "Mr. Proudfoot was horrified. But after it was over, he just had to rear back and laugh. Oh, he was a man of splendid qualities!" (136). Obviously, the story serves as a way to remember Tol after his death, particularly for the splendid generosity that overlooked her suspicion of him and dismissed as nonsense Miss Minnie's self-indictment. Tol's comment and laughter rescue her from shame that could have become a source of division between them. His love and real knowledge of her help her to see the comedy of her assumed superiority, her self-sacrifice, and her equally silly self-castigation. Andy finds it "odd" that she should enjoy telling this tale, but I'm not sure the reader does. She may recognize that it is a great gift to have a story that enables her to face her own foolishness because she knows herself accepted by a love that cannot be lost.

Perhaps the most tender of the Proudfoot stories concerns Tol and Miss Minnie's childlessness. Set in Depression times, "The Solemn Boy (1934)" opens with sixty-two-year-old Tol beginning to recognize he is getting old. He can still work but finds it takes him longer to get started. The last of the once large Proudfoot clan, he works alone. After doing so one cold morning late in the year, Tol is driving a wagonload of corn back to the barn when he meets a man and his son, both "poorly dressed for the weather."[15] Tol and Minnie have seen and assisted such men, out of work and drifting, but "till now they had seen no boy" (188). Tol points out his place ahead and invites the two to come share some biscuits. Concerned for his pride, the man refuses, but when Tol suggests it would be good to get the boy warmed a bit and fed, the man indicates he'd be "mightily obliged" (188).

Tension marks the following scene in the Proudfoots' kitchen. The shame the two feel is evident in their eating "hungrily without looking up, as though to avoid acknowledging that others saw how hungry they were"

(191). Both Tol and Miss Minnie "long" to see the boy smile, but he remains solemn. Perhaps he is reluctant to smile unless his father can also smile; perhaps he senses that even the slightest break in their grim resignation may undermine their ability to contend with life on the road. Undoubtedly, he's learned that to receive, in need, is shameful, a sign of personal fault, as many felt in the Depression, however unreasonably. Tol tries repeatedly to get the boy to smile or laugh, but the boy will do neither. It almost seems as if the boy may be permanently in danger of losing all capacity for joy: "He was a solemn boy, far too solemn for his age" (191).

Tol inadvertently puts solemnity to rout, however, when he reminds the boy to drink his buttermilk from the near side of the glass. "Drinking from the far side, as you'll find out, don't work anything like so well," he says, and then, as if to test this wisdom, he "applied the far side of the glass to his lips, turned it up, and poured the rest of the buttermilk right down the front of his shirt" (192). The boy begins to laugh, first as if there's an obstruction in his throat, but then with the "free, strong laugh" of a "boy who was completely tickled" (192). Tol laughs, Miss Minnie laughs, and then the father. Temporarily, shame is banished, and they are simply together: "The man and boy looked up, they all looked full into one another's eyes, and they laughed" (192).

The laughter "made the table a lovely place to be" (193), but the last note of the story reasserts the difference between the Proudfoots and the strangers. After the man has accepted one of Miss Minnie's old coats for the boy but rejected a much patched work jacket of Tol's for himself, Tol says to him jokingly, but in a line that suggests the Proudfoots' great need, "You might as well leave that boy with us. . . . We could use a boy like that" (194). This prompts a last smile from the man, who responds in a way that suggests what the childless Tol and Minnie will never know: "He's a good boy. . . . I can't hardly get along without this boy" (194). To Tol, he's a "boy like that"; to the father, there is no "boy like that." He is "this boy," irreducibly particular. Tol will never really know what the father means when he says he couldn't "hardly get along" without his son.

After the two leave, Tol and Miss Minnie set back to work, and "for the rest of that day, they did not look at each other" (194). Like the man and his son as they first eat, neither Tol nor Miss Minnie wants to acknowledge that the one sees the other's hunger. As Andy frames the story at its end, he remembers Miss Minnie, "looking down at her apron and smoothing it with her hands," and saying, "Mr. Proudfoot always wished we'd had some children. . . . He never said so, but I know he did" (195). Part of how she knows he did is, of course, that she did too.

More than once Berry refers to Tol as "slow to anger" (80), and I believe we are to hear the completing phrase from Exodus, Psalm 145, and the liturgy: "and abounding in steadfast love."[16] Tol's fidelity, his steadfastness—together with the breadth of his charity—is evident in "Watch with Me (1916)." The primary biblical allusion of the title is to Christ's importuning the disciples to "watch with me" as he prays in Gethsemane.[17] But the command to "watch," to be wakeful and ready, recalls other passages as well, most of them having to do with the uncertainty of the hour at which the Son of Man will come. God's good time is not our time. None of us knows even our own hour. We are to follow, in loving obedience, the one who goes ahead of us.

Tol and several of his Port William friends spend most of the story following Thacker "Nightlife" Hample—so named because of his "poor vision," shared with his family, but in his case so extreme that local theory holds "he could not tell daylight from dark, and therefore was liable to conduct his nightlife in the daytime" (82). His time is not common time. He is "incomplete" (82), subject to "spells" of what our therapeutic culture would call depression or perhaps schizophrenia. The member of a family whose overworked farm yields only enough to keep them "marginal," Nightlife is a "stranger to everybody"—perhaps even to himself—when one of his spells is on him (86–87).

An incident during a revival in the Goforth church precipitates just such a spell. Nightlife has wanted to preach, "wanted to tell what it was like to be himself," as Tol and his friends come to understand later, "because at that time anyhow, it was all he had in him" (82). The preachers refuse, because however well they knew the Son of Man would come in his own time, they "were in fact not prepared for anything unscheduled" (82–83). Thereupon Nightlife "throwed a reg'lar fit," preaching some healthy dialectical theology in the process. He told them they acted as if they thought it was "their church," but it was not. It was "Jesus's church," and he would return to claim it. But he also ended his message with hope that they would be lost, that when Jesus came back, "He would fork the likes of them into Hell as quick as look at them, and he, Nightlife, would at that time enjoy hearing them sing a different tune." Tol is called upon to quiet Nightlife, and he succeeds in doing so, knowing, however, that "he would have to deal" with Nightlife again (83).

The next day begins for Tol with reminders that our lives are out of control. His cows fail to come when called, his favorite cow puts a foot covered with manure into the milking pail, he blows a hole in the side of the henhouse with his ten-gauge trying to kill a cowsucker snake. Missing his shot, he reloads Old Fetcher, named for the certainty of its killing power, and leans it against the door of his workshop. There Nightlife finds it as he comes to talk to Tol. Taking the gun, Nightlife enters the woods, disappearing as if completely. The following, watching, and waiting now begin for Tol and the neighbors who join him. "Almost in the twinkling of an eye," Tol crosses "the boundary between two worlds," leaving one "where at least some things happened more or less as he intended" for one "in which he intended only to follow Nightlife and foresaw nothing" (85).

Tol follows Nightlife all day and through the night. He is joined early on by Sam Hanks, a little later by Braymer Hardy, and then again by Walter Cotman and Tom Hardy, all of whom stay till the end. Put Woolfork accompanies them for a while, and Burley Coulter finds them as he searches for a hound. He also stays. There is some risk to them all. While their primary concern is that Nightlife will shoot himself, a man lost in the darkness with a ten-gauge and poor eyesight might feasibly kill any of them. Yet for all except Put there is no question about following. As the men fan out in order to increase their chances of keeping Nightlife in sight, their "only clarity was their intent not to let Nightlife be further divided from them" (92). They do "watch with" Nightlife, trying to keep him in sight and reminding him of their presence in order to keep him from slipping entirely out of the world. Tol wonders momentarily whether it would have been better not to be involved, but he knows that is not a choice: "Helpless or not, hopeless or not, he would go along with Nightlife until whatever happened that would allow him to cease to go along had happened" (101). Nightlife is their neighbor; he is alone in a way no human being should ever be alone; following him has caused the men to acknowledge what the sanity of ordinary daylight keeps at bay: that we are all walking every moment "between this present world and the larger one that lies beyond it and contains it" (97).

Berry uses Christlike language for Nightlife, but I do not think we should regard him as a "Christ figure," in large part because, as Hans Frei argues, there can be no Christ figures precisely because Christ has once and for all preempted that figure.[18] Nevertheless, when Nightlife is at Uncle Othy and Aunt Cordie Daggetts's table, he prays, "not for them or at them; he prayed as if he were off somewhere by himself" (95), as Jesus often does. In the middle of the night when the followers have gone to sleep, he appears in their midst, asking repeatedly in a way that makes them astonished and "most of all ashamed," "Couldn't you stay awake? Couldn't you stay awake?" (116). Of course they could not, for, like the disciples, it is not possible for any human being to remain continually watchful. But unlike Jesus, Nightlife is not himself, he has no idea where he is going, he stares at the Daggetts as if he "had no idea where he was" (96). He seems as if "the vehicle of something he suffered," but what that is is something the men "had not suffered" (92), whereas Jesus's true humanity is to suffer precisely what all have suffered. Thus, if Nightlife confuses himself with Christ, something more complex than figuration is going on here.

During one of the night's silences, Tom Hardy says, "A man would think of killing hisself, he ain't at hisself, surely." "He's at hisself, all right," Tol replies. "He ain't nowhere *but* at hisself." Though paradoxical, both of these are true: Nightlife is so thoroughly "at hisself," lost in himself alone, that he is not "at hisself," because he has lost any ability to locate who he is as a being with and among others. As Tol says of him, "He's just wandering around inside hisself, looking for the way out. In there where he is, it's dark sure enough" (115). If he thinks of himself in Christlike terms, it may be because he is so utterly lost in himself that he cannot imagine anything good from the everyday world ever happening to him again. He knows he is lost, knows he has gotten there by too much dwelling on his own efforts to save himself, and cannot imagine anyone else, including Christ, except in his own terms—which, if he has any residual memory, he will know to be absurd. Such are the self-tightening knots of major depression as Berry suggests them in Nightlife.

Nightlife "comes to himself" at midmorning of the second day. He has circled back toward Tol's place when a hard rain begins to fall, sending his soaked followers to take shelter in Tol's shop. There they are laughing after their "wild run" when Nightlife comes through the door, "cradling the gun in his hands as if expecting a covey of quail to flush at any second." "Brethren," he says, "let us stand and sing," beginning himself "The Unclouded Day" (120). All except Sam Hanks join in lifting "the fine old song up against the rattle of hard rain," as if "in them the neighborhood sang, even under threat, its love for itself and its grief for itself, greater than the terms of this world allow" (121). Then Nightlife begins to preach, his text Matthew's version of the parable of the lost sheep: "How think ye? if a man have an hundred sheep, and one of them be gone astray, doth he not leave the ninety and nine, and goeth into the mountains, and seeketh that which is gone astray?" (Matt. 18:12). The sermon moves his hearers, prompting the plainspoken Walter Cotman to declare when he is later asked if he felt for Nightlife, "*Course* I felt for him! The son of a bitch could preach!" (122). Nightlife understands the text "entirely from the viewpoint of the lost sheep"; he can "imagine fully the condition of being lost and even the hope of rescue, but could not imagine rescue itself" (121). "Oh, it's a dark place, my brethren," Nightlife says, "a dark place where the lost sheep tries to find his way, and can't." The lostness of depression, the absolute inability to imagine any return to something like ordinary life, is understood from the inside out by Nightlife, and the men know this to be so. "The shepherd comes a-looking and a-calling," and "the sheep knows the shepherd's voice and he wants to go to it, but he can't find the path, and he can't make it" (121).

A biblical hen gathering her chicks ends Nightlife's spell. As he preaches "right in front of her nest," she walks "back and forth at Nightlife's feet, crying out with rapidly increasing hysteria," an obvious allusion to Luke 13:34: "My children! My children! What will become of my children?" (122).[19] She launches herself toward her nest, misjudges Nightlife's height, and winds up "flapping and squawking, right in Nightlife's face." He responds by striking her a hard blow with his open hand, and by the time she has "hit the ground," "a change had come over Nightlife." He has "awakened," come to himself, which, for him as for the Prodigal Son, involves being back in relation to others—back, we might say, in this world, no longer ahead of himself pushing at the boundaries between this world and that beyond. "It was plain to the others that he saw that they were there with him and that he knew them" (122), that he now knows himself again as a part of the membership—a kind of relationality that is prior, for us, to our cherished individuality. Tol tests Nightlife to see if he has any memory of what has occurred, and he does not. From being completely in and "at hisself," he has been turned outward toward others and the common life of ordinary time.

Miss Minnie glosses the story with a theologically astute tribute to that old hen's role in Nightlife's preservation: "And don't you know that old hen survived it all. She hatched fourteen chicks and raised them, every one!" (123). The hen, like the shepherd of Matthew's parable, has sought not to lose a single one. Those who have followed Nightlife have also known that the membership is not simply a matter of their choosing: that it antedates them and is there for them and thus requires their going in search of the lost. (Tol extends this care that none be lost even to Put Woolfork, something the others have a more difficult time doing.) Finally, it needs to be said that there is danger in this passion for seeking to find every one. This is to give oneself to a love and grief "greater than the terms of this world allow" (121). It is to put oneself in danger, as perhaps Nightlife does, of being carried right out of the world. Thus, the effort to lose none must be a matter for the membership, gathered together as they follow the shepherd who goes ahead, knowing where he goes.

In "Watch with Me (1916)," the membership manages to avert murder and suicide. In "Pray Without Ceasing (1912)," both occur, the murder of Ben Feltner, the suicide of Thad Coulter. The titles of the stories suggest their further connection. Christians are implored to "pray without ceasing" because no one knows the hour at which the Son of Man comes.[20] Praying, like watching, is the disciplined practice of attention, of learning to ask to stay in connection to God, and through God to others, in order to glimpse what may be going on that one would not imagine otherwise.

The story comes to Andy Catlett from his Grandmother Feltner as his grandfather Mat Feltner is dying. Andy has known the germ of the story, but he has found also that his grandfather does not like to speak of the events leading to his father's murder. Prompted by Braymer Hardy and feeling "incomplete" in his knowledge of his grandfather, Andy goes to his grandmother. To feel "incomplete" about his grandfather is to be incomplete in himself as well, for as Andy knows, much like Faulkner or T. S. Eliot, the past is not simply past, but "present also." Even when it is unknown, it is "present in us, its silence as persistent as a ringing in the ears."[21] As Andy puts it:

> Nothing is here that we are beyond the reach of merely because we do not know about it. It is always the first morning of Creation and always the last day, always the now that is in time and the Now that is not, that has filled time with reminders of Itself. (39)

In learning the story, Andy comes to recognize how fully he is a child of the story—and of those other stories that led to this story's taking the shape it did.

In its outline, the story is simple. The year is 1912. Ben Feltner and Thad Coulter are friends, the seventy-two-year-old Ben Thad's best friend. Thad and his wife, Rachel, have worked "hard and long" (51), and at great cost to themselves, to own, free and clear, a hundred-acre hillside farm. But Thad and his son Abner have contracted the characteristic disease of the century, "the suspicion that they would be greatly improved if they were someplace else" (49). Thad mortgages the farm so that Abner can buy a grocery in Hargrave, Abner fails, and Thad finds himself faced, at best, with working to pay for his farm again. Outraged, Thad goes on a two-day bender, then approaches Ben for help. Ben is patient with his friend, but when he sees that Thad is not himself, he stops the conversation and sends Thad home to get sober, getting him out the door finally with persuasive, though not excessive, force. Thad continues to drink, rides into Port William on Saturday afternoon, and shoots Ben in the head. In town with his father, Mat runs to the body, then rises with "elation" as the single desire "to kill the man who had killed his father" surges through him (59). Seeing Mat break from the crowd around Ben's body, Jack Beechum, Ben's friend and later Mat's, runs to Mat, catches him, and holds him. The two "str[i]ve together" (60) in the dust until finally Mat relents and starts home to tell his mother. Thad's escape is cut short as the weight of what he has done comes home to him, and he becomes aware of being followed by his loving daughter Martha Elizabeth. He turns himself in to the sheriff in Hargrave, where Martha Elizabeth waits the better part of the day to see him. By evening a vigilante crowd has assembled at the Feltners' house, offering to "put justice beyond question" if Mat will only say the word. Mat responds by asking the crowd "not to do that," and he is followed by his mother's gentle request: "Let us make what peace is left for us to make" (74). Soon thereafter Thad Coulter hangs himself in the Hargrave jail.

Rage moves Thad Coulter to kill Ben Feltner: rage against himself, against time, against the fact that what is done cannot be undone. His life has been, in one sense, a project of systematic self-rejection: he has, in a quite literal way, objectified himself in the farm he loves while simultaneously believing that such a life is unworthy of his son. Now he can no longer "bear to look at" the farm, for "it was his life, and he was no longer in it." He is "ashamed in its presence," his countenance falls, and he can no more "look directly at it" than he can, after his demise, look "Martha Elizabeth full in the eyes" (51). His shame lies in his own role in his dispossession: now another possesses the place of his labor, his years, largely because he did not sufficiently value that labor or the farm itself, but saw them ultimately only as means toward the acquisition of the currency of a now failed dream. He has caused himself to lose his life, and he knows it cannot be given back to him. His rage is against time, because once spent, it cannot come again.

Andy tells us his grandmother counted on his knowing stories like those of Adam and Eve and Cain and Abel. The latter bears particularly close relation to the story of Thad's killing Ben. We hear one feature after another of Cain's story as we read Andy's telling of Thad's reaction to Ben's first attempt to close their conversation:

> Thad did not have to take Ben's words as an insult. But in his circumstances and condition, it was perhaps inevitable that he would. That Ben was his friend made the offense worse—far worse. In refusing to talk to him as he was, Ben, it seemed to Thad, had exiled him from friendship and so withdrawn the last vestige of a possibility that he might find anywhere a redemption for himself, much less for his forfeited land. (46)

One terrible quality of the Cain and Abel story is that Cain does not have to take God's regard for Abel's offering as an insult to him, and yet, if we know ourselves even a little, we sense it inevitable that he will. And the offense to Cain is surely "far worse" because God's regard is for the offering of his *brother*. Much, indeed everything in Cain's eyes, is at stake precisely because Abel is the brother. Because the one God has regard for is, specifically, his brother, it seems to Cain that God has forever fixed the difference between them, even though God makes it clear that Cain, too, can be accepted if he can master sin. Unable, like Thad, to believe he will ever find "a redemption for himself"—rightly, in a sense, as redemption is God's—Cain seeks to fix the judgment of the moment once for all, exiling himself forever from God and brother. His rage is against time, against the fact that his acceptance, like Abel's, is a matter of God's good time and not his own.

Berry's insights into anger become clearer as Thad prepares to kill Ben.

Thad uses the whiskey to bring his anger to him "full and clear," and he feels "summoned by an almost visible joy." He feels a "singular joy" again as he goes to the barn to get his mule. He strips off the mule's harness carelessly, letting it fall to the ground as "he had never before in his life. . . . But he was not in his life now, and his rage pleased him" (52–53). The rage brings clarity, the singular joy of acting once and for all to exact judgment on Ben and on himself and thus to bring to an end the waiting, the daily endurance and submission to time. He is out of his life, out of time, free of bondage. Mat feels similar "elation" when it comes to him that he must avenge his father. The clarity, the singleness of purpose, is what brings joy: "All that he had been and thought and done gave way to his one desire to kill the man who had killed his father. He ached, mind and body, with the elation of that one thought." Time falls away, history is no more, Mat and Thad are enemies, no other description will ever be possible, the future— God—can change nothing. "New-created by rage," Mat "and his enemy were as clear of history as if newborn" (59). Mat will fix the difference between them once and for all, using the power that stands over all without distinction, death. Thus, the fierce joy of Thad and Mat, perhaps of war itself, lies in escape from the indignity of dying daily to wield as a power for good the death that bears us down.

"Pray Without Ceasing (1912)" ends with three acts of love. The first is Jack Beechum's holding Mat forcefully in the street. An ordinary man might have simply stepped aside, willing enough to allow a son to avenge his father in such a case, particularly if the victim was his longtime friend. But Jack knows he must hold Mat because he has loved Ben. He knows Mat is not acting as himself, but that he will come to himself, and that when he does so it will be as the son still in relation to his father, Ben, who would not have willed such revenge. In their struggle Jack feels something go "out of him that day, and he was not the same again" (60). A strength comes into Mat that holds his "grief and his anger," and Jack knows this strength not because it "enabled Mat to break free but because it enabled Jack to turn him loose" (60–61). They step back in a moment of recognition. Mat comes to himself, yielding the elation of a rage powerful enough to kill. What comes into Mat is nothing less than strength to live, call it love, the ability to go on in time without needing to fix a difference between himself and Thad that cannot be undone. It is a decision for God's good time.

The second act of love is Mat's and his mother's quieting the crowd. Berry stages this beautifully by having them come out together onto the porch where Nancy once went to face the men pursuing the "hurt man." Then Mat had to stay inside, where he watched his mother's courage with awe. Now they stand together, she still wearing her mourning for three children, and Mat acts from what he has learned from her: to try to make what peace can still be made even knowing how much that peace will have cost. The third act of love is Martha Elizabeth's. Thad's suicide represents a Cainlike judgment on himself, an act—parallel in a way to the proposed lynching—of usurping God's judgment and closing the possibility of redemption. But Martha Elizabeth remains absolutely steadfast in her love of her father. Tol and his neighbors witness and wait as Nightlife wanders in the dark; Martha Elizabeth extends that refusal to yield connection even beyond death. Thad feels the strength of her love as he journeys toward Hargrave to turn himself in: "It seemed to him that she knew everything he knew, and loved him anyhow. She loved him, minute by minute, not only as he had been but as he had become. It was a wonderful and a fearful thing to him that he had caused such a love for himself to come into the world and then had failed it" (65). As she sits waiting to be admitted to see her father, the Hargrave crowd leaves "a kind of island around her, as if unwilling to acknowledge the absolute submission they sensed in her" (68), an absolute submission to what has happened with the simple commitment to love.

This love, in fact, is what Thad cannot bear, as Andy's grandmother has come to understand, because Martha Elizabeth's steadfastness has not allowed this part of the story to be dismissed from memory:

> "You see," my grandmother said, "there are two deaths in this—Mr. Feltner's and Thad Coulter's. We know Mr. Feltner's because we had to know it. It was ours. That we know Thad's is because of Martha Elizabeth. The Martha Elizabeth you know." (68)

Andy remembers her as a woman "always near to smiling, sometimes to laughter" (68). Hers "was a face that assented wholly to the being of whatever and whomever she looked at" (68). Josef Pieper said of Thomas Aquinas's understanding of love that love consists, in effect, of a simple affirmation: "It is good that you exist."[22] Such is Martha Elizabeth's love. She "had gone with her father to the world's edge" (68) and come back with a love that affirms and consents to being. But her father could not bear this love, perhaps because he recognized he could not escape it or, like Cain, put himself beyond it. It meant the last word over him would not be his. "It's a hard story to have to know" (70), Andy's grandmother tells him, part of "the hard history of love" in this place. But Andy must know it in order to be complete, for, as he recognizes, he is "the child of his [grandfather's] forgiveness" (75). Though there are no longer Feltners nor Coulters in Port William, those lines continue, joined together in him. He is Abel and Cain, like the rest of us, called to "pray without ceasing" (73) for the love that enables us to sustain the good even through and in the hardest of history.

The story of Mat's last months and death is told in "The Boundary (1965)" and "That Distant Land (1965)." The first concerns a day in late spring or early summer when Mat is eighty-two. Mat leaves the house, telling Margaret, "It's all right, my old girl," his ostensible purpose being "to walk that length of the boundary line that runs down Shade Branch."[23] The young growth, the promise of the year, the "cast[ing] off" now of "all restraint" (291), as perhaps only an old man can do, bring him joy. His life has come to a fruitful issue, and he knows, "I am blessed" (293). He's come to check the fence line and finds that Nathan Coulter, now his son in all but name, has been ahead of him. The competence Mat knew in his own mother can now be counted on in Nathan. There will be care for all that is his beyond his life. As Mat walks the steep descent to the stream, his mind moves easily into the past, a past not simply past, however, because it is now his present. The marking of the world around him does not follow human accounting of time. The woods and stream are subject to "continuous little changes of growth and wear," but they are otherwise much as they were "when Mat first knew" them (292). At one shallow pool, Mat remembers a fencing crew from seventy-five years ago and young Jack Beechum vaulting over the water using two of the tamping rams. Next he recalls his own son Virgil making the same vault "forty-some years later" (293). A little further on, he comes to a larger pool he made with Virgil in the drought of summer 1930. On that day, Virgil had made a little nook for their water jug by placing a rock against the root of a young sycamore. They forgot the jug that day, and it is still there, broken now by "force of the tree trunk growing against it" (295), but still sheltered under the rock, fastened now to the tree by the sycamore itself as it has grown around it. This natural shrine and sign of healing causes Mat to weep, and he must "deliberately" turn away and give "his mind back to the day and the stream" (296) in order to find again that good nothingness that lies in "deep peaceable attention to that voice that speaks always only of where it is, remembering nothing, fearing and desiring nothing" (296).

As Mat turns to make the uphill climb back home, Berry moves him into a present in which he is with his father and with Virgil. First he follows his father up the branch, Ben turning to him to encourage him when he is tired: "It's all right. It ain't that far" (298). Then "he can hear Virgil behind him," calling him to wait as he pushes ahead, as a father will, to move the boy to effort. When Virgil stops following, believing "he has been left alone in the darkening woods," Mat goes back to him, speaking those words that reverberate through Berry's short fiction and that Mat has learned from his mother, to whom they have not come cheaply: "Well, it's all right, old boy, . . . It's all right" (298). He continues talking with Virgil until he is aware of both his father and his boy "moving along up the opposite side of the branch" (301). Mat's other dead are there, too: Jack Beechum, Joe Banion, Old Smoke. Many readers might call Mat's experience dementia, but Berry prefers simply to suggest that Mat is now with friends who are part of his realest, deepest experiences, those to be carried to his end and beyond. He is both with these companions and apart from them, dying alone as we all must, "going the one way that he alone is going" (301).

Mat does make it home, though he must be helped by Nathan, Elton Penn, and Wheeler Catlett. He has had "an accounting he must come to" (304) with Margaret, the one whose "smile of assent" to their love has been a "time that he has not surpassed" (305). In the last moments of his climb, "a shadowless love moves him," a love "not his," but one "that he belongs to, as he belongs to the place and to the light over it" (305–6). He senses here something like what the Christian means when she says that one can love "because God first loved us."[24] One finds oneself in love, not as something one created or made, but rather as something that has been there for one from the first, as a reality that one comes gradually to trust.

Mat wanders in his mind for several days after his return. Then he is suddenly present to himself and to Margaret, but he never rises from bed again. His is a good death. He is largely free of pain and completely free of medical and technological interventions. He is lucid, in his own bed, able to meet daily with visitors, and willing to be helped. He exhibits the marvelous freedom for death of a man who has arrived at simplicity, one content to attend to each moment without desire or compulsion of any kind. He dies at tobacco-cutting time. The Coulters, Elton Penn, the Rowanberrys, and young Andy spend day after day going down each row's "long, lonely journey that, somewhere in the middle, we believed would never end."[25] Andy calls it beautiful and "touchingly mortal" (315) work, the kind that leaves no doubt that what one spends in physical labor is one's life. Storytelling, mostly by Elton and Burley, forms an important part of the work, and Burley breaks at times into hymns like "That Distant Land": "*Oh, pilgrim, have you seen that distant land?*" (317). They are just readying to load the wagons at the end of one day's work when Wheeler Catlett drives up to tell them that Mat Feltner has died. Nobody speaks, and Andy realizes they are waiting for Jarrat Coulter, "now the oldest man," to take the lead. After a pause, Jarrat says, "Let's load 'em up" (318). He has become the one to follow, the man farthest down his row, nearest to the boundary that separates the living of this world from the life that surrounds it. There is nothing to do except continue the work Mat Feltner loved, remembering him in the stories of their membership in one another.

As Mat Feltner nears death, Andy's grandmother presents him with a pair of his grandfather's shoes, urging him not just to keep them, but to wear them. When Andy arrives at the tobacco cutting wearing them, Burley Coulter puts his arm around Andy, smiles, and says in such a way as to make "the truth plain and bearable" to them both, "You can wear 'em, honey. But you can't fill 'em" (316). Who shall wear the shoes of those who have gone before—the question of rightful inheritance—constitutes a central concern of several of the later stories in *That Distant Land*. Wheeler Catlett, Andy's father, plays a central role in these. Wheeler has gone away to the university and to law school before returning, by choice, to take up practice in Hargrave. Wheeler loves the land and is at least as much farmer as lawyer in imagination. He also sees the changes brought to Hargrave and Port William by modernity, the failure of the lines of succession, the fragility of the membership. Both lawyer and friend to the local farmers, he serves less as an adjudicator among competing interests than as a shaper of events, particularly when what's at stake is the land finding its rightful steward.

The loyalty of children to their parents, particularly of those who have moved to the cities, can no longer guarantee the rightful inheritance of the land. In "It Wasn't Me (1953)," the daughter of Jack Beechum, Clara Pettit, and her husband, Gladston, refuse to honor old Jack's intention that his farm be sold to Elton Penn for two hundred dollars an acre at his death. Jack's legal will is clear: Clara is to have the farm, but Elton—who has been Jack's tenant—is to receive an amount equal to half of what Jack regards as a fair price for the farm. Later Jack has scrawled a note telling Wheeler to "see to it" that "the boy has his place 200$ acre be about right."[26] There is no question the note is her father's, but Clara refuses to honor it. An auction is held, and Elton has two competitors, including an ambitious farmer who seeks to add "house to house and field to field" (276). Encouraged by Wheeler, Elton pays three hundred dollars an acre for the farm, a price far higher than he would have bid on his own. Aware that he has cost Elton at least an additional sixty-five dollars an acre, Wheeler resolves that freedom for him in this transaction will mean standing by Elton financially if necessary.

The story closes with a fine conversation between Wheeler and Elton, one not without tension. The Pettits have acted from within a strict construction of the law; Wheeler has acted from a vision of the good, not in defiance of the law but in recognition that law alone is not enough to ensure the good. In doing so, he has acted not only in fidelity to Jack Beechum's will but also from a knowledge of the good much like Jack's own. Jack had known what "a good one" was in all the appropriate contexts of farming; he judged a horse, a hog, or a man according to standards of "excellence represented by the known, proved, and remembered good ones of their respective kinds" (267). Judgments about the good were, for him, inseparable from practices aiming at the good and impossible without knowledge of the practices' history. It is according to the standards of good work that Jack has recognized Elton and Mary Penn to be the appropriate heirs of his work.

Three things are at stake for Wheeler: loyalty to Old Jack, ensuring the right stewardship of the land, and maintaining the membership—for, as Isaiah 5:8 tells us, if those who seek to "join house to house" and "field to field" are not kept within limits, they end up "left to live alone in the midst of the land!" At stake for Elton are his future and his sweat. After Wheeler makes it clear he is willing to help Elton financially if necessary, Elton struggles between "gratitude and resentment," wanting, as he says, in a way typical of the young, "to make it on my own. I don't want a soul to thank" (283). Neither Wheeler nor Berry dismisses this attitude simplistically.

Elton has been on his own since he was a teenager. He is rightly wary of being made part of a succession seemingly engineered by Wheeler.[27] He represents the eros of the young, the drive for distinction. After all, one must *learn* to thank, to receive gratefully and gracefully. Something like this ability to learn to thank is what Old Jack has seen in Elton, an ability to learn that it is the farm finally that expects something from us. The true "succession" consists of those who understand the land as a gift entrusted to them for a little while only.

Analogous to the gift of the land is Wheeler's gift of friendship to Elton. Wheeler explains that he has become Elton's friend because Old Jack, the farm itself, and a host of unknown predecessors had wanted it to happen. This imaginative flight causes Elton to laugh, adding, "You're going to be my friend, it sounds pret' near like, because you can't get out it." When Wheeler responds that because Jack Beechum wanted it, he "can't get out of it," Elton comments, with considerable rightness, "Wheeler, that's pretty tough" (287). No one wants to be told that another has befriended him as a matter of duty. Elton wants to be liked for himself, befriended for who he is, not because Wheeler cannot escape what has come down to him from the past. Generational difference is again central to their differences in perspective. Fifty-three-year-old Wheeler has come to understand himself as part of a familial and communal history in a way that one twenty years younger simply cannot. Moreover, Wheeler's story has been part of a family story in a way quite unlike that of the early orphaned Elton. Wheeler's family has sent him to university and law school; Elton has made a crop himself every year since he was fourteen. The inside back cover of *That Distant Land* contains a genealogical chart of the interconnected families at the center of Berry's story of Port William—Feltners, Catletts, Coulters, Beechums, Wheelers. Elton Penn does not appear on the chart.

What resonates most with Elton is Wheeler's substituting the language of gift for that of debt in describing our relationship to the past. Elton is left in a nearly intolerable position: unable, as he says, to "repay" (287) either Old Jack or Wheeler. A weaker man, one less in love with the farm, might have walked away from it, not wanting to think of himself as forever in another's debt. But perhaps because of his love for the farm, for the work, and for Old Jack himself, Elton begins to understand that the history he has become part of consists of relationships that cannot be understood solely in terms of debt. He is in debt to Jack Beechum, and "it's *not* payable—not to him, anyhow" (287), Wheeler insists. Elton can only do what both he and Old Jack would have him do: work the farm carefully and well, live from what it gives, and pass it on to another who will do likewise. This is not a matter of price, of everyday accounting, or quid pro quo. "The life of a neighborhood is a gift" that cannot be sustained simply as a system of contractual relations. Once "the account is kept and the bill presented," friendship and neighborhood end, and "you're back to where you started. The starting point doesn't have anybody in it but you" (288). With no one to thank, one would become a thankless man. Fortunately for Elton, as he himself knows very well, Old Jack has not allowed him the choice to be thankless.

The second book of the Torah begins, "These are the names of the sons of Israel who came to Egypt with Jacob," and though Christians call this book Exodus, the Hebrew title, rendered into English, follows the opening phrase and is commonly shortened simply to Names.[28] It is a keeping of the names, a record of fidelity to a history, that makes Israel a people and culminates in the giving of the law. To keep Torah is to remember the names. That, too, is Wheeler Catlett's fidelity, to be, "through dark time and bad history," the "keeper of the names that bear hope of light to the human clearings, and an orderly handing down." Wheeler is a passionate "preserver and defender of the dead." "How, as a man of law," Berry asks, "could he have been otherwise, or less?"[29] In "The Wild Birds (1967)," this fidelity to law comes into conflict with another fidelity, that of love, and Wheeler must ultimately yield. Yet we see that love, too, seeks to preserve the names, doing so in ways that disrupt the all too orderly schemes of rightful succession we envision, often with the best of human wisdom.

The scene is again Wheeler's office, the issue again the passing of land. Nathan and Hannah Coulter have come with Nathan's uncle Burley, who asks Wheeler to make his will. What must be brought now into the light, into the clearing, is something Wheeler has suspected but has attempted to discount, both in his own mind and in the history of Port William's doings. "It has been a comfort to Wheeler to think that the Coulter Place, past Burley's death, would live on under that name" (349), passing first to Nathan and then to his boys. But now Burley names Danny Branch, son of Kate Helen Branch, his heir. At this point, Wheeler begins an argument he knows to be half doomed from the first, an argument he sincerely takes to be on behalf of the land, but that also springs from his fear. Burley's word "*wayward* . . . names the difference" they must "reckon with." Wheeler has not been one to "settle for things as they are" (345). As a lawyer, he has rightly been committed to considerations of order, regularity, and merit. Burley, on the other hand, has come into all that he is and has in wayward fashion. For him, talk about rightful succession often represents an after-the-fact patching together of justifications for what has happened without much thought or intention. "I know it seems wayward to you," he tells Wheeler. "But wayward is the way it is. And always has been. The way a place in this world is passed on in time is not regular or plain, Wheeler. It goes pretty close to accidental. But how else *could* it go? Neither a deed or a will, no writing at all, can tell you much about it" (344).

For Burley, what's at stake is a matter of honesty and love. He has come to Wheeler paradoxically out of respect for the regularity Wheeler represents: to make formal acknowledgment, in legal terms, of what has taken place and should have been acknowledged earlier. He seeks to give Danny and Kate Helen a "standing" that he has given them partly in his care for them, but that needs to be given wholly. Burley has been a "night hunter," but he recognizes, too, that "when you have rambled out of sight, you have got to come back into the clear and show yourself" (354). He quotes the psalmist to Wheeler, "Cleanse thou me from secret faults" (351), and as the conversation continues, it becomes clear that the fault has been the "secret love" (356) of Kate Helen, love that should have taken the open form of marriage. Burley has come to ask Wheeler, in effect, to be witness to his marriage to Kate Helen.

Burley, now seventy, also needs to "turn it loose" (351), something Wheeler, with perhaps less faith and more need for control, finds difficult. Burley's whole life has been a kind of turning loose. It's evident in the abandon with which he enters the woods. He's never lost because he's always present in the moment. His characteristic response to where he is, "right here," is the response of biblical faith from Abraham onward. He's always held his life loosely, knowing that the best of it has come to him through events beyond his control. He never really "took to" (350) farming like Jarrat or Nathan; he came home from service in 1919 without any firm intention to stay; he stayed to help his father in hard times and then to help Jarrat with his boys "after their mother died" (350) and later to help his mother after his father died. "Somehow or other along the way," he found that this was his life, and he began to stay because he "wanted to" (350). His experience leads Burley to perhaps the widest charity of any figure in Berry's fiction, spoken plainly to Wheeler: "I ain't saying we don't have to know what we ought to have been and ought to be, but we oughtn't to let that stand between us. That ain't the way we are. The way we are, we are members of each other. All of us. Everything. The difference ain't in who is a member and who is not, but in who knows it and who don't" (356). The history of love is there before us and for us; our role is to find our place in it. Burley's place is with Kate Helen and Danny.

Burley's place is also with Wheeler. His last move in the story surprises even Nathan and Hannah. He risks opening a gap in the membership for the sake of inviting Wheeler to be his brother. He begins by asking, "Wheeler, do you know why we've been friends?" (362). When Wheeler, puzzled, asks why, Burley responds, "Because we ain't brothers" (362). "If we'd been brothers," he continues, "you wouldn't have put up with me," but "as it was, [my doings] could be tolerable or even funny to you because they wasn't done close enough to you to matter" (362). But now in the question of Danny's succession to the Coulter place, Burley has pressed something on Wheeler that matters to him. It might not be too much to say that he has put himself and Wheeler in the kind of situation pondered in so many biblical stories of rival brothers—where each has enough at stake in the person of the other that they must either part forever or be one another's keepers. In short, Burley asks Wheeler not to tolerate him or find him amusing, but to love him. "I think you've got to forgive me as if I was a brother to you," Burley laughs, and then adds, "And I reckon I've got to forgive you for taking so long to do it" (363). Wheeler knows a "deep dividing valley has been stepped across" (363), perhaps the valley of the shadow of death itself that keeps each man in his own prison waiting for the key. Wheeler has been loosed by Burley's generosity, his faith—hard-won—that love can be trusted to run its improbable history. "Burley, it's all right," Wheeler says, and the older man responds, "Thank you, Wheeler. Shore it is" (363).

Just how "all right" things are is the subject of the last two stories of *That Distant Land*. The title of the first of these, "Fidelity (1977)," points to what makes them right. The word works in several interconnected contexts in the story. Danny's fidelity to Burley in rescuing him from anonymous death in the hospital is also an act of faithfulness to himself and to his history with his father. It allows Burley to die faithful to himself, to the life he has lived, and to the woods he has loved. Lyda, Hannah, and Nathan all recognize the rightness of Danny's action and do their parts to remain faithful to him and to Burley. Part of what moves them, of course, is that they recognize they have lost Burley—and that he is lost to himself—when they have allowed him to be put in the hospital, an act itself undertaken from a desire to be faithful to him. The hospital is a place of infidelities where one is stripped of one's identity and connections, where the language of treatment and cure seems utterly divorced from bodily realities, and where our society's desperate fear of death issues in the patient's too often becoming, as Wheeler puts it, "hostage to his own cure"—stripped in a few days not only of dignity but of a life savings he might well have wanted to pass on to another.[30] Kyle Bode, the young officer who comes to Port William to solve the "crime," is a study in infidelity, caused as much by a comprehensive bewilderment as anything else. Third child and second son of a farm-equipment dealer in Louisville, Kyle has spurned becoming part-ner with his brother in the dealership because he has "higher aims" and does "not want to spend his life dealing with farmers" (398). Uprooted and with little more sense of himself than the vague desire to be a "hero," he combines "lethargy" with a tendency to "sudden onsets of violence" de-signed to "drive back whatever circumstances his lethargy had allowed to close in on him." After marrying and joining the police, he experiences the "countercultural revolution," becoming sexually liberated—which leads to his wife's catching "him in the very inflorescence of ecstasy on the floor of the carport of a house where they were attending a party" (398). After she does not pursue a divorce, he decides she is "limiting his development" and "divorce[s] her in order to be free to be himself" (399).

Detective Bode comes close to being a caricature of the young man as fascist in the making. Ignorant of himself, lacking in any real fidelity, he believes himself devoted to the creation of order and to the law. Actually, he lacks any sense of the depth or complexity of human motives and even feels vaguely distressed by the fact that people continue to live in such hills and hollows as those around Port William. What seems to trouble him most about the "crime" is that Danny has acted without "authorization" (411), approval by superior power. Fortunately, Berry allows Bode a few minor moments of greater humanity, as when he cannot resist asking Mart Rowanberry—who has been telling a hunting story about Burley—whether the "Bet" he has mentioned was a dog. Bode "knew he was a fool" to ask, but "he wanted to know" (423). At the story's end, too, Bode is "not even sorry" when he "s[ees] his defeat" after Henry Catlett tells him to sit down. He feels only "small and lost, somewhere beyond the law" (427).

"Fidelity (1977)" closes with the Port William membership giving a spontaneous eulogy for Burley, offered in the form of stories. The gathered witnesses avoid or simply discount Detective Bode's questions, telling faithfully instead a history of Burley that evokes his presence and finally gives Bode no choice but to sit down, aware of his own irrelevance. Mart Rowanberry remembers how Burley often called him "out after bedtime to go with him" (422) into the woods and then tells how Burley came finally not to know him except when he did mention "old Bet," a blue tick he had owned years earlier. Wheeler Catlett speaks the longest and last, remembering Burley's wildness as a young man, his getting into trouble in the army for punching an officer who had called him "a stupid, briar-jumping Kentucky bastard," and his breaking his mother's heart. While Burley "never gave up his love of roaming about," Wheeler recognizes that he had done one of the things most difficult for us to do: he changed, becoming "a different man from the one he started out to be" (424). Fidelity in Burley was not a rigid commitment to an idea of himself, but rather a responsiveness to what was required of him, from moment to moment, by those he loved.

Wheeler is not sure "when that change began" in Burley, but he suggests it was after Jarrat's wife died and the boys, Tom and Nathan, "started following him around." Later Burley "took his proper part in raising" Danny, cared for his mother, and "was a good and loyal partner to" Jarrat. He acknowledged Danny, took Lyda and Danny to live with him, and "at last he fully honored his marriage in all but name to Kate Helen." "A true friend to all his friends," Burley was "a faithful man," one who knew how to take pleasure "in pleasurable things," one whose laughter will remain, one who "looked at the world and found it good" (424–25). Burley's own last words reflect the fidelity Wheeler has remarked. When Burley awakes a last time in the old barn, Danny asks him if he knows where he is. "Right here" (392) is, of course, the answer, as always from Burley, who is now, thanks to Danny's fidelity, back again present to the moment and the place in his characteristic way. He says only "drink" (392) after that when Danny asks what he wants: he thirsts, desiring and honoring to the last the great gift of life.

Fidelity, the rightful ownership of land, and right honoring between those in the membership are all central motifs of "The Inheritors (1986)," the closing story of *That Distant Land.* The central characters, Wheeler and Danny, are Burley's inheritors, and part of what they have inherited is each other. Danny and Wheeler have been together in honoring Burley in "Fidelity (1977)," and Wheeler, despite his earlier opposition, has come to see that Danny is the rightful inheritor of Burley's land. Danny is one of Wheeler's "last comforts" (433) as he enters old age, "when the darkness that surrounds all our life in this world beg[ins] to close in on him" (428). Danny "embodied much of the old integrity of country life that Wheeler had loved and stood for." He has no desire to expand his farm, despite the endless propaganda that he must do so or die; he does not covet anything of his neighbors; he and his wife, Lyda, "ate what they grew or what came, free for the effort, from the river and woods" (433). Clearly, they are the heirs of the old free life, satisfied with being right here, of Burley Coulter.

Danny works his farm with mules, and he is hauling a load of wood with his team when Wheeler drives up one fall morning to ask if he would like to go to Louisville, where Wheeler is selling some calves. The story simply follows their day together, culminating in Wheeler's indirect acknowledgment that Burley had been right earlier in his passing the land to Danny. Wheeler gestures his trust in Danny by asking him to drive, something he never asks of anyone, and Danny feels somewhat "odd" in having the older man take up "the passenger seat in his own car" (430). As Wheeler has come, in time, to rightly honor Danny, so Danny, too, rightly honors Wheeler, fellow inheritor not only of Burley's legacy but of the life of the whole membership of which they are parts. Danny watches Wheeler "with solicitude, interest, affection, amusement, and pride," aware of how his own elders have looked on this man who is now his friend. Danny knows that they are both "survivors and heirs of a membership going way back," one that now has more members "dead than living" and whose "living members" are "fewer than they [have] been in a hundred and fifty years" (432). It's become increasingly "wayward" simply to stick to the land and one's people, resisting much that passes for progress.

Wheeler's sale goes well, and after it, he is "feeling good" (432), expansive and delighted. He buys Danny's dinner and talks happily from his deep long-standing feeling, "as inward and powerful as lovesickness" (433), for the life of the fields, the animals, and the earth. As they leave Louisville, Wheeler returns to the driver's seat, announcing, "We'll just go home another way," and then proceeds to take Danny through a number of places he knows Wheeler cannot recognize because they are being developed and bear no resemblance to how they looked "only a short time ago" (434–35). Confident in his sense of direction, Wheeler continues on at "an ambling gait," happily remembering the past, "tak[ing] the world as it came" in a way "not always" his habit but worthy of Burley himself (435–36).[31] After turning on to an interstate highway, only to discover they are on the wrong side of the road, Wheeler drives home in the emergency lane, still in "his level mood, evidently enjoying himself" (437) as he waves at onrushing drivers blowing their horns or making obscene gestures in his direction. Burley's presence continues to be felt in the story, for Wheeler has now made his way home by a way that is "wayward," against the rushing tide that understands itself as the way things must be. As if to acknowledge this, and with the specific purpose of letting Danny know he has been wrong in his earlier judgment about him, Wheeler tells a story as they pass the farm of a former client of his.

The client, Mr. Buttermore, died as an old man with "no children," and Wheeler settled the estate. But a fellow named "Rowd Dawson contested the will," claiming to be "Mr. Buttermore's natural son" and citing as evidence the fact "his left eye was cocked at precisely the same angle as Mr. Buttermore's." Dawson's lawyer "had several witnesses" lined up "who were experts on the angles of cocked eyes," and Wheeler confesses his fear of going before a jury of farmers "every last one" of whom "believed in the inheritability of physical traits." Fortunately, Wheeler learned "just by chance, and nearly too late" that Dawson had, "as a young man," been "hit on the head with a beer bottle in a saloon fight," and he found "witnesses who swore that that lick was what had cocked his eye" (439). "So I won the case," Wheeler says. "But, you know, I've had to wonder" (440). That wonder springs, of course, from Wheeler's seeing that Burley has been right in passing on the Coulter place to Danny, the natural son whom Wheeler, in his passion for order and the law, sought to have denied. Acknowledging his wonder to Danny is Wheeler's way of honoring him as the rightful steward of the Coulter place. If Wheeler's been wrong about Rowd Dawson, as he could have been about Danny, then he may have lost the case he's won. One thing is certain: he's won the argument he thought he lost to Burley, which is maybe just a way of saying that between him and Burley winning wasn't "a very important idea."[32] What Wheeler's won is what Burley had all along: Danny Branch, and the right estimation of him as "a good one," a faithful inheritor of the Port William membership and the hard history of its love.

Chapter 5

Remembering the Names

Andy Catlett, Nathan Coulter, A World Lost, Remembering, and The Memory of Old Jack

During his visit to his Catlett grandparents shortly after Christmas in 1943, nine-year-old Andy Catlett spends part of a day with the men working in the tobacco barn. Gathered there are his grandfather Marce, now aged beyond most work; Dick Watson, the family's African American hand; the Brightleaf brothers, Jess and Rufus, tenant farmers working on shares; and another man, "officially" named Hackman but called behind his back "Old Man Hawk." All except this last man acknowledge Andy when he enters; all except Hawk participate in the banter and storytelling that is part of the work. With "a reputation for various acts of dishonesty and violence," Hawk prides himself, "when working," on "acknowledg[ing] the existence of nothing but work," a strategy Andy recognizes for what it is: Hawk's way of "pass[ing] his harsh judgment, his utter contempt in fact, upon other people by paying them no mind at all, as if a known chicken thief might regard the world from an exalted standpoint of indifference."[1] As Andy remembers the moment well over sixty years later, all the men "who were there" seem "to be gathered into a love that is at once a boy's and an aging man's" and also "into a love older and larger that is grieved, amused, grateful, and merciful." "Only Old Man Hawk," standing "alone on his own small dignity," seems not to belong. "He did not give a damn," Andy recalls of Hawk (72).

Andy retells his encounter with Hawk in *Andy Catlett: Early Travels*, which, appearing in 2006, is the most recently published of the five short novels considered in this chapter. I treat it here together with *Nathan Coulter, A World Lost, Remembering,* and *The Memory of Old Jack,* reserv-

ing the following chapter for Berry's three longest novels, *A Place on Earth,
Hannah Coulter,* and *Jayber Crow.* The way I've gathered the works for consideration is based first on Berry's identifying *Nathan Coulter, A World
Lost,* and *Remembering* as "short novels" by bringing them together in a
collection under that name. As *A Place on Earth* and *Jayber Crow* are obviously long novels, the two that present something of an organizational dilemma are *The Memory of Old Jack* and *Hannah Coulter.* I have grouped
Old Jack here with the short novels in part because it is somewhat shorter
than *Hannah,* but primarily because it shares their central concern with
memory. I consider *Hannah* together with the long novels because of the
determining influence on all three of war and the economy, especially after
1943, that year in which the world seems to have "broken in two" for Berry.[2]
The centrality of Virgil and Hannah's story in *Place* makes it appropriate to
treat together with *Hannah,* while the rich treatment of marriage in *Hannah*
is shared especially by *Jayber Crow.*

   Old Man Hawk defines one of the alternatives to which time, with its
losses, can bring us: to not give a damn anymore. Near the end of *Andy
Catlett,* Andy defines something like a counterresponse: "continuing in
gratitude for what is lost." "The great question for the old and the dying," he
has come to believe, "is not if they have loved and been loved enough, but
if they have been grateful enough for love received and given, however
much" (119–20). "No one who has gratitude is the onliest one," a phrase
Andy remembers from the "happy-sad" drinking songs of Maze Tickburn,
the self-described onliest stone mason in Port William (120).[3] The "onliest
one" is what Old Man Hawk has hardened himself into becoming; it is the
nearest anyone approaches to damnation in Berry's world.

   Andy Catlett is divided into two parts, the first devoted to Andy's visit
to his Catlett grandparents, the second to his stay, immediately following,
with his other grandparents, the Feltners. The two households represent
different worlds, as Berry suggests through the way Andy is met by his
grandfathers. Grandpa Catlett and Dick Watson meet Andy at the bus stop
in a wagon drawn by a pair of mare mules. Granddaddy Feltner—Marce
Catlett's junior by nineteen years—comes to pick up Andy in his car. The
"creaturely" world of the Catletts is a "sun-powered" one of "horse and mule
teams," whereas the Feltners have begun movement into "the petroleum-
powered world of cars and trucks and tractors." Looking back in memory,
"where hindsight" seems "strangely mixed with foreknowledge" (87), Andy

can "see doom clearly written upon the older world," though "the whole cost of that doom is still unpaid" (88). Andy has come to believe the "old world" to be the "true" one, the new one, based on "cheap energy and ever cheaper money," to be "mostly theater" (93).

The year 1943 is also Andy's "last year of innocence, of the illusion of permanence and peace." Shortly before his tenth birthday, in 1944, his uncle Andrew is "shot and killed," an event that inaugurates a "series of deaths and losses" that "change the world" as Andy has known it and also change him. As he writes the memoir of his travels, Andy alone is "still alive" of all those he remembers "from those days in Port William" (118). He now is "the onliest one" (118), remembering, as he must, "the ancestry of [his] mind" (28) and those whose actions and interactions formed "the net" that "has gathered [him] up and kept [him] alive until now" (77). The novel seems somewhat more the story of the Catletts than of the Feltners, perhaps because Berry has treated the Feltners so much more fully elsewhere. But perhaps this is also because Andy's "heart was given more finally than [he] knew to the creaturely world of Grandpa Catlett" (87) and because that world has been quite insufficiently honored by the "world of pavement, speed, and universal dissatisfaction" that within a few years "extended itself into nearly every place and nearly every mind" (18).

Among those whom Andy remembers from the Catlett place are Dick Watson and the woman with whom he lives, known to Andy as Aunt Sarah Jane.[4] Andy's memories of them are noteworthy both for their very personal treatment of racial matters and for their suggestions about the task and limits of fiction. Andy loved Dick, with a love "the years have not diminished" and that, at least as Andy recalls it, was not "affected at all by considerations of race" (24). To Andy, Dick "was merely himself," and "perhaps," Andy thinks, acknowledging the gap between them, "in his affection for me, I was merely myself" (24). Now, as the mature Andy knows, it is impossible to think "of that long gone aging couple and their household" without thinking of "the history of racism," itself difficult to think about accurately for those so deeply implicated in it. What Andy does believe with some conviction is that now "the two races are more divided than ever" and that the "history has acquired a conventional oversimplification, implying that what we came to call 'segregation' was a highly generalized circumstance in which the two races disliked or hated each other, and which assured the happiness of one race and the misery of the other" (26).

It being one of the tasks of fiction to remember accurately, even at the risk of offending both "current political etiquette" and "the racism to which it is opposed," Andy says, perhaps not so simply, that "in and in spite of the old racial arrangement into which we both were born, I loved Dick Watson, and he treated me with affection and with perfect and unfailing kindness" (26).

This is not to say that the child Andy was unaware of what he might now understand as an adult to be bitterness in Dick. Andy remembers hearing Dick, "one time, ventriloquize rather bitterly a dialogue between 'Sambo' and 'Massa.'" For Andy this was mostly an occasion for "puzzlement," particularly since his only association for "Sambo" was with "little black Sambo," whom he "regarded as a sort of hero," and he had never heard the word "Massa" before. But Andy knows, at the time, both from "Dick's tone" and from "Aunt Sarah Jane's wish to hush him," that there is something in Dick's mimicry that ought to make him, Andy, "properly disturbed" (27). Andy's "first preceptor" in matters of race, Aunt Sarah Jane spoke often "of the rights that her people had been promised but had never been given." She made Andy "feel responsible," though he could do this but "vaguely," for he "could not precisely locate" within himself "the cause" of any "injury" to her or Dick (75). Andy now looks back with gratitude on his conversations with Aunt Sarah Jane, for he recognizes that the "fester" she introduced "into the conscience of a small boy" (76) has become the starting point for his mature sense that "the old structure of racism" was a "malevolent convention," though one whose malevolence was "hard to locate in the conscious intentions of most people." It was an "inexcusable" violation of justice, "accommodated and varyingly obscured not only by daily custom, but also by the exigencies and preoccupations of daily life" (75). It was one of those "abominations" to which a "customary indifference" silently assents and from which it is so difficult to break. "We were used to it," Andy says simply, and "what is hardest to get used to maybe, once you are aware, is the range of things humans are able to get used to. I was more used to this once than I am now" (76).

Andy knows that Dick Watson "must have had" bitter moments beyond that of the "Sambo" and "Massa" story. But in order to be true to Dick Watson as he has known him, Andy insists he "did not know him as a bitter man," but as one "who had achieved an authentic gentleness" (27). Though Grandpa Catlett's life was largely one of struggling to hold on to what he

had, and Dick's was one of "not-having" (25), both men were "born farmers, utterly reconciled to the demands of weather and work," living lives
nearly "unimaginable" to most people today. They were alike in living and
dying in a "society that depreciated their work, took it for granted, and increasingly held them and others like them in contempt for doing it" (28).
As he lies dying of stroke, Dick looks at Grandma Catlett as if he "had
something he longed to say, but he could not speak." Dorie Catlett has
passed that story on to Andy, and it has stayed in his memory, even as Dick
seems otherwise to have been forgotten. Dick's grave in the "colored graveyard" has had a "metal marker" for some years, but that has "finally rusted
away," and those who knew him have died. "Now nobody knows" the grave
site, and perhaps no one but Andy knows any of Dick Watson's story (25).

One in similar danger of being forgotten is Tom Coulter, who has, at
the time of Andy's travels, already died while serving in Europe. When the
Brightleaf brothers speak of Tom's death as they work in the tobacco barn,
Andy has the sense that Tom's name "enter[ed] the day like a bell stroke"
(46), perhaps the one John Donne said tolled for all of us. The Brightleafs
speak Tom's name as if "with the awareness that now his name would be
spoken less and less until it would be spoken no more, for they were silent
again afterwards" (46). As in the case of Dick Watson, Tom's name is in
danger of being lost unless one remembers, and it is Andy's task as a fiction
writer to remember, to be keeper of the names. It is a complex task, one
never finished, never accomplished in even remotely satisfactory fashion.
Just how difficult it is Andy suggests through a memory of looking with
Grandma Catlett at her "keepsakes," "pictures and cards" of kinsfolk and
others bearing names "that brought forth stories" (82). One who "felt keenly" the "lostness of Paradise" as "the prime fact of her world" (37), Grandma
Catlett is a "faithful keeper" of "memories." She and Andy speak "of the
absent and the dead," and their talk takes on "the charm of distance and
history almost like the stories of King Arthur" that Andy has been reading
during his visit. "But this was *our* history and these were *our* people," Andy
recalls, and "their names and stories and pictures had a worth to us that
was timely and bodily and never to be put in a book" (83). Yet Andy/Berry
has spent more than forty years putting the names and stories of his people
into books, trying to do so in ways that represent them in as "timely and
bodily" a fashion as possible. Doing so is always a work, in some ways,

failed, for those particular lives can "never" really be "put in a book," but for those like Andy called to it, it is the necessary enactment of gratitude, a way to escape becoming the "onliest one" (120).

Near the end of his memoir, Andy thinks of time in a manner reminiscent of St. Augustine: "Time is only the past and maybe the future; the present moment, dividing and connecting them, is eternal." Time disappears into the past, which "is there, somewhat, but only somewhat, to be remembered and examined." We "believe" in the future, "for it keeps arriving, though we know nothing about it," since it is no longer future when it arrives and past even as we bring it to consciousness. Since we cannot arrest the present, it "exists, so far as [Andy] can tell," only "as a leak in time, through which, if we are quiet enough, eternity falls upon us and makes its claim." To the extent that we can "hold and redeem" time, we do so by telling it as a story of life and death, of love that "is always present." Time "is told by love's losses, and by the coming of love, and by love continuing in gratitude for what is lost" (119).[5] It would be difficult to characterize any more accurately the overarching conception of the four short novels that I turn to now.

Nathan Coulter focuses on its title character's coming of age, a process marked by the early death of his mother, a violent break with his brother Tom, the even more violent break between his father and brother, and finally the death of his grandfather. The hard wisdom Nathan comes to can be summarized in two propositions: that we suffer because of who we are and that loss is real and permanent. For a child, the loss of a beloved other can be tantamount to losing a world, as is suggested by the title of *A World Lost*, Andy's account of his attempts to make sense of the murder of his uncle Andrew. Occurring when Andy is nine and knowing "exactly where" he is, the crime places him suddenly in another world.[6] Lacking those adult commonplaces by which we distance ourselves from death, Andy must narrate his feelings in order to restore some kind of wholeness to Uncle Andrew and the world they once inhabited together. As he seeks to fathom the manner of man his uncle was and the reasons for his shooting, Andy comes to understand how the complex art of truth-telling amid uncertainty requires commitments to charity as well as knowledge. *Remembering* tells the story of Andy's losing his own adult world and finding it again. After losing his hand in a farm accident, Andy suffers in exile from all that has made him who he is. While remaining incognito in San Francisco, where he is supposed to speak at a college, Andy begins the return to himself, a return moved by his response to others in the streets and to the beauty of the world. Andy's return to himself, and ultimately to Kentucky, involves his remembering the patterns of leave-taking and return that have marked the lives of both his grandfather Feltner and his own father. Similarly, Andy has made his own earlier return after leaving journalistic work for *Scientific Farming* in order to farm among his family and neighbors. The novel ends with Andy re-membered, reconciled with Flora and caring for their children and farm, aware at last, through a dream, of the goodness of the way others have left for him.

The Memory of Old Jack is the story of one who has lost nearly everything yet gained it again by living it deeply and well. Although this novel displays less self-reflexive concern with narrative as an art of memory than *A World Lost* or *Remembering*, it could be regarded as Berry's fullest treatment of memory, thus my placing it last here. On the last day of his life, Jack Beechum has become nearly wholly his memory. Jack's recent memory is uncertain, but his longer-term recollections come to him in a kind of order that has established itself over the years. Much of Jack's life could be regarded a failure: his marriage has been unhappy; he and his wife have lost their first child, a son; his relationship to his second child, a daughter, is strained at best; an attempt to expand his farm has ended in failure and five brutally hard years of work to pay for it; an affair with a woman who does truly love him as he is cannot take the form it should have, leaving him a grief that only the grave will heal.[7] Yet Jack is passionately committed to his farm, and through long years of labor he comes finally to an abiding peace as the true husband of the land. He is a friend to many, particularly Mat Feltner, and is respected, at the last, by all. He finds a rightful inheritor in Elton Penn and dies at peace, having given his blessing to Andy and Mat and Hannah and her baby. He has staked his life, passionately, in everything he's done, and at the end, he finds it enough.

Nathan Coulter tells three stories. One involves the history of a family over three generations as it becomes established in the land; a second concerns the differentiation of brothers over two of those generations; and a third relates the coming-of-age of its narrator, Nathan. This is patriarchal history. Dave Coulter dominates his wife; Nathan's mother becomes ill after his birth and dies when her sons are still young boys; the other most promi-

nent women in the story are either carnival freaks or memories. My point
is not to criticize Berry for being inadequately sensitive or feminist. This is
hard history. Dave Coulter and his son Jarrat are difficult men because the
work they must do is hard. Making a place on earth exacts a price: in labor,
in time, in life. That truth must be acknowledged and met, day by day. It
wears one down in the daily death of physical labor. The work depends, for
some, on the disciplined channeling of outrage, the learned process of directing one's anger into effort to make the world habitable. But that rage
can also break out, into cruelty or destructive rivalry, unless it can be
checked by humor. These are particularly masculine themes perhaps, but
the novel also implicitly regrets the loss of the feminine voice, which, in the
Coulters' world, is either muted or driven heavenward. Berry suggests how
the life-denying, otherworldly Christianity he often deplores can develop
from the simple desire for a place free from what bears us down on earth.

"The first thing anybody remembered about our family," Nathan tells
us, concerns a woman, his aunt Mary, youngest daughter of his great-great-
great-grandfather Jonas Thomasson Coulter.[8] Just about the time she "was
grown" (7), Jonas Coulter and his neighbor Jeff Ellis quarreled about the
placement of the fence line dividing their properties. When Mary died of
scarlet fever, her father "dug a grave where he thought the fence ought to
run, and he made the rest of the family bury her in it." Fearful of ghosts,
Ellis had the fence built ten feet his side of the grave, making "Jonas's farm
ten feet wider than even he thought it should have been." Aunt Mary's grave
has never been moved nor even properly marked or tended. No one "even
put flowers" on it (8). Her ghost is left to roam.

If Aunt Mary's grave suggests one kind of inappropriate relationship to
the place, the huge Coulter family monument suggests another—perhaps
compensatory—inappropriateness. It sits at the top of a rise, "jutting up
even taller than most of the cedars" (17), hoisting an angel up on a tall shaft
from a square base, all of granite. Purchased by Grandpa's mother "from a
traveling salesman when she was old and childish"—though perhaps not
nearly so "crazy" as he believes—this pointer to a heavenly life far above the
earth has cost Grandpa at least five years of work beyond her death (17). Its
base is so heavy that it required the work of "twenty mules" to pull it from
the railroad station seven miles away. Perhaps Grandpa's mother has ex-
acted a kind of revenge, or at least a tribute, in effectively commandeering
so much human and animal labor. Or perhaps she has simply wanted to

remind her son, the only child left on the place, of how much his life has been dependent on her expenditure of life and time. This seems the intent of the monument's engraving, recording the dates of Father and Mother on its front, but also including on the other side the name and birthdate of Nathan's Grandpa, "THEIR SON, *David Coulter,* 1860–." Grandpa "still got mad every time he thought about" this: "it was as if she'd expected him to write his other date up there and die right away to balance things" (17). What rankles Grandpa is the thought of mortality, limitation. Crazy or not, Grandpa's mother will not be like Aunt Mary, cast into a shallow grave by order of a man so angry at death as to leave his daughter's burial to others.

"Blessed are they that mourn: for they shall be comforted," Jesus says in one of the Matthean beatitudes.[9] To fail or be unable to mourn ensures only that one will never be comforted. Yet when Nathan and Tom's mother dies, their grandma tells them specifically "not to grieve," for she "was in Heaven with all the angels, and she was happy there and never would have to suffer any more" (31). "Oh, it's a pretty place up there, boys" (31), she adds, as if to suggest the contrast with this place on earth. The language of "pretti-ness" and of a place so "far away that you couldn't think about it" (34) is unlikely to have much purchase in a man like Jarrat who must have his place in mind all day long. Jarrat drives his grief into work and seems nev-er to find comfort. When his wife dies, Tom and Nathan go to live with their grandparents and Uncle Burley. Soon after her death, Jarrat goes to chopping wood, enclosing himself within work, not looking at anybody. People who come to express their sorrow must turn "away from him" be-cause "the look of him didn't allow it" (27). Jarrat responds to his loss and guilt with unrelenting effort, not only on this day but for the remainder of his life. We might read this as a refusal of comfort on his part, but I believe a more charitable reading would stress the failure of the available religious language—with its prettified images of heaven—to reach into Jarrat's soul.

Jarrat's grief—both honorable and futile—drives the powerful struggle against the fire that destroys his barn. Nathan has been with Burley, Big Ellis, and Jig Pendleton drinking at Burley's place down on the river when lightning strikes the barn. They run to help and assist in fighting the fire all night, saving the outbuildings, though not the main structure. Nathan sees his father go toward the blaze again and again, "without looking back or asking us to go with him, and without any hope, but going anyway." Jarrat wets his clothes in order to get closer to the blaze. He takes the buckets from the passers and throws the water furiously, "as if he were trying to bruise it." His main ally in the fight is Grandpa. He and Daddy, Nathan comments, "kept us going. They hated the fire and they had to fight it, and none of us would leave them to fight it alone" (66). Jarrat and his father exhibit a determined resistance to all that bears us down, to that which brings all human effort finally to dust and ashes. It seems impossible not to admire their courage or to acknowledge that such fury when controlled can lead to making the earth more habitable. But for Berry, such resistance alone is not enough.

The alternative to Grandpa and Jarrat is Nathan's uncle Burley, who "didn't own any land at all" or much of anything except "his dogs and a couple of guns" (6) and a camp house down by the river that nobody else wanted. Burley's father considers him a disgrace because he refuses to own a farm. His mother frets over his sinfulness. After serving in World War I, he returns to Port William without any particular plan to stay, but after the death of Jarrat's wife, he takes on an important role in rearing Tom and, especially, Nathan. Burley serves as Nathan's guide to the life that takes place around the edges of Port William. He leads the boys on an excursion to a Fourth of July carnival, where he shows at least as much imagination as the professionals in setting up an unwinnable game. Burley's involves players' throwing rings over ducks swimming in a barrel. This seems easy until the ducks "duck" under the water each time they see a ring approaching. The game goes well for Burley until the ducks tire, at which time his earlier marks return to recapture their losses. Finally he manages to break even only by shooting the ducks with a rifle from the shooting gallery next door. As in most American stories about swindles and confidence games, there's a rough lesson in justice here: what's easily come by is just as easily lost.

Nathan learns a more complex lesson in justice at the carnival. In order to have five dollars apiece for the carnival, he and Tom have worked for a week cleaning a fence row for Big Ellis. The one thing Nathan wants to do at the carnival is ride the Ferris wheel, but he goes along with his brother when Tom wants to see "BUBBLES: BEWITCHING ENCHANTRESS OF THE FAR EAST" (46). Nathan spends fifty cents to enter, then gets lured into losing a dollar in a pick-the-card game before the main attraction begins. After Bubbles's initial bump and grind, Nathan and the others learn they must pay an additional fifty cents to see the full "secrets of the mysterious East" (49). They all stay, though when Bubbles begins again, Nathan keeps his head "turned away" from the two others he knows there, the Montgomery twins, "so they wouldn't recognize" him—perhaps as ashamed of himself as fearful of being seen. Nathan comes away feeling only "sorry for her then, standing there without her clothes in front of a crowd of men who'd paid a dollar to look at her. It was a cheap thing, and she couldn't grin enough to change it" (49). Later Nathan pays a quarter to have his fortune told, then finds he's had another two dollars stolen by the fortune-teller. The last of his money goes to cover bets Tom has made on a sure thing in a wheel game. "We never did get to the Ferris wheel," Nathan remarks, and "I didn't mind that either. I guessed that if we'd paid the dime or quarter or whatever it cost to get on, somebody would have made us pay a dollar to get off"(52). Nathan has learned something very important for his five dollars: that the world is filled with the cheap and deceptive and that exchanging hard work for these is a bad trade.

Nathan and Burley inadvertently add to the cheap themselves after they catch a huge catfish on Burley's trotline. Thinking to have a fish fry, they take the fish to Beriah Easterly's store to put it on ice. Soon the fish attracts a crowd, and Nathan has the sense that Beriah is turning "the fish and uncle Burley and me into some sort of freak show" (80). The experience is further cheapened when Big Ellis comes by with his brother-in-law J. D. and another man from Louisville, William, who are taking their vacation in Port William. J. D. is from town but has not returned for thirty years; no one really remembers him, and yet he talks on and on about his experience. William, not wanting to be outdone, tries to bait the crowd into a debate over the comparative sizes of river and ocean fish. When he fails to get attention, he declares, "I'll show you all how to catch fish" (85), disappears briefly, and returns with a half stick of dynamite—which he then lights and throws into the river, bringing dead fish to the top. Later the game warden arrives, suspicious that Burley has done the dynamiting. When the man refuses to believe that Burley only fishes "for fun," Burley rows him and Nathan to the middle of the river, lights the other half of the stick of dynamite (which William has left behind), and drops "it under the game warden's feet" (87). Looking at Burley in disbelief, the warden throws the dynamite into the river, bringing, by Burley's estimation, about fifty pounds of fish to the top—which Burley then offers him for ten cents a pound. They collect the fish for the warden, and he pays them his last three dollars before driving off. "It's a shame we had to mistreat him," Burley says, and Nathan realizes they've spoiled the experience by getting "all wound up together" (88) with people who did not care about the great catfish, or fishing, or the river. "It takes the pleasure out of fishing" (88), Nathan remarks, pleasure that must be in the fishing itself or in the free life of the river. As they pass Beriah's store, they see "that Beriah had hung our fish outside the door so everybody could see it." One of the men asks Burley if it's his fish, and he says only, "It's Beriah's fish" (88). Burley, who owns next to nothing, has made the mistake of trying to own the fish. He and Nathan have dishonored it—as Bubbles is dishonored—by exposing its own loveliness to an utterly alien kind of valuation, the cheap fascination of those who do not care.

Commenting on their part in spoiling the fishing, Burley says to Nathan, "Well, let's go home. We've stayed a day too long already." Being a day behind, or ahead, of himself in this way is rare for Burley, whose way of taking life is to be right where he is at all times. Even when engaged in the very disorienting following of a hound, he is never lost in the woods. When others ask him where he is, his standard reply is, "I'm right here." "Here I am" is the characteristic response to the Lord's voice of biblical faith, and for Burley, knowing where he is similarly involves a kind of faith response, one that affirms his being present to what is going on in a particular place and at a particular moment. Like Thoreau, he seeks to live in the very "nick of time," at the intersection of the moment and eternity, persuaded that every instant is the acceptable time. This is not an easy faith. Burley knows life's hardness. In *A Place on Earth,* he remarks that "we've all got to go through enough to kill us."[10] When Nathan realizes that Tom has left for good after the fight with their father—and that all of us suffer inescapably because we are "ourselves"—Burley responds, "It's bad. . . . It's bad. . . . We're going to have a fair night. Let's you and me hunt a while" (104). This is not said to diminish the force of Nathan's recognition, but rather simply to say that suffering, while pervasive, is not the whole of life. One needs to develop a steady way of dealing with that suffering, and a fair night, the woods, and hunting can provide an important part of that way.

Nothing is more important to Burley's way of taking things than his sense of wonder and his rough, generous humor. Others frequently remark the way Burley enters the woods with an abandon that signifies his delight in living in a world much larger than his notions of it. He is able to be surprised, as when he looks in awe at his and Kate Helen Branch's baby "smiling in its sleep." "Look at him," Burley tells Nathan. "He's seeing the angels. . . . Well I'll swear" (40). He can joke about Judgment Day and the granite angel atop Parthenia Coulter's tomb "flying up out of the smoke and cinders and tearing out for Heaven like a chicken out of a henhouse fire" (18). Yet he entertains also a more serious feeling for the eschatological and, with it, a profounder humor. When Nathan, thinking of his mother's death, asks, "Uncle Burley, . . . it's a bad thing to be dead, ain't it?" Burley offers no easy consolation or forgettable adult platitude. Instead he replies, "Well, this world and one more and then the fireworks" (40).

Burley cares not one whit, however, about separating out sheep from goats. On the way to the carnival, he offers a preacher traveling afoot a lift in his wagon. The man begins "to talk about unbelievers and the sin of the world, and who was going to Hell and who wasn't." Burley tries to hide his aggravation while the man says "the Lord had appointed him to be a witness" to "all the people he met." When Burley rolls a cigarette, the witness proclaims, "A cigarette is as much of an abomination in the sight of the Lord as a bottle of whiskey." Burley lets this pass, then lights up, prompting the preacher to say, "If the Lord had wanted you to smoke He'd have give you a smokestack, brother." This is too much. Burley stops the team and, looking at the preacher, replies, "If He'd wanted you to ride, you'd have wheels. . . . Now you get off" (43).

Another passage about tobacco suggests the kind of preacher Burley can respect, his friend Jig Pendleton. When Burley remarks that Nathan and he are about to "start stripping tobacco the first of the week," Jig remembers, "Tobacco . . . I used to raise tobacco once. But I quit. I was plowing one morning, and the Lord said, 'Jig, how'd you like for your daughter to smoke?' And I said, 'I wouldn't like it, Lord. It's a sin for a woman to smoke.' And I unhitched the mule right there in the middle of the row, and I left" (100). No talk here of the mote that is in another's eye, just simple recognition of the log that has been in Jig's own. Jig has a deep sense of sin, one that will perhaps sound excessive to the postmodern ears of a culture of therapy. But his concern for sin is primarily directed at himself, and he has a sense of human solidarity in sin. When he arrives at the burning barn, he stops and points at the fire: "That's what it's like. . . . The fire of Hell, my brothers in sin" (65). But he immediately goes to helping his brothers put it out: "He grabbed the pump handle and began pumping" (65). Jig has as well a lovely, and entirely Christian, feeling for creation. He loves to fish, can tell "mellow-ripe" whiskey from the raw kind, and remembers Isaiah's wonderful image of the people as grass. He asks Burley why the Lord "made the stars," and when Burley says he doesn't know, Jig replies, "He liked to hear them sing" (100). When two mules come up to the trough after he and the others have fought the fire, Jig "[gets] up and pump[s] water for them," saying, "Bless you, God's creatures" (67).

Jig's language seems more often eschatological than Burley's, but Burley, too, is capable of imagining an end. Jarrat and Grandpa, however, inhabit almost wholly the world of everyday time in its passing. Nathan's experience is one of generational passing. The novel's last image is of him gathering the body of his just dead Grandpa into his arms and carrying him home.[11] Grandpa's "life couldn't be divided from the days he'd spent at work in his fields" (117): whatever judgment he'd have acknowledged would be of the good or damage he'd created together with the place. Time's passing brings the estrangement of Nathan and Tom, accelerated by Tom's beginning to "court" and imagining a life of his own away from his father and brother. A seemingly unhealable break between them occurs after Nathan has spied on Tom and his girlfriend necking on a hillside. When the brothers encounter one another later that night, Nathan feels the need to acknowledge what he has done, to be on honest terms with Tom. But when Nathan says he "saw" Tom with "that girl," Tom strikes him "square in the face." They "quit being brothers," and Nathan acknowledges that "it was my fault" (70).

The break between Tom and his father is even more violent. It occurs as Jarrat and his sons, along with Burley, Grandpa, and Gander Loyd, cut tobacco. Jarrat begins, as he has in the past, to tease the boys into racing him at cutting the rows. His voice contains that mixture of challenge and belittlement that marks the father's prideful distancing from the son: "The boy may be coming. But the old man's going. Right out in front where he always is. Nobody been to the end of the row ahead of him. And damn few can get there very soon afterwards" (94). Nathan seems to understand that in the struggle Jarrat is affirming his immortality: in relation to the son, he will always be first, always be ahead. "The strain of it suited Daddy," Nathan comments. "He was happy in it, as if he'd just made the world over to suit himself, feeling the demand on his strength and endurance close to him, and feeling himself good enough" (94). Jarrat seeks to be equal to the task, good enough for anything the Lord sends his way, free of all need and dependence.

Tom hears Jarrat's taunts as they are meant, as insistence that the son will never be good enough to surpass the father, to merit what the father has done for him in preparing the way by giving the life and time that are uniquely his and for which he can never be compensated—at least according to the world's economy. Tom presses in his work and, in doing so, makes mistakes, slowing him down. Jarrat's taunts take on more edge: "These little boys just barely weaned come out and try the old man. And they want to put it on him so bad, and they work at it so hard. But they just can't quite make it" (95). At this point, Tom goes for Jarrat, and they "come together" with a "thump of bone and muscle that sounded as if they'd already half killed each other." As they fight, Tom curses, "nearly crying, he was so mad and hurt over losing" (95), while Jarrat laughs. The end brings humiliation for Tom, as his father straddles him, "slapping him in the face" and laughing. When Burley manages to pull him off, Jarrat says to Tom, "You God-damned baby," and Tom replies, "Go to hell." Nathan puts the meaning of the fight for Tom in a particularly striking and incisive way: "Brother had been beaten and insulted until it would be a long time before he'd know what to think of himself" (96). One thing is certain: Tom must leave, and he does so that night.[12]

Nathan feels "sorry for both" (96) his father and his brother. The fight contributes to his sense that we suffer because we are the way we are. Suffering seems part of the structure of experience, an inevitable consequence of the tension between our need and drive to exist as individuals and our relatedness to others. For Nathan, as for many characters in Berry's fiction, suffering is bound up with life in the mystery of time. Some months after the fight, Burley and Nathan encounter Tom and learn that he is getting on well. That night they tell Jarrat what they've learned as he finishes his supper. When Nathan concludes by saying, "He's not mad at you anymore," his father cries, silently looking down at his plate. "I could have cried myself," Nathan remarks. "Brother was gone, and he wouldn't be back. And things that had been so before never would be so again" (103). Here Nathan echoes what his grandmother has said to Tom and him after their mother's death: "Oh, Lord, boys, you never will see her any more" (31). Speaking from the experience of long years, she knows what that statement means in a way impossible to them. By the end of *Nathan Coulter,* Nathan has begun to understand a little of what she meant.

Just how radically the death of another can alter a child's world is suggested by the title of *A World Lost,* narrated by Andy Catlett. The novel's donnée is the murder, under ambiguous circumstances, of Andy's namesake, his uncle Andrew. Not only does Uncle Andrew lose his world, but Andy loses the only world he has ever known, one with his uncle in it. The novel suggests how the loss of a beloved other—perhaps particularly for a child— can become a motive for narration. Andy narrates the story of his uncle's life and the details of his killing in order to reassemble something of a world lost. The importance of story emerges, too, as a motif within Andy's tale, as his uncle has largely been without a story sufficiently coherent and powerful to allow him to "transform fate into destiny," to borrow a phrase from Stanley Hauerwas.[13] Particularly moving is Andy's coming to understand that his grief, while deep and authentic, is nothing like that of his father, Wheeler, who is Uncle Andrew's brother, or that of his Catlett grandparents. The final section of the novel focuses on Andy's attempt to sort through the varying accounts of the crime in order to understand both what happened and what "manner of man" (325) his uncle was. The process of delving into the crime and attempting to tell his uncle's story leads Andy to recognize the limits of his own understanding. What little we can see, he concludes, is rather a matter of love finally than knowledge.

Andy was visiting his Catlett grandparents when his uncle died on a July day in 1944. He had wanted to accompany Uncle Andrew to Stoneport on the river, where his uncle and several other men had gone to take down the buildings of a former lead mine in order to get building materials, made scarce by the war. Uncle Andrew, who routinely took Andy with him to work on the farms he managed for Wheeler, had refused—properly so, as Andy later recognizes, for the work was hard and dangerous. Andy's account of that day centers on his going swimming alone in the pond on his grandparents' farm—something he was "absolutely forbidden" (230) by his mother to do. As he recounts the day, the mature Andy sees in this transgression an attempt to "maintain for at least a while the illusion that I was no more than myself, Andy Catlett, as ancestorless as the first creature, neither the son of Bess and Wheeler Catlett nor the grandson of Dorie and Marce Catlett and Mat and Margaret Feltner" (230). In a moment reminiscent of Melville, the storyless Andy has a sense of his own absence, his absorption into the all, as he floats on his back: "The sky was huge, the world almost nothing at all, and I apparently absent altogether" (230).[14] The absolute freedom from constraint by connection or history can mean the blotting out of self by the all, by fate, but the young Andy senses nothing threatening in his utter self-sufficiency: "I was nine years old, going on ten; having never needed to ask, I knew exactly where I was; I did not want to be anyplace else" (231).

Andy's uncle's death leaves him aware of the difference between where he is and where he was, where he is now and where he wants to be. This difference becomes, in a way perhaps unrecognized even by him, the motive for narration. As the adult Andy remembers, with understandable difficulty, what he felt as a nine-year-old, he thinks that he "did not grieve in the knowing and somewhat theoretical way of grown people, who say to themselves, for example, that a death of some sort awaits us all." Because he "had no way of generalizing or conceptualizing [his] feelings," they had to be narrated (241). He is aware of one occasion on which he tried to "enlarge" himself in the eyes of a girl by "attaching to [himself] the tragedy that had befallen [his] family." When she is silent, a "fierce shame" comes "upon [him] that did not wear away for years" (242). He has tried to use his uncle's death to garner pity or attention for himself. He has violated, in a way, the integrity of his uncle's death while failing to see, too, that he is no more distinguished in being touched by death than anyone else. This is not the way to speak of his uncle or of his own grief. He must tell his uncle's story—including its intersection with his own—in as nearly disinterested a fashion as possible. Lacking those adult commonplaces about death, Andy thinks that his "loss must have been beyond summary." It was "exactly commensurate" with what he had lost, "Uncle Andrew as [he] had known him." The adult Andy knows too much to be certain whether he came to understand as a nine-year-old that he "would not be able ever again to think of" the world "as a known world." But in re-creating his history, he speculates that this was the case. It is as if Andy's world divides into one before Uncle Andrew's death, and one after. The world before was whole, intact, fully understandable, the one after incomplete, broken, knowable "only in part." Having "lost what [he] remembered," Andy seeks to "remember" what he has lost, both by restoring wholeness to his Uncle Andrew and by bringing him back into the membership of the living (242).

One of Uncle Andrew's buddies, Yeager Stump, said of their adventures, "We did everything we thought of. . . . Our only limit was our imagination" (258). Andy comes to doubt whether this is precisely true, but it certainly catches many of the features of Uncle Andrew's personality: his impulsiveness, lack of restraint, exuberant energy. Andrew loves women, and his taste runs, as Andy puts it, "to the available" (295). He is charming, often jazzy in his slang, immensely creative in his humor. He loves to dance and is remembered for his dancing. One friend recalls that he had seen Andrew too drunk to walk but never to dance. Uncle Andrew spent a brief time at the University of Kentucky, and when Andy attends there forty years later, he finds that some local memory of his uncle persists. Frequently, when Andy does his banking in Lexington, one of the women salesclerks will remark, "I knew an Andrew Catlett once. . . . He was *such* a dancer!" "They always spoke of him as a dancer," Andy recalls. "They always smiled in remembering him," and they "always sounded younger than they were, and a little dreamy" (293). Andy himself has loved his uncle, loved being with him, particularly on those days when they have worked Wheeler's farms together. Uncle Andrew has been Andy's buddy, as well as his namesake, and, for a time, even a fantasized father figure. At school Andy takes to signing his name "Andrew Catlett, Jr.," and he sometimes thinks it "unfair" that he is not his uncle's son. "I wanted to be a man just like him," Andy recalls (248).

As Andy tells his uncle's life, he comes to see that Uncle Andrew's expressions of freedom were almost exclusively temporary escapes from a fate that he could not change. Much of that fate came in the form of Aunt Judith, who herself came along with her mother, Momma-pie. Regarding themselves "would-be aristocracy of the Hargrave upper crust," both women exhibit a "self-centeredness" that manifests in "constant appeal to others to fulfill" their "unfulfillable needs." Aunt Judith's is a "hopeless emotional economy" in which the demand for pity and affection "always outran the available supply" (256). Wheeler Catlett puzzles for much of his life over "why Uncle Andrew married Aunt Judith," concluding only that Momma-pie must have set some sort of "mantrap" for him. A story Andy hears "after [he] had grown up" suggests "at least that Uncle Andrew was not an ecstatic bridegroom." "On the night before his wedding Uncle Andrew got drunk and fell into a road ditch," answering the friends who tried to get him up, "Aw, boys . . . just leave me be. When I think of what I've got to lay with tomorrow night, I'd just as soon lay here in this ditch" (254). Why, Andy wonders, had Uncle Andrew "accepted" this "fate," having seen and "named it" so clearly? That remains a mystery to Andy, who does see, however, that in marriage the characters of his aunt and uncle somewhat perversely complemented one another in a way that made change impossible. Andy's mother puts this additional unresolvable question thus: "Did your Aunt Judith have so many health problems because your Uncle Andrew drank and ran around with other women, or did your Uncle Andrew drink and run around with other women because your Aunt Judith had so many health problems?" (254–55). The question suggests the couple's symbiosis: perhaps Uncle Andrew ran around to escape the impossible emotional demands of Aunt Judith, in doing so giving Aunt Judith treasured justification for additional self-pity and ensuring himself justification for further escapes.

Much about Uncle Andrew, as about any of us, remains opaque. Insofar as Andy can understand him, he seems, despite all his freedom from restraint, to have been largely unable to change. Uncle Andrew seems to lack a consistent story that would enable him to retain a kind of integrity while also allowing for change. He seems unable to anticipate the future: consequences, Andy says, were always something that he discovered rather than expected. He would then either laugh them off, if possible, or bear them, as part of the fate of being himself. Perhaps what he lacked can be described as vision. Andy recognizes this possibility after a vision of his own, which he has during the summer of his uncle's death. Hoeing tobacco one morning with the men, Andy "saw how beautiful the field was, how beautiful our work was. And it came to me all in a feeling how everything fitted together, the place and ourselves and the animals and the tools, and how the sky held us." The "immediate result" of this vision is that Andy becomes "frantic to own a mule," because, by doing so, "a boy could become a man, an economic entity, dignified and self-sustaining, capable of lovely work" (318).

"It was a boy's dream," Andy knows, "sufficiently absurd," and yet it has troubled him that his uncle thought it merely "funny, when he did not think it a nuisance." Andy came to realize that as "much as [he] wanted to be like" his uncle, they "were not alike" (318). Indeed, Andy is, in this regard, more like his father, Wheeler, who is sustained over a whole adult lifetime by a vision of beauty, order, and abundance that he associates mostly with cattle feeding on green grass. That vision takes Wheeler out of himself, moving him to learn to love what must be done in order to achieve it. In sharp contrast with Uncle Andrew, Wheeler is "determined to do what he had to do; he would look for no escape; he was free" (315). Wheeler's vision enables him to love external requirements and thus to be free in a way quite unlike the sporadic freedom from restraint of Uncle Andrew. Yet no story of a human being is simple, and Uncle Andrew was not without awareness of his need to change. After his grandmother's death, Andy discovers among her things a packet of letters from Uncle Andrew to his parents written as he was struggling with jobs and alcohol in South Carolina. One in particular, written shortly after Andy's own birth, comes home to Andy. After expressing his gratitude for the love and affection of his family, he writes, "And little Andrew, bless his heart—if for nothing else, I would be a man for him." That sentence—with its "hopeful" yet ultimately "hopeless" desire to live for something beyond his own impulses —"binds" Andy to his uncle more closely even than his name (297).

A particularly fine feature of *A World Lost* lies in the way Andy comes to recognize that his own grief for his uncle is, in many ways, quite unlike that of his grandparents and his father. "Only once" was he "ever admitted into the unqualified presence of the family's grief" (271). One evening some months after Uncle Andrew's death, Wheeler sits after supper with his mother and father in their living room. Andy sits "off to [himself]" by a little table where his grandma keeps a radio. He wants to turn the radio on but does not, and he has "an obscure feeling that it would be politest to be somewhere else but that there would be no polite way to leave." All at once the three adults begin to cry, "without moving or speaking, each as if alone" (272). Then they cease. The experience prefigures what Andy will later know. His grandparents and his father reach back farther in time with Uncle Andrew than he does. What has been lost from their worlds with his death is different from Andy's loss, and their sense of the world Andrew has lost differs as well. Their time is not easily equivalent to Andy's time. "Time is out of joint" for each, but differently.

Some years later Andy is able to frame these matters clearly after spending time visiting with his grandma. Every evening "she would begin again to grieve" for her son, and Andy feels as "divided" from her as on the night when he sat by the radio. "My loss was nothing like hers," Andy knows, because "it was answered, beyond anything I felt or willed, by my youth and unbidden happiness and all the time I had to live" (289). She, however, would never outlast her grief, would never live "beyond" it. She "had come to loss beyond life" (289), one greater than any quantity of time could assuage. Perhaps Wheeler, too, has felt a similar kind of inconsolability, one evoking anger as well as grief. After his father's death, Andy learns from his mother that Wheeler had come very close to killing Carp Harmon and thus to succumbing to the attractiveness of what Andy calls the "ultimate oversimplifier," murder—"the paramount act (there are others) by which we reduce a human being to the dimension of one thought" (308). Fortunately, Andy's mother had interceded, turning Wheeler from his design, and, in the process, exemplified the way marriage partners can provide one another freedom in a way undreamt by Uncle Andrew and Aunt Judith. From acting as if outside of time—fixing it at least for Carp Harmon and himself once for all—Wheeler is able to return to time, to "quiet himself," bear "what he had to bear" and, with his wife's help, keep "alive in his life" the lives of his children "as they would be" (316).

Andy's attempt to understand what has led to his uncle's death gives another turn to the novel's title. For apart from the barest facts, nothing is verifiable: a world has been lost. Carp Harmon has come to the site where Andrew and his friends are dismantling buildings. Just prior to the shooting, Andrew and Jake Branch have taken a break and gone to get a cup from a thermos jug in Andrew's car. Harmon then shoots Andrew as the latter says, according to Branch, "It was 'my mistake' and 'don't shoot me'" (299). His friends rush Andrew to the hospital, where he dies. Harmon is tried and convicted, but sentenced only to two years. The obvious question concerns Harmon's motive. The defense's story is that earlier that day, at a store in Stoneport, Andrew made a sexual remark to Harmon's daughter, and Harmon knocked him down with an oilcan. The store owner claims "he heard Catlett apologizing to Harmon, stating he did not know the girl was his daughter" (299). Yet a companion of Andrew's—R. T. Purlin, Jake Branch's sixteen-year-old stepson—says Andrew made no sexual insult and that, in fact, the girl was talking to him, R.T. At the trial, the defense's story has been elaborated still further. According to it, Harmon went to the job site simply to nail a covering over an exposed well. Catlett warned him off, threatening him with a two-by-four and thus precipitating the shooting. When asked why he was carrying a gun, Harmon responds that "somebody was running his trotlines," and he "was prepared to shoot whoever it was" (307).

Something Andy articulates after interviewing R. T. Purlin illuminates the nature of memory and its relationship to fiction. R.T.'s "memory," Andy learns, "was not safe from his imagination." On one occasion, he remembers seeing Harmon come "up the road before the shooting." On another, he says he had not seen him. On the same day, he tells Andy two versions of who first heard the shots: "In the first version, R.T. had said, 'What the hell was that?' and in the second, Col Oaks had said it." Andy comes to understand that these are not "falsehoods in the usual sense." Rather, they are more like the results of prolonged "brooding" over painful events, imagining them "from shifting points of view" (306), much as a writer of fiction might. One thing is clear: the jury found the defense's story believable. It fit Uncle Andrew's character, as Andy freely assents. On the other hand, if R.T. was the one who spoke to Harmon's daughter, then "Uncle Andrew's fate had nothing to do with his character and everything to do with chance and the character of Carp Harmon." R.T. has told Andy that local gossip had it that Harmon had been looking to kill somebody for a long time in the hope of making "a big name for himself" (307). Andy senses the fit between this description and one who might find Uncle Andrew peculiarly fit to kill. A fearful man worrying about being "held in contempt" might well have seen in Uncle Andrew "the very holder-in-contempt he had been expecting, whose every gesture identified him as a lifter of skirts and trotlines, a man insufferably sure of himself." If this has been the case, then again Andy must entertain the "thought that Uncle Andrew's character was his fate, and Carp Harmon the agent of it" (308).

Andy knows "finally grief has no case to make" (308). Grief is not about making a case, but rather about remembering as the "heart instructs." This involves a choice of sorts: one can cultivate suspicion, believing always the worst that can be imagined, or one can accept "the bonds of faith and affection" and "believe the best you can imagine in the face of the evidence." Andy, then, can "imagine it as it might have been" in an account that honors what can be established as fact and yet speculates on the story's gaps and on matters of motive as capaciously and generously as possible. Andy chooses "not to argue with the story of the 'remark' to Carp Harmon's daughter, because it seems both likely and unlikely, and now it makes no difference." He chooses to disbelieve the story about self-defense because it seems very unlikely that any man, armed only with a two-by-four, would go after a man with a gun. Uncle Andrew's final plea, "Don't shoot me,"

Andy accepts, "for it is too plain and sad to be a lie" (309). Andy hears in that plea a prayer, "not to Carp Harmon, but to another possibility, his own sudden vision of what he means to the rest of us—of what we had all meant and the much more that we might have meant to one another" (310). Andy reads his uncle's plea in the light of the letter in which Uncle Andrew has expressed the desire to "be a man" for little Andrew. Thus, Andy depicts the plea as his uncle's final expression of hope that the future might yet be different, spoken even as he is about to be overwhelmed by the fate he has largely prepared for himself.

At the end of *A World Lost,* Andy articulates, insofar as possible, the sense he has gained of the relationship between understanding and love. I would call that sense Johannine because it finds the source of our understanding in a light that has come into the world prior to us as love. Andy begins by acknowledging that he is still left with his original question: "what manner of man" was Uncle Andrew? Andy's story has not been able to answer that question, for a story "follow[s] a line; the telling must begin and end." To tell the story of another may be, as we have seen, a requirement of grief that knows no summary is adequate to loss. But a story cannot be equivalent to a life because, while it can be fixed in time, a life cannot, "for it does not begin within itself, and it does not end." As he realizes "how little we can understand," Andy expresses what his story has done—what fiction can do—somewhat differently, and in a way that perhaps suggests why Berry's fictions seem so often focused on a single individual. He "seem[s] to have summoned" Uncle Andrew "not into view or into thought," as one might an object or idea, but rather "just within the outmost reach of love," where his "presence" can be felt "as a living soul" (325).

The last page of *A World Lost* invokes St. Paul and Plato, as well as John's Gospel. Aware that even his very partial knowledge depends on a "light" that "can come into this world only as love," Andy must believe that the dead are risen into the fullness of that light, there to "know themselves altogether for the first time" (326). Although Berry has sometimes sharply criticized Pauline Christianity, here Andy confesses his belief that "the whole groaning and travailing world" will not come to rest in oblivion, however much at times he might wish that.[15] It will be raised, and those dead who have known in part—like Andy after his uncle's death—will know as they are known, first suffering the "light's awful clarity" and then seeing "its forgiveness and its beauty" as they come to know that "they are loved completely." "Not enough light has ever reached us here among the shadows," Andy remarks, in language reminiscent of Plato's Allegory of the Cave. Sitting in the "darkness of [his] own shadow," Andy knows his "true home" is "not just this place," but "that company of immortals" with whom he has lived.[16] Yet he knows, too, that he "could not see at all were it not for this old injury of love and grief," his uncle's death, which thrust him into a broken world and caused his longing to be whole again. The light of that love-longing is the "little flickering lamp" that he has "watched beside for all these years" (326).

If it is allowable to make Plato and St. Paul go together one more time, perhaps we can add something about a likeness between Andy and his uncle Andrew that Andy does not see. Andy and his father, Wheeler, are moved by a vision of the beauty of the world, which is also, as Simone Weil said, the order of the world. Weil thought that "carnal love in all its forms, from the highest" down "to the worst, down to debauchery, has the beauty of the world as its object." Feeling love for the "splendor" of the world, for matter that cannot respond, we "turn this same love toward a being who is like" ourselves "and capable of answering" to our love, "of saying yes, of surrendering."[17] Perhaps we should understand Uncle Andrew's erotic adventures as his way of responding to the beauty of the world. His despair over his marriage might represent an awareness that Aunt Judith will never really be able to answer to his love, to say yes. I do not mean to suggest an excuse for Andrew's philandering. Simone Weil would have nothing of that. Sins in the area of carnal love are "serious" precisely because such love *is* a form of "the longing to love the beauty of the world": "They constitute an offense against God from the very fact that the soul is unconsciously engaged in searching for God." The nature of the crime involves a "more or less complete determination to dispense with consent." The strong version of this dispensing with consent would presumably be rape, "perhaps the most frightful of all crimes." The "exchange of love" is still "unlawful," however—"whether there is physical union or not"—when the consent issues "from a low or superficial region of the soul," when "it does not come from that central point in the soul where the yes can be nothing less than eternal." St. Paul, Weil remarks, "has emphasized the kinship between vice and idolatry," and it is something like idolatry that marks Uncle Andrew's offenses.[18] Seeking what Andy and Wheeler also seek—the beauty of the world—only without knowing it, Uncle Andrew consents time and time again to finding it in a superficial way, at the cost of diminishing the ability of his soul to give consent at the deepest level. What Andy's narrative restores to his uncle is the hope to be able to give that kind of consent to the beauty—which is the order—of the world. Andrew's "don't shoot me" confesses his need and longing for a return to "the world lost," perhaps to know it for the first time.

Andy's story of losing his own adult world is Berry's novel *Remembering*. He begins the novel in exile—from his home, his family, his body, his name. He awakes in a San Francisco hotel room, having dreamed that "a great causeway" has been built "across the creek valley where he lives" and that "all he knew and loved" has been lost, left only as "the little creature of his memory" (122–23). He has come to San Francisco the previous day from participating in an agricultural conference at a Midwestern university where he has been on exhibit as the contrarian holding out for the small farm against the enthusiastic advocates of industrial farming. Having listened to a series of papers with titles like "The Ontology and Epistemology of Agriculture as a Self-Correcting System" (137), Andy has tried to voice his sense of how the influence of academic "enclosures" has contributed to real damage to "actual fields and farms and actual human lives" (138). He has told the story of finding a bill among his grandmother Catlett's papers recording a charge of $3.57 assessed against his grandfather Marce for tobacco warehouse commission in 1906. That year the whole of Marce's crop had failed by that amount to pay the "commission on its own sale."[19] On the back of that bill, Andy's grandmother Dorie had written, "Oh, Lord, whatever is to become of us?" but then, "as if to correct" herself, she had added, "Out of the depths have I cried unto thee, O Lord." As Andy tells this story in the luxurious conference room, he has only the sense that he has "damaged himself" and lost his grandmother, who has "departed from him" as he's spoken (139). In his angry frustration, he's closed, then, by naming his neighbors, living and dead, against the systems and numbers and ideas of industrial agriculture and its academic theorists. But as he's spoken the names of those for whom he wishes to speak—Mat and Margaret Feltner, Jack Beechum, the Coulters, Danny and Lyda Branch, the Penns—they, too have "departed from him," leaving him empty (140).

Andy has acknowledged his exile on arriving in San Francisco, where he is to speak at a college. When a young woman, sent to meet him at the airport, asks, "Are you Andrew Catlett?" he responds, "No mam." One can read this denial as an act of self-preservation, for Andy is aware that "a man could go so far from home" that "his own name" could "become unspeakable by him, unanswerable by anyone." His name might, then, "if he dared to speak it," "escape him utterly," leaving "him untongued in some boundless amplitude of mere absence" (124). Immediately behind his crisis is the seeming "finality" of his parting from Flora just before leaving for the conference. They have quarreled, and in his self-pity, he has said, "Flora, you don't love me. You never have." She has thrown a dishrag into his face and given him a look that he has read correctly as the sign of a kind of ending: "She was *done* with him as he had become. There was nothing for him to do but change his clothes and go" (126). What he has become—an embittered man seeking angrily to have others confirm his own sense of worthlessness—is, of course, largely the result of the accident he had the previous fall in which he lost his hand while trying to clear fouled stalks in a corn picker.

Andy grieves the loss of "his body's wholeness." His dismembered body has become a problem to him, as is evident in his longing for a time in which his body could, for instance, dress "itself, while his mind thought of something else." He remembers his "poise as a two-handed lover" (143), reaching out with his now lost hand to touch and hold Flora. But now he must consider the damage to his body in all of his movements. Thus, his condition metaphorically suggests that of all of us in middle or post–middle age, after we have ceased inhabiting our bodies with the unconscious grace and ease of youth. It also suggests an analogy between Andy's body and the land itself as treated under the assumptions of industrial agriculture.[20] Andy carries in himself a damage analogous to that done to the land, attributable in part to our coming to think of the land as a mere problem to be tackled rather than the sustaining context of our existence. Andy might be seen, then, as one particularly susceptible to the temptation of Gnosticism, the "American Religion," as Harold Bloom has characterized it in an overgeneralized but still suggestive way.[21] Salvation, of whatever sort, might involve for him an escape from the maimed body of creation into a superior knowledge or spiritual awareness denied to others. Asserting that superior knowledge is what he has been about at the conference, where he has spoken more from his own woundedness than from concern for the membership of neighbors or the land. This is why his grandmother and those other names have deserted him: he has known them too well and too long in the living flesh of their story together to use them to demonstrate his superiority to the conferees. Their presence, and his own heart, will not allow it. As he loses them, he becomes aware of his exile from himself and thus, in exile, begins the movement toward redemption.

Andy's inability to accept his loss reflects his unwillingness to forgive himself, as Flora points out. What seems paradoxical about this is that Andy has done nothing culpable. He has not intentionally maimed himself. For what, then, should he forgive himself? Perhaps for his not being perfect, immortal, immutable, as he should have been, he must believe, not simply as a matter of selfishness or egocentricity, but rather as he should have been for others—to serve, protect, and care for those who matter most to him. He has failed them by being woundable, damaged, mortal. His insistence on his own failure derives from an inability to trust God for them. He was to have been perfect for Flora and the children, and now he has failed. In his arguments with Flora, he seeks pridefully and angrily to manipulate her into confirming him in his own sense of worthlessness— which would be his ticket to an Uncle Andrew–like freedom from responsibility. "He could not win his quarrel with her," and yet "he could not quit it." He returns obsessively to his wound in a way reminiscent of some of Hawthorne's characters.[22] He recognizes the rightness of Flora's comment, "You have no faith," and he knows that he "could not win." But he does know how to perform "flanking movement[s]" in their quarrels and to attack again and again (149). Each time he attacks, he succeeds in pretending that the problem is hers, not his. He avoids adopting the only path really available to him, a narrow one: to forgive his own imperfection and to go forward into the mystery of time with faith.

Andy's return from exile begins as he walks the streets of San Francisco at 4:30 in the morning. It begins with an experience of that mysterious appeal to us that comes from the other. A "frail-looking" woman passes Andy by, trying to maintain her dignity despite being drunk. "Watching her, he feels his silence," realizing that to be able to speak to her would be tantamount to crossing into "an unknown world." "Yet something in him for which he has no word cries out toward her," for without that word, "the world between them fails in their silence, who are alone and heavy laden and without rest." Andy thinks, "*This is the history of souls. This is the earthly history of immortal souls*," and yet he is aware of himself as one of the city's "night walkers," moving about noiselessly as in a kind of netherworld (154).[23] Soon his self-absorption is disrupted by a more direct appeal of another, a man asking him for a buck for breakfast. Immediately Andy's body becomes a problem. If he takes out his wallet, the man may easily seize it and run. The need to help, to respond, in Andy overrides his fear, and he awkwardly uses his left hand to pull six dollars from his wallet, clutched against his body by his right forearm. "Far out!" the man declares. "Thanks, Tex. You a man of a better time." "*So would I hope, if I hoped, to pray to be,*" Andy reflects, unaware as yet that he *has hoped,* most obviously in assisting the man but also in not allowing his body to provide an easy excuse for not doing so (158).[24]

Hans Urs von Balthasar has argued that "love alone is credible," that the Word known to Christianity must be "self-interpreting."[25] "Christianity disappears," Balthasar writes, "the moment it allows itself to be dissolved into a transcendental precondition of human self-understanding in thinking or living, knowledge or deed" (51). Balthasar seeks to avoid both "blind faith" and Gnosticism in order to "perceive the genuine evidence of the light that breaks forth from revelation without at the same time reducing that light to the measure and laws of human perception" (51–52). Two experiences can provide particularly suggestive signs or analogies of the way we can come to perceive that light. I mention these here because there is a kind of astonishing convergence between Balthasar's thinking and Berry's depiction of this phase of Andy's return. The two experiences to which Balthasar alludes are the I's experience of the Thou, which, in its utter freedom, "will always remain an 'other' to me," and the experience of "extraordinary beauty—whether in nature or art," which simultaneously "binds and frees" as "it gives itself unambiguously as the 'self-manifesting freedom' (Schiller) of inner, undemonstrable necessity" (52–53). It is the experience of the Thou that has moved Andy in his night walk through San Francisco: he has heard it as a call that seeks response from him and yet makes clear that any response must involve a word that preserves the distance between himself and the other.[26] Andy's experience of the beautiful begins as he sits in Washington Square, gradually feeling "the touch of the light of the sky around him." He watches the "slow waking" of people in the streets as the daylight drives the darkness before it and extinguishes the lights of the streets. At full light, "he stands in front of the church and reads the legend engraved across its face: LA GLORIA DI COLUI CHE TUTTO MUOVE PER L'UNIVERSO PENETRA E RISPLENDE" (158–59).[27]

"The glory of Him who moves all things soe'er / Impenetrates the universe, and bright / The splendour burns."[28] The motto comes very close to the heart of Balthasar's theology, which has sought, above all else, to recapture the significance of beauty for Christian thinking. Modern theology has suffered greatly, in Balthasar's view, from the loss of a cosmological framework within which it was possible to speak of God's glory, shining radiantly everywhere, possessing "compelling plausibility" for us, evidencing its own gratuitousness, and seeking our response in love. For Balthasar, "the two approaches converge": "Already in the realm of nature, eros is the chosen place of beauty: whatever we love—no matter how profoundly or superficially we may love it—always appears radiant with glory; and whatever is objectively perceived as glorious—no matter how profoundly or superficially we experience it—does not penetrate into the onlooker except through the specificity of an eros" (54). What we love appears glorious; for its glory to penetrate us, we must love it. From this one might conclude that the best way to teach children to love God is to teach them to love something in particular in order that they might see its glory and later be open to the experience of beauty—the experience of inner necessity in a particular gestalt that cannot be reduced to one's imagination of it. A particular figure from Berry's work is helpful in suggesting the nature of this experience: Wheeler Catlett is sustained through his whole adult life by a vision of cattle feeding on green grass. Most American Christians would probably be disinclined to believe Wheeler's vision to be of any theological significance, but from the standpoint of Balthasar, we might say that Wheeler has a particularly strong experience of the analogy of beauty—and thus might be inclined to see the definitive form of God's glory in the particular story of Jesus of Nazareth.

Beauty's role in Andy's returning to himself is evident in the scene following his reading of the legend on the facing of St. Peter and St. Paul's church. At the bottom of Hyde Street, Andy reaches a place "outside the network of the streets," where he stands "in the great fall of dawnlight over the bay and its islands, the Golden Gate, the Marin hills and Mount Tamalpais beyond." The air "opens and lightens around him, freshening, bearing the cold pungence of the ocean" (160), and he walks out past expectant fishermen on a pier, noticing as he goes the head of a sea lion that pokes up through the waves, looks round "with the intelligent gaze of a man," and then disappears "with so little disturbance" that Andy "cannot be sure when it went." At the end of the pier, he comes to a limit. Nobody knows he is here; no communication could find him. He could slip under the waves into an absence as complete as that of the sea lion. "He wants nothing that he has," and "all choice is around him" (161). But to want nothing, to be able to choose anything, is to be nothing in particular, to experience oneself as nonbeing. It is not even to be lost, for one is lost only in relation to somewhere where one would be found. But at this point, the beauty of San Francisco Bay, of the great bridge reaching into the fog, and of the Marin hills beyond penetrates Andy, and he is recalled to particular loves, first in the passionate cry of the psalmist, heard, though he is not thinking of her, in "his grandmother's voice": "*Out of the depths have I cried unto thee, O Lord*" (162).[29]

What follows, then, is a series of memories integral to forming Andy as the particular person he has come to be. The first is of a moment in 1868 when young Jack Beechum sees a man ride up to his house, dismount, introduce himself as Ben Feltner, and ask if Nancy Beechum, the woman he will marry, is Jack's sister. "Thus was the shuttle flung," Andy knows, for "his making." His grandfather Mat "wakens, crying, in his cradle," then later Andy's mother, Bess, wakens, then Andy himself, and finally Andy's own children, "Betty, named Elizabeth for his mother, and Virgie, named Virgil for his mother's brother, missing in action, presumed dead, in the Pacific in 1945" (163). The next memory is of another man riding, this time Andy's Catlett grandfather Marce, coming to introduce himself to, and inspect, the young man now working Jack Beechum's farm, Elton Penn, whom Andy comes, in his turn, to respect and love. Next Andy remembers time spent with his Catlett grandmother, Dorie, after Marce has died and "the old ways [are] ending," the days of "tractors and other large machines" coming (166). Andy and the "grieved old woman" have a project of raising chickens up to frying size from the eggs. When Andy asks how long people have been raising chickens this way, his grandmother responds, "Oh, forever," and he, with a child's obliviousness to time, says, "I hope we always do it forever." Now Andy recalls that she clutched him to her and said, "Oh, my boy, how far away will you be sometime, remembering this?" (166).

Andy is now far away, but he is far away from something, no longer in danger of slipping into nothingness. The Golden Gate Bridge "has begun to shine," not simply because the fog has lifted. Andy finds himself "held," "caught up again" in a complex "pattern of entrances: of minds into minds, minds into place, places into minds." He "returns now to himself," alive in his own skin, singled out "in his own flesh," the product of a particular history and of people "whose love has claimed him forever." He thinks specifically of Thoreau's overburdened neighbors from the "Economy" chapter of *Walden,* happy now to be one of them "pushing in front of him a barn seventy-five feet by forty, and a hundred acres of land" (167). He remembers, then, a story told him and Elton Penn, now himself dead, by his grandfather Mat Feltner. It was of "a long time ago," when Mat, as a child, was helping Uncle Jack to "chop out a field of tall corn in a creek bottom." The heat was so "close" that Mat thought he could no longer stand it when they reached the end of a row, and Jack said, "Let's go sink ourselves in the creek." "It made that hard day good" and gave Mat a way to think about all the times he'd worked hard and in a hurry "to get to a better place." "It had been there all the time," Mat said and when Andy asked him, "What?" he laughed and answered, "Redemption . . . a little flowing stream" (167–68).

By now "all the Marin peninsula is in sunlight," so "far away, so bright" as to seem "the shining land, the land beyond, which many travelers have seen, but never reached." Indeed the "whole bay is shining now," and Andy's return to himself closes with the phrase on the facing of the church in Washington Square: "The glory that moves all things resplendent everywhere" (168). Andy has been prepared for penetration by that glory by a long history of particular loves, and that glory has, in turn, moved him to remember those loves that have made him who he is. Now what remains is the "long choosing" of the particular ways in which to live out the part chosen for him by the "long choosing" (169) of those before him.

Andy will return to Kentucky, to Flora and his children, to his farm and the membership of Port William and his neighbors. In doing so, he will reenact the pattern of others before him, a pattern of leave-taking and return. He remembers the story of his grandfather Mat, sent away, reluctantly, to boarding school in Hargrave and then later spending two years at the college in Lexington before coming home. As Mat steps off the gangplank in Port William, an old man asks him whether he's been to college, and when Mat answers yes, the man opines that he'll soon be "going away . . . to make something out of [him]self." Mat answers, "Nosir," having come home to make something out of himself, together with Margaret Finley, Andy's future grandmother, who "is coming down the bank to meet him" (172). Andy remembers that this same Margaret Feltner sent him off to the university with a "tin of cookies," the admonition to "study hard" because it would be a shame to waste a "good mind," and a reminder that there are those who love him: "Listen. There are some of us here who love you mighty well and respect you and think you're fine. There may be times when you'll need to think of that" (172–73).

As Andy walks more hurriedly "up Columbus Avenue on his way to Port William, Kentucky," he thinks of his father, Wheeler, himself "on a train in the mountains west of Charlottesville, thinking of his father" (174). Wheeler is headed home, after success both in college and later as a student in law school, while working simultaneously in Washington for Forrest Franklin, the congressman from his district. Mr. Franklin has arranged a job for Wheeler as a lawyer in a "large packing house in Chicago." "You can grow and develop and go to the top. You can be something your folks never imagined" (175), he has told Wheeler, and yet Wheeler knows that what he most wants is "to see good pastures, and the cattle coming to the spring in the evening to drink" (176). Andy knows that his father held himself "answerable" to this vision—and with it, to the vision "of a community well founded and long lasting"—ever since his return (176).

Andy has himself completed an earlier pattern of escape and return. "Fated to be charmed by cities," he has found himself in San Francisco, and later in Chicago, after college—having been advised by his teachers, and believing, that getting off the farm and into the city was "the purpose of an education" (178). In Chicago, he worked as a journalist for *Scientific Farming*, devoted to the promotion of large-scale, industrial agriculture and agribusiness. On an assignment in Ohio, however, Andy comes to realize how much the assumptions of industrial farming conflict with the vision of a community well founded and harmonious. He is to interview Bill Meikelberger, who farms two thousand acres exclusively in corn on land south of Columbus that he has "acquired by patiently buying out his neighbors in the years since his graduation from the college of agriculture at Ohio State." While Meikelberger is "the fulfillment of the dreams of his more progressive professors," he has ceased, in any meaningful way, to live on the land (180). He is heavily in debt, which he accepts as "a permanent part of an operation like this"; depends on the income of his wife, Helen, who works in town; stays so busy—as does she—that they "don't do much housekeeping" and "eat in town, mostly" (181–82). He regularly pops anti-ulcer medication, but discounts his stomach damage as part of the price of "getting ahead," rather than seeing it as his body's sign that his way of life is unsustainable. Perhaps above all, he seems terribly alone, which is, of course, a consequence of adding one former neighbor's field after another to his own. Meikelberger's farm contrasts sharply with that of the Troyers, an Amish family whom Andy encounters and visits on his way from Ohio to his next stop in Pittsburgh. As he drives eastward and north from Columbus, Andy notices a change in the "character of the country" (182) as it becomes hillier. Fields are smaller, farms closer, woodlands remain. The beauty of a particular field arrests Andy, and as he stops the car, Isaac Troyer comes by, plowing the field behind three black mares. He invites Andy to ride, to drive, and later to take dinner with his family. What Andy sees and hears is that the Troyers regard the farm as a home in a way repudiated by Meikelberger. Here there are outbuildings, a garden, martin boxes, and an orchard with beehives. In addition to horses, the Troyers keep "fifteen guernsey cows," pigs, and hens (185). They are close enough to neighbors that Andy can see other farmers plowing and hear the sounds of children's voices. Economy here centers on the household; Isaac carries no debt and would rather have neighbors than more land. He resists the call not only of expansion but also of mechanization, recognizing that to reduce the need for labor on the farm is to send his children to work in factories. The Troyer farm is "a place of work, but a place too of order and rest" (187), a word nearly forgotten by Meikelberger. Struggling for a word to describe the Troyer place, Andy thinks it might be called "cordial or congenial or convivial" (186). All of these are appropriate, as the farm seems filled with a sense of generous and pleasing abundance created by human work and life in accord with the genius of the place. Here what Andy sees is "that a man could live with trees and animals and a bending little tree-lined stream; he could live with neighbors" (186).

Andy has been prepared to read his experiences with Meikelberger and the Troyers by his memories, particularly his grandfather Feltner's finding "redemption" in a little flowing stream and his father's vision of a well-ordered community. Thus, when he cuts his ties with *Scientific*

Farming and returns to Kentucky to buy and restore the Harford Place, he remembers in both senses of the word. His action is moved by memory, which itself gives him the way to see what constitutes a good and sustainable way of life in the present. His memories re-member him, providing him a way to regain wholeness by joining him to those, living and dead, who have found a way of life worth living and passing on. He is again re-membered in the process of remembering during his exile after his wound and the break from Flora. His very particular memories of the beloved community—together with the penetrating glory of the Lord resplendent in San Francisco Bay—move him outside himself, beyond his wound. The experience of exile, together with the memory of God's faithfulness, formed the words of the psalmist that come to Andy in his grandmother's voice, as she considers the possibility that Marce and she may lose their land: "*Out of the depths have I cried unto thee, O Lord*" (162). Memory of the beloved community, memory that creates and nourishes hope, is literally what one lives from, manna in the wilderness. Remembering brings Andy to himself for a second time, returning him to Kentucky, to Flora and his children, and to neighbors waiting to regard him not as the damaged object of their benevolence, but simply as one capable of gracious exchanges.

Remembering closes with a dream that comes to Andy. It is at first very disturbing: he enters "such a darkness as he has never known," knows "nothing except a hopeless longing for something" he cannot even name, and hears "sounds of crying and of tearing asunder." But soon "from outside his hopeless dark sleep," he feels a touch "laid upon his shoulder," and he senses "his flesh" entering again into his mind and his "mind into flesh" (219). "Though dark to himself," he "is whole" as he finds himself on a hillside just before the dawn of a day in spring. There are flowers in bloom; he hears "birdsong"; a stream, once dry, has begun to flow. Rising, he sees "a man, dark as shadow," walking "away from him up the hill road," and he begins to follow, knowing the man once looked at him "face-to-face" but will not do so again and will not "look back" (219–20). The identity of the man is never specified, for he is a composite figure of all those who have walked this way before Andy. Andy follows the man as he did when he was a boy "follow[ing] older hunters in the woods at night, Burley Coulter and Elton Penn and the Rowanberrys"—men who not only "knew the way" but "who *were* the way of the places they led him through" (220).

As he walks, Andy hears a singing "more distant" than the birds' song, one "filling the sky and touching the ground," eliciting the birds' answer. He is "hearing the light" as it draws "everything into the infinite, sensed but mysterious pattern of its harmony" (220). What he hears, and then sees, is what Dante described: the "glory that moves all things resplendent every-where" (168). His final vision is of "Port William and its countryside" clar-ified by love. He sees "the signs everywhere" of the "care of a longer love than any who have lived there have ever imagined" (221). "The one great song sings" over everything and is "answered everywhere," and people rest and talk together "in the peace of a sabbath profound and bright." They are "people of such beauty that he weeps to see them" (221).[30] What he has come to, following the dark man who is the composite of all those who have come before him, is the awareness of his own contingency. He is a gift, utterly gratuitous, unable and unneeding to establish his own justification for being. There is nothing necessary about him. He is left simply to follow a way taken by others before him, to find it good, and to believe himself and others part of a much larger story of love than any of them could ever have imagined. As he "prepares to leave" those who can never be lost, their "names singing in his mind," he "lifts toward them the restored right hand of his joy" (222), that utterly gratuitous emotion Thoreau called "surely" the "condition of life."[31]

In perhaps the most famous poem in English of the last century, T. S. Eliot located the cruelty of April in the modern waste land in its mixture of "memory" and "desire."[32] If only April, spring rain, and desire would let us rest, we might be able to keep a little life warm on the way to the grave's peace. Berry depicts one who will not consent to peace on these terms in *The Memory of Old Jack,* which is devoted simultaneously to the last day and to the whole of Jack Beechum's life. As Jack lives out his last day in Port William's membership, his memories come to him in the kind of inevitable order they have established for themselves. On that last day, Jack has very nearly become his memory, and what he is for others is largely the memory they have of him. He has been a man of tremendous, almost fierce desire, one who was "nearly sixty" before he learned what his best friend, Ben Feltner, had tried to teach him, "Let tomorrow come tomorrow, my boy." He is also a man of deep memory, one who "never has learned" the other half of Ben's teaching, "Let the past be gone. Let the dead lie. . . . Let it go by, Jack, my boy."[33]

Now past ninety, Jack is losing his day-to-day memory. He often forgets names, sensibly adopting the habit of calling men "Irvin" and women "Suzy" when he cannot remember their names. When he begins using "Irvin" for his son-in-law, Gladston Pettit, his daughter, Clara, considers him "childish" (139). He has, for some years, been unable to live at home and has allowed Wheeler Catlett to persuade him to take up residence in town at Mrs. Hendrick's boardinghouse. Today Old Jack would likely be diagnosed as a victim of dementia, perhaps even Alzheimer's disease. But perhaps we might read his story as a witness to the logic of dementia: as the mind comes to terms with its own limitations, it pares away all but the most essential memories. Perhaps the mind forgets away all but the shape of the memory when, in the failure of desire, memory is all that one is. Today Old Jack would also likely reside in some regimented facility with a euphemistic name like the Port William Health Center or Hargrave Life Care. The novel is, among many things, the story of good care for an old man, who is truly part of the town's care without becoming an object of benevolence. It is also the story of a good death, which comes to Jack in the fullness of time and when he "has been around long enough to know that death is the only perfect cure for what ails mortals" (24).

Old Jack commands the respect of the Port William community, but not because his life has been a success in the ways success is commonly understood. In important ways, Jack's life has been a failure. His marriage has been unhappy, he has left no heir of his own to inherit his land, and he is largely alienated from his daughter and his son-in-law. Yet Old Jack has won through to the end: his life challenges the terms of success, suggesting the triviality of most of our ways of estimating it. His story is also one of fidelity, somewhat paradoxically, as a major episode of it involves three years of infidelity to his wife, Ruth. It might be most accurate to say of Jack that on his last day he has come to that point suggested by Shakespeare's "Ripeness is all."[34] Jack has come to his end as one with loyal friends of long standing, as one who lived so deeply and honestly that he has become a standard to which others turn for clarifications and as one able, finally, to bless.

Jack's life is marked by a tension, ultimately unresolvable, between house and land. Though he is repeatedly told he was too young to see it, he has "kept all his life a strange, unfocused vision" of the departure of his two brothers, Confederate cavalrymen, in September 1862. As he sees that memory, "they have already seen the house for the last time and their backs are turned to it forever." Mat dies a month later, Ham in 1864. His father sits "long at a time by the dead hearth" (18), looking at the floor. His mother dies before the spring of 1865. Thus, "by the war's end," the "old house was infected with a sense of loss and diminishment, and with a quietness" (19). Jack's father keeps "vigil" over him, fearful constantly of loss. In him Jack comes to recognize a "tender kindness," but Jack must learn of "manhood" from his friend Ben Feltner, for his father has lost that quality, that power to act tempered by faith, forever (21). From early in life, Jack's mind turns "away from the house, from the losses and failures and confinements of his history, to the land," to its "endlessly abounding and unfolding promise" (19). He seeks to bring that promise of endlessly renewing life into the house itself through his marriage to Ruth, whose name recalls ironically Ruth the Moabitess, who comes from outside Israel to bring a son, an heir, and life itself to Naomi after she has lost her husband and two sons. Perhaps Jack can be read as a representative of the older agrarianism of the South, as one hopeful that the strength and promise of the land might revitalize a lost way of life. That hope proves impossible; there is too much history that needs to be lived out, and lived down, before a new agrarian beginning can be made. Jack lives some of that history.

A splendid horseman and dancer, the young Jack Beechum incarnates values typically associated with the class of southern yeomanry. He abounds in energy and desire, feeling the passion of the land around him in his own body. He first sees Ruth Lightwood in church, where he sits "full of pleasure in the day" (34) and paying little attention to the sermon. He and Ruth are a mismatch from the first. He looks to give himself entirely to her, feeling within himself the "opening" of "depths of a generosity that he had never known" (41). He hopes that his own complete self-offering will evoke a similar opening in her and that they will become a couple fully united in embodied love. As such, they together would revitalize both house and land, bringing forth a new generation united in body and soul, dwelling on and drawing strength from the land. But Jack's dream of redemption through passionate love is the product of his own desire. With her Gnostic, otherworldly Protestantism, Ruth finds Jack's "dark energy" (39) fascinating primarily as the grounds for a moral project, that of transforming Jack into something he is not, some "hypothetical and shadowy figure" who would be more like the "young minister or lawyer or doctor" (42) whom Ruth's parents had assumed she would marry. Their sexual life is a failure. Ruth "could not bear" being touched by Jack's hands, which did "willingly and even eagerly what, before, she had seen only black hands do reluctantly" (44). Jack's hands do what is necessary for life, covering themselves in the process with dirt and filth and blood. Ruth stands in "moral fear" (43) of him, able to accept him "as a challenge to her hope and to her will" (40), but not as a husband in the full sense. Their son is stillborn. Later they have a daughter, Clara, who is always Ruth's child and who enacts the life her mother had been "appointed" to have, marrying a banker and moving to Louisville.

Jack and Ruth's marriage illustrates problems within Protestant Christianity that Berry has frequently commented on in his essays. Exclusive focus on spiritual experience and preparation for the next world leads to a devaluing of this world—of bodies, physical labor, the environment. What results is a compartmentalization of experience particularly useful to the reign of technology. The world ceases to be our dwelling place, the mysterious and sustaining context of our experience, and becomes instead so much "standing reserve" available to be transformed for our—that is, technology's—purposes. For Americans, this has meant becoming Franklinian economic self-maximizers while relegating the body to the status of object—today an often carefully sculpted and perfected object, but an object nevertheless. We may no longer "use Venery" only "for Health or Offspring," but American popular culture and advertising thrive on the promotion of sexuality as primarily the exercise of "Venery."[35] What Ruth cannot reconcile herself to in Jack is not unlike what American advertising could hardly accept in either man or woman: integrity, integration, self-acceptance. Thinking, passion, love, work—all are bound together in Jack. He offers his integrity to Ruth, his wholeness, born of his work in consort with the inexhaustible promise of the land and yet tragically lacking in the house from which all life but his has departed. As a yeoman, he possesses a "sufficiency to himself" and "faithfulness to his place" (44) that prevent him from needing to engage in ceaseless self-improvement, real or ersatz.[36] Ruth sees this being in place, however, only as a lack of ambition on Jack's part. He will never be the man she has wanted, one who distinguishes himself from the labor of the earth and is ever on the way to a success that is the material analogy of heaven seen as the ultimate escape from our human bondage.

In the "Afterword" to his 1989 edition of *The Hidden Wound,* Berry argues that the "root of our racial problem in America" lies not in racism, but in "our inordinate desire to be superior" to "our condition," a desire that leads to a devaluation of physical labor and the creation of a class of people whose role is to do work that no one else wants to do. Much of this work involves caretaking of one sort or another—"of ourselves, of each other, or of our country." To consider this work beneath what we aspire to is to forsake the "obligations of stewardship" and to undermine the commonwealth.[37] Jack Beechum temporarily forsakes his obligations of stewardship without even intending to do so. Influenced by Ruth's dissatisfaction with him, he decides to become one who adds fields to fields. He buys more land, the Farrier place, outwitting Sims McGrother, whose abuse of others and himself ought to be a warning to Jack of the dangers of owning more land than one can honestly work oneself. To help him redeem the Farrier place, Jack hires Will Wells, an African American who is proud, hardworking, intelligent, and competent in every way. In two years of work, they bring healing and an "assured sense of order" (59) to the farm, and a "new adjustment" begins between Jack and Ruth, who sees in him a new sense of direction and perhaps the aspiration to be a "gentleman" (60).

Jack's expansionism is undone by the reality of work itself and by his own integrity. "A sort of brotherhood" grows between Will and Jack, who are—if master and servant economically—"equals before the work." Jack's "principle and his pride" will not allow him to ask of Will what he would not do himself. They work "side by side," knowing "the same hardships of labor and weather," coming to like and respect each other (59). Will has been allotted a house as part of his wages, and with his wife, Marthy, he sets about creating an orderly and productive homestead. Jack sees that this work makes Will belong "more particularly" (60) to the Farrier place than he ever would. He knows this, of course, because he has done similar work of his own, investing his effort and sweat in good work that enables the thriving of human beings, animals, and land. Jack admires the "pleasant, frugal order" Will has made, but he finds also, and "to his surprise," that he "fear[s]" the "claim" it makes "on his respect and his feelings." He cannot help but see the "sorrow" that must inevitably accompany Will's work as long as his relationship to the place is "almost accidental" (61).

Jack knows Will to be utterly competent to farm land of his own and to live with Jack in full equality as a neighbor. The goodness of Will's work has made it impossible for the two to continue as master and servant. Gradually, each man comes to resent his "dependence" (61) on the other, and their relationship follows the pattern outlined by Rene Girard in his analysis of imitative desire.[38] As the difference between the two men diminishes, they need to reassert it more emphatically. Eventually they fight, Will must leave, and Jack must accept his very costly error in taking on land he cannot work himself. Jack and Will "cannot be reconciled," for "no real peace ever existed between them, and they are far off in history from the terms and the vision of such a peace" (64). Actually, that vision has existed, though the failed example of its most famous proponent has done a great deal to undermine it. The self-sufficiency and property ownership necessary for truly neighborly equality are, after all, tenets of Jefferson's agrarian republicanism.

Jack's attempt to expand his holdings forces him to face an irreconcilable contradiction: he cannot simultaneously own more land than he can work without turning others into dependents. He cannot be Will's master and equal. As he will not ask another man to work on the terms he had with Will, there is nothing to do except abandon his expansion and work off the loss. Irreconcilable contradiction similarly marks Jack's three-year affair with Rose McInnis, who, unlike Ruth, knew Jack "as he was, and loved him" (100). She offers—as pure gift—a passion equal to Jack's own. She requires nothing of him, indeed insists on his freedom. Yet he knows that she yearns for a more fully and formally committed relationship, marriage, in short. She "wants what she cannot ask and he cannot give." Jack can do little except to bear this contradiction, to live it out. It "makes a sorrow in him that only his grave will heal." There is little comfort for Jack in Rose's assuring him he owes her nothing, for this means he cannot do anything "to justify or redeem or safeguard Rose's gift." Despite her assurances to the contrary, he feels she is letting him "use" her (103). The very freedom she offers him exacerbates his sense of the unhealable breach between his love and his work. If Ruth had been able to open to him as he had hoped, then he could have united love and work as "two eyes make one in sight," to borrow a phrase from Robert Frost.[39] Or if he had not known Ruth and had married Rose, Jack's passion and his labor might well have found an answering response in a fully living marriage. Jack is too honest and deep a man—one insistent on giving himself with every act—to relinquish or lose his feeling for Ruth. He sees that his infidelity "touche[s] her as his love had not," that she "now helplessly and deeply bore his wound" (102). The strength of their bond is such that he must bear "the wound he had given her." A kind of "fierce justice" demands it. He cannot be unfaithful both to one whom he has loved so much and to his own word without those commitments recoiling on him. He feels what he has done to her because he cares for her and will be "forever yearning and grieving after the loss of what perhaps they never could have had" (102). These are griefs that only the grave will heal, ills for which death is the only cure.

The "incompleteness" of Jack's love for Ruth and for Rose enables him to recognize completeness when he sees it—in Hannah Coulter and her marriage to Nathan. Theirs is mortal love. Hannah has lost her first husband, Virgil Feltner, in World War II; Nathan has lost his brother Tom and served in the Pacific himself. Hannah's love could be "irreparably divided," as Berry describes Jack's, but it is not. Hannah is not torn between a remembered love for Virgil and her current love for Nathan. She loved Virgil as fully as possible and now loves Nathan wholeheartedly, perhaps with a depth of passion and generosity she had not known with Virgil because they were so young. An "understanding of mortality has been Hannah Coulter's great suffering," and "now it is her peculiar gift" (72). She "has known and borne and accepted it" (72), and she is not afraid. Her marriage to Nathan realizes what Jack had wanted long before in his marriage to Ruth: a mutual self-giving so complete that it would make them "one flesh" (to use the biblical phrase for which there is none better). A sure sign of the completeness of their bond is the way Nathan has accepted Hannah and Virgil's child, Margaret, to be his own.

On Jack's last day, Hannah is eight months pregnant with her second child with Nathan. She is aware of Old Jack's "isolation, his remoteness, now, from the daily life the rest of them are living," but "it has come to her" that "of all those near her Old Jack most carefully understands the fullness she has come to, and most exactly values it." She is "what he has failed," but never relinquished or renounced; she is "his consolation and his despair," the confirmation of the goodness of a full human love he never had. "How much," she recognizes, "of his vision of the world comes right in the figure of a woman fulfilled and satisfied, her man's welcomer, at home in the world!" (79). As they walk together, Hannah feels "completed" by Jack's attention, by simply standing in the sight of one who has, through long effort, come to know "that all human labor passes into mystery"—and to accept this, joyfully, as the truth. Hannah's voice, "strong and full of hope, knowing and near to joy," pleases Jack, who hears in it "what he wants to know"—that life, despite everything, is good, abounding, worthy to be lived, ultimately triumphant. And he, Old Jack, can praise and bless her from that same generous trust in life. "You're a fine woman. You're all right," he says to Hannah, in a tone that implies: "Believe it of yourself forever" (81).

For Old Jack, as for us all, life has become a pattern of departures and returns, of seeing loved ones go away and then of turning back to those people and things that remain. The eighteen-year-old Andy Catlett is about to depart for college on Jack's last day, and he, like Hannah, receives Jack's blessing. The two men talk as Old Jack sits on the hotel porch, his awareness of present reality growing increasingly intermittent. Old Jack "sees that he has come to an end in this boy" (119), so devoted to books in a way that Jack has never been. Jack cannot even imagine the future toward which Andy moves, although Berry suggests that in one feature, at least, Andy faces a dilemma much like one Jack faced. With the energy of the young, Andy finds his mind turning to his own concerns whenever Jack's attention fails, specifically to the meeting he anticipates with his girlfriend, Kirby, who is herself about to depart for a "fashionable Eastern school" (117). Andy thinks that all the "contradictions" in his life would be resolved if Kirby "would only love him as he is." Some things do not change. Kirby loves Andy "as raw material" (118), much as Ruth loved Jack. Reading this in the light of Jack's story, we hope that Andy discovers his Rose before his commitment to Kirby has become too deep. Old Jack, of course, knows nothing of this. All Jack sees dimly before him is a boy he has loved who is about to go off into a future that he cannot fathom and in which he will have no part. He has been holding onto Andy's arm, but now there is nothing to do but "turn him loose" (119) and bless, with the generosity of one who knows that the abounding promise of life is not his to bestow but to transmit. "Learn your books," Jack says, meaning "more than that," with his hand "opened and raised in benediction and farewell" (119).[40]

Of all his friends, Mat Feltner is the one to whom Jack's mind returns most insistently. Jack has played the part of the elder man to Mat, particularly after the murder of Ben Feltner. To Mat, Jack has spoken those words that he has needed to speak to someone, words the father must speak to the son for the sake of both. After taking the losses on the Farrier place, Jack has worked fifteen years to pay off the mortgage, to get back again to where he started. He thinks of this time as laboring in "the shadow of death," working "longer than Jacob labored for the daughters of Laban." The last five years were "the darkest and the worst" (119). He worked from dark until dark, barely looking up from the ground, driven by "his creditors and his own honesty," thinking repeatedly of the "dead woman who had loved him as he was, and of the living one who could not" (120). Yet Jack does come through; he repays the past and finds himself on the other side, renewed in his sense of the abounding possibilities "contained inside the boundaries of his farm." The biblical language of losing and finding describes his experience accurately. He "lost his life"—fifteen years of it—but now "he has found it again" (122), back where he began, perhaps knowing it for the first time. Like Esau and then like Jacob when he sees Joseph alive, Jack learns it is "enough" simply to see the promise again. He has been through the first death and found a "peace [that] would abide with him to the end of his days" (123). This experience must be told, and so Jack passes it on to Mat, "letting him see in his eyes with what fear and joy he meant it." Gesturing "to the ridges and hollows that bore indelibly for them both the memory and mark of Ben," Jack would say, "That's all you've got, Mat. It's your only choice. It's all you can have; whatever you try to gain somewhere else, you'll lose here. . . . And it's enough. It's more than enough" (124). Jack is not a religious man in any conventional sense, but his sister Nancy did insist he learn some of the Psalms as a child, and he now knows the truth of the Twenty-third. He has lived the lines he quotes to Mat: "Yea, though I walk through the valley of the shadow of death, I will fear no evil: for thou art with me; thy rod and thy staff they comfort me. Thou preparest a table before me in the presence of mine enemies: thou anointest my head with oil; my cup runneth over" (124). The cup runs over; it is enough, more than enough, just to be here, today, in this particular place, with these mortal companions, trusting that the work one is called to is good.

Old Jack dies "well" (147), at the end of his life, in his rocking chair in his boardinghouse room. Mat finds him and goes to the fields to tell the men first. Mat tries to keep the funeral simple, telling Brother Wingfare to limit it to a handful of Jack's favorite Psalms. But Clara and Gladston Pettit ultimately take control, and Brother Wingfare concludes the service with a sermon assuring his hearers that "toward the end of his life the departed showed unmistakable signs of turning toward an acceptance of Jesus Christ as his personal Savior" (159–60). Brother Wingfare's performance is not so much bad as simply irrelevant. One could say of Jack, in Christian terms, that he had been a devoted steward of Creation, one who cared for what he had been given to care for and made no attempt to shirk the pain his actions sometimes caused. He labored, hoped, trusted, refused to exploit others, and won through to the end, blessing those who followed him. He lived out, and lived down, some of the history that had to pass before a new agrarian start could be made, leaving his own land to the rightful inheritor, Elton Penn. Above all, Old Jack was a man of passion, one who sought—joyfully—to stake his life and his character in all his actions. The novel ends with a tribute to Old Jack much more fitting than Brother Wingfare's. As they work at tobacco stripping, Jack's friends remember his characteristic ways of speaking, and Berry gives one last turn to his novel's title. For now Jack's memory is something these men share, binding them together "in common knowledge and common loss." "The like" of Jack Beechum "will not soon live again in this world, and they will not forget him" (170).

Chapter 6

Imagining the Practice of Peace in a Century of War

A Place on Earth, Hannah Coulter, and Jayber Crow

A Place on Earth. Wendell Berry's novel offers rich possibilities for meditation on its title. The novel is about a particular place, Port William, Kentucky, during a time, World War II, in which the life of that place has come under the influence—perhaps the tyranny—of places far distant on earth, unknown to those in Port William except through the thin details of radio broadcasts. As those in Port William live through the war, they experience the increasing necessity of connection to their place on earth and its human membership. Some lose their place on earth. Tom Coulter is killed in Italy while bulldozing dead soldiers into a mass grave; Virgil Feltner is reported "missing in action," his body never discovered. Maintaining a place on earth for them becomes a matter of grief, memory, and hope on the part of those left. Even those not killed in war can sometimes lose their places on earth almost as profoundly as Tom or Virgil. Gideon Crop is missing in action for months after the drowning of his daughter, Annie. Ernest Finley, maimed in World War I, establishes what seems a viable place for himself until the hopelessness of his attraction to Ida Crop makes him aware of just how lost and homeless he is.

Each of us begins at home, as the child of specific parents, the carrier of a lineage. As embodied beings we carry about the visible marks of relationship to other embodied beings. We are more than just reminders of one another; we are more or less related incarnations of one another. Our first place on earth is our mother's body. The womb is the first of a series of homes through which we pass on the way to our inevitable resting place on earth, the grave. Whether that grave, however, is truly a place on earth—

marked out and known, cared for—is a matter of others' fidelity, individual and communal. Like Uncle Stanley, the aging gravedigger who turns over his trade to Jayber Crow, the older we get, the more difficult we find it to get out of the grave. Berry is himself more than a little "incorrigible" in the same way he attributes to Jayber during the graveyard scene. "No matter how near home he sets his mind to work," Berry says of Jayber, "it always beelines for the final questions."[1] Perhaps that's because those final questions are the ones nearest home, those that face up to the way we live day by day in our particular places on earth in the light of the sure knowledge of our final earthly home. Or as Jayber, Burley, and Big Ellis sing: "Yes, that old dark and silent / Ground is finally going to get us" (296).

Some, like Brother Preston, the preacher who comes to console the Feltners, deny too easily the seeming finality of the grave. His "hastening to rest in the hope of Heaven" (98) runs the risk of devaluing our life here in this place on earth. His belief comes to seem too much a "safe abstraction" (99) divorced from mortal realities: sorrow, grief, labor, mental and physical pain, dependence on the earth itself for daily bread. *A Place on Earth* is, I think, finally a "Christian novel," if it makes sense to speak of such a thing, but its eschatology is much more nearly Burley Coulter's than Brother Preston's. As part of his report to Nathan on the preacher's visit to the Feltners, Burley writes, "I ain't saying I don't believe there's a Heaven. I surely do hope there is. That surely would pay off a lot of mortgages. But I do say it ain't easy to believe. And even while I hope for it, I've got to admit I'd rather go to Port William" (105).

Port William is a place within a larger place, the United States of America, engaged in World War II in global conflict, war seeking to become the reality of every place on earth. Implicit in the novel, then, is the question of the relationship between locality and nation. To put it succinctly, "What had boys from Port William to do with the nation's involvement in war with distant nations?" Berry puts very little emphasis in the novel on the moral, ideological, or national purposes of the war. Rather, he focuses on how conflict a world away affects a particular place in Kentucky. What seems to move young men like the Coulter brothers, Virgil Feltner, and Jasper Lathrop to serve is what I suspect accounts for most participation in the nation's wars: local solidarity, the desire to do one's part, a sense of justice in the sharing of risk, a felt commitment to a particular place on earth. World War II was America's "good war" of the last century, the one so clearly justified it seems unimaginable for us not to have fought. As such, it continues to exercise enormous influence over our thinking about war, particularly its seeming unavoidability. One of the effects of Berry's minimizing the historical and ideological justifications of the war is simply to remind us that even this "good war" reached deeply into little places on earth like Port William, Kentucky, places policy-making elites hardly know exist. Our more recent wars have done the same, and the nation's ability to muster forces still depends, in large measure, on the fidelities of people in localities very far removed from the places where war is planned or conducted. *A Place on Earth* should at least cause us to ask whether the nation cynically uses local fidelities for ideological purposes quite alien to the reasons young Americans enter military service. How legitimate is it to depend on the commitment of young people to their own places on earth to wage wars for such abstractions as the extension of democracy or free markets?

As the title of a World War II novel, *A Place on Earth* cannot help but carry additional suggestions. A spurious mythologizing of mystical organic connection between a people and a place on earth was a prominent feature of Nazi propaganda. Germany justified expansionist claims on the grounds that certain territories belonged to it as a matter of its people's historical destiny. What Germany needed was *Lebensraum*, living space or room—in short, a more expansive place on earth. The people targeted for extermination, Jews, had been denied the ability to buy land, their own places on earth. The history of Israel might well be characterized as several millennia of a people's searching for a place on earth, only to be displaced time and again. After the war, the United Nations sought an end to Israel's agony by making provisions for a state. Israel would, at last, have its own place on earth. But as every schoolchild knows, the establishment of the Israeli state has meant the displacement of Palestinians. Israel's gain of a place on earth led to the Palestinians' loss.

What this history bears out is the truth of Pascal's observation regarding the distinction between "mine" and "thine": "*Mine, thine.*—'This dog is mine,' said those poor children; 'that is my place in the sun.' Here is the beginning and the image of the usurpation of all the earth."[2] To take up a place on earth is to exclude others, to assert ourselves over against others. Yet we all need a place on earth, a place in the sun. To be without one is to be disposable. Perhaps this taking up of places leaves us, then, with eternal war. For Pascal the maxim "that each should follow the custom of his own country"—of his own place on earth—proves that human beings are igno-rant of justice. For if they had known justice, they would surely not have established this principle, "the most general of all that obtain among men" (100). Sometimes "men admit that justice does not consist in these cus-toms but that it resides in natural laws, common to every country." But the "farce" in this is that every kind of action under the sun—"theft, incest, infanticide, parricide"—has, at one time or another, "had a place among virtuous actions." "Can anything be more ridiculous," Pascal asks, "than that a man should have the right to kill me because he lives on the other side of the water, and because his ruler has a quarrel with mine, though I have none with him?" (101). Berry comes close to Pascal's spirit when he asks in "To a Siberian Woodsman,"

> Who has invented our enmity? Who has prescribed us
> hatred of each other? Who has armed us against each other
> with the death of the world? Who has appointed me such anger
> that I should desire the burning of your house or the
> destruction of your children?
> Who has appointed such anger to you?[3]

If our particular loyalties, our ties to specific places on earth, are largely responsible for human conflict and war, then one strategy for the promotion of peace might seek to detach people as completely as possible from those particularist commitments. If we could become sufficiently "cosmopolitan," in the way advocated by Martha Nussbaum and others, then we might find peace in the very abandonment of the idea that a particular way of life is worth defending, with violence if necessary.[4] As Richard Flathman has sug-gested, however, the problem with accounts of "world citizenship" is their "echoing political emptiness." As Flathman argues, we learn to rule and be ruled within the context of very specific obligations of citizenship, them-selves "supported by sanctions that may include the loss of the status of citi-zen itself."[5] As it is very difficult to specify just what we would be obliged to do as "world citizens"—or what the sanctions for failure are—the term seems limited in its helpfulness. What we need is a more particular account of how peace might be fostered even within a community that is part of a nation engaged in war. Perhaps such a thick account requires narration—the kind of dense, multilayered treatment that the novel can offer.

The three novels treated in this chapter—*A Place on Earth, Hannah Coulter,* and *Jayber Crow*—can be read, I believe, as accounts of the practical peacemaking required of us, in Berry's view, as citizens and patriots. They are novels of love set in time of war, one haunted by the constant possibility of what Hannah Coulter calls "absolute loss."[6] What this means is suggested by the experiences Art Rowanberry recalls as he approaches Hargrave in "Making It Home (1945)."[7] After surviving Bastogne, where "he had expected to die," Art was sitting "by his gun one afternoon, eating a piece of chocolate cake" and "talking to an old redheaded, freckle-faced boy named McBride," when a shell hit nearby and "McBride just disappeared."[8] That possibility of imminent disappearance seems to hover over everything for Art—as it must have for his whole generation of soldiers— as he approaches his hometown. When the buildings of Ellville come into sight, they seem "only accidentally there, and himself there only accidentally." It is as if "he and the town ahead of him and all the long way behind him had been taken up into a dream in which every creature and every thing sat, like that boy McBride, in the dead center of the possibility of its disappearance" (228) . What Art dreams is simply what most of the twentieth and now twenty-first centuries has taught us to accept as inevitable, perhaps even desirable as the price of progress. As Jayber Crow would put it, we have been living the process by which War and its ever more "closely related" partner, the Economy, have brought every place on earth under the power of transformation and mobilization.[9] "The world is flat," we're told today, in what some claim is a good development. What has been flattened in the process, however, is too little taken into account, perhaps because we have become so habituated to seeing things in the way Art Rowanberry has learned in war: as always already on their way to destruction and disappearance.

The kinds of peaceableness evident in *Place, Hannah,* and *Jayber* are unlikely to move the policy-making elites who have persuaded us that making peace is their purview alone: and that often the way to peace means the initiation or continuation of war. For Mat and Margaret Feltner, who lose their son, Virgil, and to a lesser degree for all of Port William, peaceableness may mean something like keeping watch over life, finding the adequacy of life in one's own place and thus avoiding the zero-sum assumptions that drive the need for restlessness and expansionism. For

Hannah, who also loses Virgil, it means developing ultimately a rich kind of imagination grounded in love, one concrete and particular enough to resist the abstractions by which things and people are rendered unreal and thus eligible for destruction. For the returned soldier Nathan, peaceableness means choosing and imagining against the war for the rest of his life. For Jayber Crow, peaceableness involves a vision of harmonious and loving marriage, intended and undertaken in spite of all that threatens it. Such marriages would form households that would relate to one another in "friendliness," constituting something like a Heavenly City living and growing among us—but knowable, now, perhaps only in faith, hope, and love. In seeking to be a trustworthy witness to the City, Jayber comes to understand that he will have to relinquish his hatred and envy of Troy Chatham, becoming a man "unimaginable" not only to Troy but to himself (241).

A Place on Earth opens in a place changed by the war, Jasper Lathrop's store, owned jointly by Jasper's father, Frank, and Mat Feltner. Since Jasper's entrance "into the Army at the beginning of the war," it has been a "carefully tended emptiness anticipating an arrival" (5). Here Frank and Mat, longtime neighbors, friends, and business partners, began to meet in the afternoons of winter 1941–42. When both their sons went into the service, "their friendship changed from a casual fact to a necessity" (12). Soon they are joined by Jayber Crow, Burley Coulter, and Jack Beechum, and a kind of perpetual game of rummy develops, the scores—which no one ever intends to tabulate—scribbled on a long roll of brown paper hanging on the wall. The game is a ritual enactment of solidarity, a necessary vigil and acknowledgment of the tremendous facts before which they stand powerless. It derives from the need—unspoken, perhaps unspeakable—for mutual presence, the sustenance of simply being together in honest awareness of shared vulnerability. Scores are recorded as a way of remembering the game has been played, but the idea that anyone could win is preposterous (somewhat like some people thinking they are better Christians than others). What Old Jack thinks about why he never wants to win an argument with Wheeler applies equally well to the card game: "Jack never admits that he has lost, but he can never bring himself to think that Wheeler has lost, either—not for a minute. What he does believe, what he keeps very firm in his mind, is that between him and Wheeler it does not matter who wins, which is to say that between them the idea of winning is not a very important idea" (55).

One helpful way to consider Berry's depiction of the gathering at Jasper Lathrop's store is as an exercise in citizenship. After all, the occasion for their meetings is the participation of Port William's young people in the nation's war. High citizenship theory, deriving ultimately from Aristotle, holds that human beings become most themselves only by leaving behind the household, *oikos,* and entering the *polis,* to enter into deliberation over how to rule and be ruled. Such political participation is, according to one theorist of civic republicanism, "the highest form of human living-together that most individuals can aspire to."[10] Yet the game at Lathrop's store suggests an even higher form of "human living-together," one where rummy is put to service as an exercise in friendship approaching to worship—if we think of worship as involving human presence to one another in the face of ultimate reality. Here there can be no putting the household behind: life is being lived under the apprehension that what one most dreads, the loss of one's child, has already taken place. For Mat, after the first scene, the good and the only son, Virgil, is missing. That absence determines the life of the *oikos.* Questions, moreover, of how to rule or be ruled would seem terribly out of place in the store. All the men are being ruled by realities they did not will and that they barely understand. Their very high form of living-together involves responding to violence for which they are in no way responsible by upholding the life of the place.

Civilians often think war ends when armistices or treaties are signed, but for participants, particularly combat soldiers, war sometimes never ends. Ernest Finley, Margaret Feltner's brother-in-law, returns to Port William in 1919 after being severely wounded and permanently crippled in the Great War. He returns knowing he has suffered a defeat that is "real and final, allowing for no recovery or revenge, permitting no illusion to mitigate its permanence" (34). Like so many veterans, he "came back with his mouth shut, permanently," unable to "speak of" or to "forget" his experience, left instead to live out what remains of his life in war's continuing presence (34). Though renamed "Shamble" by the townsfolk, Ernest manages to reestablish his dignity through hard and skillful work as a carpenter. He astonishes people with his ability to climb, carry weight up ladders, frame structures, put on roofs of all sorts. He "h[olds] up his face" and looks at people with "a direct straight look in his eyes." He builds a shop, establishing clear order within it, "perfecting" its "neat and convenient" work spaces. In the manner of other American literary carpenters, like the one aboard Melville's *Pequod* or Faulkner's Cash Bundren, Ernest sets about making a perfect, limited, controllable order as a way to prevent himself from being overcome by what threatens him. He "withdraw[s] into the established certainties and clear limits" of his trade, perfecting his shop, "perfect[ing] his silence" (36).

Ernest's silence contributes to his undoing. His habit of living so much within himself makes it difficult for him "to give up his deceptions" (198) regarding Ida Crop. Participation in the ongoing daily casuistry of everyday life may have restrained him from allowing his dreams of her such freedom. Burley sees, for instance, that there is danger in Ernest's feeling for Ida. In a letter to Nathan, he dismisses the town gossip about Ernest and Ida with very accurate insight: "You don't have to be around Ida long to know that she's as mindful of Gideon as she ever was. If I ever see a woman whose ways gave the signs of belonging to one man, it's her. And I'm just about certain that Ernest don't even know how to make the sort of proposition the talkers are accusing him of" (238). But Burley does not conclude from this "that everything is right." He's noted how Ernest always arranges things so as not to be at dinner with Ida when Mat and Burley are there. This suggests to Burley, rightly of course, that "Ernest has Ida on his mind in a way he don't want us to see." "All this worries" Burley, who sees "a possibility of pain in it" (238).

The sadness of Ernest and Ida's relationship is that she gives Ernest what he most needs. Precisely because she is so fully and unselfconsciously "a woman of her own kind and place and way," she communicates a similar acceptance to Ernest, who "feels himself made natural, made as if whole, by her look" (168–69). She seems able to reach "into him with her hand," setting free what the war and his wounding have not been able to destroy, the simple desire for a normal life rooted in affection for another. Ernest's indulgence of his dream seems both self-destructive—given Ida's unwavering devotion to Gideon—and heroically insistent that the war will not determine the terms of his life. He puts the perfect because limited order of his carpentry shop behind him, taking a total risk toward what might be. He knows that even if he "could escape and make his way back" to the life he's reconstructed, "it would no longer serve" (200). Ernest's nearly hopeless gamble fails when Gideon returns, and his suicide follows. Ernest seems almost to act out in his own body what he has learned of war. His desperate attempt at a breakout from his personal stalemate reminds one of the hopeless efforts of infantrymen in the Great War to escape the deadlock of the trenches. Ernest, too, has learned that in some games winning is everything, even perhaps when there's no apparent game being played. Life is, as the strategists of war always insist, a zero-sum game, a competition structured by scarcity. There is only one Ida Crop. When Gideon returns, Ernest loses, as he must have known he would. His breakout has been hopeless all along, like those he has perhaps seen in the war he cannot forget.

Ida Crop's self-possession mirrors the good order that Gideon and she have brought to their place. The Crops rent from Roger Merchant, who has refused to sell the land to Gideon's father, himself an able farmer who has told his son, "Don't let *any*body tell you it ain't hell to do good work for another man who don't care if you do it or not. Who, by God, don't *know* if you do it or not" (114). Gideon has inherited John Crop's desire to own the farm, but he knows this to be a very unlikely possibility. Nevertheless, his farm gives "evidence everywhere—around the other buildings, the house, the garden—of the presence of a strong, frugal intelligence, the sort of mind that can make do, not meagerly but skillfully and adequately, with scraps" (113). Berry describes Gideon's quality of mind as a kind of "peace"; as he looks at the bottom fields "awaiting the new season's crops, they seem to him to have the same serenity that he feels in himself, the same poised free rest between one time and another" (116). The raging waters that sweep Annie away carry with them Gideon's peacefulness—and later Gideon himself—but Ida remains always curiously confident that he will return, to both his presence of mind and his place on earth. Gideon's homecoming marks a return to peace understood as a "poised free rest" capable of letting the past be past and allowing the future to come to be without too much active forcing of its shape.

Roger Merchant is this novel's exploration of the dangers warned about in Isaiah 5:8–10. His father, Griffith Merchant, has been the one who joined fields to fields, leaving Roger to live alone in the middle of the vast acres he controls. Griffith had "lived on his land like a blight, troubled only by the slowness with which it could be converted into cash" (109). Perhaps this paternal ruthlessness has been part of what Roger himself—"born a idiot," according to his father, and "educated a fool"—has sought to deny in considering himself "the descendent of gentleman farmers and one himself"

(109). Actually, Roger is no farmer at all: his place is falling to ruins, all the farming is done by tenants, he lies abed drunk and fouling himself for weeks at a time. The disorder of one generation is passed on to the next: what Griffith Merchant has "plundered," Roger has "ignored" (110). Neither has developed a healthy, peaceful relationship with the land, one in which the human being objectifies his or her life in the place itself, but in a way that respects the place's own integrity and invites its own undoing when the human maker dies. The heirless Merchants will leave nothing but their damage. "In all his life," Roger "has built nothing, added nothing, repaired nothing" (111).

Learning how much damage one can do to places on earth is a crucial part of one's education. Mat knows his "daddy hurt some" of the farm's "hillsides badly in his time," and though Mat has tried to learn from his father's mistakes, he "has made some bad ones" of his own (180). As Mat explains to Hannah, Virgil broke his ground "farther over the brow of the hill than he should have" in planting his first crop. When heavy rains came, the ground washed badly and was "hurt" in a way that could not be easily repaired. Mat was unsparing in his explanation to his son: "Virgil . . . this is your fault. This is one of your contributions to the world." Virgil had to avoid the dangerous irresponsibility of thinking his "doings" temporary. As Mat puts it, "A man's life is always dealing with permanence." One has to "keep before" oneself the knowledge that "what you do on the earth, the earth makes permanent" (180). Knowing this, one's first care must always be to do nothing that cannot be undone unless one is certain that it is good.

One place in Berry's novel remains a place primarily in imagination and yet is no less real for that. This is the house that Virgil and Hannah give to each other during Virgil's two-week furlough, the last time they see each other except in Margaret, who is conceived during this period. Walking over the land toward the river, they come upon a knoll that overlooks the woods, the bottomlands, and the long and broad valley. In this "loveliest place," Virgil pledges to build Hannah a house, only to be gently corrected by her comment that he should "build *us* a house" (57). In tones reminiscent of Frost's dialogues, particularly "West-Running Brook," they agree to the rightness of what both say, concluding that when a house is properly a house, it must be given, like love, wholly, from one to the other and then back again, without diminution. Recalling these moments later, Hannah remembers "the sound of her laughter" as she said, "I'll give you all of it.

And you can give me all of it" (57). To which Virgil responded, "And that's the way it'll be. We'll give this house to each other. We'll pass it back and forth, like a kiss."[11] Theirs is a moment of "free joyfulness," a relief from the tension and estrangement they feel as Virgil's departure nears (57–58). Again one hears Frost's tones, here those of "Directive," as they are "made . . . glad" by "this house that was no house," this "no house that was their house" (58–59).[12] The spontaneous joy, the free acknowledgment of their desire—against everything—for a house, "was like a bet made, making the thought of winning possible." There is a kind of winning already present for them as well as they refuse to let themselves be bound by the future's uncertainty. They take a risk, in faith and love, "gambl[ing]" in this "hope of house . . . toward what might be" (59). Their risk-taking results in no house atop the knoll, but rather in a daughter, a living embodiment of love given and given back, wholly and without calculation.

Berry describes Hannah's pregnancy as being "like a long lovemaking, a long continuance of Virgil's body in her own" (239). Virgil continued to have a place on earth within Hannah's body. After Margaret's birth, Hannah "feels her body going to waste" as her "mourning over Virgil is also a mourning over herself—is the same" (239). This is one consequence of that whole and radical self-giving they have playfully pledged each other earlier. As Virgil has given all that he is over to Hannah, and received from her all that she is, her mourning must encompass them both. Virgil continues to have a place on earth even in his absence. As if within her own body, Hannah is aware of what declares itself there in its absence. Her body has become a house where the missing one remains precisely as missing: "She feels his absence *within* herself, a vacancy, as though some vital part of her own body was removed in her sleep" (239). Virgil both is and is not lost to Hannah. She finds herself increasingly uncomfortable within the Feltners' house, for there everything reminds her of "Virgil's absence, her loss, the life she will never have" (240). Outside she is better, for she feels there, "just outside her reach," that something of him is still "present in the life of the place" (241). She remembers carrying water to Virgil one day as he worked hard in the hot sun. What "came to her then"—and does so again—"was the sense of the abundance of strength in him that accepted the heat and the tiredness of that day with a kind of joy" (241). Virgil gave joyfully from an abundance that knew itself so full and confident of replenishment that it rejoiced in its own diminution. Hannah knows that what is so wholly given cannot be wholly lost. As she climbs toward the top of a ridge, "that country so charged with her memory of him" comes increasingly into sight, and she knows "a strengthening in her of the sense that what he was still is. And with a kind of yielding, she receives him into herself, not to be lost again" (241).

Margaret refers to a similar inability to lose Virgil as she responds to the brokenness Mat feels after they are able to acknowledge their son's death. After they receive the news of Virgil's being missing, the Feltners continue to maintain hope as well as possible. There is really nothing to do except to wait for further information that never arrives. Some things must simply be borne, though there is small comfort in this truth. Finally Mat must confront what he knows to be true, and he does so in anger, as one might well expect, as if anger at the very nature of things is what one requires to confront the previously unthinkable. He insists that they all begin to think of and refer to Virgil as dead. Margaret cannot banish Mat's anger, but she does manage to begin to turn him back to her and Hannah and the young Margaret. Whereas Mat focuses only on the loss of the beloved son, Margaret explains that she has always known Virgil would die, from the time she has carried him in her body. She cannot now "turn away" from his life "any more than [she] could when he was a little child." She must love his life "and be glad of it," for she has no other choice (262). He must be let go, and can be let go, because he has a place on earth with her that cannot be lost.[13]

Perhaps this is the place at which to say a word in defense of Brother Preston, or "Piston" as Burley calls him. When the dutiful young preacher comes to visit the Feltners, his words of comfort surely move too quickly and abstractly to "the final hope, in which all the riddles and ends of the world are gathered, illuminated, and bound" (99). Even as he speaks, he "is aware of something failing between them" (98). Burley writes to Nathan of his irritation at what the preacher has said to him after the news of Tom's death had reached Port William. Burley's major complaint is that the preacher never knew Tom and thus does not know "what it is that's gone" (104). "I say that a man has got to *deserve* to speak of the life of another man and of the death of him" (104), Burley writes. The right words about Tom will have to be spoken by those who knew him, worked with him, lived and laughed with him. Remembering who young men like Virgil and Tom were is important to places on earth like Port William. As Burley puts it, "We don't forget them after somebody who never knew them has said, 'Dead in the service of his country' and 'Rest in peace.' That's not the way these accounts are kept. We don't rest in peace" (105).

It is difficult not to love Burley here for this frank, passionate expression of solidarity. We have all heard enough of the justifying abstractions for war to be cynical of such ideological blessings as "Dead" or "He died" in the "service of his country." One wants to insist, like Hannah in *Hannah Coulter*, that no one has the right to speak about one's life-giving service except the lost one him- or herself. But the keeping of accounts—even, perhaps especially, the accounts kept in the love for which Burley has a genius—can lead to war. As Stanley Hauerwas has powerfully argued, two compelling justifications for war will have to be confronted and disarmed if we are ever to lay war to rest. One is our tendency to sacrifice in order to justify sacrifices already made, to ensure that those who have died have not done so in vain. A second, closely related, is our need to demonstrate ourselves worthy of our history. War offers an all too fertile field and compelling opportunity for sacrifice and demonstrations of worthiness, the exercises of love.[14] Burley is right. We do not "rest in peace." Indeed, we often find it difficult to rest at all. We need something "to do" (186), like Old Jack at Mrs. Hendrick's cutting the weeds or plowing up her back lot for a garden "for the good of the world" (191). But we also need to be able to rest in the hard truth that sometimes there is nothing to be done. To begin to move the Feltners toward facing the unfaceable, imagining the known but unimaginable possibility, is Brother Preston's role. Even in that early moment of the history of their loss, Mat's "fear, which he has kept silenced until now, begins to take its words" (98). This marks the first distancing of Mat from pain far worse to confront than his own death. It begins the process of grief and thus—if not of recovery, for there is no recovery—of continuance in hope. Someone must speak a word to the Feltners or Burley and Jarrat or all the others like them that enables them to begin to believe again that hope is possible. No doubt Brother Preston does his work clumsily, too safely because too abstractly, but it must, after all, be done. And it is not easy.

Despite the difficulty of its attainment, there are intimations of peace in Berry's novel. As Gideon searches for Annie, he becomes aware, after the rain has stopped, of a "flock of mallards feeding on the open water ahead of him." As he watches them "settled" and "calmly feeding," Gideon feels momentarily "let into" a "depth of intimacy—the peacefulness of wild things among themselves," a "peacefulness [that] stretches among them, holding them at rest on the shining surface of the water" (125). We have seen that kind of restfulness in Ida, in Gideon himself before Annie's death, in Margaret and her acceptance of Virgil's inevitable death, perhaps even in Hannah after she has come to know that Virgil will continue with her in his absence.

The restfulness of fulfillment comes to Old Jack when he finds rightful heirs in Elton and Mary Penn. Succession to various places on earth has long been a source of conflict, often violent. Old Jack has had no heir to his place. His only child, Clara, has moved to Louisville and has no interest in the land apart from what it will bring monetarily. But in Elton and Mary, Old Jack finds people who care as much for the land as he has, people who combine an orderly intelligence, the capacity for hard work, and an inexhaustible interest in the possibilities of life in this place. As Jack walks over the land he now rents to the Penns, he stops "now and again" and "stands a long time, looking. He is studying his land, the shape of it, the condition of the growth on it, with the interest in it that he has had all his life" (212). For Jack the land has proven to be good in the sense Cato wrote of in *De Re Rustica,* cited and translated here by Thoreau in "Where I Lived and What I Lived For": "When you think of getting a farm, turn it thus in your mind, not to buy greedily; nor spare your pains to look at it, and do not think it enough to go round it once. The oftener you go there the more it will please you, if it is good."[15]

An intelligence that allows itself to be guided by the land's own possibilities can find within it a constant source of promise and pleasure. Thus, it does not need to aggressively extend its territory—something Jack tried to do and failed, something Elton shows little interest even in attempting. Elton's excellence brings for Jack "the terms of an unexpected happiness," the "possibility of an orderliness in his history that he has not dared to hope for." "It is as though" Jack "has come to a window looking out onto a lighted country where before was only darkness" (211). Jack can simultaneously find connection with the young man and let go in freedom. All of this is made possible by the excellence of Elton Penn, that "accurate man" who has learned intelligent responsiveness to this particular place on earth. Thoreau noted wryly in *Walden* that the only thing he ever found missing from his unlocked house was a copy of Pope's Homer, which he trusted that "a soldier of our camp has found by this time." In a community where all lived simply, "the Pope's Homers would soon get properly distributed" (218). Proper distribution is at stake, too, in Jack Beechum's passing his land to Elton Penn. It is the mark of a good community that not only the Homers but also the homesteads get into the right hands. Jack manages that passing to Elton and Mary, but only because Wheeler Catlett understands his role to involve service not simply to the law but to the good—to a Thoreauvian idea of equity that insists a "proper distribution" of things of permanent value cannot discount the character of recipients.

Mat Feltner describes himself to Hannah as "a great one for places." His farm is "just full of places" he looks forward to "spend[ing] a day sitting in." He has traveled much on his own place and in Port William and still finds them inexhaustible. There are some places on his own farm he has thought of "nearly all" his life and yet never had time to go there, rest, and "be still" (184). The novel closes with Mat at rest, and happy, in one of those places, sitting at the foot of a tree in a grove where he can see the river and the older trees on the other side. He can see rock cairns there, meaning these were once cleared fields, but the age of the trees indicates that the work "done there was done long before his time, and no doubt before his father's" (320). The passage might be read as a gloss on Thoreau's saying we need to "witness our own limits transgressed" (*Walden,* 366). Perhaps seeing our limits transgressed is the way to seeing just how limited we are and how caught up we ordinarily are in struggling with our limits without even being aware of it. Mat "feels the great restfulness of that place" and the "difference between that restful order and his own constant struggle to maintain and regulate his clearings." His is no easy absorption into nature: he remains a mortal human being whose "devotion" to those clearings "remain[s] firm in his mind." He is a creature of meanings, poised on that place between nature and civilization, knowing "without sorrow" that "the order he has made and kept" will be "overthrown" (321). He has become one who can keep and lose in peace.

A Place on Earth offers no program for peace, no guidelines that realist policy makers would deem even worthy of consideration. But if peace is, at least partly, dependent on our imagining alternatives to war, then Berry's novel might well be pondered as a contribution to peace. Perhaps part of thinking peacefully is to imagine the inexhaustibility of particular places and then—having imagined it—to find out how it is true. Such inexhaustibility would have nothing to do with consumption or expansion of one's territory. In fact, too much expansion of territory—by an individual or nation—would almost surely seem irrational, a form of technological-consumerist thinking in which everything can be thought of only as a resource to be transformed into something else. Obviously, nothing conceived of simply as a means can be inexhaustible. To think peace would be to accept that one's efforts, one's "doings," should never be damaging to the earth or to the possibilities of others coming after one. It would be enough to "keep watch," like Mat Feltner at lambing time, over life, knowing that "whatever is born will be born into his wakefulness and his care" (87). One would cherish and find satisfaction in the task of holding up "the life of his place," finding peace with oneself, as Mat does, when "his labor has been his necessity and his desire" (88). Peace might involve thinking ourselves out of zero-sum games and the fear of scarcity, while acknowledging that resources of all kinds are limited. An old ewe that Mat fails to get to in time loses her first lamb as she struggles in labor with the second; she has been prevented from "attending properly to the lamb she had already got born" (89). Birth, sustenance, rearing require dedicated attention and care: too often what is given to one must come away from another. But it can be our part—the role of an accurate and orderly intelligence directed toward the real—to minimize these effects of scarcity. Mat's mind has, in this case, "fallen short of its subject" (89). If we wish to see what there is to be done, we must first learn adequate attention, a quality that itself depends upon restfulness, for we will never understand the requirements of our subjects if we are always busily seeking to put intelligence to work. Part of avoiding zero-sum thinking would be to learn, as Old Jack has in his friendship with Wheeler, that winning is not a very important idea.

A politics of peace might begin with something like the conviction Jack keeps firmly in mind in arguments with Wheeler: "Jack never admits that he has lost, but he can never bring himself to think that Wheeler has lost, either—not for a minute." "As a matter of fact," Berry adds, "nothing would trouble him more than to beat Wheeler in an argument" (55). The only way to arrive at the resolution Jack would accept—win-win, no parties needing to save face—is to continue the argument as long as it takes, with all parties involved, until no person, people, or country felt itself diminished by the others. Such a politics would be the near antithesis of the concluding events of World War II, as Mat understands them. After hearing the news of Hiroshima over the radio, Mat has the sense that war has now come to its fulfillment, accomplished its totality, proven itself capable of dominating and destroying every place on earth. He feels himself borne along "like a man in a little boat, on the crest of history, in a violence of pure effect, as though the event of the war, having long ago outdistanced its cause, now escapes comprehension, and speeds on. It has seemed to him that the years of violence have arrived at what, without his knowing it, they had been headed for, not by any human reason or motive or wish but by the logic of violence itself" (259). Violence, purest product of the fear of scarcity, the fear that, as Pascal saw, there will be no place on earth for me.

News of the end of World War II comes to Port William on the day before Ernest Finley's burial. Jayber has already dug Ernest's grave, and the men sit in mourning on the Feltners' porch when Frank Lathrop bursts from his house, doing a dance across his own porch across the street. Mat will keep in his mind a long time "the sight of Frank dancing for joy, oblivious to the mourning he danced in the face of" (278). The joy at the words *"It's over! It's over!"* (278) cannot be suppressed, and soon nearly all are drawn into the celebration with its dancing, bonfires, and bootleg whiskey. When they become sufficiently lubricated, Jayber, Big Ellis, and Burley decide to conduct a mock funeral and burial of Whacker Spradlin, the bootlegger who has been provider of the drink and who is so sufficiently "stinking" as to seem dead. The dirge suggests the "unimpeachable class" of the proceedings:

> We are hauling,
> We are hauling
> His aaaaass
> To the graveyard.
> We'll bury this peckerwood
> In six foot of ground. (295)

As the procession and singing continue, Jayber—"once a preacher, always a preacher"—moves almost in spite of himself to a more sober turn, creating a "true grave digger's tune." Once he's "sung his way into it," there's "nothing to do but dig in and sing his way out of it": "If you think that stops the story / And puts an end to the matter / Maybe so. But maybe there's a glory / Where you'd rather we'd all gather" (296). The scene's wonderful blend of seriousness and farce continues as Burley and Big Ellis let Whacker down into Ernest's grave, where Jayber stands ready to help. The two cannot hold the huge Whacker, and Jayber finds himself fighting "off the impulse to turn loose and run, knowing there is no place to go," as he "shov[es] at Whacker's great buttocks for dear life, his voice rising up quick and small under his burden" (300). Once Whacker is properly placed, Jayber speaks "slowly and with feeling," his words taking on a weight and seriousness wholly unintended or unexpected:

> Water into water, earth into earth,
> Breath into breath, light into light,
> Singing into singing, birth into birth,
> Thought into thought, sight into sight,
> Let this man's makings be unmade,
> Let stillness be, let peace come
> To this place that was a man. (300–301)

Burley, Jayber, and Big Ellis stand with heads bowed, recalled to the occasion: "the end of the war, the dying, the deaths—the graves of the millions that, beyond knowing, peace has come to" (301). They sleep and awake the next morning—"Resurrection morning" (305), Big Ellis calls it—to find Whacker gone. And it's a good thing, too, for they had neither plan nor strength to get Whacker out of that grave. No one sees Whacker's resurrection nor the power by which it is accomplished. He simply gets up and walks on another day. That he does so is both a matter of high seriousness and farce—perhaps of farce put to the service of high seriousness.

Mat Feltner is uncertain whether to be offended or not by the goings-on inspired by the cry "It's over," and surely Berry presses us to ponder their appropriateness. One way to see Jayber, Big Ellis, and Burley's antics, with their fine Shakespearean feel, is as a form of Christian comic defiance of the devil. Their spirit recalls the two wonderful epigraphs from C. S. Lewis's *The Screwtape Letters,* one from Luther, one from Thomas More. "The best way to drive out the devil, if he will not yield to texts of Scripture, is to jeer and flout him, for he cannot bear scorn," Luther writes. And in a similar vein, More comments, "The devil . . . the prowde spirite . . . cannot endure to be mocked."[16] As they work at getting Whacker out of the trunk of Big Ellis's car, Big whispers, "We look just like devils in this red light," and Burley responds, "We'd look like the devil if it was daylight" (298). And so they do and would, for the devil they mock is within them—and us—as

well as without. Our proud spirit is his greatest resource as he seeks to persuade us that death has dominion everywhere, that the power of scarcity—
scarcity of life—rules over every place on earth. Mat Feltner has himself
been drawn into the spirit of the procession as it has passed his house on
the way to the graveyard. Something of the burden of that night—"that the
dead have lost and are absent from victory"—has been "start[ed]" by the
"unabashed glee" of the celebrants "toward something else—though he was
not able to say what" (303). Berry does not "say what" in any specific way,
but perhaps part of what the procession moves us toward is peace, grounded in a power not our own that enables us to mock the Devil's so seductive
claims that there will never be a place on earth, or under the sun, for us all.

Jayber Crow, barber and Augustinian, holds to the idea that "in Port
William, or beyond it, or above it," there is a "kind of Heavenly City."[17] One
here is a resident traveler in an earthly city while knowing also that another city, the City of God, has come into our midst, lives and grows among
us, and calls us to itself as ultimate reality. Perhaps like many moderns,
Jayber has somewhat more sense than Augustine of simultaneously exist-
ing in both cities, but the conception itself is distinctly owing to Augustine's
Civitas Dei. For Jayber, the City is, as it was for Augustine, a true commonwealth, ordered by justice and by virtue, whose true end is peace. Marriage
is central to the City, a witness to the possibility that human relationships
might be ordered by love. For the bachelor Jayber, who sometimes thinks
of himself as "the most married" of all Port William's men, marriage has
become "a kind of last-ditch holy of holies: the possibility that two people
might care for each other and know each other better than enemies, and
better than strangers happening to be alive at the same time in the same
town; and that, with a man and a woman, this caring and knowing might
be made by intention, and in the consciousness of all it is, and of all it
might be, and of all that threatens it" (72). Jayber's larger vision of the City
is one in which "each house would be built in a marriage and around it"
and "all the houses would be bound together in friendships." Peace would
prevail over conflict within a continuous harmony of loving difference, or
"friendliness," in Jayber's idiom, which "would move and join among them
like an open street" (72). Jayber has staked his life on living this ideal in his
own life in Port William, bearing "the descent of the town from that ideal"
in his own person and taking responsibility for continually giving "birth to

the new real morning and the real town" (72). His is a work of hope. But he also knows himself to be an adulterer, one unfaithful to his ideal, one who slips "away from his Heavenly City" to "become the lover of all the perishing lights and substances of Port William and of the weather over it and of the water under it." He has come to think of himself as a "native and occupant of both places," one who "passes freely between them, and in serving either serves both" (72–73).

A pair of marriages is at the center of both *Hannah Coulter* and *Jayber Crow*. In *Hannah*, these marriages follow one another: Hannah first marries Virgil Feltner and then, some years after Virgil's death in the war, Nathan Coulter. In *Jayber*, the marriages are simultaneously ongoing: Mattie Keith is married to Troy Chatham, but Jayber Crow, for a variety of reasons, decides to take upon himself the role of being her true husband. Both novels explore how marriage might be, as Jayber has put it in *A Place on Earth*, a place where "caring and knowing" (72) could come to their fullness by intention and even in the face of all that threatens to destroy them.

Hannah's memoir is a work of piety, a loving giving of thanks for the goodness that has made her life possible. To tell her story, she knows, is to situate it within a much larger story begun long before her and continuing long after. Her "Grandmam" first "shaped" Hannah's life, making the "connections that made" that life after Hannah's mother had died and her father had remarried a woman, Ivy Crutchlow, with two sons of her own (11). Ivy teaches Hannah nothing except to beware those who look on all of life as a zero-sum game. Grandmam's influence on Hannah's story is incalculable. "Determined to mold me into something that could stay alive" (19), as Hannah remembers, Grandmam moved her to the house of her old friend Ora Finley in Hargrave after Hannah had finished high school. There she began to work for Wheeler Catlett, entered—without intending to do so— the Port William membership, and met Virgil Feltner. As she and Virgil came to love each other, they were coming—as she recognizes, looking back—"into the presence of something good that was possible in this world" (28). Virgil's descriptions of the "shape" (28) of a life that he anticipated and loved—like those of a good novelist, one might say—caused Hannah to come to love it. They would have their part in making that life, but their marriage would also "have to be part of a place already decided for it, and part of a story begun long ago and going on" (33). Virgil's love for Hannah was his own, but it, too, was part of a "love that had been borne to him, by people he knew" (33), people he loved. Hannah became a part of that people, came to love them and know them. Indeed, she came to love them in a way unknown to Virgil, for she loved and knew them dead.

World War II diminishes, but does not utterly destroy, the goodness that Hannah and Virgil commit themselves to bringing into the world. Before Virgil is called to duty, the whole Feltner household feels the war as "a bodily presence," something that "was in all of us," Hannah remembers, "and nobody said a word" (36). As the Feltners' Christmas gathering for 1941 draws to an end, young Andy Catlett hides in a corner of the dining room, crying, aware "that what we were that day was lovely and could not last" (40). Hannah speaks for a generation of Americans when she recalls the way the war altered forever her sense that she lived in a local world. That "small old local world of places like Shagbark and Hargrave"—with their "daily work and dreaming of themselves"—looked "small and lost" in the "new world made by the new war" (41–42). War had become total; it had succeeded in establishing itself as *the* reality, capable of coming into and transforming every household on earth. "Total mobilization," Ernst Junger called it, everything set into motion and capable of transformation.[18] Or, as Hannah feels it, "Our minds were driven out of the old boundaries into the thought of absolute loss, absolute emptiness, in a world that seemed larger even than the sky that held it" (42). When Nathan and Hannah later marry and begin to farm, Hannah senses that Nathan is recreating a place on earth for them beyond the war. He has returned to this homeland—to these hillsides and bottomlands and woods—because "this place" was "what he wanted," a desire formed "in the midst of killing and dying, terror, cruelty, hate, hunger, thirst, blood, and fire" (67). I am not one to think much of ranking generations, but a part of the simple greatness of men like Nathan is that so many returned from total war to take up the old ways of carrying on a good human life—loving and marrying women, having families, cultivating places on earth, renewing memberships.

War disrupts time, usurping it for itself, claiming no other pursuit worthy to stand alongside it. As soon as Virgil leaves home, Hannah and the Feltners begin "holding something back inside" themselves, something they "didn't want to give to that time" (44). When Virgil comes home for two weeks in August 1944, he and Hannah find themselves in "a no-time that led on to a time" they "could not imagine," one that makes them "strange to each other" (47). One of Virgil's great gifts to Hannah is his imagining—on their next-to-last evening together—the house they would build, "now and always," and marking out the spots for the walls and rooms. Hannah describes that house as "the kindest" of "all the kind things he did for me." It represents a time both when they "were together on the condition only of loving each other" (48) and when Virgil risked a future against the war himself by letting it be imagined, spoken, and begun. Virgil leaves Hannah with Margaret, with the house, and with a kindness that later leads Hannah to realize she cannot speak of his love in the past tense. As she and the Feltners wait through the time defined by Virgil's being "missing," "kindness kept [them] alive," kindness rooted in their constant awareness of one another's struggling grief and hope. "By kindness I was coming to understand what it meant to be in love with Virgil," Hannah remembers. "He and I had been, we were, we *are*—for there is no escape—in love together" (50).

Coming to know what it means to lose Virgil helps Hannah to understand what it means for others to lose him too. So grief performs its office of binding together those who have lost with a "sort of heartbreaking kindness" (50). Hannah begins "to know" her "story then," that it will be, "like everybody's," the "story of living in the absence of the dead" (51). Perhaps grief is the motive for story itself, part of the way we resist war's claim that all time belongs to it. Hannah is well aware that others will gladly tell Virgil's story if she does not. Her telling is an act of resistance against those who would make Virgil's death "official," a "government property or a public thing" (57). She does not know whether Virgil would consider "the life and freedom of the living a satisfactory payment to the dead in war for their dying" (56). She dislikes "for the dead to be made to agree with whatever some powerful living person wants to say" (56). What she knows is altogether more simple: "What I know is this. Virgil loved his life. He loved me. He loved his family. He did not want to die. He wanted to come home and live with me and raise a family, and farm with his dad. He knew we were going to have a baby. He never knew he had a daughter. He never knew her name" (57). The great responsibility that can come with grief is something Hannah feels intensely. Her grief for Virgil "made his death his own," protected from appropriation by political or patriotic rhetoric, however well intentioned. Her "grief was the last meaning of his life in this world" (57), and thus it was extraordinarily difficult to give up.

Hannah's sense of grief here is somewhat reminiscent of Augustine's grief over a lost friend in Book IV of the *Confessions*. Augustine comes to understand that his extreme, nearly inconsolable grief for his friend derives, in part, from his own sense that only his—Augustine's—memory prevents his friend from utter extinction. Augustine's anxiety over his own death increases enormously—something not true of Hannah—for fear that with his death "one whom [he] had loved so well might then be wholly dead." Fortunately, as Augustine recalls,

> Time never stands still, nor does it idly pass without effect upon our feelings or fail to work its wonders on the mind. It came and went, day after day, and as it passed it filled me with fresh hope and new thoughts to remember. Little by little it pieced me together again by means of the old pleasures which I had once enjoyed.[19]

Time pieces Hannah together again, too. She finds the "living can't quit living because the world has turned terrible and people they love and need are killed." They can't quit "because they don't." She knows herself, in her own Johannine way, to be called on into life by the "light that shines in darkness and never goes out" (57). But to allow herself to move beyond grief for Virgil and to desire a life with Nathan is an extraordinarily difficult and delicate matter for her.

Hannah and the Feltners have become members of one another during the war, especially after Virgil is reported missing. She has become, in effect, their daughter and given birth to Margaret, Virgil's child. She has come to know in her own grief what grief must be for them, and—as Augustine feels for his friend—she feels that her grief gives Virgil a continuing place among the living, a place on earth. To allow her grief to pass, to allow herself to acknowledge her desire for Nathan, must seem a betrayal not only of Virgil but of the Feltners, from whom she has received nothing but kindness. Fortunately, neither of the Feltners thinks of life or love as a zero-sum game. For them, Hannah's love for Nathan in no way diminishes Virgil. Her continuing to grieve for him at the expense of her own life and happiness would be only to allow the war to continue to determine the present—and the possibilities of good—for all of them. It is a mark of the extraordinary kindness and generosity of the Feltners that they sense Hannah's dilemma, give her permission to take up her life again, and happily bless her marriage to Nathan. Such generosity derives from their knowing themselves to be participants in a much larger and longer-running story of love—one in which Virgil is so surely loved by God that the Feltners are freed to simply love where Virgil has loved, Hannah, and then where she comes to love in turn, Nathan.

Hannah's story of her life with Nathan is a love story. Perhaps, on her terms, all stories are, at least in part, love stories. Hannah knows in the light of love, a love that we have not invented, one that we could not have conceived. That love has come into the world, goes ahead of us, and shines on in the darkness, drawing us on and opening up a way for us, however little we understand. Like Jayber Crow, Hannah believes that Port William, Kentucky, is "an immortal place" (43), where nothing really is lost. Even the name of the place is something of a mystery, as the town sits atop a ridge and is half a mile from the river. Townspeople get used to being asked why the place is called a "Port," and Hannah is fond of remembering Ben Feltner's habitual answer: "They didn't know where the river was going to run when they built Port William." Hannah understands this to mean that Port William "has never been the same place two minutes together," that it is continually being changed by time (and no one yet knows where the river will run). But she thinks, too, that "any way it has ever been it will always be" and that, finally, the whole story of its life will be recapitulated in the *hieros gamos,* the marriage of heaven and earth: "Some day there will be a new heaven and a new earth and a new Port William coming down from heaven, adorned as a bride for her husband, and whoever has known her before will know her then" (43).

For Hannah, all things partake of love-longing, "the longing" to be "together, and to be at rest together" (110). Our hearts are restless, we recall from Augustine, until they rest in God. Her marriage to Nathan is one of the ways Hannah lives now from this eschatological vision of peace, itself grounded in that vision of an original peace that is the great gift to us of Genesis 1. Hannah knows no diminution of life here as she waits for some fulfillment that will only arrive later. Indeed, she waits on God, and yet she lives quite fully in the present from the love that moves all of creation. This love does not "come out of thin air," as she puts it. "It is not something thought up. Like ourselves, it grows out of the ground. It has a body and a place" (88). Nathan and she made their "love for each other" on a particular place, which they loved, and among "its stories remembered and forgotten." Their love for their children, lost and alive, "was made" there (88). As they lived by their work, they fortunately were able to love it. They loved the membership of people of whom they were parts, and they were blessed to understand themselves as part of the "one piece of work," as Burley puts it. Sometimes in the midst of communal work, Burley will "preach the membership, mocking a certain kind of preacher, yet meaning every word he said." His theme is that all are part of the membership: "The difference, beloved, ain't in who is and who's not, but in who knows it and who don't. Oh, my friends, there ain't no nonmembers, living nor dead nor yet to come. Do you know it? Or do you don't?" (97).

Hannah and Nathan know it. They know also that one must love one's life and the place that sustains one. Much of the latter part of the novel is given to Hannah's accounts of her children—Margaret, Mattie (M.B.), and Caleb—and particularly to the way their college educations make them unsuited for life on the farm. Hannah's criticism of education as currently conceived—and it is Berry's—is that it involves a kind of systematic training in restlessness. "The big idea of education, from first to last, is the idea of a better place," Hannah puts it, "not a better place where you are, because you want it to be better and have been to school and learned to make it better, but a better place somewhere else" (112). With regard to farming, part of American education's consistent message has been "that farming people are inferior and need to improve themselves by leaving the farm" (114). Fortunately for Nathan and Hannah, when they need someone to farm the Feltner place, left to Margaret, and finally to assist Nathan, Danny Branch and his clan have avoided contracting the conviction that they are not good enough just as they are. No doubt this immunity derives, at least literarily, from their ancestor Burley, who is always content to be right where he is. Berry allows some possibility, too, that perhaps some members of the present generation will find the return to farm life desirable. As the century turns toward 2001, Hannah remarks that nothing very remarkable has happened in Port William except that Virgie, Margaret's son, has come back, saying he wants to farm. There is no way of knowing, apart from time, whether that is true.

When Margaret comes back to Port William to tell Hannah and Nathan that her marriage has failed, Nathan encourages her with, "Margaret, my good Margaret, we're going to live right on." Hannah says that she heard Nathan "say that only three or four times in all his life" and "only when he knew that living right on was going to be hard" (141). He says it again when he knows he is dying, shortly after a diagnosis of metastatic cancer: "Dear Hannah, I'm going to live right on. Dying is none of my business. Dying will have to take care of itself" (161). Nathan dies a good death, choosing not to avail himself of the therapeutic options offered by his physicians, committed to living as himself to the end. Death is perhaps the supreme crisis of our lives, and yet, as Nathan helps Hannah to see, "it had to be, it could only be, dealt with as an ordinary thing" (161). Nathan has seen plenty of the business of dying—and killing—at Okinawa, and he chooses to have no more of it. This is not to say that the war has had no effect on him. Rather it is, as Hannah believes, "the circumstance of the rest of his life" (167)—that which must be chosen against, imagined against, outnarrated, if you will, every remaining day of his life. After Nathan's death, Hannah turns to reading about Okinawa from the need to know more of this circumstance of Nathan's life—one he spoke about very little, as is characteristic of World War II veterans.

What Hannah's reading about Okinawa leads her to is one of Berry's most explicitly theological understandings of war. Glossing Sherman's famous phrase, she sees that war "is the outer darkness beyond the reach of love, where people who do not know one another kill one another and there is weeping and gnashing of teeth, where nothing is allowed to be real enough to be spared" (168). "What is needed" is imagination, for it is "want of imagination" that "makes things unreal enough to be destroyed" (168). Without imagination, we are helpless before the wielders of power, who tell us that only power is real. To imagine the real means living every day in Port William with a loving, compassionate knowledge of the concrete lives of people whom the powers would have us believe are our enemies. It means remembering and keeping vividly alive what the reality of Okinawa was for American soldiers like Nathan and their Japanese counterparts. Christ enables this kind of imagination. He does not bring an end to suffering, although "he asked us to end it" (171). But he is "born into" this "body of our suffering," to "suffer it Himself and to fill it with light, so that beyond the suffering we can imagine Easter morning and the peace of God on little earthly homelands such as Port William and the farming villages of Okinawa" (171). To "give yourself over to love" is always to give yourself over to suffering, to experiencing the "old suffering over and over again" until you finally, "in loving," come to see "that you have given yourself over to the knowledge of suffering in a state of war that is always going on" (171). Hannah concludes that "The Battle of Okinawa" was "not a battle only of two armies making war against each other," but also "a battle of both armies making war against a place and its people" (172). Perhaps, theologically speaking, it was a battle against suffering itself, which one could pretend to defeat by turning it into a power to be used against others. Perhaps it was a battle against the very possibilities of good in that place and that people.

As Nathan has decided consciously to have no truck with dying, Hannah teaches herself to remain in the "room of love" (158), dwelling on the possibilities of good in the present—even as she knows, like a good Augustinian, that the present is swept away into the past even before one apprehends it. As she first experiences Nathan's absence in the house after his death, she "turned again to that other world" she "had taught [herself] to know, the world that is neither past nor to come, the present world where we are alive together and love keeps us" (166). Part of the way love keeps us in the present is by our telling our stories, patiently, repeatedly, to "get [them] right." Hannah imagines herself telling her story to Andy, who "has been listening to [her] all his life." Telling and retelling the story is a way, as she puts it, of "perfect[ing] these thanks" (158). What she describes is very close to, indeed is, prayer. As she retells her stories, intensely aware that our minds are part of one another's and that the love we share is surely no invention of our own but something that comes to us, she thinks her mind "has started to become, it is close to being, the room of love where the absent are present, the dead are alive, time is eternal, and all the creatures prosperous" (158). It is in this space that the novel concludes with a brief chapter called "Given." Hannah is "standing at the gate," Nathan "salting the cattle down at the edge of the woods." He begins up the hill, at first just walking, then walking toward her as he sees her. She knows he is going to give her a hug and "how it is going to feel, the entire touch of him." "He looks at me with a look I know. The shiver of the altogether given passes over me from head to foot" (186). That looks says "we're going to live right on, old girl," and they will, for the altogether given cannot be altogether lost.

The Life Story of Jayber Crow, Barber, of the Port William Membership, as Written by Himself is less centrally concerned with the direct effects of war than *A Place on Earth* or *Hannah Coulter*, but it, too, is ultimately a novel of love set in time of war. Jonah Crow—later J., then Jaybird, then Jayber—was born "on August 3, 1914—and so lived one day in the world before the beginning of total war" (11). That war, as Jayber understands it, did not end in 1918; it only paused. Peace broke out while the powers reloaded for the next coming of the killing phase in 1939–45, itself followed by more episodes in the life of War—and its partner, the Economy—episodes we know by names like Korea and Vietnam. War and the Economy sought and successfully completed the transformation of places like Port William, destroying both local self-sufficiency and complacency, displacing people from the land, promoting the desirability of debt, teaching everyone that, above all, their lives should be focused on constant self-improvement—therefore simultaneously teaching them that nothing is ever good enough. Transformation itself is the essence of War and the Economy under technology. War seeks to transform the living into the dead as efficiently as possible. The Economy seeks to transform everything into something whose value is assessed only in relation to other things. Its central lesson is that nothing has value in itself.[20]

Jayber makes the reader feel the indirect effects of War and the Economy throughout his life story. Jayber's enemy, Cecelia Overhold, originally "of the Hargrave upper crust" (151), lives in constant dissatisfaction with most everything about Port William, including her husband, Roy. She longs for California, where she's gone to visit her sister Dorothy (set down there, presumably, by a tornado). "Oh," she says about it, "it's a real place, a wonderful place. You can see the stars of the picture shows alive" (152). She realizes this old dream of going after Roy dies, and she sells the farm, expecting a nephew of hers in the Promised Land to provide her a "joyous welcome." He welcomes her "by enrolling her into an old folks' home where, forsaken, she did not live long." About all she accomplishes, as Jayber puts it, is transferring "the pretty penny she got for the Overhold place" from Port William to Los Angeles (355). Similarly, Troy Chatham rejects the conservative, ecologically attuned farming methods of his father-in-law, Athey Keith. Impressed by the propaganda of land-grant universities, Troy believes that only bigness will allow farms to survive and succeed. He turns increasingly to monoculture, to keeping ever more land under continual cultivation, and to financing his expansion with increased debt and leverage. Finally, in an unsuccessful attempt to save his land, he cuts the Nest Egg of old-growth timber so long preserved by Athey and

Mattie. Indeed, it's not even clear whether Troy thinks the timber can actually service his debt. One might just as well say he has the timber cut because he's completely at the service of the powers he has admired. He serves to perform the ultimate meaning of War and the Economy: that nothing is safe from being transformed into something else.

Jayber's barber shop falls victim to the ever greater rationalization of life in Port William in the name of public safety. Its plumbing is pronounced substandard by the Inspector, a version of "the man across the desk" (289) whom Jayber spends a lifetime eluding. Burley Coulter has delighted over the years in pointing out how Jayber's shop has allowed him to have his work and his living in the same place. That unity of life and work is a casualty of the Economy, for Jayber as well as the generation of farmers who have provided his primary clientele. Jayber moves to Burley's camp house on the river; the barbering and socializing that were once features of Main Street life in Port William now take place on the margins. Economic life still goes on as ever. Barbering is an organic vocation. Hair grows and therefore must be cut, calling forth the barber. But while the stylists take over in town, Jayber ends his barbering life trading work with Danny and Lyda Branch, inheritors of the old liberty of Burley and Port William, a liberty that now must be maintained by an increasingly conscious refusal of engagement in mainstream economic life.

One of the consistent themes of Jayber's life concerns the question of his calling or vocation. Jayber first hears the "call" to "full time Christian service" (43) in the summer before his last year at the Good Shepherd orphanage. Brother Whitespade preaches frequently on this theme, and Jayber begins "to suspect that [he] might be called to preach" (42). "Perhaps," Jayber recalls, this "suspicion may have been no more than fear, for with all my heart I disliked the idea of becoming a preacher" (42). At this point, the reader familiar with the prophetic books of the Bible will begin to suspect that there is something authentic in Jayber's call. Reluctance and the sense of unworthiness are surely characteristic of the prophets, or, to put this another way, anyone too desirous of becoming a preacher had perhaps better not be one. Aware of the stories of his namesake Jonah and of the young Samuel, Jayber knows this matter of calling to be an awesome one. Lying awake one night, he implores the Lord, in the words of Samuel, "Speak, Lord; for thy servant heareth." "Then," Jayber recalls, "so help me, I heard the silence that stretched all the way from the ground underneath my window to the farthest stars, and the hair stood up on my head, and a shiver came into me that did not pass away for a long time" (43). At this early point in his tale, Jayber's reader may not know quite how to understand this experience, but as it unfolds, we can see it clearly as one of his first intimations of the holiness of all creation. In biblical language, Jayber senses that the Lord surely is in this place, a fact that ought to make the hair stand up on our heads (calling forth the barber).

Jayber's declaring his call to Brother Whitespade "set[s] the stage for well-paying hypocrisy and self-deception"—quite without any intention of his own. Brother Whitespade feels vindicated in having one of his "once-lost lamb[s]" called to the ministry. Jayber finds he has created "the perfect camouflage" for himself, one that allows him to go on just as he was without official or self-criticism. "Hypocrite and fool" that he later judges himself to have been, Jayber speaks in chapel on "I Samuel 3, the story of the young Samuel and the voice of God" (44). From the later standpoint of mature vocation, this early confusion between his own call and that of the true prophet seems absurd—but Jayber's seeing that may indicate a certain authenticity even in his early, confusedly interpreted, summons. For Jayber ponders his "call" with considerable care and biblical fidelity. Jayber knew that he had actually "heard no voice," but he "could not dismiss the possibility that it had spoken" and that his failure to hear it was the result of a "deficiency" or moral fault in him. He resisted any too easy conclusion, remaining in "fearful uncertainty" for months while recognizing that his growing attraction to the "siren song of girls" may be the source of his "trouble." Finally, as he says, "I reasoned that in dealing with God you had better give Him the benefit of the doubt. I decided that I had better accept the call that had not come, just in case it had come and I had missed it" (43). Whether this is authentic response to a God who is wholly other or elaborate self-deception on Jayber's part seems undecidable. If we knew that Jayber sensed the advantages his "call" would bring at the Good Shepherd, we'd be likely to consider him self-deceived. But he says he had no intention of ingratiating himself with Brother Whitespade. What should we believe? That question of faith—of good faith, fidelity, faithfulness—is one raised not only by this part of Jayber's story but, as we will see, by the whole of it.

As we know from *A Place on Earth,* Jayber is a bit of a preacher in spite of himself and his lack of a pulpit. His barbering is an integral part of that vocation. This is not to say he preaches while others are in the barber's chair. He is not that kind of barber. What he prefers is to listen, and in doing so, he learns "the outlines of a lot of stories" and begins to "see how the bits and pieces of knowledge fit in" (94). He sees the generational process of Port William's male life, watching the young mature, the middle-aged get old, the old prepare to die. He holds people's heads in his hands, sometimes noting quirks of genetic resemblance not in accord with the official accounts of lineage. He can sometimes see from men's eyes and carriage that they know their time is short. Who but the barber would come closest to that kind of Godlike knowledge of the number of hairs on each of our heads? Jayber, too, must reckon with the hatred in his own soul, for he stands often with a razor in his hand, inches away from the throat of one like Troy Chatham, whom he despises. Just knowing how easy it is to contemplate killing one's enemy causes Jayber to recognize his need for a love greater than his own. Uncle Stanley might be said to have chosen rightly when he picks out Jayber to carry on Port William's grave digging, for, as Jayber learns, grave filling is grieving, a task of one who has come to love them all, one story at a time—as Jayber does, for the most part, through a life of cutting hair.

Jayber's call to the barbershop of Port William comes to him less from the voice of God spoken on high than it does from specific people, events, and places of his early life. Prominent among these are the love of an elderly uncle and aunt, a little landing on the Kentucky River, a five-dollar bill, and the image of a man standing restfully in a boat while fishing in a flood. Jayber is orphaned early, his young parents dying "only a few hours apart in late February of 1918" (13). His "first clear memories" are of the "terrible winter of 1917 and 1918," when very heavy snow was followed by thaw, rain, and flood, the waters forming "great ice gorges" that "sheared off or uprooted the shore trees and wrecked steamboats and barges." Nothing "could stand against" that ice when it broke off. Jayber has always associated these early images of that winter with the war that was ongoing in 1918. His parents seem to have "just disappeared into the welter of that time: a war off somewhere in the dark world; a river of ice off somewhere, breaking trees and boats; sickness off somewhere, and then in the house; and then death there in the house, and everything changed" (13). What rescues Jayber from disappearance is the love of a grand-aunt, Cordelia, and her husband, Othy Daggett, who take him in and rear him until he is ten. Jayber loves them both, loves their little farm and store at Squires Landing, and loves the river there "from the day [he] first laid eyes on it" (18). The river has "entranced and mystified" him from that day forward, seeming when it is still to offer a glimpse "into another world that is like this one except that it is quiet" (20).

The five-dollar bill that has a part in bringing Jayber to Port William is given him by Sam Hanks after Jayber has left his preministerial studies at Pigeonville College. Hanks frequently drives livestock from Port William to Louisville but is taking a truckload to Lexington when he picks up Jayber, who lies to him about where he's from when Hanks asks. After Hanks has dropped him off at the trotting track, Jayber finds a five-dollar bill Hanks has stuffed into his jacket without his knowing it. Thus, Jayber's new life begins with a lie he feels the need to redeem and a gift he'd like to consider a loan—and thus repay. When Jayber later tells Sam the story of their ride into Lexington, Sam denies ever having made such a trip and also refuses Jayber's attempt to give him back five dollars. Jayber has wanted, rightly, to make it even between them. Sam indicates that it already is, his gesture implying too that no one begins without a measure of forgiveness and gifts from others.

Jayber's experience at Pigeonville is critical to his changed sense of the call. He soon realizes there that his theological questions disqualify him for full-time Christian ministry (at least as it's understood at Pigeonville). He wonders how Christians can go to war when Jesus teaches us to love our enemies, why we pray in public when we're told to do so in private, how denigration of the body can be consistent with faith in the Incarnation and bodily resurrection. Most of all he rightly shrinks from praying, "Thy will be done," when that will almost surely includes suffering for us. The questions "change" him, as do his prayers, perhaps because he is praying seriously for the first time and thus "dwind[ling] down nearer and nearer to silence" (52). When he goes to the professors with his questions, the answer is invariable: he needs to have more faith. Unable to sacrifice his intellect, Jayber goes to the "feared" Dr. Ardmire, "a hard student and a hard teacher" of the Greek New Testament (53). Ardmire makes no attempt to answer Jayber's questions, and he does not counsel greater faith. He leads Jayber to see that he cannot preach in good faith. Yet when Jayber feels "ashamed" because he had "had this feeling maybe [he'd] been called," Ardmire responds, "You may have been right. But not to what you thought.

Not to what you think. You have been given questions to which you cannot be *given* answers. You will have to live them out—perhaps a little at a time" (54). How long will that take? Perhaps a whole life, perhaps—in what Ardmire calls a "further mystery"—even longer. Jayber leaves the interview thinking Ardmire was the "kindest" professor in the school, no doubt because he was the most honest (54).

Jayber's time in Lexington is one of anonymity and negative freedom from the questions he has been given. After he progresses from the trotting track to barbering, he becomes a self-styled "cut-rate prodigal" (68), reveling in the delights of the world at least insofar as his income allows. He enjoys taking literature courses at the university simply because he likes to read and to hear people talk about books that matter to them. By fall 1936, however, he's experiencing what seems clearly depression (in the midst of the Great one). By that time he understands that the university wants to be an "island" unto itself, a world turned inward just like the other institutions he knows. He's preparing for nothing in particular and cannot imagine himself doing anything the university would train him to do. He finds himself crying repeatedly, hearing in his mind "Aunt Cordie's voice saying, 'I don't know. Honey, I just don't know'" (72). His memories of Squires Landing are "more real than anything outside," and yet his mind's picture of that place is "getting ever smaller and farther away and harder to call back" (72). As he looks back on this time, Jayber can see that here he was being called, not by a divine voice from above, as he had earlier imagined, but rather by the particulars of a life he had loved and still loves:

> I had completely lost the feeling that I should make something of my-self. Aunt Cordie's voice troubled my mind, but it told me I didn't look down on my humble origins and didn't yearn to rise above them. It took me a long time to see what was happening to me then. I have known no sudden revelations. No stroke of light has ever knocked me blind to the ground. But I know now that even then, in my hopelessness and sorrow, I began a motion of the heart toward my origins. Far from rising above them, I was longing to sink into them until I would know the fundamental things. I needed to know the original first chapter of the world. (73)

"The life in us is like the water in the river," Thoreau says near the end of *Walden*. "It may rise this year higher than man has ever known it" (381). The Kentucky rose to unknown heights in January 1937, calling Jayber to a life that could be loved. Hearing Aunt Cordie's question about him, fearing he might lose Squires Landing forever, and wanting to pay back five dollars, Jayber sets out for the rest of his life.

When Jayber sets off from Lexington, he has it in mind to go to Louisville to see the waters. As he journeys afoot, however, his destination changes, becoming the first chapter of his world. He becomes "more and more excited" as he goes, feeling his "old life" come back, though he does not yet have "the words" for what is happening to him (76–77). At Frankfort he persuades a policeman to let him cross a bridge that is just about to go, saying "something that [he] had never thought of saying": "I've got to get to my people down the river" (78). From the middle of that span, everything seems to be in flux, shaken and shaking, moving and ready to move. Suddenly the opening words of Genesis "were just right there" in Jayber's mind, and he knows they are "true": "the earth was without form, and void; and darkness was upon the face of the deep. And the Spirit of God moved upon the face of the waters" (79).

Jayber is not engaged here in framing his experience intellectually; indeed, "even now," he's not sure he knows what was happening to him. Rather, "after all [his] years of reading in that book and hearing it read and believing and disbelieving it," he "seemed to have wandered [his] way back to the beginning—not just of the book, but of the world—and all the rest was yet to come. I felt knowledge crawl over my skin" (79). The biblical language depicted the world in which he was moving in a way he could recognize—at least if the hair standing up on the back of one's neck amounts to recognition. One might say Jayber found himself in the world made, articulated, by the biblical language. The knowledge that makes the flesh crawl is that the world is real, that it matters, that God is alive in it, that it's good because loved from the beginning. Jayber has a sense that he's back on a path, "J. CROW'S PATH," that even "in all [his] years of wandering" and being lost, he's somehow been crossing and recrossing (86). The particulars of his life seem now to form a pattern directing him to a specific place and vocation, a call uniquely his to take up in the world.

The last detail in this episode of Jayber's story is his meeting with Burley Coulter, who speaks to him from the boat where he is lifting fish baskets. Jayber is certain Burley will not know him, and he does not by sight, but he does remember "the one that lived with Uncle Othy and Aunt

Cordie" and who "went away when [he] was just a little bit of a boy—after Aunt Cordie died" (91). Immediately Burley gives Jayber back a history, a place, a sense that he is part of a longer story of life as it has been lived there. "All of a sudden I was afraid," Jayber remembers, when Burley remarks what a coincidence it is that Jayber is a barber and Port William is "fresh out" of one (92). It's as if a place has been prepared for him, as if the Lord is doing something that Jayber has only begun to sense. Rightly fearful that he's about to begin something that matters—a life in which he counts, precisely as himself—Jayber takes up the tonsorial call in Port William, getting and doing his living in the same place.

"Ignorant pilgrim" that he is—living forward but understanding backward—Jayber remarks that he has "for a long time" been "unable to shake off the feeling that I have been led—make of that what you will" (133). What he is led to ultimately is the love of Mattie Chatham, a calling complicated by the presence of Troy Chatham, whom Mattie unquestionably loves and with whom she has three children. Jayber does not like Troy Chatham; to say he hates him is perhaps not too strong. A high school basketball star, Troy is handsome, athletic, confident, proprietary in his attitude toward Mattie when they are still students. One might say he is everything Jayber is not yet would like to be. Troy represents attitudes toward farming and the land that Jayber considers destructive. He is the industrial farmer on the move, convinced of the logic that bigger is always better; that the conserving ways of his father-in-law, Athey Keith, are contemptible; that permanent debt is merely the cost of doing business; that wherever he is going must surely be better than what he leaves behind. In short, Troy Chatham represents much that Jayber Crow—and Wendell Berry—despise. Yet Mattie loves Troy, and Troy, despite his infidelity, can probably be said to love her. She probably comes to love Jayber as well by the end of the novel, but that is less important than whether Jayber's story—and thus his life—is finally one of love or of self-deception and envy.[21] The text will surely support a suspicious reading, one that would reduce Jayber's motives to imitative desire and resentment. But it offers us the possibility, too, of being read as a love story—told, despite much counterevidence, in good faith. Readers must make of it "what they will," though, for this reader at least, the will is directed by all the particulars of the story to irresistible faith in Jayber's account.

Jayber's status as rival-double of Troy—conferred by Jayber himself—is evident when he looks into the schoolbooks Mattie leaves in the shop. Inviting himself to read Mattie's friends' inscriptions, he takes "offense" at one by Troy: "Remember me and bear in mind / That a gay bird's heel sticks out behind. / You know who" (135). What bothers Jayber about Troy's inscription might well be applied to him as he snoops anonymously among the private communications of a high school girl: "Troy Chatham's inscription was a claim; beyond anything it actually said, it announced that he felt entitled to a lot of room in the mind and life of Mattie Keith. It bothered me in particular that, having claimed her, he did not sign his name" (135). Later, as Jayber watches the young men playing basketball, he's offended again when Troy takes a "pass, fake[s] at the goal, and then, leaping, drop[s] a perfect over-the-head shot" into a bushel basket that Mattie is holding as she watches from the sidelines. "It was the most beautiful thing he had done, and yet it was proprietary and aggressive, a kind of violence," Jayber remarks, and yet "you could see nevertheless that she was pleased." "Why, you impudent son of a bitch!" Jayber thinks, not yet sufficiently aware of how well that describes himself as well as Troy (138).

The story of Jayber's love for Mattie does not exist in isolation from the other chapters of his story, at least as he recollects it in the light of its end. World War II begins, and what this means is first "brought home" to Jayber when he sees his "usually cheerful next-door neighbor, Miss Gladdie Finn," crying as she hangs wash on the Monday after Pearl Harbor. Remembering she has lost her son in World War I, Jayber says, "as consolingly" as he can, "Maybe it won't last long. Maybe it'll be all right." But Miss Gladdie has been thrust "back into the midst of her loss" and answers, "Oh, honey, boys will be killed" (140). Jayber decides to report for service, and though he is rejected as 4-F, what he discovers about his reasons for doing so is important: "I will have to share the fate of this place. Whatever happens to Port William must happen to me" (143). During the war, he becomes a member of the ongoing rummy game at Lathrop's store, where he learns, among other things, that winning is not a very important idea and grows closer to two friends marked by loss, Burley Coulter and Mat Feltner. As he goes about his grave-digging duties, he feels increasingly "tender toward" all who "now could be changed only by forgiveness and mercy." The many stones of children are especially moving, and he becomes unable to "forget that all the people in Port William, if they lived long, would come there burdened and leave empty-handed many times, and would finally come and stay empty-handed." Jayber "began to be moved by a compassion that seemed to come to [him] from outside," and he wanted to make his "heart as big as Heaven to include them all" (158). He begins to see that this undying feeling for life, this love, is what moves the gathered church even though its often life-denying theology seems preoccupied with other concerns. One day he falls asleep in a pew while going about his janitorial duties, and then somewhere between sleeping and waking, he sees "all the people gathered there who had ever been there" and he "seemed to love them all with a love that was [his] merely because it included [him]" (164–65).

The trouble with these kinds of thoughts is that they make one accountable. Even the densest of us can't go around for long thinking of a love that includes us all without realizing our own particular hates will have to be discarded or at least apologized for. Jayber's readers find themselves drawn into the process of keeping him accountable. Thus, it troubles us when Jayber speaks of Athey and Della having to give their blessing to a marriage they do not like, "enduring what could not be helped" (177). Or to hear that "Troy brought nothing to the marriage but himself and an automobile" (177) and that he "had no idea, not a suspicion," about what it meant to belong to a farm in Athey's sense—that instead, in his selfishness, Troy thought only that "the farm existed to serve and enlarge him" (182). These may be relatively accurate assessments of Troy, but coming from Jayber, they ring of envy. How, after all, does he know what Troy brings to the marriage? Can such a thing even be known to one outside the marriage? Isn't marriage the form of a particular kind of knowing that makes Jayber's judgments ridiculous in principle? Only Mattie can really know what Troy brings to the marriage because marriage is that form of knowing in which the spouses come to know both one another and themselves in ways unknown by others (or by themselves when in the role of others rather than spouses).

The discovery of erotic love is what most people would call "the most deciding event" of their lives, after which they are "not the same ever again" (191). Jayber describes a day in summer 1950 this way, a day "(at the start of another war)" when he sees Mattie guiding the play of and playing with the children of the Vacation Bible School. She seems "free as a child" and yet "with a generosity and watchfulness that were anything but childish" (191). "She was just perfectly there with them in their pleasure," and Jayber feels "overcome with love for her" (191). What follows is a passage of Jayber's life about which he still rightly "feel[s] a kind of shame" (193). "Overruled" by the love to which he now "belongs," Jayber begins to imagine the failure of Troy and Mattie's marriage; he meditates "without compassion" on Troy's loneliness (fruit of his "self-centeredness") and envisions Mattie and himself escaping Port William in the Zephyr he has purchased for his own escapes to Hargrave (194). In Jayber's mind, at least, he and Troy have become rivals: "The lower Troy Chatham fell in my estimation, the better I thought of myself" (195). He reasons that Troy must be objectionable to Mattie and that thus "she might be attracted" to him "as one who truly loved and appreciated her" (196). Fortunately, Jayber is able—at least, on later reflection—to recognize that this "process of reasoning" was "entirely invented by [him] and had nothing to do with anything in this world" (196).

Perhaps the place in Jayber's narrative requiring most faith of us is his account of Liddie's death. This is something Jayber "must tell," and yet he did not "see [it] happen." Nevertheless, "it is as clear to [his] mind as anything [he] ever saw," and he cannot think of it "without seeing it happen"— something in which he is "not alone" (198). Perhaps it is so compellingly real because it is something we all fear, do our best to protect against, and yet know ourselves finally unable to prevent. The death of a child touches the deepest place in us—that place Simone Weil thought the source of justice where we ask, "Why am I being hurt?"[22] Jayber's first feeling for Mattie has been that one we all feel when we see the young—the hope that somehow the world will deal kindly with this innocence, that somehow she will get through relatively intact. Yet we know this is very unlikely to be, that none of us gets out of the world alive, that we will all ultimately be hurt in that place that cries out like the child. Liddie dies at five years old as she is gathering asters with her mother. She is struck by a car as she dances down from a bank into the road in order for Mattie to see her. "Look how beautiful I am!" she says, just before the car lifts her into the air "like a tossed doll" (199). Both Mattie and the boy driving the car know that what has happened in that moment can not only never "be undone" but never be unknown again in their lives (200). The boy had no chance to avoid Liddie. Joy in the world's beauty and her own movement has simply resulted in a death beyond anyone's control and the concomitant scarring of many lives.

It would be intolerable for Jayber to tell this story in such a way as to elevate himself at Troy's expense: to suggest, for example, that he was the one who understood what Liddie's loss meant to Mattie in a way that Troy did not. Still, one might ask about the appropriateness of Jayber's making the story part of his own narrative, particularly when he makes no attempt to comment on Troy's response to the loss of his daughter. While that suspicious reading is possible, I believe three features of Jayber's narrative in particular tend to prevent it. One is the detached, pictorial way in which Liddie's death is described. The highly visual quality of Jayber's account gives the event a status in its own right, independent of all but Liddie, Mattie, and the young driver. The final effect of Jayber's description has the quality of statuary: "the stricken boy, the mother on her knees at the roadside holding her dead child, the sun suddenly gone beyond the hilltop, and the chill of the evening coming down" (200). The picture has a kind of completeness; these three figures have been bound together in a way that excludes any other—Jayber or Troy—from having comparable knowledge of the loss. Jayber's compassionate response to Mattie in the graveyard also enhances our sense that he is no longer moved by the desire to be recognized—even just by himself—as a better husband for Mattie than Troy. When he discovers Mattie lying "on the raw mound" of Liddie's grave, crying and seeming to want "to shelter it with her body," he "kne[els] beside her, according to [his] calling in this world" (206). That calling is to love Mattie, as barber, grave digger, and preacher in spite of himself in Port William, as one who now has abandoned his sense of the gathered church for an even more inclusive "vision of the gathered community," which, "in the midst of all the ignorance and error," was a "membership" and finally a mystery to be completed and perfected in eternity in ways we know only darkly here (205). When Jayber says gently to Mattie, "You can't stay here" (206), he speaks from the culmination of all the details of his life, pressing as they do irresistibly toward his vocation.

The third reason to trust Jayber's narrative is that he is coming to see how much like Troy Chatham he is. While dancing to "Smoke Gets in Your Eyes" with Clydie at Riverwood, Jayber finds himself face to face with Troy, dancing with a woman whose "long blond hair could not have been Mattie's." Troy gives Jayber "a wink and a grin, raising his hand" with the "thumb and forefinger joined in a circle" (237). Jayber gets sick, goes to the bathroom, climbs out a window, falling to the ground, and leaves Clydie a note in the car, ending their relationship. Jayber insists to himself, "We're *not* alike!" (238), yet he isn't sure. He sounds at first like the Pharisee he has been, congratulating himself that at least he is superior to Troy.[23] He does not want "to be like him," but he sees now "that it would also be a fearful thing to be unlike him" (241). Jayber is trapped in the dialectic of distinction. There are good reasons not to want to be like Troy. Yet so long as he is merely being unlike Troy, then Troy determines the conditions of Jayber's existence. As Kierkegaard put the problem, Jayber continues only to work for distinction as long as he seeks to be either like or unlike another.[24] Love offers a way out of the ceaseless working for distinction. As Jayber puts it, "I saw that I had to try to become a man unimaginable to Troy Chatham, a man he could not imagine raising his hand to with the thumb and forefinger circled—but to do that I would have to become a man yet unimaginable to myself" (241). What Christian readers will hear here is the process of dying in Christ, the paradoxical dying to self that leads to one's truest—and previously unimaginable—self being born, a self no longer needing to establish itself by ceaseless distinction from others. Jayber asks himself, in a chapter called "The Way of Love," whether he has not just been engaged in elaborate self-deception—at which he knows himself to be adept. How does he know he would or could have loved Mattie "all her life"? (247). The answer is that he did so, did "love her all her life," and does so still—"all her life." In language very suggestive of Kierkegaard, Jayber adds, "That is my answer, but in fact love does not answer any argument. It answers all arguments, merely by turning away, leaving them to find what rest they can" (248).

Jayber begins his life story with a two-line epigraph from Andrew Marvell's "The Definition of Love": "Magnanimous Despair alone / Could show me so divine a thing." Near the end of that poem, Marvell describes an impossible love—binding yet "enviously debar[red]" by Fate—as a pair of parallel lines, in contrast to the oblique ones of realized love:

> As lines so Loves oblique may well
> Themselves in every angle greet:
> But ours so truly parallel,
> Though infinite can never meet.[25]

These lines are echoed by Jayber's description of the river after he has moved to Burley's camp house. The move is accomplished in "the way of love" (248), Jayber not so much resisting the inevitable man across the desk, the Inspector, as simply turning aside to his own path. "Sometimes," Jayber says, "living right beside it, I forget it," but then "it seems just to flow back into my mind. I stop and look at it. I think of its parallel, never-meeting banks, which yet never part" (310). The riverbanks suggest infinity as well as Jayber and Mattie's love. The river itself seems an image of love, not belonging "to the workaday world" or "the vacation world either," but "keep[ing] to its own way." Jayber thinks of the river as a single course of life running its own way, "a single opening from its springs in the mountains all the way to its mouth" (310). "It is a beautiful thought," he concludes, "one of the most beautiful of all thoughts. I think it not in my brain only but in my heart and in all the lengths of my bones" (310).

The notion of sublimating infinitely frustrated desire into Aristotelian "great-souledness" may be a beautiful thought, but even more beautiful is love mutually acknowledged and capable of healing our small-souledness. Jayber's story is not finally a book about "Magnanimous Despair," but rather "a book about Heaven," though it narrowly escapes being a "book about Hell" (354). The heaven Jayber refers to is not one based on a rejection of life on earth. Rather "earth speaks to us of Heaven, or why would we want to go there? If we knew nothing of Hell, how would we delight in Heaven should we get there?" (354–55). One way earth speaks to us is of the mystery Dr. Ardmire alludes to in sending Jayber away from Pigeonville to find his calling. We know there is much we have left undone, unlearned, unhealed. We know love's tense is present. We believe Jayber loves Mattie all her life. We sense that whatever perfection we are being called to involves a continual *ecstasis,* in the Orthodox sense, a being led beyond ourselves in a process that continues beyond what we call death.

Like the rest of us, Jayber has more small-souledness to get over than a lifetime will allow. As War and the Economy move into that phase we call Vietnam, Troy becomes a "fierce partisan of the army and the government's war policy" (286), especially after his son Jimmy enters the service. When Troy castigates the war's protestors, saying it would be a good idea to let them and the "damned communists" kill one another, Jayber quotes the New Testament at him: "Love your enemies, bless them that curse you, do good to them that hate you." When Troy asks, "Where did you get that crap?" Jayber responds, "Jesus Christ"—thus using lines that are among Christ's most precious gifts to us to establish his superiority to Troy.

Reflecting on this particular bit of small-souledness, Jayber notes, "It would have been a great moment in the history of Christianity, except that I did not love Troy" (287). Jayber never manages—at least not so far—to love Troy. For him to do so might stretch our capacity for belief too far. But when he encounters Troy in the futile process of cutting the Nest Egg, he sees "an exhausted man" whom he can only commend to "mercy" (360). "The time would come," Jayber remarks, when he would have his own "deliverance, [his] Nunc Dimittis" (361), and be able to call Troy a friend. Troy is "redeemed" finally, in Jayber's eyes, "by Mattie's long-abiding love for him" (361), as he has been himself by love of her.

Jayber and Mattie are like the banks of the river in their few chance meetings in the Nest Egg. Brought together by love of the place, its quiet and beauty, and by love of Mattie's father, the man who preserved it, the two arrive at an unspoken understanding. When Mattie goes into the hospital to die, Jayber resolves to stay away, knowing he will be sorry but knowing also that his going will be an embarrassment to them both. But a dream he has after seeing the Nest Egg cut changes Jayber's mind. It is a dream of War and the Economy, the dream of a "dreadful sleep that maybe was my death itself" (361). In it Jayber hears "the motors speeding along the pavements and the rivers, the tractors in the fields, the airplanes in the sky, and always, always that chainsaw in the woods. I heard the big trees tearing and breaking their way to the ground, and the thumps of little creatures run over on the road" (361). Nothing in the dream is good enough to resist transformation. Nowhere is one saying, "It is good that you exist." To say something like that to Mattie takes Jayber to her hospital room, where Mattie is crying over the loss of the woods. When Jayber cannot say "the words [he] had so long wanted to say," he asks instead, "But what about this other thing?" She says simply, "Yes," taking his hand, acknowledging their love, their lives no longer infinitely parallel lines, but joined now in meeting. Jayber feels "covered" all "over with light" (363), knowing now love both so fully its own thing, so other, and yet so compellingly and beautifully here.

Chapter 7

The "Art of Being Here"
The Poetry

Wendell Berry has repeatedly posted his poetry with signs saying, "NO EXPLAINING." In "Stay Home," the opening poem of *A Part,* he gives a turn to the well-known invitation, "You come too," of Frost's "The Pasture":

> In the labor of the fields
> longer than a man's life
> I am at home. Don't come with me.
> You stay home too.[1]

One is reminded here of Thoreau's insistence that he was not looking for followers, but for those who would discover their own homes, their own ways to live, the dimensions of their own fields—if only to jump over the fences.[2] In "For the Explainers," Berry challenges reductivists of all stripes to account for the beautiful curl in the "plume" of the mallard "drake's tail" or the "white ring round his neck" (*Selected,* 149). In "Sabbath VI, 1980," he points out how we are bearers of an "intellect so ravenous to know" that it threatens to obscure the light in which we stand. Instead of insisting on "disclosing what is so and what not so," we need to learn to be "dark and still," to remember that all the "orders made by mortal hand or love / Or thought" are "lost in order we are ignorant of."[3] Leaving behind the compulsive explanations and divisions of "word and argument," we may "grow as unopposing, unafraid / As the young trees, without thought or belief; / Until the shadow Sabbath light has made / Shudders, breaks open, shines in every leaf" (*TC,* 31).[4]

The great liberty of the Sabbath, as Berry's poems remind us, is in God's gift and command of rest. Those of us who sometimes weary of argument—and of the selves we become in argument—can rejoice in Berry's "dream" of "a quiet man / who explains nothing and defends / nothing," a man whose wisdom lies in knowing simply to "smile" when he finds "the rarest wildflowers" in bloom.[5] Poems like this suggest a case could be made for Berry as an ecological poet, an advocate for the environment. But Berry doesn't want any cases made for him, and as he's made plain any number of times, no one lives in an environment. People, animals, and plants live in particular places. The abstract thinking that has given us "the environment" has also led to the systematic exploitation of real places and real people.[6]

Robert Frost began a famous essay on poetry by observing that "abstraction is an old story with the philosophers, but it has been like a new toy in the hands of the artists of our day." Frost knew how important abstraction is. As he said, "Our lives for it."[7] Every schoolchild knows, of course, that our language is never fully commensurate with what it seeks to describe or convey. Our descriptions are always abstractions from all that is, and thus the need is for responsive and responsible ones. Keeping language responsible is an ever more difficult task, and it is preeminently the task of poetry, as Berry sees it, to be the last refuge of the particular. A vulgarly understood pragmatism too often enlists language simply as part of the technological enterprise of constructing reality in whatever ways "we" deem most desirable. It's perhaps that kind of extreme, pragmatic social constructionism that Berry is reacting to when he says bluntly that "abstraction is the enemy *wherever* it is found."[8] That statement, together with the relentless particularity of Berry's poetry, recalls us to the ethical recognition that the textual worlds we pride ourselves on creating and inhabiting invariably leave out many of the blessed "things of the world" to which love calls us, as Richard Wilbur puts it.[9] Berry's insistence on particularity represents an act of resistance to technology's way of framing the world as so much standing reserve on the way to transformation into something else. Such resistance is Berry's way of taking his stand, one that no doubt derives, in part, from his seeing his homeland transformed into a colony of that most abstract of abstractions we now call the symbolic or information-based economy.

So we come to the problem of abstraction. If it's an enemy, then it is a necessary one, for we clearly cannot do without it. At the same time, remembering it's an enemy should cause us to be ceaselessly aware of what we're leaving out—and to modify or discard our abstractions altogether when we leave out too much. Perhaps our attitude toward abstraction should be precisely that Christianity insists we take toward other enemies: love. We can cooperate with abstractions when they can be made consistent with the purposes of love; otherwise, we lovingly resist in the name of all those glorious particulars of the world to which we are lovingly faithful. But we must first know some of those particulars or risk getting lost in the abstractions of today's increasingly total economy. Knowing the particulars is, then, the task of several analogous disciplines: theology, marriage, farming, and most important here, poetry. A brief word first about theology. It's a discipline of particulars because it never has the luxury of leaving something out without reckoning the cost. Everything matters because it is all from God. As Berry makes plain, God's love includes everything we have abstracted; it allows nothing to be lost. Its nearest natural analogue is the river in flood that, as it "spread[s]" its "mirrors out upon" the "valley floor," is "like God's love or sorrow, including / at last all that had been left out" ("Sabbath V, 1998," in *Given*, 59). The world begins in love, for Berry, and will end there as well, with everything included in the story. Part of learning to live as a creature is to know that we live continually from what is given, not created by us, and therefore to know that we must use it humbly and with care for its renewal. It will be remembered, whether we do so or not. If or as we are drawn into the life of God, we will remember more— and *more particularly.*

Short of the last day, our task, though, is to find responsible abstractions with which to speak, and poetry can play a critical role in that process by ceaselessly guiding us back to the particular. My focus in this chapter will be on the way Berry's poetry constitutes a way of making the particulars of people and places "real" for us, as he says we must do if we are ever to imagine our country differently—not as something simply to be used up, but as a home for a settled people. Berry understands this real-making quality to be the authentic work of imagination, as he says in "American Imagination and the Civil War."[10] Imagination must not be understood simply as the ability to "make things up" (30). The kind of imagination we need, according to Berry, is situated and disciplined. It seeks no escape, but rather wants only to be the "art of being here" (*Selected,* 100–101). Poetry written from such imagination resists excessive abstraction. It insists on engaging the common world, refusing to address itself only to specialists or to become so self-referential as to be about little more than its own possibility. It refuses our age's despair, affirming the goodness of a world simultaneously perennial and new. Rooted in place, it seeks an audience among the poet's neighbors, those who have contributed to it. Like marriage and farming, poetry constitutes a way of living in form, committed to the faith that forms can bring forth something wonderful even in a world of severe limits—sometimes doing this most wonderfully, in fact, when we find ourselves baffled and at an impasse. Ultimately, these disciplines of the real can bring us to a quiet in which we simply see and hear the things of this world. A poem then can be so utterly without the pretensions of ego as to be content to point to a "tanager" or "columbine" and say "There!"[11] Finally, being faithful to making things real for us is part of the poet's discipline of hope, to which Berry remains as committed as ever. For it is by seeing how real people, places, and animals are that we come to understand the requirement to honor them, to regard them in ways appropriate to their places in creation and not simply as means to whatever ends we devise.

Such disciplines of the real as poetry or marriage are needed perhaps now more than ever, when people have become as abstract to themselves as the placeless boaters Berry observes in "Sabbath VIII, 1998." Watching the river, Berry notes that nothing "given" in the scene could "have foretold the sudden / apparition of these two / speeding by as if late / for the world's end, their engine / shaking the air, breaking / the water's mirrors." As the boat's wake settles, he asks sadly "how many years / of labor" it has taken for the boaters to "become completely / anomalous everywhere" (*Given,* 63). The boaters have succeeded only in making themselves at home nowhere. They exist in the abstractions of speed and power, of getting someplace as fast as possible where they will be just as superfluous as they were in the place from which they came.

In "Sabbath II, 1997," Berry suggests the political danger represented by people so abstract to themselves. The poem presents a dream-vision so disturbing that Berry says he "prayed" even as he dreamed "that what I saw was only fear and no foretelling" (*TC,* 208). In his dream, Berry sees "the last known landscape destroyed for the sake / of the objective, the soil bulldozed, the rock blasted. / Those who had wanted to go home would never get there now." Variants of the military phrase "for the sake of the objective" recur throughout the poem's description of a kind of war waged against every specific place and creature. Nothing is acceptable, valuable, or beautiful in its own right. The poem suggests how difficult the poetic defense of the particular can be, for in a condition of near total displacement, no one can remember or begin to conceive what it might have meant to be placed. Each generation seems left utterly to itself. "The graves and the monuments" of the past—the past itself—are not simply neglected but "obliterated," for such exclusive focus "on the objective" induces a forgetting that is total, one in which "those who have forgotten forget / that they have forgotten" (*TC*, 208).

One concrete political result of domination by the objective is the extraordinary empowerment of elite planners who establish the objectives, themselves never met, of course, because total transformation is, by definition, unlimited. After "every place ha[s] been displaced, every love / unloved, every vow unsworn, every word unmeant," all that remains is an anonymous "crowd" straining to see "the objective" that they do "not yet perceive in the far distance" (*TC*, 209). The political question implicit in such a vision is whether a democratic social order can be maintained among people so displaced from every traditional source of stability, meaning, or comfort: place, marriage, neighbors, faith. Surely doing so will require ever more nimble politician-managers and ever more imperative objectives—among which none, we should remember, is more compelling or more potentially unending than war.

Nowhere does Berry's poetry, however, allow us to take refuge in comfortable despair. The poem immediately following his dream vision in *A Timbered Choir* opens with his being "wakened" from his "dream of the ruined world by the sound / of rain falling slowly onto the dry earth" of his own "place in time" (210). Nothing is more fearful to Berry, as he puts it in "Sabbath IX, 1998," than despair "for the world and us: forever less / of beauty, silence, open air" (*Given*, 64). These seem at first reasons or confirmations for despair, but they are also its dire consequences. If we despair of beauty, we will see less of it, and we will do less to create it or allow it to come to be. If we despair of "silence" or "open air," we may stop insisting that these are fundamental goods, as necessary to a life worth living as food or water. A danger of despair is its self-perpetuating quality, its denial of the grace by which we live. Among the fortunate consequences of the doctrine of original sin, according to Berry, is that "it preserves us from the pride / of thinking we invented sin ourselves / by our originality, that famous modern power" ("Original Sin," in *Given*, 35). Without this reminder that "something is bad the matter / here," we would never "know / forgiveness, goodness, gratitude, / that fund of grace by which alone we live" (35).

Despair is a closing in of the self and thus closely connected to death and our claiming the "freedom / to kill one another," a freedom that is but the other side of our illusory desire "to belong only / to ourselves." In "Sabbath IV, 2003," an Easter poem, Berry asks that "we too" may "rise" with Christ, "as out of the dark grave" represented by such illusion (*Given*, 125). Arising from such sleep, in accord with the reality of the resurrection, means renouncing not only killing but also the hatred that Jesus understood to be forbidden by the commandment. It "would be easy" for us "to bear" if the "Lords of War" hated the world, "hated / their children and the flowers / that grow in the warming light." If this were the case, Berry notes in "Sabbath X, 2003," we could rest comfortably justified in our hatred. But it is incumbent on people who live in the light of the resurrection to do something much harder: "to imagine the Lords of War / may love the things that they destroy" (*Given*, 132). I do not know if Berry wants to go so far as Stanley Hauerwas has in suggesting that the source of our violence lies in our loves—which accounts, in part, for the difficulty of putting an end to violence and war.[12] The poem seems to press in that direction, suggesting that our freedom from death lies in our belonging to a larger love—the love of God evident in the risen Christ—and that that love requires us to recognize that our enemies are included in it. Only through that recognition, we understand, can reconciliation and peace be found.

Berry is under no illusion that loving our enemies is an easy matter. But, as in the poem "Enemies," he poses us a stark choice: if we are not to become monsters, we "must care what they think," but if we do care what they think, we are likely to hate them and thus become monsters "of the opposite kind." The "love for your enemy / that is the way of liberty" can come only from forgiveness, as hard as we find that to accept: "Forgiven, they go / free of you, and you of them" (*Selected*, 160). Notice what Berry does not say here: that "forgiving," we go free of them. To advocate forgiveness for that reason—as one often hears suggested—leaves forgiveness a kind of therapeutic power we exercise to rid ourselves of harmful emotions. Berry does not put forgiveness so easily within our reach. When we forgive, our enemies go free of us, and our going free must depend on forgiveness from them. They are free of us, and we of them, only in forgiveness precisely because we are so completely linked to one another—so much so that we will become monsters if we do not care what they think or if we care what they think and respond in the way of unforgiveness. This is to put us ineluctably in the hands of our enemies more fully than any of us cares to accept. We are dependent on our enemies' forgiveness, not simply so that they will not harm us, but so that we, too, can begin to forgive them (as well as ourselves) and walk together in the way of forgiveness—which is the way of enemies walking together in mutual freedom from becoming the mirrored monsters they would otherwise be.

At the risk, then, of being exiled by Jayber Crow to the "desert island" reserved for explainers, I will try here to set out some of the major features of Berry's poetry and his nonfiction writing about it. I promise not to treat Berry as if he is dead, become a literary "name" or "a part of mere geography"—fates that come to the writer, as he says in "To a Writer of Reputation" (*Given*, 21). I promise, too, not to write about the poetry as if it doesn't matter, in the manner of too much that is produced in university departments devoted to literature. Again, here is Berry speaking to the writer:

> Or perhaps you have become deaf and blind,
> or merely inanimate, and may
> be studied without embarrassment
> by the disinterested, the dispassionate,
> and the merely curious. (*Given*, 21)

I will say, anecdotally, that I think Berry need not be too worried about his readers in these terms. The young people I know who are attracted to his writing are anything but dispassionate or merely curious about it. They care deeply about it because they care deeply about the same things Berry does: land, people, and specific places; finding good work and an appropriate scale for human life; discovering again ways to live in real community with neighbors; liberating the American idea of liberty from equation with the unlimited power to consume; redirecting American policy in the world so that we do not need to wage unending war over control of resources and markets.[13] I do think there's a place in literary criticism for being "disinterested," at least if we understand this to mean, as it used to, being committed to getting the ideas of others as close to right as possible before evaluating them.

Resisting excessive abstraction is at the heart of Berry's task as a poet, which is to say that he aligns himself with the poet's traditional role of renewing the language. In "Below," he speaks as one who "aspire[s] downward" and thus in contrast with "flyers" who "embrace / the air," the realm of symbols like "banner, cross, and star."[14] The "mode of those / who live by" such "symbols" is "air war," or the "pure / abstraction of travel by air." The suggestion of this poem so reminiscent of many of Frost's—"To Earthward," for instance—is not that earth is the only place for life or love or that we can do without symbols altogether. Berry takes note of one church spire on which an angel points heavenward as if "to admonish that all's not here" and then goes on to grant that "All's not." We cannot live without symbols or abstractions or pointers toward realities greater than those we can observe. But the poet's role is to find words that we can stand on and stand by, concrete and particular words whose truth lies in our witness to them. To renew the bond between word and deed is Berry's aim as poet and human being. Or, as he concludes the poem, "What I stand for / is what I stand on."

Part of the poet's problem is audience. To whom is he or she speaking? To whom is he or she responsible? The audience for poetry today is limited and specialized, much of it consisting of people who are themselves poets or aspiring poets and who are associated with departments of creative writing and the little magazines they produce. In a university made up of highly specialized fields, poetry becomes a specialized discipline of its own. In "The Specialization of Poetry," Berry notes the growing popularity of the genre of interview-with-the poet. The essay is some thirty years old, but its general conclusions still seem accurate. The popularity of this genre suggests to Berry that poets have become a species of rare birds, "different from other people," leading lives that "are constantly 'different' and exciting"—in contrast with the "routine and dull" lives of the rest of us. Berry is, I think, insufficiently discriminating in his treatment of interviewers as a group, but amusing and partially accurate in saying they are all too often "poet watchers," who with "their intended readers are so convinced of the poet's otherness that they need to stand in his presence and say, 'Well, well, so this is a poet.'" Berry notes further that the poets themselves seem now convinced "that they are of a different kind" and "hence have some special explaining to do."[15]

Berry has no desire to be a rare bird. He wishes instead "to live and work within a community, or within the hope of community, in a given place." Others, he writes in "Sex, Economy, Freedom, and Community," seem to "wish to live and work outside the claims of any community, and these now appear to be an overwhelming majority."[16] This majority might be seen as the vanguard of the "public," that curious and empty term whose function we have seen is often no more than to act as entering wedge for economic invasion of every specific community. Playwright Arthur Kopit serves as an example, for Berry, of the artist as "public person." Prior to the premiere performance of *Bone-the-Fish* in 1989 in Louisville, Kopit was quoted in the newspaper as saying of the play, "*I am immodestly proud that it is written in consistently bad taste. It's about vile people who do vile things. They are totally loathsome, and I love them all. . . . I'm almost positive that it has something to offend everyone*" (quoted in SE, 154). For Berry, Kopit simply evidences a conventionalized "antipathy to community life and to the moral standards that enable and protect" it (SE, 158). This is not to say that art must never offend: anybody seeking to be truthful will often enough offend simply as a matter of integrity. But at present "our public art" often "communicates a conventional prejudice against old people, history, parental authority, religious faith, sexual discipline, manual work, rural people and rural life, anything local or small or inexpensive." "At its worst," it "glamorizes or glorifies drugs, promiscuity, pornography, violence, and blasphemy," as a trip to any video store will confirm (SE, 158).

Berry is not interested in any argument to suppress freedom of expression, but he also insists on going beyond "advocacy of the freedom of speech to deplore some of the uses that are made of it" (SE, 158). One problem I believe he underestimates is the degree to which the word "community" has itself become so broadly used as to be virtually meaningless. This may not be apparent to Berry because he does live and work within a very specifically defined and situated community, but the rule that those who have forgotten forget that they have forgotten applies to community life as well. Or one might say that those who have never had any experience of community life will have little idea what Berry is invoking. Now that "community" is routinely used to refer to groups like the "bond-trading community" or the "arms-manufacturing community," the word seems to have lost much of what it means for Berry. This is not to say we should abandon the word, only to suggest that the work of renewing the concept will perhaps be even more difficult than Berry has conceived.

Berry wants nothing to do with the elevation of poetry to the status of a substitute religion, something he sees happening among the cult of specialist poets. He distances himself, too, from the so-called language poets, who, in his view, no longer understand the poem as "a point of clarification or connection between themselves and the world on the one hand and between themselves and their readers on the other." These poets have lost the sense of the poem as an "adventure" into "reality or mystery outside themselves," preferring instead to seek the "self in words, the making of a word-world in which the word-self may be at home" (SOP, 7).[17] I'm not sure the sharp distinction Berry draws here is entirely tenable, as we can see by looking at his "Words" and "Creation Myth." After asking, in "Words," what one is "to make of a life given / to putting things into words," Berry asks whether there is "a world beyond words." After answering the question in the best way possible—"There is"—he pleads that we will "just stop" before going on into the arguments for a reality independent of language, "the tree unqualified," and so forth. If we do stop, we may come to know what "only silence knows," the extraordinary diversity of a world in which living and even inanimate things "call themselves / by whatever they call themselves, their own / sounds, their own silence." But as the poem closes, Berry recognizes that we "must call" all of these things "out of the silence again to be with us" and that calling must be "by name," by that language which is our way of being in the world (*Given,* 20). At least since the second creation account in Genesis, we have understood ourselves as the namers, those who know a world of separate things in language and know themselves to be separate as well. I could go on here to point out how even the beings Berry has invoked to give us "their own sounds" have come before us, as for all since Adam, in the names we have given them. I could add that a world in which stones speak their own language can only be imagined in ours. But I will just stop.

"Creation Myth" announces itself a "story handed down" from the "old days" (*Selected,* 118). It is the story of Bill, Florence, and "a lot of their kin" who lived in a little house near the woods at the bottom of a hill. During the days, Florence worked in the house while the men and boys went up the hill to work in the fields. In the evenings, they all came home to take "their ease around the porch / while the summer night closed." One night Bill's "young brother," McKinley, "stayed away late, and it was dark / when he started down the hill." As he smoked while leaning against the door jamb of the house, Bill listened to McKinley "coming down" in a darkness that seemed "joined to all the rest / of darkness everywhere," a disorienting darkness so "huge" as to cause "things" to "com[e] close / that never had come close before" (*Selected,* 118–19). Bill smoked on, amused, as McKinley became lost and even as he began to run about in the dark. As the older brother who has gone on ahead, Bill "knew where / McKinley was, though McKinley didn't." But when McKinley neared "something really to fear"— not self-imagined darkness and chaos but "the quarry pool"—Bill "quit his pipe" and stepped out, "barefoot, on the warm boards" of the porch:

> "McKinley!"
> he said, and laid the field out clear
> under McKinley's feet, and placed
> the map of it in his head. (*Selected,* 119)

Bill's voice speaks a world into being. McKinley is able to know where he is by finding himself in relationship to a voice he knows and can trust. Each of us finds him- or herself in relation to those who have gone before and who know the dangers in the landscape. If we are lucky, the maps in our heads will be accurate. Those who have laid them out for us cannot clarify every inch of the terrain—that can only be accomplished by repeatedly going over it, up and down—but they can help us to know where the greatest dangers lie, and their love can provide points of orientation without which we would be truly lost.

Thus we come again to language and naming, to our inhabiting a world mapped by language. However much we need the renewal of darkness and lostness, of seeing our "limits transgressed," as Thoreau put it, we locate and understand ourselves within the stories that come down to us.[18] This is just to say that Berry's objection to what is often called "language poetry" is not so much a linguistic one—having to do with whether or not we only know through language—as it is a broader political, cultural, and economic one. What has largely been lost is the common world in which a meaningful poetry can be written. The hyperspecialization of today's fast capitalism obscures any remaining sense of the ways we "get our living together" or the ways that living is ultimately dependent on the natural world. Berry quotes Denise Levertov's observation that contemporary poetry consists largely of "an unexampled production of *notations*" (SOP, 16), a development that signifies the loss of common experience and common speech. It becomes enough for the poet of notation to try to fix and hold some moment of experience before it vanishes forever into the absences caused by our rapid pace of change. Berry comments, too, on "the emphasis upon personal terror and suffering and the fear of death in much recent poetry."[19] While he attributes this to a kind of poetic narcissism—in which "the world" once "mirrored by the poet has become the poet's mirror"—it may also reflect a desperate reaching for common experience, for the one thing we still must all endure, though each in his own way (SOP, 8).

If there is a preponderant emphasis on "personal terror" and "the fear of death" in contemporary poetry, as Berry suggests, it can also be explained, I believe, by poets' desire for authority. After Auschwitz and Hiroshima, a kind of everyday nihilism has been orthodoxy among those interested in the humanities, understandably so.[20] To speak in a believable voice to Western culture in the second half of the twentieth century or the first years of the twenty-first, the poet has had to witness in her own person to an anguish sufficiently intense to qualify her to speak. By now, this has often come to seem mere posturing, but the crisis of meaning and belief it reflects must not be overlooked. Berry has called that which is required "A Discipline," one that begins by "turn[ing] toward the holocaust" that "approaches / on every side" (*Selected,* 64). What's required is a steady gaze into the fire where "man's despair" threatens to consume all and yet to "be still, and wait." If we can learn to rest from restless will, then we may yet see "the world go on with the patient work / of seasons, embroidering birdsong / upon itself as for a wedding." Our "time's discipline" has been "to think / of the death of all living, and yet live" (*Selected,* 64).[21] Berry's discipline has been to acknowledge the worst possibilities of human hubris and yet to insist that we can find again the perennial world—and find it, moreover, as it has been from the beginning, good.

My point, then, is simply that the task of renewing the life of poetry, as Berry sees it, requires freeing it from the specialized setting where it is now largely written and read. What Berry seeks to do in his poetry is consistent with the effort of his nonfiction and fiction, as one would expect from one who wants to write as a whole human being. Berry wants to live and write as a man who knows, respects, and, in some cases, loves his neighbors (believing he should love them all). He wants to be able to do his work and do it well, and he hopes for others who will understand it and be able to see its goodness. He hopes to be able to enter into exchanges with his neighbors based on mutual trust and respect, a condition that requires some degree of shared history, community, and knowledge. He wants to be able to exchange his good work for the good work of others, and he knows, too, that to be able to call his and his neighbors' work "good," it must not diminish the possibilities of life for those who come after him. Declaring himself "an old-fashioned man," Berry defines his "purpose" in "Some Further Words" to be "a language that can pay just thanks / and honor for" the manifold gifts he cherishes: "the natural world," a good domestic life that knows its limits and "pays its debts," the "promise of Heaven." Such language would be one, too, "set free from fashionable lies" (*Given*, 28).

How does one learn a language capable of paying "just thanks and honor" for the gifts one has received? "Remembering My Father," itself a returning of thanks, suggests that learning right poetic speech begins with right teaching, which is grounded in labor understood as service, driven by love and hope, and guided by the awareness of what one owes to the sources that make life possible. Right speech, labor, and service are inseparable from right remembering, itself grounded in a vision of the goodness of things that it endlessly renews. Berry learned to speak in "sentences, / Outspoken fact for fact," from his father, who taught him simultaneously "the difference / Between good work and sham" (*Selected*, 169). This was a difference Berry's father learned while serving the oldest, simplest kind of human hope: a small, self-sufficient homestead where "no year" was "lived at the next year's cost." In doing so, "he kept in mind, alive," his own father's vision, so reminiscent of Wheeler Catlett's, that a place whose care is good should be abundant and alive everywhere, its grass in bloom. Berry's father remembers the very language in which his father had expressed his vision, "A steer should graze and thrive / Wherever he lowers his head," and Berry remembers, in turn, his father's helping him to see rightly as they watch the animals graze a hillside:

> "Look. See that this is good,
> And then you won't forget."

I saw it as he said,
And I have not forgot. (*Selected*, 169–70)

His father connected the words to the vision and pronounced it, as loving
fathers have from the beginning, good. But he also gives Berry a charge,
one not forgotten, to uphold the goodness he sees in every act of speech,
for every word witnesses to the first and last.

We come, then, to the question of how to "unspecialize poetry," something
Berry has provided helpful "Notes" for in *Standing by Words*. One way this
can be done is by bringing poetry into relationship to other disciplines,
marriage and farming specifically. But before we look at the way those disciplines figure in Berry's poetry, it is instructive to look at some of his
"Notes," which happen, too, to be delightful in the best way of aphoristic
writing. A place to begin is with Berry's remark that "there are obligations
to 'identity' that must precede an escape from it," a comment that seems to
endorse a more individualistic conception of poetic voice than one might
expect from Berry.[22] But this reading is only possible if we understand
"identity" to point to what is most unique about us, as it is so often used in
modern talk of finding our identities and so forth. The very fact that Berry
refers to our having "obligations" to "identity" suggests he is not using the
term in this way, but rather to point to all those people and things who
have made us who we are—family, history, place, tradition, religion, region, nation. The poet must learn to write from a full sense of those alle-
giances and not simply from uniquely personal experience. Berry comes
close to a similar observation in another of his "Notes": "By taking oneself
too seriously one is prevented from being serious enough" (85). One becomes serious enough not by registering one's unique personal "notations"—which may simply be idiosyncratic—but by writing from all those
connections that constitute one's identity.

Perhaps no connection is any more important than one to place. In
another of the "Notes," Berry declares himself "endlessly in need of the
work of poets who have been concerned with living in place, the life of a
place, long-term attention and devotion to a settled home and its natural
household, and hence to the relation between imagination and language
and a place" (88). Berry hopes to see action again "become the subject of
poetry" and wonders whether we are perhaps even "near to a revival of

narrative in poetry." For action to again take on this importance, however, requires a commitment of poets to place, for the "meaning of action in time is inseparable from its meaning in place" ("Notes," 88). Commitment to place might also encourage a proper seriousness, one capable of recognizing the poetic worthlessness of both weighty attitudinizing and the endless multiplication of notations. Place is essential to our coming to understand the consequences of action over an extended period of time. When we live, work, and think in places that aspire to be like every other place, we are necessarily turned in on ourselves, invited to believe ourselves more important than we are and to believe thinking itself more important than it is.

The poet "concerned with the life of a place" is likely to retain a feeling for that quality Berry calls, in still another of his "Notes," the "chief criterion of thought": "propriety" (89). A sense of propriety depends upon our coming to know ourselves in relation to the concrete purposes that develop as we learn to fit our lives into what a place makes possible and forbids. Staying at home may seem, for the poet, dull or static, but Berry suggests that it is rather "paradoxically to change, to move." For what the placed poet (or someone in "any other calling") moves away from first is "professionalism" and "professional standards"—that is, standards established by largely placeless specialists. Freed from "primarily literary" standards, the poet rooted in place and concerned with propriety can begin to ask different questions of his or her work: "What good is it? Is it at home here? What do the neighbors think of it? Do they read it, any of them? What have they contributed to it? What does it owe to them?" ("Notes," 88).

The way poets—and all too often other academics—have learned to leave out the issue of propriety is by focusing on themselves, making the question irrelevant but also leaving themselves hard put to differentiate "between what interests [them] and what interests everybody" ("Notes," 85). Connection to place and to a community other than one's academic peers might cause poets to again think hard about "what, or whom, the poems are *for*." Regaining a sense of "what poems are *for*" (or just the sense that they are "for" something other than the process of writing them) will lead, Berry hopes, to a renewal of "the art (the technical means) of writing them." "And so we will renew their ability to tell the truth," he adds, presumably because poems written "for something" will enter again into a life of dialogue with communities capable of responding to and evaluating what they say ("Notes," 84). The "specialized imagination" institutionalized by society in the university has been one "free and unfettered." The "unspecialized imagination," on the other hand,

> may imagine a farm, a factory, a community, a marriage, a family, a household, a city, a poem—but only as a first step. Having imagined one, it will then strive to imagine the relation of that one to all the rest. It is, thus, a disciplined imagination. It is a formal imagination. It is concerned with relation, dependence, propriety, proportion, balance. ("Notes," 89–90)

When we know the end in view, and that end must fit with the ends of other complex human practices, we will know where to begin, the first principles: "If the builder knows where the house is to be built and who will live in it, and if he respects that place and those people, then he must necessarily strive to build a good house" ("Notes," 81). So the poet, too, will write well who knows the people who will live in her poems and has learned to respect them by hearing what they have to say about her work.

Poetry needs to be freed, then, from too easy ideas of genius and originality. Flight from discipline—poetic form, marriage, other forms of cultural continuity—may mean only that one never confronts the hardest and yet possibly richest human experiences. This is the claim of Berry's fullest piece on the analogy of poetry and marriage, the 1982 essay "Poetry and Marriage: The Use of Old Forms," collected in *Standing by Words*. Both poetry and marriage begin in a "giving of words" that "implies the acceptance of a form that is never entirely of one's own making."[23] The joining of a couple in marriage can only be accomplished by their "joining the unknown." The couple commit their lives "to a way" that is not going where either of them alone thinks it is, but rather "where the two of [them]—and marriage, time, life, history, and the world—will take it" (PM, 92). There is a sobriety and depth about Berry's description of marriage that puts it at odds with today's celebration of the institution as the site of personal and sexual fulfillment within a union of enhanced consumer power:

> Marriage rests upon the immutable *givens* that compose it: words, bodies, characters, histories, places. Some wishes cannot succeed; some victories cannot be won; some loneliness is incorrigible. But

there is relief and freedom in knowing what is real; these givens come
to us out of the perennial reality of the world, like the terrain we live
on. One does not care for this ground to make it a different place, or
to make it perfect, but to make it inhabitable and to make it better. To
flee from its realities is only to arrive at them unprepared. (PM, 92)

Poetry, too, particularly that "of the traditionally formed sort," accepts various givens, various limits, as "imposed *before* the beginning." It does not
propose to solve the difficulties it meets in running its course "by skipping
or forcing a rhyme or by mutilating syntax or by writing prose" (PM, 93).

Poetry and marriage are, for Berry, two mutually illuminating aspects
of the larger practice of living in form, which is itself "a way of accepting and
of living within the limits of creaturely life." What we learn, if we take them
"seriously enough," is that such forms enable us to live generously and hope-
fully in a world of limits. The forms "acknowledge that good is possible; they
hope for it, await it, and prepare its welcome—though they dare not *require*
it," knowing that to do so is "to forsake the way" and thus "to forsake the
possibility" of the form itself—one that human beings have learned over
time can only be had by fidelity to the form (PM, 93). The form, "strictly
kept, *enforces* freedom," for it can only be fulfilled "by a kind of abandonment to hope and to possibility, to unexpected gifts." Thus, it is a mistake to
think of freedom and form as opposing terms; rather "form, like topsoil
(which is intricately formal), empowers time to do good" (PM, 96–97).

Paradoxically, forms do some of their best work when they create difficulties. It is through obstruction and bafflement that we learn "patience,
forbearance, inspiration—the gifts and graces of time, circumstance, and
faith." Failure is a possibility, in poetry and in marriage, but "it is this possibility of failure, together with the formal bounds, that turns us back from
fantasy, wishful thinking, and self-pity into the real terms and occasions of
our lives." "It may be," Berry continues, "that when we no longer know
what to do we have come to our real work and that when we no longer
know which way to go we have begun our real journey." What do we do
when we no longer know what to do? One possibility is to begin the slow
process of consenting to forms that have been valid, a self-abandonment in
hope that the forms that have borne others through will do the same for us.
If we can abandon expectation for the hope that is born of fidelity, we may
yet come to find "the world, the truth, is more abounding, more delightful,
more demanding than we thought" (PM, 97).

That forms can make something good of us never ceases to stun some of us, as Berry makes clear in "A Warning to My Readers." Confessing himself a man "crude as any, / gross of speech, intolerant," Berry remarks that if he has "spoken well / at times," it is "not natural. / A wonder is what it is" (*Selected*, 117). I am reminded here of a line of Stanley Hauerwas's that resonates closely with my own experience. Hauerwas has said he's a Christian pacifist because he knows himself to be a violent person and he needs the church to keep him peaceful.[24] Thus valid forms serve us, insisting on a discipline that can bring the wonderful out of the merely natural.

Disciplines move us toward the goods that are available within a world of limits, while simultaneously reminding us that we are forever on the way toward the realization of our fullest goods. They shape us, guide the ways we shape ourselves, and remind us that we are never complete. Remarking in "Marriage" how his wife Tanya has "quieted" his restlessness, Berry acknowledges that such quietness is no final state, but rather more a matter of continually learning how to be healed after being "broken" or "torn open" (*Selected*, 31). Indeed, to be married is perhaps to be broken and torn more deeply than one would be otherwise, for it is to commit oneself to an emotional vulnerability quite unlike that of any other relationship— particularly if one's vows are taken to be unalterable. But it is not only vulnerability that is a source of pain, but also the ego's restless need to assert its independence of the one it needs most. As long as we are burdened by that "fat relentless ego," as Iris Murdoch called it, no final wholeness is possible between a couple.[25] But what can take place—if we learn to be willing— is a kind of continual healing:

> I turn against you,
> I break from you, I turn to you.
> We hurt, and are hurt,
> and have each other for healing.
> It is healing. It is never whole. (*Selected*, 31)[26]

Part of what makes marriage a place of tearing and healing is suggested by another early poem, "The Design of a House." The house is brought forth out of love's labor, which is itself the labor of life loving itself as it articulates itself in the living facts of the world:

> the seed doesn't swell
> in its husk by reason, but loves

itself, obeys light which is
its own thought and argues the leaf
in secret; love articulates
the choice of life in fact (*Selected,* 14)

What "love foresees" is a "jointure / composing a house, a marriage / of contraries, compendium / of opposites in equilibrium" (*Selected,* 14). What the house is trying to keep, for the sake of equilibrium, at the present moment of the poem, is "a spare dream of summer" within as the winter nights bring a "dark and depth" of snow outside:

the Queen Anne's lace
—gobletted,
green beginning to bloom,
tufted, upfurling—
unfolding
whiteness:
in this winter's memory
more clear than ever in summer,
cold paring away excess: (*Selected,* 12–13)

In the sixth section of the poem, Berry declares directly that "This is a love poem for you, Tanya—" and then cites its occasions: "among wars, among the brutal forfeitures / of time, in this house, among its latent fires, / among all that honesty must see, I accept / your dying, and love you: nothing mitigates" (*Selected,* 15). Here is plain speech about one source of the tearing in marriage's flesh: the death of the spouse that "nothing mitigates." The commitment to love unto death takes upon itself what Emily Dickinson declared she could not do in the great poem that begins, "I cannot live with You—": "I could not die—with You—/ For One must wait / To shut the Other's Gaze down—/ You—could not—."[27] Each spouse must, as Berry puts it, "accept" the dying of the other, perhaps a harder task than accepting one's own death, for each puts so much of his or her hope for life into the beloved. Accepting the death of one who has elicited so much of one's hope can cause the pulling away that marital partners feel, one grounded in a resentment that is self-pitying and yet completely understandable. At its most destructive, such resentment leads to the bitterest loss of all hope.

Such is the "fear of love," one that makes us shrink from it and one that is part of it, fear that we do not have enough of it to last, that if we give it all, we will never be filled again. Perhaps also we fear its simplicity: what to do cannot be so simple as just to love and then love more, drawing forever on a source that seemingly never runs down or goes dry. Yet fortunately, as Berry puts it in "The Fear of Love," we are mostly wise enough to know "what must be desired" and "what must be done" (*Selected,* 107). Life, more life, and perhaps happiness are what must be desired. As Aquinas thought, we are so constituted as to desire happiness; to want to be happy is not a choice that we make.[28] If we have lived long enough, gotten old enough in body, or committed ourselves to a discipline like marriage, we come to know that "what must be done" is love, the self-giving that leads to an exhaustion that leads, in turn, to our dependence on a source beyond ourselves for renewal. That daily and counterintuitive resurrection overrides our fear, causing us to will the repetition of the process as we come to understand it as the way that leads to life. There is "no remedy for love but to love more," Thoreau put it.[29] Or, as Berry says, "Only love can quiet the fear / of love, and only love can save / from diminishment the love / that we must lose to have" (*Selected,* 107). The allusion here, of course, is to several New Testament passages on the paradox of losing and finding, on dying and rebirth. Given Berry's fondness for the Gospel of John, perhaps it is best to cite John 12:24: "Except a corn of wheat fall into the ground and die, it abideth alone; but if it die, it bringeth forth much fruit" (KJV). No wonder then we fear. To live from the Resurrection is to enter into death daily, learning the discipline to trust and even will what we could not do but for love.

In "The Country of Marriage," Berry speaks of how marriage's "ways" must "be made anew day after day" (*Selected,* 84). Life in that country "reminds" him "sometimes" of "a forest in which there is a graceful clearing / and in that opening a house, / an orchard and garden, / comfortable shades, and flowers / red and yellow in the sun, a pattern / made in the light for the light to return to" (84). This gracefully ordered place depends on going into the forest, "mostly dark," in order to continually remake the way to the clearing, a process that leads in time to awareness that the dark itself is "richer than the light and more blessed, / provided we stay brave / enough to keep on going in" (84–85). The "bond" created by spouses coming together as ones "lost" and "wholly trusting" is "no little economy based on the exchange / of my love and work for yours, so much for so much / of an expendable fund" (85). The idea of exchange becomes irrelevant, based as it is on some prior assumption of quantities owned and controlled, and the fund is not expendable, not even a "fund," in fact, with that word's inevitable monetary connotation. "We don't know what its limits are—" Berry continues, "that puts it in the dark. We are more together / than we know, how else could we keep on discovering / we are more together than we thought?" As one is "more blessed" in the beloved than one can know, one can "possess nothing worthy to give," for anything worthy to be given is "belittled" by the claim that it can be possessed in order to be given away. Thus "even an hour of love is a moral predicament, a blessing / a man may be hard up to be worthy of."[30] One cannot do anything to deserve it; there is nothing to be done that will somehow cause one to receive it as the product of a fair exchange, so much for so much. "He can only / accept it," begin to understand it as a grace, as something we did not make but that, fortunately, was there for us as the way of life we did not have to make (85).

What we can give, paradoxically, is our death: "What I am learning to give you is my death / to set you free of me, and me from myself / into the dark and the new light. Like the water / of a deep stream, love is always too much." Our death is not a possession, however much we would like it to be, however much we treasure it up as the precious thing that is wholly ours, the sign of our distinction. To give that up is to enter into the country of marriage, into an "abundance" that "survives our thirst," a "commonwealth" of what can only be received freely as the unbidden, the grace of the purely incalculable, "joy." What each of us can give a spouse is something it takes discipline and sometimes long years to risk, the life that we cannot "have," because it cannot be had, but that can come to life in and through us if we are courageous enough to let go of having altogether: "I give you the life I have let live for love of you: / a clump of orange-blooming weeds beside the road, / the young orchard waiting in the snow." As the poem has its source in nothing that belongs to Berry but in the "country of marriage itself," he concludes by giving it to Tanya, declaring it rightly "no more mine than any man's who has loved a woman" (*Selected*, 86).

Fortunately, it is a country for old men as well as for the young. In "Thirty-five Years," Berry speaks of how Tanya and he "have kept to the way we chose / in love without foresight / and long ago" (*TC*, 162). It is a way that "has come / to light only in the daylight / of each day as that day has come," a way involving "daily faithfulness" to the past, to hopes and griefs, to "one another," and to the "difficult, beautiful place" where their lives are being made. Their anniversary marks a moment in their following of an "old road," one that is "yet always renewed by growth / of the trees that lean over it / by weather never two days the same, / and by our own delight" (162–63). As in "The Country of Marriage," the way leads to a clearing, an "opening" discovered again and again, now "familiar / as the oldest dream," a place "where we know / we are, even as we do, / the work of love" (163).

Those who know themselves to be the work of love have arrived at "the lasting world," as Berry puts it in "Sabbath I, 1998," and they "will not leave, / whatever happens" (*Given*, 55). Yet much can and does happen to us, and modern medicine has perfected ways to keep us here in this world even after we have ceased really to be here, a possibility Berry faces in "Sabbath X, 1998." Speaking directly to Tanya, he acknowledges that "the time may come" when he will "have gone" either "beyond / all remembering," as his father did, or "into a time of pain, drugs, and still sleep" like his mother (*Given*, 65). Imagining himself on "time's edge," Berry knows he "will be longing / to return, to seek [Tanya] through the world," to reaffirm the life they have together. He wonders, too, if in the "light / of that place beyond time," he may see "the world / as perhaps Christ saw it before His birth"—a world "imperfect," of course, but perhaps paradoxically fortunate in its imperfection, for "to whom would love / appear but to those in most desperate need?" Berry sees that Tanya and he "would err" and "suffer/ again," but "provided you would have it," he says to her, "I would do it all again" (66). Love's discipline in marriage is capable of bringing us to the fullest affirmation: that all that is is good, though fallen, and that one can be so mortally in love and married to the world that one would do it all again gladly. We can give it up only because we do not really need to do so, for in death we enter more fully into that love we have glimpsed and come to trust, a love that goes ahead of us, opening for us a way into the clearing and preparing the renewal of all creation.

The farmer experiences a mortal longing for the world as an aching in the flesh. He is married to the earth, to the particular place where he receives "the current" of life from his ancestors and "is made their descendant," hoping, in his turn, that "The current flowing to him through the earth / flows past him" to his own descendants (*Selected*, 76). "The Current" begins in a way that, by now, should seem familiar to us, though no less compelling. Berry gives up the life of air, of free movement above the earth, in order to give himself to the life of the earth where his body will ultimately lie. What he enacts is hope, which, once enacted in this realest of ways, will bring him back, causing pain in his body itself if he tries to deny or pretend that he has not so given himself:

> Having once put his hand into the ground,
> seeding there what he hopes will outlast him,
> a man has made a marriage with his place,
> and if he leaves it his flesh will ache to go back.
> His hand has given up its birdlife in the air. (76)

The farmer's connection to the earth is a mortal bond, one that acknowledges fully what human beings perhaps uniquely know: that we live not only on other life but *at the expense of* other life. This knowledge of good and evil brings with it the question of our worthiness. If we, wedded to the world, live from other life, then we must honor it, as Berry does in the prayerlike "For the Hog Killing." "Let them stand still for the bullet, and stare the shooter in the eye," Berry says, reminding us of the life that goes into our "provisioning." "Let this day begin the change of hogs into people, not the other way around," as we saw happen in the story "Don't Send a Boy to Do a Man's Work (1891)."

The farmer learns to go by contraries, dependent on what he cannot control, serving what will not last, aware that confessed ignorance is the beginning, and perhaps ending, of knowledge that matters. "Men think to be immortal in the world," Berry says in "The Farmer, Speaking of Monuments," but the farmer's discipline is to learn that "he remains in what he serves / by vanishing in it, becoming what he never was." Like the poet, "He will not be immortal in words." "All his sentences," like those of men wooing the ground, the weather, or women, "serve an art of the commonplace, / to open the body of a woman or a field / to take him in" (*CP*, 139). The farmer sows in desire and receives, by grace, what he needs, what satisfies, not because it comes in the form of what he has desired, but because it is wonderful enough to reform his desire. He comes to love the sowing as going free of himself.

If he has been paying enough attention, or is ignorant enough to know by now he needs to learn something he had not expected, the farmer may understand, as Berry's Mad Farmer puts it in one of his "Prayers and

Sayings," that "the *real* products of any year's work are the farmer's mind and the cropland itself" (*CP,* 131). These are intimately connected, for the ability of the cropland to continue in good health depends on the farmer's mind learning what the place has to teach him about its good care, its possibilities and limits. Knowing "The finest growth that farmland can produce is a careful farmer," the Mad Farmer prays that the husbandman "will receive the season's increment into his mind. Let him work it into the soil" (131). Berry's Mad Farmer is a figure of contrariness, one who delights in setting himself against popular pieties, challenging unchallengeable beliefs, suggesting the world is a great deal wider and more mysterious than our views of it. In "The Contrariness of the Mad Farmer," he announces himself "done with apologies. If contrariness is my / inheritance and destiny, so be it" (*CP,* 121). He has been caught often "laughing at funerals" because he "knew the dead were already slipping away, / preparing a comeback," and he has "gritted and gnashed" his teeth at weddings because he knows "where the bridegroom / had sunk his manhood, and knew it would not / be resurrected by a piece of cake." He has refused to dance when told to do so and then danced while others "stood / quiet in line at the gate of the Kingdom." He has laughed when told to pray, covering himself "in the earth's brightnesses," and then stolen "off gray / into the midst of a revel, and prayed like an orphan." If there is a time and a season for all things under the heavens, as the Preacher says, the Mad Farmer insists that human beings may not know either the times or the dates with any precision. "Going against men," he has "heard at times a deep harmony / thrumming in the mixture," but when others have asked him what he's heard, he says he doesn't know, perhaps for fear that if his words become enshrined among men, he will have to reject them (121–22).

The Mad Farmer's contrary voice would be cherished by a culture confident and healthy enough to understand its own ignorance and need of prophetic challenge. In "The Mad Farmer Manifesto: The First Amendment," he declares in a voice reminiscent of Blake, "The world / is a holy vision, had we clarity / to see it—a clarity that men / depend on men to make" (*CP,* 154). This is not to say that wisdom lies only in contrariness, for Berry, although perhaps it does more now than usual in this "mad time," this time of "*ignorant* money," when to be sane "is bad for the brain, worse / for the heart" (154). But there is wisdom yet in the "old ways"—the communal ways of the commonwealth—that sometimes still can come to clarity, "as at a country funeral" where "the usages of old neighborhood" persist (*Selected*, 91). In the lovely poem "At a Country Funeral," Berry depicts the "Friends and kinsmen" as they "come and stand and speak, / knowing the extremity they have come to." They do so as those who farm have done for generations, knowing however today that often the death they grieve means the loss of a "lifework" and one of the recognizable places in their world. The "blood kin" gather "for one last time, to hear old men / whose tongues bear an essential topography / speak memories doomed to die" (*Selected*, 91–92). But the speaker insists those memories not be allowed to die, for they are "what we owe the future." What the future needs from us is not "a new start," but precisely "the past," the "long knowledge" of "what has happened" that is itself "the potency of time to come." As the poem ends, the speaker turns home, for where else can one go who is pledged to being a keeper of the "memories of the dead"? Where else can one go who would be "faithful to the fields, lest the dead die / a second and more final death"? (92).

In "History," Berry comes to his land after two hundred years of "history's despite / and ruin," arriving at the place where he will make "the beginning / of a farm intended to become / my art of being here" (*Selected*, 100–101). Part of that art is to learn to "instruct" his "wants" so that his farm and art "should belong / to one another and to this place." Only then will he know what to make and sing of a diminished thing: "Until my song comes here / to learn its words, my art / is but the hope of song" (101). The learning of the words begins, as Berry puts it in "The Man Born to Farming," with hands "reach[ing] into the ground," entering "into death / yearly, and com[ing] back rejoicing" (*Selected*, 67). In "The Stones," song is roused in the poet-farmer as he raises stones "like buried pianos" from places "where the earth caught and kept them / dark, an old music mute in them / that my head keeps now." Wearing himself "against it," he enters into a "bond" with the earth, one that results in "singing" that is "fatal," in both unavoidability and cost (*Selected*, 68). The body that gives itself in heavy labor, that knows the resistance of the world, will sing its own diminishment, its daily death.

In "The Supplanting," the farmer comes to know himself as a supplanter who will be supplanted in turn. Setting fire to a long-deserted house and shed surrounded by choking undergrowth, Berry thinks of those he's supplanted: an "old wife" whose daffodils and white peonies still suggest a domesticity among the wild, a homeless drunk who has sometimes slept in the buildings. As the blaze continues, he knows "those old ones departed" and he "arrived," but he also feels something "rise" in him "that would not bear" his "name—something that bears us / through the flame, and is lightened of us, and is glad" (*Selected*, 69). Part of the art of being here is to learn to be lightened, and even glad, that we, too, will be supplanted by a wildness, a yearning, creation's fierce joy in renewal.

The poet-farmer may look, with a joy born of honesty, on his ultimate supplanting, but in the near term, he needs ground on which to stand, a place where he can distance himself even "from the crowd who may agree / with what" he says. The "earthly promise of life or peace" lies only in "A Standing Ground" for him because he knows, on the one hand, that to be "uprooted" is simply to be "furious without an aim," and, on the other, that he is not destined for some "public place." Berry has of course engaged in making arguments through many volumes of nonfiction prose, but the poet-farmer knows it's "Better than any argument" to "rise at dawn / and pick dew-wet red berries in a cup" (*Selected*, 73). Such rootedness enables one to go on when life seems nearly without hope, arid, incapable of renewal. "In a country without saints or shrines," Berry begins "The Springs," he knows "one who made his pilgrimage / to springs, where in his life's dry years / his mind held on. Everlasting, / people called them, and gave them names" (*Selected*, 69). In my part of the country, not far from Berry's, some country people make continual rounds of the springs, to check on their health and to drink as if from the depths of the earth itself. They know, I suspect, something like what Thoreau came to understand about why some people thought Walden Pond was bottomless: that it was good for the imagination to believe in the infinite, perhaps necessary if the mind is not to die of its own self-imposed limitations.[31]

One fruit of the farmer's discipline is generosity, which involves learning to will that one's life become, as Berry says in "The Wish to Be Generous," a "passing without haste / or regret toward what will be," a "patient willing descent into the grass" (*Selected*, 70). Such generosity brings with it a freedom achieved only by a letting go of the ego, as we see in the generous man of "Enriching the Earth," whose serving "the dark" by "slowly falling / into the fund of things" gives "a wideness / and a delight to the air." He knows that even what is "heaviest / and most mute about him"—his body—will be "at last raised up into song" (*Selected*, 71). Part of learning to be generous involves learning to praise—even in the midst of hard history—a quality grounded in remembering gratefully those whose "kindness" has made one's life possible. The speaker of Berry's beautiful "A Praise" exhibits such gratitude as he asks that his mind may "be the earth" of his predecessor's "thought." He has known the older man so well, watched him so closely and often, that now "certain wise movements of his hands, / the turns of his speech / keep with" him (*Selected*, 70). This is how we all, where there is real community, learn the art of being here: one gesture, one phrase, one hope, one kindness at a time.

Perhaps the fruit of all disciplines of the real is right hearing, which takes place in silence, depends on openness, and gives rise to praise. One capable of such hearing was "crazy old Mrs. Gaines," remembered by Berry's grandmother as "standing balanced eighty years ago / atop a fence in Port Royal, Kentucky, / singing: 'One Lord, one Faith, and one / Cornbread'" (*Selected*, 77). Following the way of her rambles into the woods in "Meditation in the Spring Rain," Berry hears what the old prophetess had heard so many years before him:

Surely
there is a great Word being put together here.
I begin to hear it gather in the opening
of the flowers and the leafing-out of the trees,
in the growth of bird nests in the crotches
of the branches, in the settling of the dead
leaves into the ground, in the whittling
of beetle and grub, in my thoughts
moving in the hill's flesh. (*Selected*, 78)

As he hears the "sounds" of "hidden water" underground together with those of the falling rain, Berry begins to "think the maker is here, creating his hill / as it will be, out of what it was." What comes to him, then, is the rightness of Mrs. Gaines's holy speech as an expression of the "thickets" themselves as they "send up their praise / at dawn! One Lord, one Faith, and one Cornbread / forever!" But aware of the inadequacy of any human speech, Berry intervenes again, reminding himself to "hush. Wait. Be as still / as the dead and the unborn in whose silence / that old one walked." The poem closes, then, by pointing to the final end of all the poet's discipline, an end that lies in knowing the limits of one's language and the moment in which one must simply abandon oneself to listening and praise. "For a time" here, Berry says, "I was lost and free, speechless / in the multitudinous assembling of his Word" (78–79).

The Word for Berry is Love, there at the beginning and the end, standing over all, entering into all. The end for the poet, then, paradoxically, is to arrive at a kind of speechlessness, a silence before the Word that creates and sustains everything. One of the impulses of Berry's most recent years of Sabbath poems, as I read them, is to create a kind of quiet, a stillness in which things can come to be and be seen in their own light. Unfortunately— and this is a second emphasis of the poems—that quiet is torn repeatedly by the violence of war and environmental destruction. Hope is still on Berry's mind as well: what it means for an older man; why we must have it; what we can learn from practicing its opposite, hopelessness, at times. There is an intimacy about these poems, too, especially those from *Leavings*, that contributes to both their emotional and their moral strength—"moral" because they remind us that a particular quality of intimacy with the world is something we must protect if we are not to lose it to the depredations of a total economy.

"Sabbath VII, 1998" suggests the way years of disciplined self-emptying can bring one quietly into "a place of water and the light" where trees, leaves, light, and birds are not the objects of thought, but rather "themselves / your thoughts," and you are "here as though gone" (*Given*, 62). In "Sabbath III, 2001," Berry implores us to seek the "true quiet" in which things "become what they are, and are nothing else" (*Given*, 97). Similarly, in "Sabbath XI, 2007," the "sounds of engines" must "leave the air" before silence can bring again "the presence / of the world made without hands," of "creatures" who are otherwise seemingly absent (*Leavings*, 98). A poem might be, like "Sabbath VIII, 2007," no more (or less) than a pointing toward something or "a whisper that says 'There!'" where "the sun enters and the tanager / flares suddenly on the lighted branch" (*Leavings*, 95). Quiet, too, is the measure of one of Berry's most beautiful poems, "Sabbath X, 2007," with its image of Tanya "as she works in the garden / in the quiet" suffused by the "passing light" that Berry has learned to love (*Leavings*, 97).

The quiet is still torn, however, by violence, greed, ignorance, and our overconfident knowledge that is often worse than ignorance. "Sabbath II, 2005" begins by remembering "the killed by violence, the dead / in war, the 'acceptable losses.'" These "gather like an ancestry / in the centuries behind us," and despite commands like "love your enemies," the killing "goes on regardless, reasonably: / the always uncompleted / symmetry of just reprisal." The pressure of the poem toward its conclusion involves a magnifying of the kinds of motives that keep the killing going, as if the ever-gathering ancestry of the dead brings from us ever more potent justifications, however absurd they might be if examined. What begins with "the angry word, the boast / of superior righteousness," ends in "centuries bloodied and dismembered / for ideas, for ideals, / for the love of God!" (*Leavings*, 34–35). "Sabbath VII, 2006" suggests that any god served by killing children "for righteousness' sake" is merely one "thoughtified to the mean / of our smallest selves" (*Leavings*, 74). If "the nation is a boat," as "Sabbath II, 2007" remarks, it is disturbing to see its descent from our original visions of liberty and abundance to that "caricature" of what is called "vision" in our own "characterless time" (*Leavings*, 83).

Berry is no less convinced than ever that we must change our lives if we are to save some part of that world that sustains us. Speaking specifically of mountaintop removal, he says in "Sabbath I, 2007," "To take the coal to burn / They overturn the world / And all the world has worn / Of grace, of health." By such overturning, the order of the world is undone, the "fist of their greed" making "small / The great Life" (*Leavings*, 82). "Sabbath XII, 2008" begins with a reminder that we continue to live in comprehensive forgetting of what we "live from," setting "ourselves / free in an economy founded / on nothing, on greed verified / by fantasy." We consume the world in fire, offering "our land as fuel" in a process that can only end by our "offering ourselves at last / to be burned" (*Leavings*, 123). If our lives have come to depend upon greed, then it is no wonder some now defend it as a virtue, "the best engine of betterment known to man," as William Safire comments in a passage Berry uses as an epigraph for "Sabbath XIII, 2008," the final poem of *Leavings*. "By its own logic, greed / finally destroys itself," Berry insists, and "only mourners survive" (*Leavings*, 124).

"Hope is our duty" no less than ever, but, as "Sabbath III, 2007" proposes, we might make it part of our discipline to "live a while without it" in order to "shrink us to our proper size" and find the world then "twice as large." Practicing hopelessness, Berry finds himself still "well," like the "springtime rue anemones," which, "hoping / not even to live, are beautiful / as Eden" in their perfect moment (*Leavings*, 86). Hope "is hard to have,"

Berry acknowledges in "Sabbath VI, 2007," and "harder as you grow old, / for hope must not depend on feeling good." Hope must live on despite one's having "withdrawn belief in the present reality / of the future." "But stop dithering," Berry commands himself in the midst of this rehearsal of what makes hope difficult. "The young ask the old to hope," and we can at least tell them what we tell ourselves. Berry advises the young to hope "to belong" to their places in the fullest sense: through knowledge of the place and care for it; through learning its speech and learning to listen to what its voices have to teach; through connection to one's neighbors in the place, human and nonhuman; through cultivation of an "imagination in place" that will be the source of one's ability to understand what others, in their places, require, by way of care. "Found your hope," even to the "hope of Heaven," Berry says to the young, on "the ground under your feet" (*Leavings*, 91–93).[32]

There is, for Berry, hope in heaven, and part of that hope is to know that the "bottom rung" of the ladder on which he rests his foot "*is* Heaven" (my emphasis), "though the ladder is standing / on the earth where" he works and where, like Jacob, he sleeps with his "head upon a stone" ("Sabbath I, 2006," in *Leavings*, 61). In a prayer to the saints in "Sabbath VI, 2006," Berry acknowledges that even pain "in eternity's once and now" would "place" him "surely in the Heaven of [his] earthly love," for it would be pain felt for "beauties overlooked," for falling short in attention or gratitude. And so such "pain would be the measure" of his love (*Leavings*, 73). Hope of heaven, like all hope, derives from an intimacy with the earth. An old man can hope in "his own / small place of peace, a patch of trees / he has lived from many years." Having kept it whole, he hopes, in "Sabbath XVII, 2005," that "after him, God willing, another / will follow in that membership / that craves the wholeness of the world / despite all human loss and blame" (*Leavings*, 54). The discipline of hope, together with living so deeply from one's own place, can bring us, at last, to will it for another, as the speaker of "Sabbath VII, 2007" understands. Knowing he must disappear "from his lifelong fields," he "foresees" this "with hope, / with thanks," saying, "Let others come" (*Leavings*, 94).

The most powerful poem of hope in *Leavings*, for me, "Sabbath XI, 2008," presents the simple narrative of an old man, a shepherd, who, "ill and in pain," gets out of bed, goes to the barn, and sends his dog to bring in the lambs. As they feed, he feels the deep hope we know as we see others fed, and Berry suggests the ritual gathers them together with "all the known and unknown / round about to the heavens' limit." Was the old man's venturing out in his sickness and hurt an act of "stubbornness or bravado?" Berry asks.

> No. Only an ordinary act
> of profoundest intimacy in a day
> that might have been better. Still
> the world persisted in its beauty,
> he in his gratitude, and for this
> he had most earnestly prayed. (*Leavings*, 121–22)

In this simple act of tending the world with thanks, a world beautiful and intimately known, the old man gives a powerful account of the hope that is in him.

Notes

Introduction

1. Berry, *Life Story of Jayber Crow,* n.p.
2. Twain, *Adventures of Huckleberry Finn,* xxv.
3. "Dante," in Berry, *Given,* 8.
4. "Imagination in Place," in Berry, *Way of Ignorance,* 50–51.
5. See, e.g., Thoreau's point that "to cooperate, in the highest as well as the lowest sense, means *to get our living together*" (*Walden,* 115).
6. Cf. Kant, *Foundations of the Metaphysics of Morals,* 46.
7. "Preface," in Berry, *Way of Ignorance,* x.
8. "The Loss of the University," in Berry, *Home Economics,* 91–92 (LU hereafter).
9. "Discipline and Hope," in Berry, *Continuous Harmony,* 124–25 (DH hereafter).
10. "The Gift of Good Land," in Berry, *Gift of Good Land,* 274 (hereafter GGL).
11. GGL, 273.
12. "The Hurt Man (1888)," in Berry, *That Distant Land,* 10.
13. Berry, *Remembering,* 154.
14. James, "Art of Fiction," 399.
15. Berry, *Life Is a Miracle,* 118 (*LM* hereafter). For Berry's objection to Wilson's claim that works of art or literature can be explained according to the laws of biology or physics, see *LM,* 105–19. I treat these matters in chapter 3 of this book.
16. On agrarianism, the new agrarianism, and the relationship of both to Berry, a helpful beginning list would include the following: Carlson, *New Agrarian Mind;* Freyfogle, *New Agrarianism;* Wirzba, *Essential Agrarian Reader;* and Smith, *Wendell Berry and the Agrarian Tradition. I'll Take My Stand* is, of course, an essential source. For a very helpful gathering of agrarian writings by Berry, see *Art of the Commonplace.* Wirzba's introduction to that volume, "The Challenge of Berry's

Agrarian Vision," is a good place to begin the process of thinking about how agrarianism can become a vital source of change for people who are not primarily farmers—something taken up, in fact, by many of the pieces collected in the readers edited by Freyfogle and by Wirzba.

17. Wirzba, "Introduction: Why Agrarianism Matters," 4.

18. Wirzba, "Introduction: Why Agrarianism Matters," 4. Berry comments on our not yet being "authentically settled" in America in "The Whole Horse," in Berry, *Citizenship Papers,* 119.

19. Berry, *Leavings,* 49.

20. LU, 96.

1. Practices, Particulars, and Virtues

1. "A Native Hill," in Berry, *Long-Legged House,* 171–72 (NH hereafter, cited in the text). For biographical material on Berry, see Angyal, *Wendell Berry,* which takes a chronological approach, as Goodrich does partially, too, in *Unforeseen Self.* Also valuable are the chronologies in Grubbs, *Conversations with Wendell Berry,* xvii–xx; and in Peters, *Wendell Berry,* 325–28. The interviews collected in *Conversations* offer many details, as do the delightful pieces by friends of Berry's collected by Peters.

2. In the "Economy" chapter of *Walden,* Thoreau remarks, "In any weather, at any hour of the day or night, I have been anxious to improve the nick of time, and notch it on my stick too; to stand on the meeting of two eternities, the past and future, which is precisely the present moment; to toe that line" (59). But closer in spirit to Berry's comment that he was born "barely in the nick of time" is Thoreau's saying, "I have never got over my surprise that I should have been born into the most estimable place in all the world, and in the very nick of time, too" (*Journal,* 160). Part of this quote is cited by Walter Harding at the beginning of *The Days of Henry Thoreau* (3). For Thoreau's saying "I went to the woods because I wished to live deliberately," see "Where I Lived, and What I Lived For," in *Walden,* 135 (hereafter cited in the text).

3. Deneen, "Wendell Berry and the Alternative Tradition," 312.

4. MacIntyre, *After Virtue,* 187 (AV hereafter, cited in the text).

5. "Feminism, the Body, and the Machine," in Berry, *What Are People For?* 193 (FBM hereafter, cited in the text).

6. "The Unsettling of America," in Berry, *Unsettling of America,* 9 (UA hereafter, cited in the text).

7. "Renewing Husbandry," in Berry, *Way of Ignorance,* 91 (RH hereafter, cited in the text).

8. For the way working with animals puts one in a living world in a way that

riding a tractor does not, see Berry's letter to Wes Jackson of Nov. 11, 1980: "As one who has farmed with both tractors and teams, I would insist (to you; I would be more cautious, at present, in a public statement) that with the use of a tractor certain vital excitements, pleasures, and sensitivities are lost. How much numb metal can we put between ourselves and our land and still know where we are and what we are doing?" Quoted in Jackson, "Letters from a Humble Radical," 157.

9. "Horse-Drawn Tools and the Doctrine of Labor Saving," in Berry, *Gift of Good Land,* 104.

10. For Berry's use of these terms, see "The Conservation of Nature and the Preservation of Humanity," in Berry, *Another Turn of the Crank,* 67–70 (CN hereafter).

11. Berry "ought to be read as much as a futurist describing better possibilities as someone looking back to what once had been." See Orr, "Uses of Prophecy," 176.

12. Aristotle, *Ethics,* Book I, 65.

13. "Preface," in Berry, *Home Economics,* ix.

14. "Going Back—or Ahead—to Horses," in Berry, *Gift of Good Land,* 192.

15. *LM,* 31–32 (hereafter cited in the text). Berry's censure of the totalitarianism implicit in Wilson's drive for perfect clarity and certainty recalls Pascal's *pensees* on the way God hides himself precisely in order to prevent such perfect certainty about him. For Pascal, God does this because he "prefers rather to incline the will than the intellect. Perfect clearness would be of use to the intellect, and would harm the will." See *Pensees,* no. 580, 190.

16. "The Way of Ignorance," in Berry, *Way of Ignorance,* 66.

17. Cf. Benjamin Franklin: "In order to secure my Credit and Character as a Tradesman, I took care not only to be in *Reality* Industrious & frugal, but to avoid all *Appearances* of the Contrary. I dressed plainly; I was seen at no Places of idle Diversion; I never went out a-fishing or shooting; a Book, indeed, sometimes debauch'd me from my Work; but that was seldom, snug, & gave no Scandal" (*Autobiography,* 54).

18. Pieper, *Four Cardinal Virtues,* 25 (hereafter cited in the text).

19. "People, Land, and Community," in Berry, *Standing by Words,* 64 (PLC hereafter, cited in the text).

20. See the opening pages of "Where I Lived, and What I Lived For" in *Walden.* Thoreau concludes his account of buying the local farms in imagination with a comment on his seeds: "All that I could say, then, with respect to farming on a large scale, (I have always cultivated a garden,) was, that I had had my seeds ready. Many think that seeds improve with age. I have no doubt that time discriminates between the good and the bad; and when at last I shall plant, I shall be less likely to be disappointed" (128).

21. Gene Logsdon gives an account of Berry's work on this hillside in "Wendell Berry: Agrarian Artist," 248–50.

272 Notes to Pages 22–29

22. Aristotle, *Ethics,* 258.

23. For Lightning, see Berry, *Memory of Old Jack,* esp. 82–84.

24. "That Distant Land (1965)," in Berry, *That Distant Land,* 314.

25. Aristotle, *Ethics,* 258–59.

26. "A Friend of Mine (1967)," in Berry, *That Distant Land,* 324 (hereafter cited in the text).

27. "The Wild Birds (1967)," in Berry, *That Distant Land,* 351.

28. "Fidelity (1977)," in Berry, *That Distant Land,* 424–25.

29. Romans 12:5 (KJV).

30. "The Island," in Muir, *Collected Poems,* 248–49. Berry cites the poem in "Unsettling of America" (9) and in "In Defense of Literacy," in Berry, *Continuous Harmony,* 167.

31. "The Ecological Crisis as a Crisis of Character," in Berry, *Unsettling of America,* 22.

32. "Health Is Membership," in Berry, *Another Turn of the Crank,* 89.

33. "The Ecological Crisis as a Crisis of Agriculture," in Berry, *Unsettling of America,* 30–31 (ECCA hereafter, cited in the text).

34. "The Work of Local Culture," in Berry, *What Are People For?* 166–67.

35. "An Argument for Diversity," in Berry, *What Are People For?* 117 (AD hereafter, cited in the text).

36. "An Agricultural Journey in Peru," in Berry, *Gift of Good Land,* 17.

37. For this essay, see *Art of the Commonplace,* 236–48, or Berry, *Citizenship Papers,* 113–25.

38. On the very important question of what is "to be *sustained* in 'sustainable' economic development," see Daly, "Sustainable Economic Development," 62–79. Daly states that two basic answers have been given to this question. One uses "*utility* or happiness" as a measure—that is, "the utility of future generations is to be non-declining"; the other focuses on "physical *throughput,* the entropic physical flow from nature's sources through the economy and back to nature's sinks" (62). Daly prefers "throughput" as the measure, arguing further that economic theory has inappropriately ignored nature's inputs, treating them as if infinite. For Daly, throughput must be built "into economic theory as a basic concept" if we are to see how what he calls "illth" is "necessarily generated along with wealth" (66).

39. A vital point about scale is made by Wes Jackson as he reflects on the changes brought to farming by mechanization and the availability of "low-priced nonrenewable energy." Jackson proposes that, as "a general rule," "high energy destroys information" of "both the cultural and biological varieties." Small scale makes possible a "culture" of agriculture, in which "the cultural information in the workers and the biological information stored in the genes of the crop" are both critical and able to work complementarily. See "Letters from a Humble Radical," 160.

40. Henry James to Charles Eliot Norton, Feb. 4, 1872, in James, *Letters,* 274. Writing from Cambridge, Massachusetts, to Norton in England, James commented, "I exaggerate the merits of Europe. It's the same world there after all and Italy isn't the absolute any more than Massachusetts. It's a complex fate, being an American, and one of the responsibilities it entails is fighting against a superstitious valuation of Europe.—It will be rather a sell, getting over there and finding the problems of the universe rather multiplied than diminished. Still, I incline to risk the discomfiture!"

41. Berry actually taught uptown at the University Heights campus of New York University in the Bronx, but I do not think this changes the Jamesian associations significantly. In fact, those associations are strengthened, if anything, by the identity of the department chair who hired Berry and who later referred to Thomas Wolfe's famous line in trying to persuade him to remain in New York. This was Oscar Cargill, who had published a major book on Henry James in 1961, *The Novels of Henry James.* For details on Berry's teaching for NYU, see Angyal, *Wendell Berry,* 20–22.

42. James, *Hawthorne,* esp. 42–44.

43. James, "Art of Fiction," 399. Worth noting is the strong similarity between James's advice to the young writer and Berry's steadfast resistance to abstraction, that primary way by which things are lost on us.

44. Townsend, *Sherwood Anderson,* 4.

45. Woodress, *Willa Cather,* 189.

46. Woodress, *Willa Cather,* 203. Without wanting to suggest that Berry even knew Jewett's advice to Cather, it seems worth pointing out how Jewett's strong distinction between "writing life" and "writing about it" parallels the contrast in Berry's opening line of "Style and Grace": "Works of art participate in our lives; we are not just distant observers of *their* lives" (64). He develops the point by contrasting Hemingway's "Big Two-Hearted River" and Norman Maclean's "A River Runs through It." Hemingway's story is a "triumph of style in its pure or purifying sense," but its fisherman, Nick Adams, is "divided from history and bewilderment." Such style, that of the observer, is "reductive of both humanity and nature," for it "deals with what it does not understand by leaving it out" (65–66). While Maclean acknowledges that there is something in fishermen that seeks to turn "fishing into a world perfect and apart," his story "refuses that sort of perfection." It "never forgets that it is a fragment of a larger pattern that it does not contain. It never forgets that it occurs in the world and in love" (69). It participates in life; it "writes life," in Miss Jewett's terms. Hemingway's art "imposes its terms on its subject"; Maclean's "subjects itself to its subject" (70). Those terms seem, to me, to capture very well what Jewett was telling Cather she must do: that she must subject herself to her subject in order to write well. Obviously, they also point to a way of describing what Berry

was doing in his return to Kentucky. See "Style and Grace," in Berry, *What Are People For?* 64–70.

47. "Writer and Region," in Berry, *What Are People For?* 86.

48. Cather, *My Antonia*, 238 (hereafter cited in the text).

49. The comparison of Berry to Thoreau is frequently made by commentators on Berry. Scott Russell Sanders has called Thoreau "an essential predecessor for Berry" ("Words Addressed to Our Condition," 43), and Jason Peters has called Berry "one of Thoreau's worthiest heirs" ("Introduction," 1). Peters stresses the similarity in economic critique of "these two dissenters" (3), though he argues finally that Berry's "critique reaches further and sustains an urgency greater than anything Thoreau ever attempted: for above all this, Berry, more than any living writer, certainly more than any commander in chief, has defended—without a standing army—*actual* American soil" (4). This last point reflects the tendency of some critics to stress the differences in the two men's attitudes toward farming and agrarianism. While finding many similarities between the two writers, Herman Nibbelink, e.g., stresses the difference between them as that "between bachelor and husband, between naturalist and farmer. Unlike Thoreau, who would live 'free and uncommitted,' Berry insists on commitment, husbandry, the marriage of agriculture that links 'nature and culture, the wild and the domestic'" ("Thoreau and Wendell Berry," 141–42). Stanley Hauerwas has said that "Berry seldom betrays any knowledge of philosophy or philosophers" ("What Would a Christian University Look Like?" 95), but this judgment is itself a reflection of the way we have divided up the disciplines, particularly in the modern university—a division that ends up with Thoreau being taught in departments of literature rather than philosophy. Norman Wirzba says that "if we turn to ancient models of philosophical reflection, what becomes clear is that the philosopher was first and foremost interested in practicing a way of life" ("Placing the Soul," 87), a description that perfectly suits Thoreau. Thoreau himself was well aware of the division in process during his lifetime between philosophy and the practice of life, commenting on it in *Walden*: "There are nowadays professors of philosophy, but not philosophers. Yet it is admirable to profess because it was once admirable to live. To be a philosopher is not merely to have subtle thoughts, nor even to found a school, but so to love wisdom as to live according to its dictates, a life of simplicity, independence, magnanimity, and trust. It is to solve some of the problems of life, not only theoretically, but practically" (57).

50. "A Few Words in Favor of Edward Abbey," in Berry, *What Are People For?* 40–41.

51. FBM, 185.

52. DH, 125 (hereafter cited in the text).

53. "Civil Disobedience," in *Walden*, 395 (CD hereafter, cited in the text).

54. "Life Without Principle," in Thoreau, *Essays*, 197 (hereafter cited in the text).

55. "Absolutely speaking, the more money, the less virtue; for money comes between a man and his objects, and obtains them for him" (CD, 399–400).

56. "Economy and Pleasure," in Berry, *What Are People For?* 136 (EP hereafter, cited in the text).

57. EP, 138. Berry's quotation from Thoreau's commencement speech is from Thoreau, *Familiar Letters*, 9.

58. Burleigh, "Wendell Berry's Community," 139 (WBC hereafter). In a related vein, Vandana Shiva remarks that "it is in the daily, responsible interaction between species that we learn our best lessons in diversity and democracy." See "Globalization and the War against Farmers," 123.

59. Berry, *Selected Poems*, 70.

60. Cf. Heidegger, *Question Concerning Technology*, 17.

61. Berry, *Hannah Coulter*, 88.

62. "Health Is Membership," 89; "The Burden of the Gospels," in Berry, *Blessed Are the Peacemakers*, 58 (BG hereafter).

2. Toward a Peaceable Economy for a Beloved Country

1. Berry, *Collected Poems*, 151 (*CP* hereafter, cited in the text).

2. See Lasch, *Revolt of the Elites*, 3–49. Lasch provides a fascinating complement to Berry on the way contemporary emphasis on "upward mobility" represents a "sadly impoverished understanding of the 'American Dream,'" once thought of quite differently as "the democratization of competence" (50), rather than the meritocratic elevation of a few. As Jeremy Beer points out, Lasch argues that meritocracy tends to isolate elites from the rest of the population, creating a class whose "tourist's view of the world" is unlikely to include "passionate devotion to democracy." As, in Beer's view, too much emphasis on meritocracy can lead only to "greater social stratification," Berry and Lasch suggest that "the only stable basis of social equality" rests in "democratizing intelligence and virtue rather than stripping away barriers to social mobility." As the descendant of landless nineteenth-century immigrants, I perhaps see this matter slightly differently. Emphasis on social mobility was an important way to diminish the hold of an earlier American ruling class, and it is difficult to see, even today, how undermining the idea of meritocracy can do anything except reinforce the hold on power of those who possess it. I suggest we need both to promote recognition of merit and to insist on the democratizing of "intelligence and virtue." One might say we need more people like Wheeler Catlett, trained in the law in Charlottesville yet committed to return-

ing home to practice and to serve. And of course, we need more communities like the one that produced Wheeler. For Beer's analysis, see "Wendell Berry and the Traditionalist Critique," 224–27.

3. This wonderful term for those who continually claim to tell us how things are derives from Saul Bellow. For a typical use, see *Herzog,* 30.

4. "The Wild Birds (1967)," in Berry, *That Distant Land,* 354 (hereafter cited in the text).

5. "Sex, Economy, Freedom, and Community," in Berry, *Sex, Economy, Freedom, and Community,* 147 (SE hereafter, cited in the text).

6. "Out of Your Car, Off Your Horse," in Berry, *Sex, Economy, Freedom, and Community,* 23 (OYC hereafter).

7. Smith, *Wendell Berry and the Agrarian Tradition,* 2. More recently, Smith has stressed the "political concern" of Berry's writings, citing her coming to see "the attack on the World Trade Center from Berry's point of view" as an experience that "brought home" to her "how deeply he is concerned with man's *political* condition: not our ultimate, transcendent destiny but how we humans (who are neither beasts nor gods) make a home for ourselves in the mutable, transitory, secular world." The language here may still hold apart what for some of us, including Berry, must be thought together: that is, how to act in the here and now in light of our ultimate destiny. See "Wendell Berry's Political Vision," 49.

8. For Berry's relationship to the Twelve Southerners of *I'll Take My Stand,* and to Allen Tate in particular, see "The Whole Horse" and "Still Standing," both in Berry, *Citizenship Papers,* 113–25 and 153–63, respectively. The latter essay plays off Tate's 1952 reaffirmation of the principles of *I'll Take My Stand* against John Crowe Ransom's dismissal of them in 1945 as "agrarian nostalgia." Berry stresses Tate's saying in 1952 that he "never thought of Agrarianism as a restoration of anything in the Old South," but rather "as something to be created" as the "result of a profound change" in "the moral and religious outlook of western man" (Berry, "Still Standing," 160). Berry considers the "great contribution" of the Twelve Southerners to lie in their "uncompromising regionalism," with its "insistence upon the importance of the local." Such thinking "stood (and still stands) opposed to that of the agri-industrialists" and is "perfectly conformable to the thinking of such agricultural scientists as Sir Albert Howard and Wes Jackson, whose guiding principle is that of harmony between local ways of farming and local ecosystems. An agriculture, thus, is good, not by virtue of its universal applicability, but according to its ability to adapt to local conditions and needs" (159). This last comment suggests one of Berry's clearest similarities to Tate: the objection to what Tate called the belief, "irrational" itself, "in omnipotent human rationality" ("Remarks on the Southern Religion," 158). This faith in instrumental rationality is part and parcel of an industrialism based on "the enemy, abstraction" (167). But

this is a "bad religion," for "nothing infallibly works," and its practitioners simply "ignore what they do not want to see—which is the breakdown of the principle in numerous instances of practice" (158). One could think of Berry's work as a pointing out of the "numerous instances of practice" in which the abstract rationality of an industrial agriculture has done great damage. Like Tate, Berry thinks we need a true religion, one that "wants the whole horse," not just "that half which may become a dynamo, or an automobile, or any other horsepowered machine" (Tate, "Remarks on the Southern Religion," 157).

For a detailed consideration of Berry's relationship to the Nashville agrarians, one that ultimately stresses their differences at least as much as their similarities, see Smith, *Wendell Berry and the Agrarian Tradition,* 28–30, 165–68.

9. "A Citizen's Response to 'The National Security Strategy of the United States of America,'" in Berry, *Citizenship Papers,* 3 (CR hereafter, cited in the text).

10. MacIntyre, "Is Patriotism a Virtue?" 209–28 (hereafter cited in the text).

11. SE, 122. For an insightful treatment of Berry as a conservative, both in Russell Kirk's sense and then in a more postmodern one, see Bonzo and Stevens, *Wendell Berry and the Cultivation of Life,* 38–48. On why Berry tends to be associated with the political left rather than with conservatism, no one has put it better than Bill Kauffmann: "If he is usually assigned to the left pen of our hopelessly inadequate and painfully constrictive political corral, that is because by the 1960's conservatives had largely renounced peace and stewardship" and "embraced finance capitalism, development *uber alles,* and a promiscuously interventionist foreign policy." See "Wendell Berry on War and Peace," 27.

12. For this point about fundamentalism, see SE, 169–70.

13. Lasch, *Haven in a Heartless World.*

14. Bonzo and Stevens refer to the household as a "unique middle territory" being mapped by Berry: "Household is the bridge between individual and community, the place where character is cultivated, where work is done both for sustenance and for the formation of virtue" (*Wendell Berry and the Cultivation of Life,* 110).

15. Weil, *Need for Roots,* 114.

16. Wes Jackson argues that community is "a direct product of our biology, consisting of countless elements, the roots of which reside in social organizations going back to the early humanoids and before." Public policy, "nearly always implemented at the expense of community," is an "abstraction arising out of large social organizations with precedents no more than one hundred centuries old." See *Becoming Native to This Place,* 53.

17. Kant, *Doctrine of Virtue,* 244.

18. "Love," in *Simone Weil Reader,* 359.

19. Berry says this of thrift "from an agricultural point of view," but I see no reason why it should be any less true of the cultural sources on which we depend—

themselves, of course, rooted in our agriculture. See "Six Agricultural Fallacies," in Berry, *Home Economics,* 128.

20. "The Idea of a Local Economy," in Berry, *Art of the Commonplace,* 251 (ILE hereafter, cited in the text).

21. Herford, *Ethics of the Talmud,* 34.

22. Eric Tretheway has suggested the possibility of a more congenial relationship between Berry and the Romantic poets in "Politics, Nature, and Value," 86.

23. "Afterword," in Berry, *Hidden Wound,* 113 (*HW* hereafter, cited in the text).

24. Jackson, *Becoming Native to This Place,* 3. Jackson proposes the universities offer a major in "homecoming" to encourage and prepare students to go somewhere, "dig in," and become native. David W. Orr suggests that "school gardens and gardening could be a cornerstone of the daily experience of children" from the earliest ages to university; such experience would reconnect children to their own communities and help develop the "ecological imagination of children in association with pleasurable activity"—a vital step in the creation of an ecologically informed public. See "Uses of Prophecy," 185–86.

25. Perhaps the most extensive survey and development of Berry's ideas about university education is Peters, "Education, Heresy." Peters's critique focuses on the commoditizing of contemporary education, proposing, as an alternative, one based on a "rediscovery of character and skill—the character to choose less and the skill to do more for oneself" (263–64).

26. Eric T. Freyfogle has pointed out, e.g., how questions like "What is good land use?" or "What kind of culture is needed to promote it?" are unlikely to be asked in the contemporary university "because they fit within no specialty." See "Wendell Berry and the Limits of Populism," 177. For an interesting example of how those questions can begin to be raised, see David W. Orr's account of efforts at Oberlin College, including his course in sustainable agriculture, "Urban-Agrarian Mind." Orr makes the case that the "transition to a better world" will "require the marriage of urban-industrial and rural-agrarian perspectives" (106).

27. Hauerwas, "What Would a Christian University Look Like?" 101. Eric T. Freyfogle has said that the "presumption" that agrarianism generally is "inherently anti-science or in all ways anti-market" needs to be clarified. "For agrarians," he writes, "science is merely a tool, highly useful when well directed," "highly destructive when it is not." See "Introduction: A Durable Scale," xxxv–xxxvi. Allan Carlson argues, however, that Berry has been more hostile to "technological innovation" than others in the new agrarian succession, defined as beginning shortly after 1900 with Liberty Hyde Bailey. See *New Agrarian Mind,* 189–90.

28. Thoreau, *Walden,* 73.

29. In an interview with Anne Husted Burleigh, Berry comments that "specialization is going to happen" because "people are differently talented and differently

called to kinds of work." Vocation implies specialization. But "what you have to regret is the *isolation* of the specialists so that they're at liberty to judge their work by professional standards to the exclusion of any other kind" (WBC, 143).

30. This would be to bring the university into line with Norman Wirzba's sense that agrarianism "represents the most complex and far-reaching accounting system ever known, for according to it success must include a vibrant watershed and soil base; species diversity; human and animal contentment; communal creativity, responsibility, and joy; usable waste; social solidarity and sympathy; attention and delight; and the respectful maintenance of all the sources of life." Perhaps what is required is an agrarian or new agrarian university. Perhaps, too, one should ask how an institution can claim to be a "*uni*-versity" if it is not committed to such a far-reaching system of accounting. For Wirzba's comment, see "Introduction: Why Agrarianism Matters," 4.

31. LU, 83 (hereafter cited in the text).

32. On Berry's own teaching, see Grubbs, "Practical Education," 137–41. Commenting on the last span of Berry's service at the University of Kentucky (1987–93), Grubbs, a former Berry student, concludes it was clear "that he preferred teaching students who would likely find work in practical service to others in small communities, such as school teachers and traditional agriculturalists" (139).

33. Tocqueville, *Democracy in America,* 663 (hereafter cited in the text).

34. Sheldon S. Wolin has invoked Tocqueville's concerns about despotism in his study of the way our "managed democracy" is becoming what he calls an "inverted" form of totalitarianism. Democracy can be managed, in Wolin's view, to the exclusion of any real politics, without even "appearing to be suppressed." "This has come about" largely "through certain developments, notably in the economy, that promoted integration, rationalization, concentrated wealth, and a faith that virtually any problem—from health care to political crises, even faith itself—could be managed, that is, subjected to control, predictability, and cost-effectiveness in the delivery of the product. Voters are made as predictable as consumers; a university is nearly as rationalized in its structure as a corporation; a corporate structure is as hierarchical in its chain of command as the military" (*Democracy Incorporated,* 47). The similarity of this characterization to Berry's comments on the "total economy" is striking. Wolin uses Tocqueville to remind us that he feared a democratic despotism "made possible because citizens have chosen to relinquish participatory politics, which he had singled out as the most remarkable, widespread, and essential element of American political life." It's our tendency to abandon "intense involvement with the common affairs of [our] communities in favor of personal ends" that threatens to leave us subjects of despotism "rather than citizens" (80).

35. As an extreme case of how a certain kind of economic rationalization affects the farm, consider the poultry man working for one of the "vertically inte-

grated" firms that control the business. As Hank Graddy points out, these integrators control nearly every decision taken in the raising of the birds from the earliest stages onward: from the feed to the design of the poultry houses. The "farmer" no longer exercises any of the judgment involved in the practice of farming and has become a "serf" on his or her own farm—or, as we might also put it, the modern worker exercising the technological function allotted to those involved in meat production. To the economic rationalizer who designs the integrators' processes, all conventional farmers must appear "mad." See "Legal and Legislative Front," 230–31.

36. Brian Donahue has argued, e.g., that agrarians will not "be taken seriously unless [they] begin with the premise that life has been brutally hard for most farm people." Movement toward a "decent agrarian future" will have to begin with this acknowledgment ("Resettling of America," 38). Jeffery Alan Triggs has also suggested that Berry sometimes neglects what is "dark" or "limiting" in agricultural life ("Kinship of the Fields," 101).

37. The quotation from Dante is from *La Vita Nuova,* 566.

38. "The Hurt Man (1888)," 10.

39. FBM, 180 (hereafter cited in the text). "Why I Am Not Going to Buy a Computer" can be found in Berry, *What Are People For?* 170–77. Barbara Kingsolver finds the "feminist ire" aroused by this essay "bizarre." She points out that her husband also "comments on [her] drafts" and "provides many other kinds of help." On hearing this, one would simply attribute "good sense" to him, but somehow that's not the conclusion if the one giving the help, as in Berry's case, is one's wife. That conclusion "only proves that women are still not adequately credited with brains by either gender" (Kingsolver, "Art of Buying Nothing," 289).

40. Ignatieff, "Myth of Citizenship," 53.

41. Lasch, *Haven in a Heartless World,* 13 (hereafter cited in the text).

42. "Think Little," in Berry, *Continuous Harmony,* 76 (TL hereafter, cited in the text).

43. "Notes from an Absence and a Return," in Berry, *Continuous Harmony,* 37 (NAR hereafter, cited in the text).

44. The quotation is from *Confucius,* 59.

45. For the quotation, see *Confucius,* 151.

46. "Irish Journal," in Berry, *Home Economics,* 30. Frederick Kirschenmann points out how acquisition and control of land by absentee "farmers" in our now globalized condition have the additional effect of "depriving local populations of the opportunity to access land to feed themselves," thus greatly increasing the likelihood of social unrest in destabilized societies ("Current State of Agriculture," 110–11).

47. "Property, Patriotism, and National Defense," in Berry, *Home Economics,* 107 (PPND hereafter, cited in the text).

48. "A Nation Rich in Natural Resources," in Berry, *Home Economics,* 134 (NR hereafter, cited in the text).

49. "Higher Education and Home Defense," in Berry, *Home Economics,* 53.

50. AD, 115.

51. "Conservation and Local Economy," in Berry, *Sex, Economy, Freedom, and Community,* 16 (CLE hereafter, cited in the text).

52. "The Pleasures of Eating," in Berry, *What Are People For?* 147.

53. "Preserving Wildness," in Berry, *Home Economics,* 144.

54. "A Defense of the Family Farm," in Berry, *Home Economics,* 165 (DFF hereafter, cited in the text).

55. CD, 403.

56. It's astonishing that the worldwide loss of biological diversity is not seen as a security threat of the greatest magnitude. Andrew Kimbrell has pointed out that well over 90 percent of the varieties of lettuce, corn, tomatoes, and asparagus were lost between 1903 and 1983 ("Seven Deadly Myths," 24); Frederick Kirschenmann notes that "rapid consolidation" in the "food retailing" sector means "that about six multinational retail firms will determine not only the size of America's farms, but also the type of management decisions made on those farms." Kirschenmann warns we are ignoring the insight of evolutionary biology that "population explosions of any species inevitably transform it into a 'plague species' that crashes in order to bring it back into ecological balance with the community of species on which it ultimately depends" ("Current State of Agriculture," 104, 110).

57. "Thoughts in the Presence of Fear," in Berry, *Citizenship Papers,* 18 (TPF hereafter, cited in the text).

58. See TPF, 18.

59. Smith, "Wendell Berry's Political Vision," 55–57 (hereafter cited in the text).

60. "God, Science, and Imagination," in Berry, *Imagination in Place,* 188.

61. "American Imagination and the Civil War," in Berry, *Imagination in Place,* 30.

62. "If you have built castles in the air, your work need not be lost; that is where they should be. Now put the foundations under them" (Thoreau, *Walden,* 372).

63. MacIntyre, "Is Patriotism a Virtue?" 209–28 (hereafter cited in the text).

3. Against the Church, For the Church

1. While he is certainly comfortable with biblical language, Wes Jackson asserts, e.g., that "agrarianism requires no moral or spiritual language for justification; it grows out of a scientific understanding of how organisms interact within natural habitats, an understanding that is too greatly ignored in industrial approaches to agriculture" ("Agrarian Mind," 140).

2. BG, 55 (hereafter cited in the text).

3. For Berry's remark on the Gospel of John, see "Health Is Membership," 89. "Sabbath Poem IX, 1999" is in Berry, *Given*, 78.

4. Twain, *Adventures of Huckleberry Finn*, 137.

5. "Toward a Healthy Community," in Grubbs, *Conversations*, 118 (THC hereafter, cited in the text).

6. For Berry's confession to being a "bewildered reader," see Basney and Leax, "Conversation with Wendell Berry," 129.

7. "Sabbath VII, 2008," in Berry, *Leavings*, 114.

8. Fisher Smith, "Field Observations," 95–96.

9. WBC, 139.

10. On this matter, I very much like Charles R. Pinches's remark that "Christians in America would do well to aspire to the sort of church that is not really a church but behaves like one, namely, Berry's Port William community." See "Democracy, America, and the Church," 257.

11. Jason Peters suggests the usefulness of Bloom's analysis of American Gnosticism in his treatment of the way Berry's work can be described as anti-Gnostic or anti-Manichean (terms Berry does not use, as Peters rightly points out). See "Education, Heresy," 270–75. Joel James Shuman has also mentioned Bloom's diagnosis of American Religion in his description of Berry's anti-Gnosticism. Shuman adds the helpful definition that Gnosticism "is a sometimes subtle distortion of orthodoxy. According to Christian tradition, it *is* true that creation has been alienated from its Creator . . . [yet] God's redemptive work neither requires nor encourages a flight from this life or this world. God, who delights in creation and desires its well–being, has given humanity the gift of sharing in that delight" ("Introduction," 2–3). Shuman opens his coedited collection *Wendell Berry and Religion* by saying it "is not a book *about* Wendell Berry," but rather a series of "contributions to an ongoing conversation" by Christians who have found in Berry's work a "kind of wisdom" that "might help them" to "work, live, and think more faithfully" ("Introduction," 1–2). Nevertheless, it is also the most important source "about" Berry and religion to date.

12. A similar point has been made by Janet Goodrich, who sees a "more conciliatory attitude toward Christian tradition" in Berry's work from the 1980s and a "constructive use" of the "language and values" of the "Judeo-Christian tradition" in writings from the 1990s (*Unforeseen Self*, 89).

13. Angyal stresses the similarity between Berry and White in *Wendell Berry*, 51.

14. After paraphrasing the earlier verses of the first chapter of Genesis, White says of the "striking story of creation" that "Christianity inherited from Judaism": "Finally, God had created Adam and, as an afterthought, Eve to keep man from being lonely. Man named all the animals, thus establishing his dominance over them. God planned all of this explicitly for man's benefit and rule: no item in the

physical creation had any purpose save to serve man's purposes. And, although man's body is made of clay, he is not simply part of nature: he is made in God's image." White goes on to say that Christianity, "especially in its Western form," is "the most anthropocentric religion the world has seen." See "Historical Roots of Our Ecologic Crisis," 24–25. For a description of the way White's argument exercised authority over environmentalists' views of religion, see Oelschlaeger, *Caring for Creation*, 22–27. Oelschlaeger describes himself as "worshiping at the altar of Lynn White's" article during the "late 1970s and early 1980s" (24). By 1994, however, Oelschlaeger considered the charge "that Judeo-Christianity caused the environmental crisis" to have "been discredited as an oversimplification of a complicated skein of historical events" (25). Pointing out that White was a "religious (Presbyterian) layperson," Oelschlaeger suggests a revised reading of White's essay "as being in the Judeo-Christian tradition of prophetic self-criticism. White was less counseling Judeo-Christians to abandon their faith in favor of Native American or Eastern religions," than "challenging them to renew their faith in the tradition of those who cared for creation" (232). To one reading White's essay now, Oelschlaeger's conclusion must seem apparent from the way White closes by invoking St. Francis as the representative of "an alternative Christian view of nature and man's relation to it" (29). But perhaps it has taken the intervening forty years from White's publication to make this as apparent as it now seems.

15. GGL, 269 (hereafter cited in the text).

16. "Holy Thursday: The Mystery of Unity," in McCabe, *God Matters*, 76–79.

17. "There is nothing to eat / seek it where you will / but of the body of the Lord." Berry quotes these lines from "The Host" in "A Homage to Dr. Williams," in Berry, *Continuous Harmony*, 57.

18. Brueggemann, *Land*, 2 (hereafter cited in the text).

19. Bloom, *American Religion*, 32 (hereafter cited in the text).

20. "Christianity and the Survival of Creation," in Berry, *Sex, Economy, Freedom, and Community*, 105 (CSC hereafter, cited in the text).

21. "The Body and the Earth," in Berry, *Unsettling of America*, 109 (BE hereafter, cited in the text).

22. *HW,* 16–17.

23. See GGL, 267.

24. "God and Country," in Berry, *What Are People For?* 98. Allan Carlson makes the interesting argument, however, that the "New Agrarians" have "*erred deeply in their opposition to sectarian, other-worldly Christianity,*" for it has been "American sectarians in the universally condemned Anabaptist, fundamentalist, Pentecostal, and monastic dispensations" who have best resisted the "full industrialization of life" and moved "rural dwellers to become good stewards of both land and community." Separation and keeping one's "eyes fixed firmly heavenward"

help to make "bearable the psychological price of renouncing the symbols and products of intensive consumerism and a highly refined division of labor." See *New Agrarian Mind,* 211, 206.

25. "Introduction," to Berry, *Blessed Are the Peacemakers,* 3–4.

26. CR, 14 (hereafter cited in the text).

27. I do not want to misrepresent Berry here. He identifies himself very clearly as a pacifist. I only wish to suggest that some of his comments could be taken to accommodate defensive military action in a time of extreme threat to one's home places.

28. "The Failure of War," in Berry, *Citizenship Papers* (FW hereafter, cited in the text), 26.

29. On this very important matter, see Hauerwas, "Sacrificing the Sacrifices of War."

30. CSC, 107. See the last stanza of Yeats's "Among School Children," which begins, "Labour is blossoming or dancing where / The body is not bruised to pleasure soul" (Yeats, *Selected Poems,* 117).

31. PLC, 70. Cf. Frost's "Birches," of course, but also "Mowing": "The fact is the sweetest dream that labor knows" (Frost, *Poetry,* 17, 121).

32. Learning to take delight in creation is at the heart of the practice of the Sabbath, as Norman Wirzba emphasizes in *Living the Sabbath.* That "Sabbath observance has a low priority for many people" today indicates "a profound confusion about what the Sabbath means," for it "ought to be our highest priority and our deepest desire." As the practice of the Sabbath involves our sharing in "God's own *menuha,*" or delight, in creation, "what," Wirzba asks, "could be finer or more desirable?" (52). Berry has contributed a "Foreword" to this book, which might be read as a companion to his Sabbath poems.

33. EP, 138 (hereafter cited in the text). Cf. "Surely joy is the condition of life," in "Natural History of Massachusetts," in Thoreau, *Essays,* 5.

34. "Beauty," in *Simone Weil Reader,* 377.

35. NH, 207.

36. Thoreau, *Week on the Concord,* 315.

37. "A Secular Pilgrimage," in Berry, *Continuous Harmony,* 3 (SP hereafter, cited in the text).

38. See Collis, *Triumph of the Tree,* 115–16.

39. Psalm 24 (NRSV).

40. Taylor, *Secular Age,* 221 (hereafter cited in the text).

41. See CSC, 98. For the quotation from Philip Sherrard, see his *Human Image,* 152.

42. Berry remarks further in a letter to Wes Jackson that it is a mistake to forget that "the Creation is only the beginning of the Genesis story. It is followed by a thoroughly fierce and unflattering history that shows humans (chosen and uncho-

sen) to be ignorant, fallible, and dangerous. That is the conclusion or the judgment that is handed down in Genesis and right through the Bible." This reading ought to be remembered as further corrective to White's argument for the tradition's anthropocentric character. Quoted in Jackson, "Letters from a Humble Radical," 171.

43. For a discussion of the "mutually informative relation between ecological awareness and biblical study" (115), particularly of the Old Testament, see Davis, "'And the Land I Will Remember.'" Beginning with an exposition of the way reading agrarians like Berry caused her to change her "professional work of reading the Old Testament," making her "readings sharper and more concrete" (118), Davis develops three "aspects" of agrarianism that seem particularly convergent with biblical thinking. First, the "agrarian project" to reconnect property to "notions of propriety" resembles the biblical writers' placing the "land within a network of relationships that are constituted and maintained through acts of mutual acknowledgment, respect, honoring," best understood as acts of remembering and, as such, acts of continued faithfulness to the covenant, which must itself be understood "as a triangulated relationship among Israel, the land, and YHWH" (120–21). Second, "the land comes first": it "sets the standard for all human actions" (121). Third, biblical thinking shares with modern agrarianism an "exacting concern with the *materiality* of human existence," with "ordering material existence in ways that are consonant with God's will and the design of the world" (125). If this last claim sounds odd, it is because we have come to understand materialism quite differently, mostly from within the illusion encouraged by "materialistic scientism" that science can cure all of our ills (126).

44. Daniel Cornell identifies Berry with an ethic of stewardship organized around three central principles: "humility, kindly use, and community" ("Vision of Stewardship," 14–15). Lawrence Buell similarly places Berry's "religiocentric" conservationism squarely in the "stewardship tradition" (*Environmental Imagination,* 512).

45. Goodrich sees a correspondence between the "three conditions that the Israelites must meet to keep the Promised Land," as Berry understands them, and the "three relationships" he has stressed in developing the "atonement metaphor" of "Discipline and Hope": "First, they must be humble in spirit (humans-God); second, they must be neighborly (man-wife); and third, they must practice good husbandry (farmer-field)." See *Unforeseen Self,* 99. For the context of Goodrich's observations, see "Discipline and Hope," in Berry, *Continuous Harmony,* 152–56.

46. Wirzba, *Paradise of God,* 13–15.

47. "Two Economies," in Berry, *Home Economics* (New York: North Point Press, 1987), 54 (TE hereafter, cited in the text).

48. SE, 166.

49. OYC, 20.

50. RH, 102.

51. Cummins, *Feed My Sheep*, 47.

52. For Kierkegaard, we ceaselessly reintroduce worldly distinctions even when we try to diminish them. Christianity, however, uses the "short-cut of the eternal" to arrive "immediately at the goal: it allows all distinctions to stand, but it teaches the equality of the eternal. It teaches that everyone shall *lift himself above* earthly distinctions" (*Works of Love*, 82–83). The eternal comes to each of us in the form of the command "You Shall Love Your Neighbor," which means, "Your love has eternal worth" (55). "The essence of faith," then, "is to be a secret, to be for the single individual," and it is not believed at all if he or she does not preserve it "as a secret" even when professing it (43). Terry Cummins was blessed by being so much in secret, we might say, where he might learn to do good work where it would not bring him any distinction. Berry says of Cummins's description that it records an "experience regrettably and perhaps dangerously missing now from the childhood of most children" (RH, 101). He leaves the nature of this experience somewhat unspecified, but I would suggest that part of what Cummins experienced was doing hard physical work and finding his own satisfaction in it—or frequently finding satisfaction either in seeing other animals fed or, like the draft horses at the end of the day, relieved of their burdens (see Cummins, *Feed My Sheep*, 46). Many children today have the experience of hard, self-expending bodily effort only in the competitive context of sports, those practice grounds for our culture of ceaseless distinction. They learn to appraise themselves and others always and only in relation to others and thus may never develop the singularity that can hear the command of the eternal.

Berry's sense of faith seems, at times, similar to Kierkegaard's, as when he says in a 1993 interview that he's been trying to "work out a sense of community that's not sentimental and is not metaphorical" (Brown, "*Bluegrass* Interview," 106). Berry notes that "it's a cliché. 'I love my community.' Well, a community is not something you love all that simply" (106). In other words, we don't love the neighbor because we find ourselves able to or because he or she is lovable; rather, we love the neighbor because we are commanded to do so, and we find that there is freedom in following the command. But nowhere is Berry more "Kierkegaardian" than in his fondness for the parable of the lost sheep. "To love one's neighbour means," for Kierkegaard, "essentially to will to exist equally for every human being without exception" (*Works of Love*, 92). The good shepherd goes in search of the lost, without exception; the Buddhist vows to save all sentient beings, without exception. Or, as Terry Cummins puts it in the title of the first chapter of *Feed My Sheep*, "Save Every Lamb."

53. "Health Is Membership," 86.

54. "Solving for Pattern," in Berry, *Gift of Good Land*, 143 (SFP hereafter, cited in the text).

55. "Two Minds," in Berry, *Citizenship Papers,* 93.

56. "Agriculture from the Roots Up," in Berry, *Way of Ignorance,* 109 (AR hereafter, cited in the text).

57. For Jackson's description of this "Natural Systems Agriculture," see "Agrarian Mind," 150–52. For an account of a visit to the Land Institute, see Sanders, "Learning from the Prairie."

58. Pointing out the inadequacy of the body-as-machine metaphor, Joel Shuman makes use of Berry's work to suggest ways for us to "learn to live, see, and speak differently about our bodies." He suggests the metaphor of body as landscape—particular, beloved, cared for properly only if understood to be mortal. See "Landscapes of Flesh," 136 ff.

59. *LM,* 13 (hereafter cited in the text).

60. "Men and Women in Search of Common Ground," in Berry, *Home Economics,* 115.

61. FBM, 194.

62. "The Agrarian Standard," in Berry, *Citizenship Papers,* 149 (AS hereafter, cited in the text).

63. CN, 80 (hereafter cited in the text).

64. Rhonheimer insists that the argument against artificial contraception in *Humanae Vitae* turns not on a moralizing of biological processes, but on "the inseparable connection, willed by God and unable to be broken by man on his own initiative, between the two meanings of the conjugal act: the unitive meaning and the procreative meaning." For him the "key to the argument" lies in the "concept of *responsible parenthood,*" which can be exercised only when decisions about contraception are grounded in the virtue John Paul II spoke about frequently in his interpretations of the encyclical: marital chastity. See *Natural Law and Practical Reason,* 113–14. For John Paul's insistence that the distinction between periodic abstinence and artificial contraception is so strong as to point to "two irreconcilable concepts of the human person and of human sexuality," see *Familiaris Consortio,* Article 32. Bonzo and Stevens helpfully compare Berry and John Paul II in *Wendell Berry and the Cultivation of Life,* 35–38.

65. Bonzo and Stevens contrast John Paul II's concern "with the issues of limit in human life and death" and Berry's greater devotion to the "terrain in between" (*Wendell Berry and the Cultivation of Life,* 37). To some extent, this way of dividing reflects something John Paul himself wants to combat. Contraceptive practices are not matters to be looked at only in their own right, for instance, but for the way they lead either to or away from the "fruitful married love" that can move us to a "manifold service to life." See *Familiaris Consortio,* sections 28, 41.

66. For an agrarian argument against the use of hormonal birth control, one based on the way it reflects a "disintegration of the household" that results in the

"division of sexuality from fertility," see Bahnson, "The Pill Is Like . . . DDT?" 93. Bahnson makes the additional suggestion that this represents a case where there is deep "connection between the way we treat our bodies and the way we treat the earth," citing as evidence the possibility that the "worldwide decline in amphibian populations" may result in part from the way "estrogen in the water supply" affects "the reproductive systems of amphibians" (94).

67. Shakespeare, *King Lear*, IV, vi, 55 (p. 1173).

68. "Letter to Wes Jackson," in Berry, *Home Economics*, 3–4 (LWJ hereafter, cited in the text).

69. For a similar treatment of scientific pretensions to speak on religious matters, see Berry's essay "God, Science, and Imagination," in Berry, *Imagination in Place*. The essay is a response to a piece by Steven Weinberg, "Without God," *New York Review of Books*, Sept. 25, 2008.

70. Wilson, *Consilience*, 248, 100 (quoted in *LM*, 29, 31).

71. "Creation," in McCabe, *God Matters*, 2 (hereafter cited in the text).

72. Brueggemann, *Land*, 58 (hereafter cited in the text).

73. 1 Samuel 8:19–20 (NRSV).

74. "The Loss of the Future," in Berry, *Long-Legged House*, 45 (LF hereafter, cited in the text).

75. "Does Community Have a Value?" in Berry, *Home Economics*, 185 (DC hereafter, cited in the text).

76. DFF, 165.

77. "Standing by Words," in Berry, *Standing by Words*, 58 (SBW hereafter, cited in the text).

78. "The Landscaping of Hell: Strip-Mine Morality in East Kentucky," in Berry, *Long-Legged House*, 20 (LH hereafter, cited in the text).

79. Premnath, "Latifundialization and Isaiah 5:8–10," 49–60.

80. Berry, *Remembering*, 180.

81. Brueggemann, *Land*, 49.

82. "Whole Horse," 119.

83. Brueggemann, *Land*, 60.

84. Berry, *Given*, 60.

85. "A Long Job, Too Late to Quit," in Berry, *Citizenship Papers*, 77–84.

86. "Sabbath IV, 2003," in Berry, *Given*, 125.

4. Port William's "Hard History of Love"

1. "The Inheritors (1986)," in Berry, *That Distant Land*, 432 (stories are hereafter cited in the text).

2. "The Hurt Man (1888)," 10.

3. "The Wild Birds (1967)," in Berry, *That Distant Land*, 349.

4. "The Hurt Man (1888)," 8.

5. "Human Personality," in *Simone Weil Reader*, 315.

6. John 11:35 (KJV).

7. Jeremiah 31:15 (KJV).

8. Cf. Berry's title *What Are People For?*

9. "Don't Send a Boy to Do a Man's Work (1891)," in Berry, *That Distant Land*, 12–13.

10. Exodus 20:2–3 (KJV).

11. "True virtue most essentially consists in benevolence to Being in general. Or perhaps to speak more accurately, it is that consent, propensity and union of heart to Being in general, that is immediately exercised in a general good will." Edwards speaks of such "true virtue" as being the most essential quality of a "general beauty of the heart," a phrase remarkably apt as a description of Tol Proudfoot (*Nature of True Virtue*, 540).

12. "A Consent (1908)," in Berry, *That Distant Land*, 25–26.

13. Janet Goodrich makes the point that the "stereotypically feminine" Miss Minnie is "an example of the female characterizations that occasionally earn Berry the charge of chauvinism." To defend Berry, Goodrich cites such characters as "Flora Catlett, Margaret Feltner, or Hannah Coulter," none of whom "suggest 'feminine' weakness." "Within the farming community of Berry's writings," these "are women of dignity, strength, intelligence, and practical accomplishment" who "establish a significant female presence in Berry's work." Where I would differ from Goodrich is simply in saying that Miss Minnie, too, exhibits the qualities she rightly attributes to Flora, Margaret, and Hannah. See *Unforeseen Self*, 137, n. 33.

14. "A Half-Pint of Old Darling (1920)," in Berry, *That Distant Land*, 135.

15. "The Solemn Boy (1934)," in Berry, *That Distant Land*, 187.

16. "Watch with Me (1916)," in Berry, *That Distant Land*, 80. For the completing phrase, see Exodus 34:6, Nehemiah 9:17, Psalm 145:8 (NRSV). The KJV translation describes Tol equally well, as in Psalm 145, where the Lord is described as "slow to anger, and of great mercy."

17. Matthew 26:38 (KJV).

18. Frei, *Identity of Jesus Christ*, 65.

19. "O Jerusalem, Jerusalem, which killest the prophets, and stonest them that are sent unto thee; how often would I have gathered thy children together, as a hen doth gather her brood under her wings, and ye would not!" (Luke 13:34 [KJV]).

20. 1 Thessalonians 5:17 (KJV).

21. "Pray Without Ceasing (1912)," in Berry, *That Distant Land*, 39.

22. Pieper, *About Love*, 26.

23. "The Boundary (1965)," in Berry, *That Distant Land*, 290. For an interesting

use of the story for the sharp contrast between Mat's attitude toward the land and "liberal, free market" views of private property, see Freyfogle, "Mat Feltner's World," 75–90. The story offers an example of a kind of land use, responsible both to ecological imperatives and to the surrounding human community, that might help people reimagine the relationship between private property and the common good—a kind of reimagining Freyfogle considers essential if property law is to be reshaped in accord with necessary land-use requirements.

24. Cf. 1 John 4:19: "We love him, because he first loved us" (KJV).

25. "That Distant Land (1965)," in Berry, *That Distant Land,* 316. For an account of the tobacco harvest, complete with extraordinary photographs, see Berry and Hall, *Tobacco Harvest.*

26. "It Wasn't Me (1953)," in Berry, *That Distant Land,* 268.

27. Sometimes commentators on this story seem a little too quick to override Elton's insistence on his independence in order to affirm Wheeler's language of gift. D. Brent Laytham says, e.g., that "we can learn to renounce independence and embrace election, trying neither to earn our entrance nor to deserve our inclusion but instead to continually live in the economy of the gift" ("'Membership Includes the Dead,'" 182). Kimberly K. Smith is somewhat more willing to allow for independence, suggesting its greater appropriateness at earlier stages of the life cycle. But she is consistently critical of Berry when he seems to endorse independence or self-reliance and complimentary when he critiques "autonomy." She, too, judges "independence as Elton imagines it" to be "illusory" (*Wendell Berry and the Agrarian Tradition,* 146–51). Identifying Berry primarily with Wheeler's voice here seems appropriate, but Elton's independence needs also to be recognized. Elton's insistence on being able to respect himself has contributed to his being chosen by Old Jack, and it will be largely the hard sweat of his own body that will pay off the debt he's incurred. As Berry puts it in "The Whole Horse," "A major characteristic of the agrarian mind is a longing for independence—that is, for an appropriate degree of personal and local self-sufficiency. Agrarians wish to earn and deserve what they have" (117). None of this is meant to deny the importance of community or the gift, only to suggest that the relationship of those terms to independence is more complicated, for Berry, than is sometimes allowed.

28. Exodus 1:1 (NSRV). As Carol Meyers points out, the English name "Exodus" comes "to us, via the Latin, as an abbreviation of the Greek title *exodos aigyptou* ('Road out from Egypt')," whereas the Hebrew title "follows ancient Semitic practice of naming a work by its opening words" (*Exodus,* 1).

29. "The Wild Birds (1967)," in Berry, *That Distant Land,* 349. Richard P. Church has argued that Wheeler's practice of law illustrates a legal "ethic of care" as articulated in the work of Thomas Shaffer on legal ethics. Following Shaffer,

Church distinguishes the ethic of care from two dominant models of legal practice, one guided by an "ethic of role," in which "lawyers are obligated to do everything within the law to aid their clients regardless of the clients' proposed ends," and a second, an "ethic of isolation," which allows for moral interchange between lawyer and client, but only of proposals developed in isolation. In the ethic of care, lawyers are not simply "agents" for their clients, but rather friends or even "ministers" who engage in "moral conversation" in a "relationship of mutuality." See "Of the Good That Has Been Possible in This World," 54.

30. "Fidelity (1977)," in Berry, *That Distant Land,* 417.

31. Wheeler's driving seems to be modeled on Berry's father's driving, as Gene Logsdon comments. Apparently, Berry's own driving is not much different. Of it Logsdon remarks, he "drove like his father, adding conviction to my fear that, at least when I was riding with him, the world could end at any moment." See Logsdon, "Wendell Berry: Agrarian Artist," 247.

32. Jack Beechum believes that between Wheeler and himself, "winning is not a very important idea." See Berry, *Place on Earth,* 55.

5. Remembering the Names

1. Berry, *Andy Catlett,* 41 (hereafter cited in the text).

2. I borrow the phrase here from Willa Cather, who said that the "world broke in two in 1922 or thereabouts." Readers have speculated on Cather's meaning, but surely she was, in part, referring to the devastation caused by the Great War and its aftermath. Andy Catlett's saying that the world divided for him between 1943 and 1944 suggests the similar sense of a decisive break in time caused, at least in part, by war. Cather's remark is in "Prefatory Note," v.

3. The phrase from Frost applies well to Maze Tickburn's songs. See Frost, "Figure a Poem Makes," 18–19. The poem "begins in delight," finds its way, and ends "in some final phrase at once wise and sad—the happy-sad blend of the drinking song."

4. Dick Watson and Aunt Sarah Jane seem to be modeled on Nick Watkins and Aunt Georgie Ashby. Berry's coming back to them in *Andy Catlett* bears witness to his saying of Nick and Aunt Georgie in *The Hidden Wound* that attempting "to tell the 'truth' about them as they really were is to resign oneself to enacting a small fragment of an endless process. Their truth is inexhaustible both in their lives as they were, and in my life as I think they were" (*HW,* 50).

5. For Augustine's meditations on time, see Book XI of *The Confessions,* esp. 261–80.

6. Berry, *World Lost,* 231 (hereafter cited in the text).

7. One who stresses the failure of Old Jack's life, e.g., is Andrew J. Angyal, who calls Jack's "the unhappy story of work without love." See *Wendell Berry*, 27.

8. Berry, *Nathan Coulter*, 7 (hereafter cited in the text). Unless otherwise noted, quotations from *Nathan Coulter* are from the 2002 revision.

9. Matthew 5:4 (KJV).

10. Berry, *Place on Earth*, 277.

11. Berry's first version of *Nathan Coulter*, published in 1960, ends not with Dave Coulter's death, but with Nathan's betrayal of his bond to the other men and his being cast out by his father. Grandfather Coulter has a stroke but does not die immediately, as in the revised text, and the men continue to work at Gander Loyd's, where Nathan becomes attracted to Mandy Loyd. On the night of Grandpa's death, Gander comes to stay late with the Coulters, and Nathan goes to Mandy, an action Berry attributes not just to desire but also to fear: "The fear separated me from Grandpa's house and his death, and I let it stay" (189). As he leaves the Loyds' house, Nathan is seen by Gander, although the latter is not certain of the identity of the person he's seen. Gander does get the story out of Mandy, however, and comes after Nathan with a knife while he, his father, and Burley sit with Grandpa's body. After Gander is restrained and escorted home by Big Ellis, Jarrat asks Nathan what he's got to say. When Nathan says he's sorry, Jarrat calls him a "damned disgrace," and Nathan responds by saying, "I don't have to take that." Like his brother Tom, Nathan must leave: "I knew I had to leave. I couldn't stay to bear his contempt, and I wouldn't accept his anger. If I'd done wrong, I thought, my guilt belonged to me; and if my guilt was disgraceful then I had to own the disgrace of it" (202). In the very last motif of the novel, Nathan dreams again of the lion that he's associated with his grandfather, "only now his voice was the sound of the wind through the grass, so soft I could hear my breathing." He dreams, too, of Burley, who tells him, quietly, smiling, "That's not a lion. . . . You're dreaming, Nathan" (204). Perhaps what's most revealing thematically in this ending is the association between betrayal of the community and Nathan's fear of death. That association suggests that the maintenance of a good community depends a good bit on the grief work of the individuals who compose it—and that good communities had better provide means for such grief work if they are to contain impulses rooted in fear and denial of death that can potentially tear them apart. This point, I believe, has far-reaching ramifications for how we understand a whole host of matters in Berry's work. If Berry has defended private property, e.g., more staunchly than many environmentalists who, like Eric T. Freyfogle, want to reaffirm communal claims to appropriate land use, it may be because he understands the work one does on one's own place on earth to be absolutely necessary as the working out of a life project, a way of doing the grief work we do to live within appropriate bound-

aries. As Berry says most directly in some of his poems to his wife, Tanya, what we can give one another paradoxically is our deaths—that is, the life that can come to be in us as we take our deaths upon ourselves, life that can then be offered to others without our diminishing the separateness required for love to be love. The quotations above are from the first published edition of *Nathan Coulter* (1960). For Freyfogle's critique of Berry's too individualist politics, see "Wendell Berry and the Limits of Populism."

12. Jack Hicks reads Jarrat much more negatively than I do, calling him "one of Berry's ruined husbands, seized in a cancerous, abstract obsession with his land." The judgment reflects a reading of the first edition of *Nathan,* as Hicks refers to Jarrat's driving "his sons from his house" ("Wendell Berry's Husband to the World," 127).

13. Hauerwas, "Story-Formed Community," 10.

14. Cf. Ishmael on the reveries of the masthead, where the "absent-minded youth" can be so lulled "by the blending cadence of waves with thoughts, that at last he loses his identity" (Melville, *Moby-Dick,* 136).

15. See Romans 8:22: "For we know that the whole creation groaneth and travaileth in pain together until now" (KJV).

16. Cf. "The Allegory of the Cave," in Plato, *Republic,* 227–35. Janet Goodrich has suggested "that light in this passage" be taken primarily "in the Platonic sense of omniscient Mind," while noting, too, how Andy's emphasis on love's entering the world through suffering seems more in accord with Christian understanding. She sees Berry "appropriat[ing]" the "vocabulary and imaginative terms" of biblical tradition "not to connote belief in Christian dogma so much as to give shape to his prophetic vision" (*Unforeseen Self,* 114).

17. "Forms of the Implicit Love of God," in *Simone Weil Reader,* 479.

18. Weil, "Forms of the Implicit Love of God," 479–80.

19. For the roots of this story in Berry's own family history, see Polsgrove and Sanders, "*Progressive* Interview," 32–33. Berry explains the background of his father's participation in "starting the Burley Tobacco Growers Cooperative Association" during the Depression, an association he served for fifty years in various capacities: as counsel, vice president, and president. Berry's father was seven, the family's crop had been sent by boat to sell in Louisville, and they stayed "up talking about what they were going to do when they got the money." Berry's father's father got up in the middle of the night, rode to the train, and went "to Louisville, to see his crop sold. And he got back without a dime. They took it all. The crop, in other words, about paid the warehouse commission." "My father," Berry adds, "saw men leave the warehouse crying and he said, when he was a little boy, 'If ever I can do anything about this, I'm going to.'"

20. Andy's maiming by the machine interestingly parallels the "tramp's" suicide in Book II of Willa Cather's *My Antonia*, accomplished when the man "jumped
head-first right into" a "threshing machine" (115) during wheat harvest. Jim
Burden and Antonia's movement from Book I to Book II of that novel is from their
family farms to the town, where Jim lives with his grandparents and Antonia
works as a hired girl. Antonia's employer, the sinister Mr. Harling, was "generally
considered the most enterprising business man in our county." He "controlled a
line of grain elevators in the little towns along the railroad to the west of us, and
was away from home a great deal" (96). The movement is thus from self-sufficient
family farming to a new economic situation where consolidation of enterprise
brings its corollary, displacement of workers like the tramp, who have now become
superfluous. Here as elsewhere, Cather anticipates Berry's point that "there is an
uncanny *resemblance*," between "our behavior toward each other and our behavior
toward the earth" (BE, 124). Like Berry, Cather frequently uses the metaphor of
mining to suggest a way of being that exhausts not only the natural world but human beings. Of Tiny Soderball, who comes to live in San Francisco after "nearly
ten years" of great success "in the Klondike" gold rush, she says, e.g., "she was like
someone in whom the faculty of becoming interested is worn out" (193–94).

21. Bloom, *American Religion*. See my discussion of Bloom in chapter 3.

22. The most extreme of these is Roderick Elliston of "Egotism; or, The Bosom-
Serpent," who "contract[s] a sort of affection for his tormentor," for it is, after all,
his tormentor. See Hawthorne, *Selected Tales and Sketches*, 289.

23. P. Travis Kroeker has described this moment in the novel as one in which
"the language of prayer, the soul's communion with that convocation of voices that
points the soul beyond itself toward divine mystery, begins to obtrude itself increasingly as an unbidden grace in Andy's memory" ("Sexuality and the
Sacramental Imagination," 126).

24. John Leax notes that in taking the risk to help the man, Andy has respond-
ed "from the character that had been shaped in him by his long membership in the
Port William community rather than from the anger that has dis-membered him"
("Memory and Hope in the World of Port William," 69).

25. Balthasar, *Love Alone Is Credible*, 56: "The plausibility of God's love does
not become apparent through any comparative reduction to what man has always
already understood as love; rather, it is illuminated only by the self-interpreting
revelation-form of love itself" (Balthasar is hereafter cited in the text).

26. Some of Balthasar's comments from the section I am citing might well be
read as a gloss on Berry's resistance to having his work understood or explained—
e.g., "I can 'understand' a love that has been given to me only as a miracle; I cannot
understand it through empirical or transcendental analysis, not even in terms of
knowledge about the human 'nature' that includes us both—for the 'Thou' will

always remain an 'other' to me" (*Love Alone Is Credible,* 52). See also, and particularly, 52 n. 1.

27. These are the opening lines of Canto I of Dante's *Il Paradiso.* They are the legend on St. Peter and St. Paul's Church at Washington Square in North Beach, San Francisco.

28. Dante Alighieri, *Paradise,* 53. For a reading of *Remembering* that stresses Dantean echoes throughout, see Esbjornson, "*Remembering* and Home Defense."

29. For an account of Andy's recovery in terms of Platonic and biblical understandings of the soul and sexuality, see Kroeker, "Sexuality and the Sacramental Imagination," 126–30.

30. Suggesting that Berry's concept of "membership" "gesture[es] toward the same reality" as that Christians have spoken of as the *communio sanctorum,* the communion of saints, D. Brent Laytham points out the way Berry emphasizes the "real presence" to Andy of the living and dead whom he loves, not simply their being experienced as matters "of thought and memory" ("'Membership Includes the Dead,'" 173, 176–77).

31. "Natural History of Massachusetts," in Thoreau, *Essays,* 5.

32. Eliot, *Waste Land,* in *Selected Poems,* 51.

33. Berry, *Memory of Old Jack,* 16 (hereafter cited in the text).

34. The line is said by Edgar to Gloucester, remembering his father's earlier despair at Dover in the scene alluded to by Berry in *Life Is a Miracle.* "What, in ill thoughts again? Men must endure / Their going hence, even as their coming hither. / Ripeness is all." Apart from the opening question, the lines resonate beautifully with Old Jack's condition, particularly if we understand "ripeness" as "perfect readiness." See Shakespeare, *King Lear,* V, ii, 9–11 (p. 1179).

35. Franklin gives to Chastity, the twelfth virtue in his project of arriving at moral perfection, the following gloss: "Rarely use Venery but for Health or Offspring; Never to Dulness, Weakness, or the Injury of your own or another's Peace or Reputation" (*Autobiography,* 68). D. H. Lawrence famously responded, "Never 'use' venery at all. Follow your passional impulse, if it be answered in the other being" ("Benjamin Franklin," 296).

36. Kimberly K. Smith treats Jack as a representative of a kind of "rugged individualism" that she considers not only shown to be a failure by the story but also "morally suspect," as "it is driven by a particularly dangerous fantasy: a seductive but ecologically destructive image of infinite human *power.*" Thus, for her, "Jack Beechum's spiritual heir is not the small organic farmer living close to the land but the agribusinessman, cultivating his vast wheat fields all by himself in a shiny new air-conditioned tractor" (*Wendell Berry and the Agrarian Tradition,* 133–36). But this is to leave out too much of what makes Old Jack himself. I'd call it his agrarianism, except that it is really the land itself. His individualism means nothing apart

from the land he works. The land and the limits of his body discipline him. Surely, too, it is Ruth's attitude toward the land as commodity that more nearly mirrors the agribusinessman's approach than Jack's love for the land as "all you've got."

37. "Afterword," in *HW,* 112.

38. In Girard's terms, we might say that the crisis begins when Jack sees that Will has a particular kind of connection to the place that he will never have. "Envy," in Jack, "covets the superior *being* that neither the someone nor something alone, but the conjunction of the two, seems to possess" (*Theatre of Envy,* 4). Jack does not simply envy Will, and, of course, he, not Will, possesses the Farrier place. What he does envy is the "conjunction" of Will and the place that he is denied. His "envy involuntarily testifies to a lack of *being* that puts the envious to shame" (4), the only time in his life that Jack, it seems to me, experiences anything of this order. With the "loss of difference," Jack and Will become "mimetic antagonists" caught in a "hostile *doubling*" (56).

39. "Two Tramps in Mud Time," in Frost, *Poetry,* 277.

40. Goodrich suggests that "Berry captures" here, in Andy, "his own perspective as a younger man whose love both for traditional agriculture and for books will later meld in his agricultural writings" (*Unforeseen Self,* 64).

6. Imagining the Practice of Peace in a Century of War

1. Berry, *Place on Earth,* 297 (hereafter cited in the text). Berry also includes an "Author's Note" with a brief "editorial history." Begun in 1960, the novel was first published in 1967, then later revised and published, in a shortened version, by North Point Press in 1983. For the 2001 edition, Berry again made changes, both "to improve the writing and to correct geographical and historical discrepancies between this" and the "other books about Port William" (xi).

2. Pascal, *Pensees,* 102 (hereafter cited in the text).

3. "To a Siberian Woodsman," in *CP,* 96.

4. See, e.g., Nussbaum, "Patriotism and Cosmopolitanism."

5. Flathman, "Citizenship and Authority," 111.

6. Berry, *Hannah Coulter,* 42 (hereafter cited in the text).

7. For an interesting comparison between this story and Hemingway's "Big Two-Hearted River," see Crowe, "Hemingway's Nick and Wendell Berry's Art." Particularly intriguing is Crowe's observation about Berry's use of the word "nothing" and its similarity to Karl Barth's reference to "*das Nichtige*" to indicate "all that is not-God and all that is not God's will, including evil" (202).

8. "Making It Home (1945)," in Berry, *That Distant Land,* 224 (hereafter cited in the text).

9. Berry, *Life Story of Jayber Crow,* 273 (hereafter cited in the text).

10. Oldfield, *Citizenship and Community*, 6.

11. Cf. "West-Running Brook," especially ll. 72–75, in which the lovers come to see the rightness in what both have said (Frost, *Poetry*, 260).

12. Our guide, "who only has at heart" our "getting lost" (l. 9), advises us, in "Directive," to "Weep for what little things" could make the children "glad," the "playthings" in their playhouse, and then to weep "for the house that is no more a house / But only a belilaced cellar hole, / Now slowly closing like a dent in dough" (ll. 43–47) (Frost, *Poetry*, 377–79).

13. Jack Hicks comments that in this moment Mat's "whole received and elected life" as "husband to the world" is "threatened." His "task" is "to re-discover man's own mortal place" and to "yield his pride before a greater scheme." In this, he "is instructed by his mystic and literal wives"—the soil and Margaret. This is, in my view, to go too far toward making Virgil's death in war a kind of inevitability ("Wendell Berry's Husband to the World," 124, 132).

14. See Hauerwas, "Sacrificing the Sacrifices of War."

15. Thoreau, *Walden*, 128 (hereafter cited in the text).

16. Lewis, *Screwtape Letters*, 5.

17. Berry, *Place on Earth*, 72 (hereafter cited in the text).

18. Junger's essay "Totale Mobilmachung" first appeared in 1930. A translation of it is available in Richard Wolin's edited collection *The Heidegger Controversy* ("Total Mobilization"). Junger's comments on the way war mobilizes every aspect of a modern economy suggest Jayber Crow's sense of the way these two powers have become part and parcel of each other: "In the same way, the image of war as armed combat merges into the more extended image of a gigantic labor process. In addition to the armies that meet on the battlefields, originate the modern armies of commerce and transport, foodstuffs, the manufacture of armaments—the army of labor in general. In the final phase, which was already hinted at toward the end of the last war, there is no longer any movement whatsoever—be it that of the homeworker at her sewing machine—without at least indirect use for the battlefield" (126).

19. Augustine, *Confessions*, 78–79.

20. For a treatment of global industrial agriculture as war, see Shiva, "Globalization and the War against Farmers," 122–26.

21. Stanley Hauerwas has called *Jayber Crow* a "sweet story," noting that he usually hates "sweetness because it always threatens to become sentimentality, and sentimentality is" the "enemy of the good." Hauerwas obviously likes *Jayber*, as he does Berry's other novels, which he thinks "do what is next to impossible in our time, and that is make goodness compelling." I share this estimation of Berry's novels, but for me, it is precisely this quality of envious rivalry toward Troy in *Jayber*—bordering on hatred—that prevents the story from being sweet. See Hauerwas, "Foreword," xii.

22. "Human Personality," in *Simone Weil Reader*, 315.

23. Luke 18:11: "The Pharisee, standing by himself, was praying thus, 'God, I thank you that I am not like other people: thieves, rogues, adulterers, or even like this tax collector'" (NRSV).

24. "Distinction can, as the word signifies, mean important distinction or the utmost distinction, but everyone who struggles against distinction in this way that he wants to have one set aside and another in its place really works for distinction" (Kierkegaard, *Works of Love*, 83).

25. For the full text of the poem, see Marvell, *Poems and Letters*, 39–40.

7. The "Art of Being Here"

1. Berry, *Selected Poems*, 105 (hereafter cited in the text as *Selected*).

2. "I would not have any one adopt *my* mode of living on any account; for, beside that before he has fairly learned it I may have found out another for myself, I desire that there may be as many different persons in the world as possible; but I would have each one be very careful to find out and pursue *his own* way, and not his father's or his mother's or his neighbor's instead" (*Walden*, 114).

3. "Sabbath Poem VI, 1980," in Berry, *Timbered Choir*, 30 (*TC* hereafter, cited in the text) .

4. Norman Wirzba comments on this poem in "Dark Night of the Soil." Wirzba asks what it means to become "dark and still ourselves" (159), suggesting ultimately that it points toward a kenotic movement often adopted by mystics as they "seek to take up the divine pattern of life within their own" (162). This humbling or kenosis does not signify "a flight or escape from the world" (in a way that mysticism is often understood), but rather "our full immersion into creation, our giving ourselves to others so that they can more fully be" (164). For the way our own "practices of attention, care, and fidelity" can be patterned after "God's own kenotic work of creation," understood as "the expression of a supreme generosity and availability for another," see Wirzba, *Paradise of God*, 13.

5. "Sabbath Poem II, 1999," in Berry, *Given*, 70 (hereafter cited in the text).

6. This is not meant to diminish, in any way, environmental or ecological poetry, only to respect Berry's reservations about the term "environment" and to insist that the value of his poetry is not dependent on its being primarily about "the environment." For an important study of Berry together with other ecological poets, see Scigaj, *Sustainable Poetry*, esp. chapters 1 and 4. Scigaj gives particular emphasis to the way Berry and other ecopoets understand language to be "profoundly relational" and "referential," rather than self-referential (134).

7. Frost, "Figure a Poem Makes," 17.

8. OYC, 23.

9. "Love Calls Us to the Things of This World," in Wilbur, *Poems*, 65–66.

10. "American Imagination and the Civil War," 30.

11. Cf. "Sabbath VIII, 2007," in Berry, *Leavings*, 95 (hereafter cited in the text).

12. In "September 11, 2001: A Pacifist Response," Hauerwas argues that "any love not transformed by the love of God cannot help but be the source of the violence we perpetrate on one another in the name of justice" (206).

13. I believe Norman Wirzba accurately characterizes the attraction of students (and other readers) to Berry when he says that "Berry is so compelling precisely because he draws our attention to what (on closer investigation) is obvious and decent but has been forgotten or overlooked." Berry taps "into a widespread sentiment that our culture is deeply flawed because of its denial and destruction of the many good sources of life. We need a better way, a way that preserves, promotes, and celebrates the gift of life" (142). The "conundrum" lies in discerning how to go about doing this, and Wirzba offers some very helpful suggestions in "Economy of Gratitude." At the heart of the process, as Wirzba sees it, is repenting of a consumerism that devalues the world in order to move toward an experience of "creation as a gift" (152) to be received in delight. Moved by gratitude, we will begin to move toward "practices and commitments that have at their core fidelity, care, and celebration" (155). Wirzba has developed similar themes in *Living the Sabbath*. The center of Wirzba's argument for enriching our Sabbath practice is that the Sabbath is not meant to be a "break" from our otherwise "frenetic, self-obsessed ways of living" (though would that it could be as little as that more regularly!). "Sabbath practice" is meant rather to be "the focus and culmination of a life that is daily and practically devoted to honoring God, the source of all our delight and the provider of every good and perfect gift, and to sharing in God's own creative delight" (20, 22).

14. *CP*, 207.

15. "The Specialization of Poetry," in Berry, *Standing by Words*, 6–7 (SOP hereafter, cited in the text). For Berry's own interviews, see Grubbs, *Conversations with Wendell Berry*. In nearly every case, these interviews seem to avoid the problems in the genre that Berry notes in his essay.

16. SE, 158 (hereafter cited in the text).

17. Robert Collins notes Berry's attraction to the work of contemporaries like Denise Levertov, Gary Snyder, and A. R. Ammons, whose poetry "is not turned self-consciously back upon itself, but rather toward the external world" ("More Mingled Music," 37).

18. "We need to witness our own limits transgressed, and some life pasturing freely where we never wander" (Thoreau, *Walden*, 366).

19. For Levertov's remark, see *Poet in the World*, 90. John Lang suggests that Berry's own poetry "returns almost obsessively" to the subject of death ("'Close

Mystery,'" 261). Asked in an interview to comment on his "attention" to "death from the focus of life's vigor," Berry remarked that he does not "think death is a disease," as people increasingly seem to feel. "If we don't think death is a disease," he added, "then we must come to terms with it. I regard my attention to the matter as merely normal." See Weinreb, "Question a Day," 40.

20. Opposition to what he calls "the Nihil of the Age" is a theme of Berry's recent collection of essays *Imagination in Place*. See, particularly, his essays on the poetry of John Haines ("Speech After Long Silence," 49–53), on the work of Kathleen Raine ("Against the Nihil of the Age," 115–40), and on Shakespeare's *As You Like It* and *King Lear* ("The Uses of Adversity," 141–78).

21. Lionel Basney has said of these two concluding lines that they are "preceptual"; they lay "an intellectual obligation on us: not to accept the discipline is to deny the reality of 'the time.'" Basney suggests it may be this kind of "explicit precept" that "bothers readers who complain" of Berry's "didacticism," for the precept "expects more of us than appreciation"—we must "grant the obligation or reject it." This nicely suggests the way Berry's poetry breaks both with notions of the poem as pure object and with the poetry of "notations." See "Five Notes on the Didactic Tradition," 177.

22. "Notes: Unspecializing Poetry," in Berry, *Standing by Words*, 81 (hereafter cited in the text as "Notes").

23. "Poetry and Marriage: The Use of Old Forms," in Berry, *Standing by Words*, 92–93 (PM hereafter, cited in the text).

24. Hauerwas fleshes out this claim by saying that he knows neither "how to be nonviolent" nor what it really means to "claim to be a pacifist." What his "declaration" of his pacifism does, however, is to "create expectations in others who can and should call me to account for living in a manner that belies my conviction that, if I am to live a truthful life, I must be nonviolent" ("Explaining Christian Nonviolence," 171).

25. "In the moral life the enemy is the fat relentless ego" (Murdoch, *Sovereignty of Good*, 51).

26. On the way health is for Berry "dynamic," involving "an infinite call to heal" and thus never complete, see Bonzo and Stevens, *Wendell Berry and the Cultivation of Life*, 28.

27. Number 640 in Dickinson, *Complete Poems*, 316.

28. On Aquinas's sense that we seek happiness by nature and of necessity, see Pieper, *Happiness and Contemplation*, 20.

29. July 25, 1839, in Thoreau, *Journal*, 88.

30. Daniel Cornell stresses the poem's metaphor of love as blessing rather than exchange ("*Country of Marriage*," 66).

31. Thoreau comes around to this recovered faith after he has fathomed the

bottom of the pond with his cod-line and stone in "The Pond in Winter." "What if all ponds were shallow?" he asks. "Would it not react on the minds of men? I am thankful that this pond was made deep and pure for a symbol. While men believe in the infinite some ponds will be thought to be bottomless" (*Walden*, 335).

32. Philip A. Muntzel has commented on the "embedded" quality of hopefulness in Berry's work. For Berry, hopefulness begins with those "proximate, localized relationships" that are always for him "the critical arena for imagining and discussing Christian invocations of God's mysterious fullness." The idea of the "membership" reflects the way "one cannot separate one's own goodness from the whole goodness that God embraces" ("Embedded Hopefulness," 191–93).

Bibliography

Angyal, Andrew J. *Wendell Berry.* New York: Twayne, 1995.

Aristotle. *The Ethics of Aristotle: The Nicomachean Ethics.* Trans. J. A. K. Thomson. London: Penguin, 1976.

Augustine. *The Confessions.* Trans. R. S. Pine-Coffin. Baltimore: Penguin, 1964.

Bahnson, Elizabeth. "The Pill Is Like . . . DDT? An Agrarian Perspective on Pharmaceutical Birth Control." In Shuman and Owens, *Wendell Berry and Religion,* 85–97.

Balthasar, Hans Urs von. *Love Alone Is Credible.* Trans. D. C. Schindler. San Francisco: Ignatius Press, 2004.

Basney, Lionel. "Five Notes on the Didactic Tradition, in Praise of Wendell Berry." In Merchant, *Wendell Berry,* 173–83.

Basney, Lionel, and John Leax. "A Conversation with Wendell Berry." In Grubbs, *Conversations with Wendell Berry,* 122–34.

Beer, Jeremy. "Wendell Berry and the Traditionalist Critique of Meritocracy." In Peters, *Wendell Berry,* 212–29.

Beiner, Ronald, ed. *Theorizing Citizenship.* Albany: SUNY Press, 1995.

Bellow, Saul. *Herzog.* New York: Viking, 1967.

Berry, Wendell. *Andy Catlett: Early Travels.* Washington, D.C.: Shoemaker & Hoard, 2006.

———. *Another Turn of the Crank.* Washington, D.C.: Counterpoint, 1995.

———. *The Art of the Commonplace: The Agrarian Essays of Wendell Berry.* Ed. Norman Wirzba. Washington, D.C.: Counterpoint, 2002.

———. *Blessed Are the Peacemakers: Christ's Teachings about Love, Compassion, and Forgiveness.* Washington, D.C.: Shoemaker & Hoard, 2005.

———. *Citizenship Papers.* Washington, D.C.: Shoemaker & Hoard, 2003.

———. *Collected Poems, 1957–1982.* San Francisco: North Point, 1985.

——. *A Continuous Harmony: Essays Cultural and Agricultural.* New York: Harcourt Brace Jovanovich, 1972. Reprint, Washington, D.C.: Shoemaker & Hoard, 2004.

——. *The Gift of Good Land: Further Essays Cultural and Agricultural.* New York: North Point Press, 1982.

——. *Given: New Poems.* Washington, D.C.: Shoemaker & Hoard, 2005.

——. *Hannah Coulter: A Novel.* Washington, D.C.: Shoemaker & Hoard, 2004.

——. *The Hidden Wound.* New York: North Point Press, 1989.

——. *Home Economics.* New York: North Point Press, 1987.

——. *Imagination in Place.* Berkeley: Counterpoint, 2010.

——. *Leavings.* Berkeley: Counterpoint, 2010.

——. *Life Is a Miracle: An Essay against Modern Superstition.* Washington, D.C.: Counterpoint, 2000.

——. *The Life Story of Jayber Crow, Barber, of the Port William Membership, as Written by Himself.* New York: Counterpoint, 2000.

——. *The Long-Legged House.* New York: Harcourt Brace and World, 1969. Reprint, Washington, D.C.: Shoemaker & Hoard, 2004.

——. *The Memory of Old Jack.* New York: Harcourt Brace Jovanovich, 1974. Rev. ed., Washington, D.C.: Counterpoint, 1999.

——. *Nathan Coulter.* Boston: Houghton Mifflin, 1960.

——. *Nathan Coulter.* In *Three Short Novels,* 1–117.

——. *A Place on Earth.* Rev. ed. Washington, D.C.: Counterpoint, 2001.

——. *Remembering.* In *Three Short Novels,* 119–222.

——. *The Selected Poems of Wendell Berry.* New York: Counterpoint, 1998.

——. *Sex, Economy, Freedom, and Community.* New York: Pantheon Books, 1993.

——. *Standing by Words: Essays.* Washington, D.C.: Shoemaker & Hoard, 2005.

——. *That Distant Land: The Collected Stories.* Washington, D.C.: Shoemaker & Hoard, 2004.

——. *Three Short Novels.* Washington, D.C.: Counterpoint, 2002.

——. *A Timbered Choir: The Sabbath Poems, 1979–1997.* New York: Counterpoint, 1998.

——. *The Unsettling of America: Culture and Agriculture.* San Francisco: Sierra Club, 1977.

——. *The Way of Ignorance and Other Essays.* Washington, D.C.: Shoemaker & Hoard, 2005.

——. *What Are People For?* New York: North Point Press, 1990.

——. *A World Lost.* In *Three Short Novels,* 223–326.

Berry, Wendell, and James Baker Hall. *Tobacco Harvest: An Elegy.* Lexington: University Press of Kentucky, 2004.

Bloom, Harold. *The American Religion: The Emergence of the Post-Christian Nation.* New York: Simon & Schuster, 1992.

Bonzo, J. Matthew, and Michael R. Stevens. *Wendell Berry and the Cultivation of Life: A Reader's Guide.* Grand Rapids: Brazos, 2008.

Brown, Katherine Tandy. "The *Bluegrass* Interview: Wendell Berry." In Grubbs, *Conversations with Wendell Berry,* 103–13.

Brueggemann, Walter. *The Land: Place as Gift, Promise, and Challenge in Biblical Faith.* 2nd ed. Minneapolis: Fortress, 2002.

Buell, Lawrence. *The Environmental Imagination: Thoreau, Nature Writing, and the Formation of American Culture.* Cambridge: Belknap Press of Harvard, 1995.

Burleigh, Anne Husted. "Wendell Berry's Community." In Grubbs, *Conversations with Wendell Berry,* 135–46.

Cargill, Oscar. *The Novels of Henry James.* New York: Macmillan, 1961.

Carlson, Allan. *The New Agrarian Mind: The Movement toward Decentralist Thought in Twentieth-Century America.* New Brunswick, N.J.: Transaction, 2000.

Cather, Willa. *My Antonia.* Boston: Houghton Mifflin, 1988.

———. "Prefatory Note." In *Not under Forty,* v. New York: Alfred A. Knopf, 1936.

Church, Richard P. "Of the Good That Has Been Possible in This World: Lawyering in Port William." In Shuman and Owens, *Wendell Berry and Religion,* 50–70.

Collins, Robert. "A More Mingled Music: Wendell Berry's Ambivalent View of Language." *Modern Poetry Studies* 11 (1982): 35–56.

Collis, John Stewart. *The Triumph of the Tree.* New York: William Sloane Associates, 1954.

Confucius. *Confucius: The Great Digest* and *Unwobbling Pivot.* Trans. Ezra Pound. New York: New Directions, 1951.

Cornell, Daniel. "*The Country of Marriage:* Wendell Berry's Personal Political Vision." *Southern Literary Journal* 15 (1983): 59–70.

———. "A Vision of Stewardship: Wendell Berry's Ecological Ethic." *Literature and Belief* 12 (1992): 13–25.

Crowe, David. "Hemingway's Nick and Wendell Berry's Art." In Peters, *Wendell Berry,* 192–208.

Cummins, Terry. *Feed My Sheep.* Lexington: 1st Books, 2003.

Daly, Herman E. "Sustainable Economic Development: Definitions, Principles, Policies." In Wirzba, *Essential Agrarian Reader,* 62–79.

Dante Alighieri. *Paradise.* Trans. Dorothy L. Sayers and Barbara Reynolds. Middlesex, England: Penguin, 1962.

———. *La Vita Nuova.* Trans. D. G. Rossetti. In *The Portable Dante,* ed. Paolo Milano, 547–618. New York: Viking, 1967.

Davis, Ellen F. "'And the Land I Will Remember': Reading the Bible through Agrarian Eyes." In Shuman and Owens, *Wendell Berry and Religion*, 115–30.

Deneen, Patrick J. "Wendell Berry and the Alternative Tradition in American Political Thought." In Peters, *Wendell Berry*, 300–315.

Dickinson, Emily. *The Complete Poems of Emily Dickinson*. Ed. Thomas H. Johnson. Boston: Little, Brown and Company, 1960.

Donahue, Brian. "The Resettling of America." In Wirzba, *Essential Agrarian Reader*, 34–51.

Edwards, Jonathan. *The Nature of True Virtue. Ethical Writings*. Vol. 8 of *Works of Jonathan Edwards*. Ed. Paul Ramsey. New Haven: Yale University Press, 1989.

Eliot, T. S. *Selected Poems*. New York: Harcourt, Brace & World, 1964.

Esbjornson, Carl D. "*Remembering* and Home Defense." In Merchant, *Wendell Berry*, 155–70.

Fisher Smith, Jordan. "Field Observations: An Interview with Wendell Berry." In Grubbs, *Conversations with Wendell Berry*, 86–102.

Flathman, Richard E. "Citizenship and Authority: A Chastened View of Citizenship." In Beiner, *Theorizing Citizenship*, 105–51.

Franklin, Benjamin. *Benjamin Franklin's Autobiography*. Ed. J. A. Leo Lemay and P. M. Zall. New York: Norton, 1986.

Frei, Hans. *The Identity of Jesus Christ: The Hermeneutical Basis of Dogmatic Theology*. Philadelphia: Fortress Press, 1975.

Freyfogle, Eric T. "Introduction: A Durable Scale." In Freyfogle, *New Agrarianism*, xiii–xli.

———. "Mat Feltner's World." In *Bounded People, Boundless Lands: Envisioning a New Land Ethic*, 75–90. Washington, D.C.: Island, 1998.

———. ed. *The New Agrarianism: Land, Culture, and the Community of Life*. Washington, D.C.: Island, 2001.

———. "Wendell Berry and the Limits of Populism." In Peters, *Wendell Berry*, 173–91.

Frost, Robert. "The Figure a Poem Makes." In *Selected Prose of Robert Frost*, ed. Hyde Cox and Edward Connery Lathem, 17–20. New York: Collier Books, 1966.

———. *The Poetry of Robert Frost*. Ed. Edward Connery Lathem. New York: Holt, Rinehart and Winston, 1969.

Girard, Rene. *A Theatre of Envy: William Shakespeare*. New York: Oxford University Press, 1991.

Goodrich, Janet. *The Unforeseen Self in the Works of Wendell Berry*. Columbia: University of Missouri Press, 2001.

Graddy, Hank. "The Legal and Legislative Front: The Fight against Industrial Agriculture." In Wirzba, *Essential Agrarian Reader*, 222–36.

Grubbs, Morris Allen, ed. *Conversations with Wendell Berry.* Jackson: University Press of Mississippi, 2007.

———. "A Practical Education: Wendell Berry the Professor." In Peters, *Wendell Berry,* 137–41.

Harding, Walter. *The Days of Henry Thoreau.* New York: Knopf, 1970.

Hauerwas, Stanley. "Explaining Christian Nonviolence: Notes for a Conversation with John Milbank and John Howard Yoder." In *Performing the Faith,* 169–83.

———. "Foreword." In Peters, *Wendell Berry,* xi–xii.

———. *Performing the Faith: Bonhoeffer and the Practice of Nonviolence.* Grand Rapids: Brazos, 2004.

———. "Sacrificing the Sacrifices of War." *Journal of Religion, Conflict, and Peace* 1 (2007). Available at http://www.plowsharesproject.org/journal/php/archive/archive.php?issu_list_id=8.

———. "September 11, 2001: A Pacifist Response." In *Performing the Faith,* 201–10.

———. "A Story-Formed Community: Reflections on *Watership Down.*" In *A Community of Character: Toward a Constructive Christian Social Ethic,* 9–35. Notre Dame: University of Notre Dame Press, 1981.

———. "What Would a Christian University Look Like? Some Tentative Answers Inspired by Wendell Berry." In *The State of the University: Academic Knowledges and the Knowledge of God,* 92–107. Malden, Mass.: Blackwell, 2007.

Hawthorne, Nathaniel. "Egotism; or, The Bosom-Serpent." In *Selected Tales and Sketches,* 279–94. New York: Penguin, 1987.

Heidegger, Martin. "The Question Concerning Technology." In *The Question Concerning Technology and Other Essays,* trans. William Lovitt, 3–35. New York: Harper & Row, 1977.

Herford, R. Travers, trans. and ed. *The Ethics of the Talmud: Sayings of the Fathers.* New York: Schocken, 1962.

Hicks, Jack. "Wendell Berry's Husband to the World: *A Place on Earth.*" In Merchant, *Wendell Berry,* 118–34.

Ignatieff, Michael. "The Myth of Citizenship." In Beiner, *Theorizing Citizenship,* 53–77.

I'll Take My Stand: The South and the Agrarian Tradition. New York: Harper, 1962.

Jackson, Wes. "The Agrarian Mind: Mere Nostalgia or a Practical Necessity?" In Wirzba, *Essential Agrarian Reader,* 140–53.

———. *Becoming Native to This Place.* New York: Counterpoint, 1996.

———. "Letters from a Humble Radical." In Peters, *Wendell Berry,* 156–72.

James, Henry. "The Art of Fiction." In *The Portable Henry James,* ed. Morton Dauwen Zabel and Lyall H. P. Powers, 387–414. New York: Viking, 1968.

———. *Hawthorne.* London: Macmillan, 1883.

――――. *Henry James: Letters.* Ed. Leon Edel. Vol. I, 1843–1875. Cambridge: Harvard University Press, 1974.

John Paul II. *Familiaris Consortio.* Available at http//www.vatican.va/holy_father/john_paul_ii/apost_exhortations/documents/hf_jp-ii_exh_19811122_familiaris-consortio_en.html.

Junger, Ernst. "Total Mobilization." In *The Heidegger Controversy: A Critical Reader,* ed. Richard Wolin, 119–39. Boston: MIT Press, 1993.

Kant, Immanuel. *The Doctrine of Virtue. The Metaphysics of Morals.* Trans. Mary Gregor. Cambridge: Cambridge University Press, 1991.

――――. *Foundations of the Metaphysics of Morals.* Trans. Lewis White Beck. New York: Macmillan, 1990.

Kauffmann, Bill. "Wendell Berry on War and Peace; or, Port William versus the Empire." In Peters, *Wendell Berry,* 17–33.

Kierkegaard, Søren. *Works of Love: Some Christian Reflections in the Form of Discourses.* Trans. Howard Hong and Edna Hong. New York: Harper, 1962.

Kimbrell, Andrew. "Seven Deadly Myths of Industrial Agriculture." In *The Fatal Harvest Reader: The Tragedy of Industrial Agriculture,* ed. Andrew Kimbrell, 3–36. Washington, D.C.: Island, 2002.

Kingsolver, Barbara. "The Art of Buying Nothing." In Peters, *Wendell Berry,* 287–95.

Kirschenmann, Frederick. "The Current State of Agriculture: Does It Have a Future?" In Wirzba, *Essential Agrarian Reader,* 101–20.

Kroeker, P. Travis. "Sexuality and the Sacramental Imagination: It All Turns on Affection." In Peters, *Wendell Berry,* 119–36.

Lang, John. "'Close Mystery': Wendell Berry's Poetry of Incarnation." *Renascence* 35 (1983): 258–68.

Lasch, Christopher. *Haven in a Heartless World: The Family Besieged.* New York: Basic Books, 1977.

――――. *The Revolt of the Elites and the Betrayal of Democracy.* New York: Norton, 1995.

Lawrence, D. H. "Benjamin Franklin." In *Benjamin Franklin's Autobiography,* ed. J. A. Leo Lemay and P. M. Zall, 289–99. New York: Norton, 1986.

Laytham, D. Brent. "'The Membership Includes the Dead': Wendell Berry's Port William Membership as *Communio Sanctorum.*" In Shuman and Owens, *Wendell Berry and Religion,* 173–89.

Leax, John. "Memory and Hope in the World of Port William." In Peters, *Wendell Berry,* 66–75.

Levertov, Denise. *The Poet in the World.* New York: New Directions, 1973.

Lewis, C. S. *The Screwtape Letters.* Rev. ed. New York: Macmillan, 1982.

Logsdon, Gene. "Wendell Berry: Agrarian Artist." In Peters, *Wendell Berry,* 241–55.

MacIntyre, Alasdair. *After Virtue: A Study in Moral Theory.* 2nd ed. Notre Dame: University of Notre Dame Press, 1984.

——. "Is Patriotism a Virtue?" In Beiner, *Theorizing Citizenship*, 209–28.

Marvell, Andrew. *The Poems and Letters of Andrew Marvell*. Vol. I. Ed. H. M. Margoliouth. Oxford: Clarendon, 1971.

McCabe, Herbert. *God Matters*. London: Continuum, 2005.

Melville, Herman. *Moby-Dick*. New York: Norton, 2002.

Merchant, Paul, ed. *Wendell Berry*. Lewiston, Idaho: Confluence, 1991.

Meyers, Carol. *Exodus*. Cambridge: Cambridge University Press, 2005.

Muir, Edwin. *Collected Poems*. New York: Oxford University Press, 1965.

Muntzel, Philip A. "Embedded Hopefulness: Wendell Berry and Saint Thomas Aquinas on Christian Hope." In Shuman and Owens, *Wendell Berry and Religion*, 190–208.

Murdoch, Iris. *The Sovereignty of Good*. London: Routledge & Kegan Paul, 1971.

Nibbelink, Herman. "Thoreau and Wendell Berry: Bachelor and Husband of Nature." In Merchant, *Wendell Berry*, 135–51.

Nussbaum, Martha C. "Patriotism and Cosmopolitanism." In *For Love of Country: Debating the Limits of Patriotism*, ed. Joshua Cohen, 3–17. Boston: Beacon Press, 1996.

Oelschlaeger, Max. *Caring for Creation: An Ecumenical Approach to the Environmental Crisis*. New Haven: Yale University Press, 1994.

Oldfield, Adrian. *Citizenship and Community: Civic Republicanism and the Modern World*. London: Routledge, 1990.

Orr, David W. "The Urban-Agrarian Mind." In Freyfogle, *New Agrarianism*, 93–107.

——. "The Uses of Prophecy." In Wirzba, *Essential Agrarian Reader*, 171–87.

Pascal, Blaise. *Pensees*. Trans. W. F. Trotter. New York: Modern Library, 1941.

Peters, Jason. "Education, Heresy, and the 'Deadly Disease of the World.'" In Peters, *Wendell Berry*, 256–81.

——. "Introduction." In Peters, *Wendell Berry*, 1–11.

——, ed. *Wendell Berry: Life and Work*. Lexington: University Press of Kentucky, 2007.

Pieper, Josef. *About Love*. Trans. Richard Winston and Clara Winston. Chicago: Franciscan Herald Press, 1974.

——. *The Four Cardinal Virtues*. Trans. Richard Winston, Clara Winston, et al. Notre Dame: University of Notre Dame Press, 1966.

——. *Happiness and Contemplation*. Trans. Richard Winston and Clara Winston. South Bend, Ind.: St. Augustine's Press, 1998.

Pinches, Charles R. "Democracy, America, and the Church: Inviting Wendell Berry into the Discussion." In Shuman and Owens, *Wendell Berry and Religion*, 239–60.

Plato. *The Republic*. Trans. F. M. Cornford. New York: Oxford University Press, 1945.

Pocock, J. G. A. "The Ideal of Citizenship since Classical Times." In Beiner, *Theorizing Citizenship*, 29–52.

Polsgrove, Carol, and Scott Russell Sanders. "*The Progressive* Interview: Wendell Berry." In Grubbs, *Conversations with Wendell Berry*, 27–35.

Premnath, D. N. "Latifundialization and Isaiah 5:8–10." *Journal for the Study of the Old Testament* 40 (1988): 49–60.

Rhonheimer, Martin. *Natural Law and Practical Reason: A Thomist View of Moral Autonomy.* Trans. Gerald Malsbary. New York: Fordham University Press, 2000.

Sanders, Scott Russell. "Learning from the Prairie." In Freyfogle, *New Agrarianism*, 3–15.

———. "Words Addressed to Our Condition Exactly." In Peters, *Wendell Berry*, 34–44.

Scigaj, Leonard M. *Sustainable Poetry: Four American Ecopoets.* Lexington: University Press of Kentucky, 1999.

Shakespeare, William. *King Lear.* In *Shakespeare: The Complete Works*, ed. G. B. Harrison, 1136–83. New York: Harcourt, Brace & World, 1968.

Sherrard, Philip. *Human Image: World Image.* Ipswich, Suffolk, England: Golgonooza Press, 1992.

Shiva, Vandana. "Globalization and the War against Farmers and the Land." In Wirzba, *Essential Agrarian Reader*, 121–39.

Shuman, Joel James. "Introduction: Placing God in the Work of Wendell Berry." In Shuman and Owens, *Wendell Berry and Religion*, 1–14.

———. "Landscapes of Flesh: On Finding More Faithful Metaphors for the Body and Its Goods." In Shuman and Owens, *Wendell Berry and Religion*, 131–47.

Shuman, Joel James, and L. Roger Owens, eds. *Wendell Berry and Religion: Heaven's Earthly Life.* Lexington: University Press of Kentucky, 2009.

Smith, Kimberly K. *Wendell Berry and the Agrarian Tradition: A Common Grace.* Lawrence: University Press of Kansas, 2003.

———. "Wendell Berry's Political Vision." In Peters, *Wendell Berry*, 49–59.

Tate, Allen. "Remarks on the Southern Religion." In *I'll Take My Stand: The South and the Agrarian Tradition*, 155–75. New York: Harper, 1962.

Taylor, Charles. *A Secular Age.* Cambridge: Belknap Press of Harvard, 2007.

Thoreau, Henry David. *The Essays of Henry D. Thoreau.* Ed. Lewis Hyde. New York: North Point Press, 2002.

———. *Familiar Letters of Henry David Thoreau.* Ed. F. B. Sanborn. Boston and New York: Houghton Mifflin, 1894.

———. *The Journal of Henry D. Thoreau.* 14 vols. Ed. Bradford Torrey and Francis H. Allen. Boston: Houghton Mifflin, 1906.

———. "Life Without Principle." In *Essays of Henry D. Thoreau*, 197–214.

———. "Natural History of Massachusetts." In *Essays of Henry D. Thoreau*, 3–23.

———. *Walden and Civil Disobedience.* New York: Penguin, 1983.

———. *A Week on the Concord and Merrimack Rivers.* New York: Penguin, 1998.

Tocqueville, Alexis de. *Democracy in America*. Trans. Harvey C. Mansfield and Delba Winthrop. Chicago: University of Chicago Press, 2000.

"Toward a Healthy Community: An Interview with Wendell Berry." In Grubbs, *Conversations with Wendell Berry*, 114–21.

Townsend, Kim. *Sherwood Anderson*. Boston: Houghton Mifflin, 1987.

Tretheway, Eric. "Politics, Nature, and Value in Wendell Berry's 'The Art of the Commonplace.'" In Peters, *Wendell Berry*, 76–87.

Triggs, Jeffery Alan. "A Kinship of the Fields: Farming in the Poetry of R. S. Thomas and Wendell Berry." *North Dakota Quarterly* 57 (1989): 92–102.

Twain, Mark. *Adventures of Huckleberry Finn*. Ed. Walter Blair and Victor Fischer. Berkeley: University of California Press, 1985.

Weil, Simone. "Beauty." In *Simone Weil Reader*, 377–80.

———. "Forms of the Implicit Love of God." In *Simone Weil Reader*, 469–91.

———. "Human Personality." In *Simone Weil Reader*, 313–39.

———. "Love." In *Simone Weil Reader*, 357–62.

———. *The Need for Roots*. Trans. Arthur Wills. London: Routledge, 2007.

———. *The Simone Weil Reader*. Ed. George A. Panichas. Mt. Kisco, N.Y.: Moyer Bell, 1977.

Weinreb, Mindy. "A Question a Day: A Written Conversation with Wendell Berry." In Merchant, *Wendell Berry*, 27–43.

White, Lynn, Jr. "The Historical Roots of Our Ecologic Crisis." In *Western Man and Environmental Ethics: Attitudes toward Nature and Technology*, ed. Ian G. Barbour, 18–30. Reading, Mass.: Addison-Wesley, 1973.

Wilbur, Richard. *The Poems of Richard Wilbur*. New York: Harcourt Brace & World, 1963.

Wilson, E. O. *Consilience: The Unity of Knowledge*. New York: Knopf, 1998.

Wirzba, Norman. "The Dark Night of the Soil: An Agrarian Approach to Mystical Life." In Shuman and Owens, *Wendell Berry and Religion*, 148–69.

———. "An Economy of Gratitude." In Peters, *Wendell Berry*, 142–55.

———, ed. *The Essential Agrarian Reader: The Future of Culture, Community, and the Land*. Lexington: University Press of Kentucky, 2003.

———. "Introduction: Why Agrarianism Matters—Even to Urbanites." In Wirzba, *Essential Agrarian Reader*, 1–20.

———. *Living the Sabbath: Discovering the Rhythms of Rest and Delight*. Grand Rapids: Brazos, 2006.

———. *The Paradise of God: Renewing Religion in an Ecological Age*. New York: Oxford, 2003.

———. "Placing the Soul: An Agrarian Philosophical Principle." In Wirzba, *Essential Agrarian Reader*, 80–97.

Wolin, Sheldon S. *Democracy Incorporated: Managed Democracy and the Specter of Inverted Totalitarianism*. Princeton: Princeton University Press, 2008.

Woodress, James. *Willa Cather: A Literary Life*. Lincoln: University of Nebraska Press, 1987.

Yeats, W. B. *Selected Poems and Two Plays of William Butler Yeats*. Ed. M. L. Rosenthal. New York: Collier, 1966.

Index

3 8950 61047 9961

818 Oeh   *C*
Oehlschlaeger, Fritz
The achievement of Wendell Berry :
the hard history of love

HOCUTT-ELLINGTON MEMORIAL LIBRARY
CLAYTON, NC 27520